Boys and Their Schooling

Routledge Research in Education

1. **Learning Communities in Education**
Edited by John Retallick, Barry Cocklin, and Kennece Coombe

2. **Teachers and the State**
International Perspectives
Mike Bottery and Nigel Wright

3. **Education and Psychology in Interaction**
Working with Uncertainty in Inter-Connected Fields
Brahm Norwich

4. **Education, Social Justice and Inter-Agency Working**
Joined up or Fractured Policy?
Sheila Riddell and Lyn Tett

5. **Markets for Schooling**
An Economic Analysis
Nick Adnett and Peter Davies

6. **The Future of Physical Education**
Building a New Pedagogy
Edited by Anthony Laker

7. **Migration, Education and Change**
Edited by Sigrid Luchtenberg

8. **Manufacturing Citizenship**
Education and Nationalism in Europe, South Asia and China
Edited by Véronique Bénéï

9. **Spatial Theories of Education**
Edited by Kalervo N. Gulson and Colin Symes

10. **Balancing Dilemmas in Assessment and Learning in Contemporary Education**
Edited by Anton Havnes and Liz McDowell

11. **Policy Discourses, Gender, and Education**
Constructing Women's Status
Elizabeth J. Allan

12. **Improving Teacher Education through Action Research**
Edited by Ming-Fai Hui and David L. Grossman

13. **The Politics of Structural Education Reform**
Keith A. Nitta

14. **Political Approaches to Educational Administration and Leadership**
Edited by Eugenie A. Samier with Adam G. Stanley

15. **Structure and Agency in the Neoliberal University**
Edited by Joyce E. Canaan and Wesley Shumar

16. **Postmodern Picturebooks**
Play, Parody, and Self-Referentiality
Edited by Lawrence R. Sipe and Sylvia Pantaleo

17. **Play, Creativity and Digital Cultures**
Edited by Rebekah Willett, Muriel Robinson and Jackie Marsh

18. **Education and Neoliberal Globalization**
Carlos Alberto Torres

19. **Tracking Adult Literacy and Numeracy Skills**
Findings from Longitudinal Research
Edited by Stephen Reder and John Bynner

20. **Emergent Computer Literacy**
A Developmental Perspective
Helen Mele Robinson

21. **Participatory Learning in the Early Years**
Research and Pedagogy
Edited by Donna Berthelsen, Jo Brownlee, and Eva Johansson

22. **International Perspectives on the Goals of Universal Basic and Secondary Education**
Edited by Joel E. Cohen and Martin B. Malin

23. **The Journey for Inclusive Education in the Indian Sub-Continent**
Mithu Alur and Michael Bach

24. **Traveller, Nomadic and Migrant Education**
Edited by Patrick Alan Danaher, Máirín Kenny, and Judith Remy Leder

25. **Perspectives on Supported Collaborative Teacher Inquiry**
Edited by David Slavit, Tamara Holmlund Nelson, and Anne Kennedy

26. **Mathematical Relationships in Education**
Identities and Participation
Edited by Laura Black, Heather Mendick, and Yvette Solomon

27. **Science, Society and Sustainability**
Education and Empowerment for an Uncertain World
Edited by Donald Gray, Laura Colucci-Gray, and Elena Camino

28. **The Social Psychology of the Classroom**
Elisha Babad

29. **Cross-Cultural Perspectives on Policy and Practice**
Decolonizing Community Contexts
Edited by Jennifer Lavia and Michele Moore

30. **Education and Climate Change**
Living and Learning in Interesting Times
Edited by Fumiyo Kagawa and David Selby

31. **Education and Poverty in Affluent Countries**
Edited by Carlo Raffo, Alan Dyson, Helen Gunter, Dave Hall, Lisa Jones, and Afroditi Kalambouka

32. **What's So Important About Music Education?**
J. Scott Goble

33. **Educational Transitions**
Moving Stories from Around the World
Edited by Divya Jindal-Snape

34. **Globalization, the Nation-State and the Citizen**
Dilemmas and Directions for Civics and Citizenship Education
Edited by Alan Reid, Judith Gill, and Alan Sears

35. **Collaboration in Education**
Edited by Judith J. Slater and Ruth Ravid

36. **Trust and Betrayal in Educational Administration and Leadership**
Edited by Eugenie A. Samier and Michèle Schmidt

37. **Teaching and Learning with Technology**
Beyond Constructivism
Edited by Concetta M. Stewart, Catherine C. Schifter, and Melissa E. Markaridian Selverian

38. **Gender Inclusive Engineering Education**
Julie Mills, Mary Ayre, and Judith Gill

39. **Intercultural and Multicultural Education**
Enhancing Global Interconnectedness
Edited by Carl A. Grant and Agostino Portera

40. **Systemization in Foreign Language Teaching**
Monitoring Content Progression
Wilfried Decoo

41. **Inclusive Education in the Middle East**
Eman Gaad

42. **Critical Issues in Peace and Education**
Edited by Peter Pericles Trifonas and Bryan Wright

43. **Children's Drawing and Writing**
The Remarkable in the Unremarkable
Diane Mavers

44. **Citizenship, Education and Social Conflict**
Israeli Political Education in Global Perspective
Edited by Hanan A. Alexander, Halleli Pinson, and Yossi Yonah

45. **Emerging Teachers and Globalisation**
Gerry Czerniawski

46. **Social Studies as New Literacies in a Global Society**
Relational Cosmopolitanism in the Classroom
Mark Baildon and James S. Damico

47. **Education Policy, Space and the City**
Markets and the (In)visibility of Race
Kalervo N. Gulson

48. **Memory and Pedagogy**
Edited by Claudia Mitchell, Teresa Strong-Wilson, Kathleen Pithouse, and Susann Allnutt

49. **Universities and Global Diversity**
Preparing Educators for Tomorrow
Edited by Beverly Lindsay and Wanda J. Blanchett

50. **Equity and Excellence in Education**
Towards Maximal Learning Opportunities for All Students
Edited by Kris Van den Branden, Piet Van Avermaet, and Mieke Van Houtte

51. **Global Pathways to Abolishing Physical** Punishment
Realizing Children's Rights
Edited by Joan E. Durrant and Anne B. Smith

52. **From Testing to Productive Student Learning**
Implementing Formative Assessment in Confucian-Heritage Settings
David Carless

53. **Changing Schools in an Era of Globalization**
Edited by John C. K. Lee and Brian J. Caldwell

54. **Boys and Their Schooling**
The Experience of Becoming Someone Else
John Whelen

Boys and Their Schooling
The Experience of Becoming Someone Else

John Whelen

NEW YORK AND LONDON

First published 2011
by Routledge
711 Third Avenue, New York, NY 10017

Simultaneously published in the UK
by Routledge
2 Park Square, Milton Park, Abingdon, Oxon OX14 4RN

Routledge is an imprint of the Taylor & Francis Group, an informa business

© 2011 Taylor & Francis

The right of John Whelen to be identified as author of this work has been asserted by him in accordance with sections 77 and 78 of the Copyright, Designs and Patents Act 1988.

Typeset in Sabon by Swales & Willis Ltd, Exeter, Devon

All rights reserved. No part of this book may be reprinted or reproduced or utilised in any form or by any electronic, mechanical, or other means, now known or hereafter invented, including photocopying and recording, or in any information storage or retrieval system, without permission in writing from the publishers.

Trademark Notice: Product or corporate names may be trademarks or registered trademarks, and are used only for identification and explanation without intent to infringe.

Library of Congress Cataloging in Publication Data
Whelen, John.
  Boys and their schooling: the experience of becoming someone else/ by John Whelen.
    p. cm.—(Routledge research in education)
  Includes bibliographical references and index.
  1. Boys—Education. 2. Sex differences in education—United States.
    3. Men—Identity. 4. Education and state—United States. I. Title.
    LC1390.W44 2011
    371.823—dc22
    2010040788

ISBN13: 978-0-415-87917-0 (hbk)
ISBN13: 978-0-203-82780-2 (ebk)

For Nola

Contents

Acknowledgments xi

Part I:
Boys in the Frame

1 Getting at Experience 3

2 The Schoolboy as Object of Study 32

3 Writing the Schoolboy 60

4 Observing Participation 91

Part II:
That Unstable Construct

5 Monday Morning 101

6 George 124

7 Year 9 147

8 The Student Body 180

9 The Aspirational Self 202

10 Conclusion: Another New Beginning 226

    Epilogue 236
    Appendix I: Reading Interview Transcriptions 237

Notes 238
Bibliography 253
Index 274

Acknowledgments

This book is based on my PhD undertaken at Monash University, Melbourne. I am particularly indebted to Anna Clarkson and Max Novick of Routledge for their encouragement and for making the Research in Education series a platform for launching new work. At Monash I was privileged to have Georgina Tsolidis as my supervisor and to receive wise counsel also from Lindsay Fitzclarence. I have also benefited from the collegial support of Mary Lou Rasmussen, Joel Windle, Cynthia Joseph, and in particular Scott Webster. I also wish to thank Becky Francis and Bob Lingard for their encouragement and to acknowledge John Loughran and the Faculty of Education at Monash for providing me with institutional support and for the opportunity to contribute to the teaching program. My thanks also go to Robyne Bowering in particular for help with word processing. Any errors whatsoever are entirely my own. Special thanks are also due to John and Deirdre Casey and Evelyn and Richard Johnson for their friendship and support during the preparation of this work.

Parts of Chapter 5 have appeared in Whelen (2008), "On the margins of education, or two stories of arriving at school," published in *Ethnography and Education*, 3:3, 297–312 and I thank the editors and publisher for permission to draw on it.

This work would not have been possible without the good will and support of the administration and staff at Hillside High School, but my most profound thanks are due to the boys who took part in the original study and to their parents for giving their permission. I hope I have in some small way repaid their trust. The names of all participants in the study, and of the school, are pseudonyms.

Above all, I wish to thank my family for their ongoing interest in this work, especially Nola, whose encouragement and support has been so constant for so long.

Part I
Boys in the Frame

> This is my question: at what price can subjects speak the truth about themselves?
>
> M. Foucault, interviewed by G. Raulet (1983) "Structuralism and Post-structuralism: An Interview with Michel Foucault," *Telos*, 55: 202.

1 Getting at Experience

INTRODUCTION

The origin of this study lies principally in my experience as a teacher in a secondary school in Melbourne, Australia. In more than 20 years there I witnessed, and was deeply implicated in, the relationships between students and teachers (and between students) that occur formally and informally and that might loosely be called schooling. Throughout this study I will return to my experience and the part it has played both in generating my interest in the experience of school and in developing an ethnographic approach to the question of how one might understand boys' experience of their schooling.

In this book I argue that the study of boys in school has been caught up in, and restricted by, the way "boys" have been understood both in and out of the academy to the detriment of what I maintain is a more fundamental issue: namely, what it is to be a boy at school. On the one hand, issues of achievement and retention have dominated discussion in the academy more recently (at least in Australia), within a gender equity discourse which aims to evaluate government policy, whereas on the other, radically conservative fears for the "plight" of boys have been framed in biological or essentialist terms, frequently outside the academy, by those who argue that schools (and often families), are failing to meet boys' alleged needs. Each of these positions, in its own way, aspires to influence education policy at state and federal levels in Australia.

What I hope to show is that in spite of both academic research and popular rhetoric concerning boys and their schooling, or more specifically concerning boys' achievement or lack of it at a time when the subject of neo-liberalism in late modernity, and the purpose of schooling, are under constant review, a significant gap lies in the failure to understand the experiences and the subjectivities of boys at school, particularly in Australia. This is in sharp distinction to studies of girls over the past 20 years which have shown how girls have been positioned within a masculinist educational hegemony, and at what cost, but amid claims that schooling is becoming increasingly feminized, panic about boys and their "plight" has deflected attention from what might be referred to as the lived experience of this so-called plight, or more simply, the experience of being schooled. Not only have boys' experiences been assumed and reified within the deterministic discourse of biological essentialism and its attendant emphasis on role model socialization, but the notion of experience has remained relatively untheorized in accounts of schooling that deal with achievement or which emphasize the school and its relationship to the construction of identity. It is in glossing, or limiting the notion of experience, I will argue, that boys so often continue to be portrayed in schools, in policy and in populist media in terms of the ubiquitous Enlightenment subject of modernism: unitary, rational, voluntarist, and self-evidently embodied; a stable, prediscursive reference point from which the construction of meaning proceeds.

In framing this study I have adopted a perspective that has been developed in feminist critiques of modernity and a poststructuralist epistemology with roots in the work of Michel Foucault and Judith Butler which proposes the discursive construction of subjectivity and leads to an understanding of the subject as positioned, multiple, decentered, and radically nonessential. In broad terms, the move to a poststructuralist perspective has problematized the humanist subject of earlier research but has by no means dislodged it from educational policy or daily life in schools. My focus throughout therefore draws on a Foucauldian frame of reference which rejects the common-sense apprehension of the pre-existing subjects of schooling (e.g., good student, disaffected boy, teacher), and argues instead for an understanding of them as constituted in discursive practices rooted in the local, the personal, and the apparently trivial, or, as Miller and Rose (2008: 4) put it, in "the small and dispersed events that (bring) something new into existence." Foucault's notions of discourse, power-knowledge, governmentality, and in particular subjectification (or the coming into being of subjectivities), are therefore central to this work and in this context I will further draw heavily on his notion of surveillant technologies that seem to me to permeate and characterize schooling.

This book is in part an ethnographic study of boys' experiences of being schooled in a state High School in suburban Melbourne, Australia, conducted over a two-year period from 2003 to 2004, and is at the same time a meditation on doing the work of ethnography. The work of doing and writing this study has to some extent been informed by the so-called "textual turn" in anthropology and ethnography generally, so a related and important preoccupation of this study is the nature of the ethnographic encounters both for myself as teacher-researcher and for the boys and teachers who took part in this study, and the way they are represented. In line with the poststructuralist position advocated earlier I have been concerned with issues of voice, reflexivity, and textual representation as will become clear in the chapters where I discuss the ethnographic work in detail. In fleeting moments or lengthy encounters, whether in conversations or unstructured interviews, and emerging from seemingly endless observation, a series of narratives has been created which has become the record of my research and the evidence for much of what I claim. Unlike more itinerant educational ethnographers, my presence in, and familiarity with the school setting have marked me as an "insider" from the start and contributed uniquely to my understanding of its institutional processes. Such immersion in the daily life of the school over a long period initially contributed to the privileged perspective from which I began work as a teacher-researcher but, as I will show, such familiarity presented its own problems and was not able to prevent a sense of rupture and even dissociation from early certainties as the study progressed.

UP CLOSE AND PERSONAL

At the same time as I was confronting the roughly drawn and crudely understood experiences that I will refer to throughout this introduction, the popular press was bringing news of similar situations elsewhere. According to some accounts, many boys were becoming alienated from school and society and a range of pathologies was revealing a crisis among boys, even a crisis of masculinity. Popular writers such as Steve Biddulph in Australia advised parents how to bring up boys to make the most of their masculinity, a theme picked up by journalists and some educationalists who saw in the disaffection and underachievement of many boys an unexpected and regrettable outcome of the previous decade's focus on gender equity for girls in schools. Stories abounded of boys' weak performance relative to girls in final school exams, of boys' poor literacy and unwillingness to read and of youth suicide (principally males) and what schools could do to combat depression and disaffection. The "cool to be a fool" syndrome was reported as entirely a masculine phenomenon and programs began to emerge to address the issue. Men continued to need parenting advice and were advised to become involved in their sons' schooling, even at school as mentors. The amorphous and distant "Men's movement" seemed to project a presence, or voice, through much of this material. Articles on bullying (by and of girls as well as boys) with accompanying psychological advice seemed never ending. Boys were said to prefer certain learning styles requiring lots of moving around and short, clearly defined tasks as distinct from girls' alleged preferred learning styles involving reflection, discussion, and extended writing. Boys, it was said, were being discriminated against throughout their schooling and especially in their final exams by forms of assessment that favored girls. Boys were starting school too soon; boys' brains were unable to cope with auditory processing in the early years, if not later as well. Would single sex classes help, especially in English? Was the curriculum becoming feminized? Why were there so few male primary school teachers? Why did boys have so few male role models at school? No wonder boys were disaffected with school by Years 9 and 10.

Set against this characterization of a generalized boys' dissatisfaction with and resistance to schooling in both public and private sectors one might read stories of allegations of rape against high-profile footballers, of violent misbehavior by a prominent film star and of high rates of young male suicide. Boys and men, it was said, needed better skills at managing anger, negotiating relationships, and simply expressing emotion. Poor parenting and poor literacy were adduced as causes. English courses at school were boring and boys said they didn't like reading. Some schools claimed success with mentoring boys at risk and others reported on father–son rites of passage into young manhood. The generalized picture remained startlingly at odds with my impression of day-to-day life in a coeducational high school in which I worked and yet something about it seemed disturbingly real.

During this time, the school offered parents information evenings with a prominent child psychologist. Year 8 had personal development programs involving visiting speakers around the topic of sexuality and gender. In staff meetings, teachers were informed of the problem of disaffected boys and from time to time teachers attended seminars on boys' education and reported back to staff. There one might hear a range of consultants entertain and inform Primary and Secondary teachers from all school systems, drawing endlessly on psychology, biology, and personal reminiscence. The development of boys' brains was a favorite topic. Together with a colleague I arranged for a group of Year 8 boys to talk to a staff meeting about their interests and attitudes and in all this activity it seemed that we, too, were addressing a major issue with due diligence. But there the matter lay. Health and personal development studies were to include sexism, homophobia, gender equity, drug, and alcohol education and personal development generally. Concern for boys' issues as they were popularly framed, however, were not perceived by staff in questionnaires as vitally important and the argument was put to me in conversation by an administrator that in this school it just wasn't a major issue: in fact, gender issues surrounding boys were no more than "a pimple on the backside of educational research." But almost on a daily basis boys continued to be sent by teachers to year level coordinators for a range of misdemeanors. In the staff rooms and the corridors, stories of boys' behavior were exchanged daily. By the end of Year 10 each year, as if by custom, a number of boys had been helped to leave the school, some to continue their schooling elsewhere, others to leave school altogether. How had this come to be normal practice? What was going on among students and between teachers and students to bring this about? And what was it like to be one of these boys?

I INTRODUCE MYSELF

The relation of the researcher in qualitative research to the process of doing the work and writing the text has received considerable scrutiny. Rather less attention has been paid to issues arising when the researcher is a teacher in the school where he or she teaches. In this context it is particularly important that I take up the task of positioning myself in relation to the formulation of the research project as well as the participants with whom I interacted and that I acknowledge the constitutive role I have played throughout (Heyl, 2001: 370). This reflexive – even confessional – task is sometimes easily mistaken for an opportunity for self-indulgent exposure of oneself rather than a means of confronting the central issue of what Walkerdine refers to as "the place of our own subjectivity in the research process" (Walkerdine, 2002: 179), yet its importance cannot be overstated if it is conceded, as it is here, that this study has produced knowledge that has been collaboratively achieved. This will be further discussed, but in this section I will begin to position myself in relation to my project, speaking of my experience as if at this distance it were a simple possession of memory. Such an impression, however, should be treated warily. "My" experience has arisen intersubjectively in countless locations and positions that have been socially (and discursively) constructed (Tedlock, 2000); in a sense, my experience is all too familiar to me, and as a result, one of the procedural tasks in this project has been to address the ethnographic injunction to make the familiar (i.e., my experience and the world around me), strange (Delamont and Atkinson, 1995). Consequently, a central issue to be addressed in this work will be to clarify what I mean by "experience."

For over 20 years I taught boys and girls at Hillside High School during which time I was a subject coordinator and a year level coordinator (Years 8 to 10) for nearly 13 years. As a year level coordinator I had a shared responsibility for the discipline and welfare (more recently the "well-being"), of up to 350 students in a year level. In this role I allotted students to classes, advised teachers in their relationships with students and students in their relationships with teachers, mediated between teachers and students and between students and students, advised parents, negotiated with parents, referred students to welfare staff for counseling and admonished and disciplined students. But this hardly scratches the surface of experience. I have coached boys in Years 9–10 football and been in charge of school debating and chess teams. I have been happy and upset in various degrees – sometimes intensely so; I have been angry, worn out, delighted, energetic; I have been thanked, abused, criticized, and sought out for advice. I have felt satisfied and been proud of students, others, and myself and I have despaired, all in the course of teaching and coordinating, but such a list only suggests the variety of experience, not the subtlety. For example, I have spoken to students: I have shouted, I have talked reasonably, I have explained, I have joked and laughed, and I have no doubt been sarcastic and judgmental. I have looked at students: I have smiled, frowned, looked stony-faced, looked upset, fixed students with a stare, and acknowledged others with a nod. I have taken up space: I have walked quietly up to students, I have stormed up to students, and I have been unobtrusive. I have called out to students over 50 meters away and I have spoken quietly to students in tears. I have been told "All teachers are shit talkers" and I have enjoyed joking relationships with classes. And I have been cheered and clapped, jeered at, sworn at, thanked, embarrassed, felt incompetent, and been gratified all in varying degrees.

The point of mentioning these inchoate experiences is to indicate that at the same time I have acquired personae and have been identified in a thousand eyes as such-and-such a person, not only by those with whom I have come into contact but by those who became the subjects of my study – the participants, both students and staff of the school. I have not been an outsider in the sense traditionally used in relation to ethnography. I have been inside the institution, inside its rules and regulations, visible, audible, materially present, accountable, and, like the students, constituted by regimes of power which I will attempt to bring to light in this work.

Throughout this experience, my colleagues and I had to deal with students – both boys and girls – who were sent to our office by teachers for a variety of reasons related to the terms "discipline and welfare." Among these students, boys were sent in greater numbers, for a greater range of issues and more frequently, than were girls, and individual boys were sent repeatedly far more often than were individual girls. In the middle school (Years 9 and 10), boys were suspended almost exclusively throughout the period of this research, as they had been for years before. The fact that boys outnumbered girls in each year level and had done so for many years by itself fails to explain the regularity of this phenomenon. Similarly, while every effort was made to balance gender representation among award winners at the annual Speech Night, awards for academic excellence and for personifying the school's values tended initially to go to girls rather more readily than to boys in the middle school year after year.

It had become clear to me at the start of this study that many teachers at Hillside High School were finding boys a trial; that while a good many of the boys achieved outstanding results in the VCE,[1] elsewhere in the school many boys were struggling to do well and in fact many were performing badly in exams and other forms of assessment. This proudly academic school had a long "tail" and by far the majority of those making it up were boys. Certainly in the middle school (Years 9–10), each year one saw distressed teachers, failing boys, and an increasingly well-defined anti-school ethic, especially among those for whom passage to Year 11 was unlikely on academic grounds or was judged to be undesirable on grounds of antagonism to teachers and to the school's values.

This welter of untheorized and impressionistic "experience" led me to want to investigate the nature of the experiences boys were having. It seemed to me that as a staff we were complicit in the production of difficult students in the same way that we might congratulate ourselves on jointly producing academic high-achievers; hence my initial intention to document the social construction of boys' experiences in whatever variety I could identify. It was clear very early in the research process that a variety of discursive regimes located within the formal curriculum and pedagogy was constituting not only subject positions in some abstract sense but deeply felt subjectivities among my research participants, and that the formal school was discursively unwilling or unable to acknowledge its constitutive role in their formation. In other words, much of what my participants felt and understood themselves to be arose out of discourses that intertwined in and around figures of authority and formal pedagogic settings and encounters in which their habitual response was resistance in one form or another. What were these students experiencing? Why was it so hard for them to find a discursive position from which they could participate in their schooling on terms that were not inimical to the aims of the school? Why have boys so often been "the problem"? To frame these questions in this way, of course, is to constitute these boys as "other" to the school and to valorize the primacy of the school and its agents, which in itself can be thought of as perpetuating the imbalance of power implicit in such a representation and to perpetuate the humanist discourse so pervasive in school settings (Laws and Davies, 2000). As such, it reflected my position as I have so far described it. My task, as I saw it, would be to step outside such an habitual framing of the issue and, as a teacher-researcher, confront the relations of power in which I was enmeshed within the school, seeking to reposition or reconstitute myself within whatever discursive formation might make this possible.

GETTING TO THE PROBLEM

As with many qualitative studies, especially those involving ethnography, changes in orientation and emphasis continued throughout the period of the research. In this section I chart the move from a social constructionist conceptualization of the issue of boys' disaffection with schooling, which privileged a unified, rational subject, towards an account seeking to understand more clearly the constitutive function of discourse as it produces the subjectivities and boys of whom it speaks.

This study was initially conceived in terms of the "what about the boys?" debate which has recently permeated educational discourse in the public domain in Australia (Walpole, 1995; Kenway and Willis, 1997;

Lingard, 1998; Lingard and Douglas, 1999; Weaver-Hightower, 2003; Lingard et al., 2009). The impression my colleagues and I had of boys in the school – of their behavior, academic progress and sociability – in spite of exceptions, seemed to fit the descriptions of those disaffected adolescents whose images and stories permeated professional development conferences, in-service presentations, staff room discussions, media accounts, and parental concerns. All, one way or another, seemed to accept that the major issue confronting schools and boys was why so many boys were doing so poorly academically and why their behavior was so often difficult to deal with.

In seeking to understand why many staff members at the school found boys in general uncooperative and challenging compared to girls, it seemed reasonable to approach the issue in terms of the social construction of their experience. Clearly, a social constructionist account of the issue as I have outlined it so far would focus not only on situations that led to the view that boys are not doing well or are resistant to schooling, but would also challenge the understandings that are produced socially in the process (Potter, 1998). Such an approach would be attuned to the situational use of language and actions and in its focus on discourse and its anti-essentialist skepticism would operate as much to deconstruct received accounts of a real world as to reconfigure it. In this view, the nexus between boyhood and pedagogy in the context of the school emerged as a possible focus for this study. The thrust of my interest, however, was not so much in terms of gender, or gender equity (as might have been expected given the "competing victim" rhetoric sustaining the popular debate about boys), as in what I took to be the more central issue of how boys experience themselves in experiencing their schooling. It was the social construction of that experiential nexus that I hoped would become the focus of the study.

Initially, however, it seemed this might be a question of how the processes of schooling contributed to the construction of gender among adolescent boys. If, as Connell and Mac an Ghaill argue, the institution of the school and its curriculum are gendered (Connell, 1995: 36–37; Mac an Ghaill, 1994), and if the gender regime of the school promotes heteronormativity, then, given the overall patriarchal structure of gender in society it is to be expected that many boys would exhibit behavior and espouse values that might be described as hegemonic masculinity,[2] and that some would become marginalized, or subordinate, in the process (Connell, 1987: 85; 156). In this view, gender is to be understood as an achievement, as performative, as socially constructed; in a word, as relational, arising out of the multiplicity of interactions and relationships between individuals, rather than as a role to be learned or as a biological characteristic of a person (Connell, 1987: 76; Connell, 1995: 44).[3] Such a view of gender suggests that there can never be a fixed and invariant masculinity or femininity, but rather a multiplicity of masculinities and femininities, some hegemonic, some not (Connell, 1987: 170; Connell, 1995; Martino and Pallotta-Chiarolli, 2003).

From the outset, therefore, it seemed that this study required a theorization of gender in order to frame the study. If education and schooling were to be understood as social processes playing a fundamental role in the construction of gendered identities, and if, as I observed daily, boys' experiences of school were problematic and in need of analysis and explanation, did this mean that the question of how boys experience their schooling was at the same time a question of how they were experiencing the way they were being constituted as gendered? In other words, could it be that to experience being gendered in the context of the school is at the same time to experience one's schooling? If contemporary writers were correct in asserting that masculinity is a highly contested and unstable concept among men, how much more so might this be true of adolescents who were becoming young men? I took the view that schoolboys were, in a sense, "apprentice men," (apprenticed to fathers, sports coaches and teachers, among others), learning the "criteria of masculinity" (Carrigan *et al.*, 1985: 585; Phoenix and Frosh, 2001: 28) in the business of acquiring an inevitably gendered identity.

Given this theoretical orientation it seemed pertinent to ask what practices are significant in the production of meanings, values, and ideas connected with the construction of gendered identities among boys in a high school? To what extent is a gender regime identifiable in the school being investigated? What identities do boys aspire to and appropriate? What is boys' experience of their schooling (i.e., of their teachers, classes, friends, sense of success or failure, and so on)? To what extent do boys attempt to assert patriarchal values in an environment where the assumptions of patriarchy are under more or less permanent review? To what extent are teachers' views of students (especially boys), attributable to the stereotyped, customary expectations of sex-role theory? How does a secondary school identify and respond to gender issues that emerge within its own institutional environment?

In its initial framing, therefore, the project sought to investigate gender relations in a state high school, focusing in particular on boys in the middle years – boys from about 13 to 16 years old. One reason for focusing on this age group was that debates about boys' achievements (or lack of achievement) draw almost entirely on final year exam results, whereas my experience suggested that questions about achievement could equally be addressed to boys throughout the school at any year level. In my role as a year level coordinator in the middle school, and as a teacher-researcher, I contemplated an ethnographic study in which participants would emerge from the daily institutional practices of the school. Given that my initial concern was with disaffected boys, I expected to be able to draw participants from those who were habitually defined by teachers (and not by me), as "difficult": boys who were poorly behaved, challenging, unmotivated, and unwilling to accept the expectations and ethos of the school. Such a focus on institutional practices, I believed, would enable me to gain access to the grounded and situated meanings of the interactions I wished to investigate.

GOING FURTHER

Three aspects of the original formulation of the project seemed problematic from the start. In the first place, my understanding of "boys" or "schoolboys" drew too uncritically on a humanist conception of the individual as rational, sovereign, and unified, even given the coarse institutional distinction between "difficult" and "good" boys that I was already committed to. The issue for me was rather one of how "identity designation" (Walkerdine *et al.*, 2001: 13) is made and lived; of how these boys experienced subjectification in the context of the school. Poststructuralist critiques of the modern individual deny that there is anything essential about them: indeed, as Walkerdine (1993: 462–63) observes, "if subjects are produced (in specific locations) in practices that are at once material and discursive (then) the subject is a textual relation, not coterminous with the person at all".[4] Thus, it would be futile to try to understand the boys I would study as "occupants of fixed, institutionally determined positions" (Walkerdine, 1990: 14). Rather, they would need to be understood in terms of the "multiplicity of subjectivities" they experienced arising from the school's many discursive practices into which they were daily drawn (ibid.).

Second, what I had come to see as behavior – as good behavior, bad behavior, rudeness, politeness, studiousness – was arguably to be understood as constitutive not only of gender but of a particular ontology. The way a student walked, wore the school uniform, spoke, looked at teachers, and related to friends and others were all now to be understood as evidence of being and becoming gendered, just as the ways teachers presented themselves were also in some way constitutive of gender.[5] It seemed strangely reductionist, however, to see the daily life of the school – what I could see and hear around me and in which I was inextricably caught up – in terms of "the project of masculinization" (Connell, 1995: 141) to the exclusion of so much else[6] unless it "intersected" with gender. Even given the hugely significant role of schools as "sites of masculinising practices" (Connell, 1995: 146; Mac an Ghaill, 1994), the question of how the collective construction of the school's gender regime promoted "adolescent peer masculinity" (Connell, 1995: 123; 129), while important in itself, seemed tangential to the interactions I wished to investigate in the everyday life of the school. Given what I increasingly thought was, on the one hand, a somewhat programmatic understanding of gender relations implied in Connell's account of the project of masculinization, and, on the other hand, the day-to-day experience of schooling, a conceptual shift favoring a discourse analytic framing of the problem of the ways boys experience and are produced by their schooling seemed more appropriate.[7] In recasting my approach in these terms I was to some extent also drawing on Joan Swann's (2002: 48) question of how to assess "whether a speaker is doing gender, or another aspect of identity?" To privilege one at the expense of whatever else might be going on seemed unwarranted.

This bore directly on a third area of concern. As this was to be an ethnographic study, the issue of the constitutive role of my presence in the research process needed to be acknowledged. It is widely understood that ethnography is not a transparent means of representing the "other" but rather a site of contested understanding and jointly produced knowledge (Denzin, 1997; Marcus, 1998; Atkinson et al., 2001). It would be essential that in situating myself in relation to the epistemological project I sought to avoid the sort of unreflective realism that had produced the "what about the boys?" debate. In taking this view I would acknowledge not only the situatedness and contingency of participants' beliefs and actions but also, crucially, that in any ethnographic encounter I would be party to the ways in which participants might be discursively constituted and positioned to produce themselves as subjects of a particular kind.

Thus, in reframing my approach to the study, I had moved from an unreflective acceptance of the unitary Enlightenment subject implied in the notions of the schoolboy and the researcher, to an understanding of the subject as multiple and discursively produced (Henriques *et al.*, 1984). Such a step therefore required a further rethinking of issues related to the processes of subjectification and agency which neither sex-role theory nor a biologically essentialist view of gender, nor an understanding of gender as relationally constructed, could address. What I had thought would be a study of disaffected boys in school would now, I hoped, become a study of subjectification brought about by the discursive regimes that constituted the functions and processes of the school. This would require an understanding not only of to what extent boys' experiences and subjectivities were constituted discursively, but, as I hope will become equally clear, of my own role as teacher-researcher and narrator of this study and how it was similarly challenged and recast in the process.

THEORETICAL SOURCES

My concern with subjectivity and the discursive practices by which subjects are constituted locates this work firmly in the disciplinary space provided by postmodernism's ascendancy in qualitative research. The perspective offered by this development rejects the unitary, timeless, rational, and prediscursive subject of humanism (the modernist subject), together with its characteristic functionalist and patriarchal "meta-narratives" and reformulates the way the social world is theorized in terms of the centrality accorded language in social relationships. In this context, language may be conceived of as the initial object of discursive analysis, and in this study, critical attention will be drawn to the constitutive function of a wide range of discursive practices in the institutional setting provided by Hillside High School.

Michel Foucault

Foucault's role in destabilizing Saussurian linguistics and the certainties offered by structuralism is well known (Young, 1987; O'Farrell, 2005). These certainties collapsed with the insight that words do not offer a transparent reflection or representation of things, or of the structure of things. In particular, the structuralist assumption of the prior constitution of meaning (e.g., "within" or "behind" the text[8]), over the social, or textual production of multiple and indeterminate signifying effects of signs was shattered. Among those who fatally challenged Saussurian dualism on which structuralism depended, Michel Foucault's proposal of another kind of language formation, namely discourse, contributed significantly to structuralism's demise and the so-called "textual turn" in cultural and other studies of society.

In his formulation of the concept of discourse,[9] Foucault drew attention to statements identifiable across disparate sites, which crucially, had "the power to constitute domains of objects . . ." (Foucault, 1970, in Young, 1987: 73). In these terms, discourses were not to be regarded merely as "groups of signs (signifying elements referring to contents or representations) but as practices that systematically form the objects of which they speak" (Foucault, 1972: 49). Such discourses as Foucault had in mind were historically verifiable, located in discontinuous practices which constitute the social world (denying any prediscursive domain of meaning), and so could be understood in terms neither of a search for origins nor of any interior, hidden thought or signification.[10] For Foucault, any discourse constituted not only the objects of which it spoke but the very conditions of their possibility – the horizon of their meaning and intelligibility (Foucault: 1970, in Young, 1987: 67).[11]

It is perhaps not surprising, therefore, that Foucault privileged the practice of speaking or writing (making statements) from within discursive formations over mundane thought (1972: 117). This distinction draws attention to the speaking subject's locatedness in time and space (so that what is said "is not said from anywhere" (ibid. 122), and to the subject's discursive constitution. The analysis of discourse, therefore, does not require reference to a prediscursive, volitional subject (cogito), collective consciousness, transcendental subjectivity or psychological subjectivity, but instead recognizes that "the speaking subject" (ibid. 122), dispersed as it is in language, is constituted and positioned within and by discourse (ibid. 54–55). This is a subject who does something other than reveal thoughts or play with the structure of language; this is a subject who in speaking shows "that to speak is to do something" (Foucault, 1972: 209; Young, 1987: 12).

This particular notion of the constitutive power of discourse was crucial to Foucault's studies of the ways the modern state had come to be governed. The modern state, he argued, required its citizens to be knowable in order to be governed. This meant, in effect, that persons became knowable, or, in his terms, "disciplined", through subjection to the various apparatuses of knowledge in the modern state. In *Discipline and Punish: The Birth of the Prison* (1991), he argues that one such "apparatus of knowledge" is the prison, and makes a compelling case for the equivalence of prisons, hospitals, workshops, and schools where bodies and the spaces they inhabit are disciplined by meticulous, often minute techniques, in order to produce "subjected and practiced bodies, 'docile' bodies" (ibid. 138).[12] In the application of these disciplinary techniques, Foucault points to "a 'new micro-physics' of power" (ibid. 139) in relations between the objects of subjection (prisoners, workers, patients, students), and the prison warders, supervisors, doctors, and teachers who are among the agents of this "disciplinary society" (ibid. 216; 209). These relations, he argues, produced privileged forms of knowledge (such as psychiatry, psychology, criminology), which have generated a vast documentary apparatus through which the associated authority figures (psychologists, confessors, teachers) apply their techniques of normalization, so essential to the modern state's management of large populations. This intersection of knowledge and the authority it conveyed he termed "power-knowledge." Thus, through such surveillant technologies as studies, files, dossiers, reports, censuses, tests, and the like, the analysis of society becomes possible and the individual becomes knowable by those discursively empowered to study, file, report, test, and so on. At the same time, in this objectification of the subject, the disciplinary effect of normalization culminates in the individual's adoption of reflective techniques of surveillance of the self to allow him/her to take an active role in his/her subjectification as a person of a particular kind. Under the normalizing judgments of power-knowledge, in "the vigilance of intersecting gazes" (ibid. 183–84; 217), the early modern subject emerged from the multiplicity of humanity.

Foucault's conception of discipline, understood as a type of power, or technology, "comprising a whole set of instruments, techniques, procedures, levels of application, targets" (ibid. 215) clearly means more than simply being organized, or managed, and finds its ultimate expression in a society where the function of discipline, and therefore the effects of power, have been infinitesimally distributed among "the most minute and distant elements" of that society (ibid. 216).[13] To Foucault, this expresses "the panoptic principle" (ibid. 216) which "imposes on those whom (discipline) subjects a principle of compulsory invisibility . . . It is the fact of being constantly seen . . . that maintains the disciplined individual in his subjection" (ibid. 187) and which subtly ensures that this individual takes up the task of continually disciplining him- or herself. In Foucault's lexicon, the penal image of the panopticon stands precisely for this function.

Foucault's revelation of the pervasive and constitutive effects of discourse has contributed in no small way to the development of a poststructuralist approach to the question of how to understand the social (Rabinow, 1991) and has been taken up widely in the context of education (Ball, 1990a; Davies, 1993; O'Farrell, 1997; Middleton, 1998). Concepts such as subjectivity, subject position, and subjectification have enabled discourse analysis (broadly conceived) to reveal the subject as a construction; that is, as the result, or effect, of being discursively positioned. This has become especially clear in poststructural feminist analyses of gender and gendered experience, such as in the work of Bronwyn Davies and Valerie Walkerdine (among others), in which subjectivity comes to be understood primarily as a sense of self that is not an essence, that is not singular, and which challenges the notion of the constant, unitary, conscious self, or subject, of modernism (Davies, 1989, 1992, 1993, 1997; Walkerdine, 1981, 1986, 1990, 1994, 2002). If subjectivity is therefore understood as constructed discursively, it is, as Davies says, because:

> each person actively takes up the discourses through which they and others speak/write the world into existence *as if they were their own*. Through these discourses they are made speaking subjects at the same time as they are subjected to the constitutive force of those discourses.
>
> (Davies, 1993: 13; original emphasis)

In this formulation, it is clear that subjectivities are unstable and constructed from "multiple layers of contradictory meanings" (ibid. 11) arising from the many discourses in which an individual is enmeshed. As a result, the self is seen to be a socially and discursively constituted achievement: "an interactive, discursive process, fragile (and) always vulnerable to the discourses through which it is spoken and speaks itself into existence" (ibid. 21).

This, of course, has clear echoes of Foucault's subject, so dispersed in discursive formations as to posit the death of the (Humanist) subject, leaving behind nothing but the body – disciplined, subjected and docile. And yet, as in the aforementioned passage, by seeming to attribute a pre-discursive voluntarism to a unified subject, Davies raises the question of agency. In some respects this question of agency has been the source of feminist unease with Foucault's thoroughly dispersed subject by appearing to deny a coherent and shared sense of experience on which to build "a politics of resistance" (McNay, 1992: 193; 2000).[14] Nevertheless, as McNay recognizes, the later Foucault revived the acting subject in his writings on the care and technologies of the self, a topic to which I will return in later chapters (Foucault, 1987, 1988). I will return to the question of agency in relation to Judith Butler's work later on.

Among writers on education and gender, both Connell and Davies have explicitly rejected the concept of "role" and therefore also of "socialization" as a process leading to the adoption of normative behavior. In the work of Davies and Walkerdine, "role" has been displaced by the concept of "positioning" which acknowledges the constitutive force of discursive practices (Davies and Harré, 1990: 43) in a way that the static, formal, and ritualistic aspects of role theory could not.[15] Positioning, in their view, is "the discursive process whereby selves are located in conversations as observably and subjectively coherent participants in jointly produced story lines" (Davies and Harré, 1990: 48). As such, discursive positioning "helps focus attention on dynamic aspects of encounters" (ibid. 43).[16] To be positioned in this sense, therefore, is to adopt discursive practices such that the meaning of actions and words is jointly achieved in speech. In the process, one is produced as a person of a particular kind; that is, one comes to know oneself (one's subjectivity) and to be known by others in terms of the positions one "takes up" within the discursive formations one enters into. This pragmatic understanding of positioning draws on Foucault, as I intend to, but is clearly far removed from a literal appropriation of his epistemology.

This has important consequences for the concept of "self" implied in the notion of experience. If one assumes that individuals "are characterized both by continuous personal identity and by discontinuous personal diversity" (Davies and Harré, 1990: 46), one may experience oneself as multiply and even contradictorily positioned in discourse. In the context of this study, such a formulation suggests the sort of dilemma students and teachers may well experience as they daily "take up" positions within discourses which constitute the domain of their work as if this were a matter of choice. It also suggests that one's commonsense awareness of one's "continuous personal identity" is the locus of the modernist conviction that the "I" of whom one speaks in grammar is a unitary, rational, and voluntarist subject. In later chapters I will draw attention to what appears to be a grim and relentless contest between the self of modernism and the postmodern subject in the experiences of boys at school.

This, then, is the basis on which I arrived at the revised formulation of the questions underpinning this study. The question of what it is to be a boy at school – that is, of how some boys come to be known as difficult and disengaged whereas others do not, and of what their experiences of school and themselves might be – may be resolved into the following questions. What discourses characterize or create the institutional practices of schooling at Hillside High School? What discursive practices do teachers and students engage in, and to what end? What sort of persons do students (and teachers) understand themselves to be, and how do students and teachers represent themselves (or, how are they represented), discursively? And, following Foucault and Rose, in what ways do students police, protect, insinuate, and even parade themselves in the face of the normalizing practices of the school? What reflective discourses of the self, or soul, are available to them? (Foucault, 1988; Rose, 1989).

In sum, therefore, I have taken the notion of discourse as a field of intelligibility within which discursive practices both position and construct speakers in a process of subjectification. This enables a conceptual distinction between persons (individuals), and subjects occupying subject positions within a discourse. Furthermore, the institution of the school may be regarded as a site within which the disciplinary techniques characteristic of the power-knowledge of teachers works to normalize the student population, suggesting the parallel discursive realms of the normative school and the pathological school, represented by those spaces, bodies, and subjectivities resistant, but not yet subject to, the dominant techniques of normalization represented by "the school."

Judith Butler

Drawing on Foucault's notions of discourse and of power (as both productive and an effect of discursive relations), Judith Butler has confronted the question of the relation of the sovereign subject to the subject of discourse by critiquing the relationship of language to subjectivity. "If we are formed in language (she observes), then that formative power precedes and conditions any decision we might make about it, insulting us from the start... by its prior power" (Butler, 1997a: 1; 135). The example she considers, following Althusser, is of being hailed, so that by being named one is constituted as a subject in language. Such interpellation, she argues, has what she calls "the character of performativity" (ibid. 2–3), or the capacity to constitute "a certain kind of effect" (ibid. 18) – in this case subjectivity – and thus to give the one so hailed "a certain possibility for social existence" (ibid. 2; also Butler, 1993: 13).

In Butler's view, the distinction between the one who speaks and the one who becomes a subject "(untethers) the speech act from the sovereign subject (and) founds an alternative notion of agency" (ibid. 15); alternative, that is, to the view that "speech is taken to be a sign of agency" (ibid. 84) in a unified, rational, sovereign subject.[17] In so far as a speech act such as interpellation has future effects, Butler argues that it signifies "a theory of linguistic agency" (ibid. 15), separate and different from conventional notions of agency as a property of the subject, and therefore of what she refers to as "linguistic existence" (ibid. 29–30). In drawing these distinctions, Butler is refusing to elide the social with the discursive and is adamant in her defence, or extension, of Foucault's notion of subjectivity by seeking the "post-sovereign subject" and its agency in a theory of discursive performativity.

Butler's notion of discursive performativity refines Foucault's claim that discourses (as I noted earlier), are "practices that systematically form the objects of which they speak" (Foucault, 1972: 49), and has been taken up in the context of education by Deborah Youdell (2006a, 2006b, 2006c). Extending the notion of interpellation, she observes:

> With this understanding of the performative, the schoolgirl and boy, the gifted and talented student, the student with emotional and behavioural difficulties, even the teacher, is so because he/she is designated as such. Indeed, while these designations appear to describe pre-existing subjects, *it is the very act of designation that constitutes the subject,* as if they were already student, teacher, gifted, emotionally/behaviourally disordered, and so on.
> (Youdell, 2006a: 36; original emphasis)

Here the performative constitution of subjects in the everyday life of the school appears as a process amenable to observation and the analysis of spoken and written language. Critical attention is thereby deflected from any commonsense, prediscursive notion of subjects as persons or individuals who precede their designation, to "the subject (as) an artefact of its performative constitution" (Youdell, 2006a: 36).

Becoming such a subject, Butler argues, requires not only that the subject be performatively constituted within a discursive frame, but that subjects repeatedly draw on (or cite) the rules or conventions of the discourse. For Butler, subjectivity is not possible if the subject is conceived as the origin of some unique utterance, forlornly hoping to perform one's subjectivity into being. Instead, what is required is a repetition of some act or utterance identifiable with a convention – a citation of a practice – conferring authority and intelligibility within the discursive frame (Butler, 1997a: 50–51).[18] For example, Butler argues that to "(be) called a name is . . . one of the conditions by which a subject is constituted in language" (Butler, 1997a: 2), and that by being both recognizable and recognized repeatedly one survives in language both as a subject and as embodied (Butler, 1997a: 4–5; 27).

As Youdell notes, Butler adds to this idea of performativity by drawing on Bourdieu's notion of habitus to suggest that "the disposition of the bodily habitus might be understood as . . . a tacit awareness of the potential performative force and limits of bodily practices" (Youdell, 2003: 6). Thus "the bearing of the body as the rhetorical instrument of expression" (Butler, 1997a: 152; Laws and Davies, 2000) is acknowledged as indissociable from the speech act. Discursive performativity, then, may be deployed, as

Youdell observes, "through bodily gestures, adornments, acts – the way students sit at their desks, how they wear (or do not wear) their school uniform, how they link arms in the corridor" (Youdell, 2006a: 36). Throughout the ethnographic chapters I will draw on this notion of performativity to illustrate the discursive effects of the relations of power; or more particularly, of "power at its extremities, in its ultimate destinations . . . at the extreme points of its exercise" (Foucault, 1976: 96–97).

The notion of discursive performatives therefore suggests a particular focus for an ethnographic study of the ways identities are constituted in bodily and linguistic practices and thus of the subjectivation of students and teachers within the discursive community of a school. A host of practices from the direct naming of social and biographical categories or the attribution of qualities, to pictorial representations that might implicitly cite specific discourses and to bodily gestures and comportment might all be understood as expressions of subjectivation within the normative school and may, at the same time, suggest the performative context of resistance as a means for appropriating the productive power of discourse.[19]

ETHNOGRAPHY

Ethnography's long history within anthropology and sociology and its extension in the era of its repatriation from colonial settings into a range of contexts including education is well known (Burgess, 1984; Delamont, 1992; Atkinson and Hammersley, 1994; Gordon et al., 2001). In relation to education, ethnographic research has been defined as "research on and in educational institutions based on participant observation and/or permanent recordings of everyday life in naturally occurring settings" (Delamont and Atkinson, 1995: 15; see also Gordon et al., 2001: 188). As such, a vast archive of ethnographic studies has accumulated and in Chapter 3 I will offer a critique of its contribution to the study of boys and their schooling. For the moment, however, I wish to reflect on my task as teacher-researcher attempting to retain as much as I could of the "everyday life" of the school around me in the way I carried out and wrote about the research. I envisaged an ethnographic project in which participant-observation would be the central methodological practice as I negotiated my way through a field within which, in one sense (as I will show), I was relatively unfamiliar. In this context the umbrella term "participant-observation," raises a number of epistemological issues, three of which I will briefly discuss.

Reflexivity

In the era of traditional, realist ethnography, representation of the "other" was taken to be epistemologically unproblematic and an author's claim to have "been there" was enough to valorize her (or, more often, his) account (Clifford, 1983; Denzin and Lincoln, 1994). It is clear, however, given feminist and poststructuralist critiques of practice, as I mentioned earlier in this chapter (see also Behar and Gordon, 1995), that the ethnographer cannot stand outside the domain of his/her object of study as detached interpreter but must accept his/her constitutive role within the everyday interactions that characterize the research site. Thus the researcher is obliged to scrutinize his/her power in relation to participants as subjects and to locate him- or herself in the epistemological enterprise. Ethnography of any sort clearly entails complicity in knowledge production in the sense that knowledge is not unambiguously "there" somewhere, waiting to be uncovered: rather, it is thought of here as a product of discourse, thus raising crucial ethical issues concerning power, honesty, respect, rapport, discretion, and reciprocity. These issues are commonly addressed by adopting a reflexive[20] stance in relation both to the research process and to the writing of the ethnography and involve what Coffey (1999) refers to as "identity work" by the researcher; work which has led some to be accused of overfamiliarity with their subjects, an issue to which I will return in Chapter 3.

The issue of reflexivity has been widely discussed among feminist writers, especially those taking a socially critical perspective (e.g., Kondo, 1990; Fine, 1991; Skeggs, 1998, 2004). According to Skeggs (2001), feminism and ethnography have in common a concern for "experience, participants, definitions, meanings and sometimes subjectivity" (Skeggs, 2001: 426) which, in combination with critiques of Enlightenment rationality, has enabled feminist ethnography to question the apparent virtues of objectivity, distance, and detachment and reveal them as "a 'god trick'" played by (often male) ethnographers seeking a position of authority (Skeggs, 2001: 437). The rationale for undertaking an ethnographic study of boys' experiences, therefore, is partly established by the prospect of my discursive participation in the production of that experience and the meanings and subjectivities arising from it; partly by precedent, and partly by the opportunity it offers in preserving the situatedness of institutional discourses within the environment of Hillside High School. At the same time, feminist ethnography's contribution to an understanding of how the "positioning and subjectivity of the researcher impact upon and necessarily inform the production of situated knowledge" (Skeggs, 1997: 13) indicates that the very act of participant observation will be as much the object of the study as are the experiences of the participants (and myself), in the research. Indeed, Skeggs' (2002) trenchant critique of reflexivity poses a considerable challenge to the researcher and in this study it will be understood as to some extent both autobiographical and surveillant, in the sense of monitoring the "complicated plays of power" involved in "who reveals what to whom . . ." (Walkerdine *et al.*, 2002: 191).

Interviews

The second key epistemological issue for this study concerns the nature of interviews and the data that arise from them. As I indicated earlier, "participation" and "observation" are not neutral or unproblematic terms. Understood as sustained and interactive immersion in a setting, participation is usually accompanied, or evidenced, by textual accounts of interviewing, whether structured or unstructured or some combination of both (Mishler, 1986; Kvale, 1996; Saukko, 2003). In fact, unstructured interviews may plausibly be called conversations, or discussions, if one is admitted into one's subjects' lifeworlds on the basis of trust and rapport (Woods, 1985; Burgess, 1988; Fontana and Frey, 2000: 654–55; Heyl, 2001: 374).[21] What has increasingly come to be accepted is that any interview is a collaborative accomplishment between interviewer and respondent(s) but there is little consensus over the uses to which it may be put. For example, Hammersley (2006a), in discussing the recent radical critique of interviews, notes that they should be used with caution rather than abandoned. In so far as there is any consensus, he claims that interviews may be analyzed as linguistic events (e.g., by conversation analysis), but the radical critique is aimed more at "the 'romantic impulse' which treats open-ended interviews as capturing the 'genuine voices' of interviewees" (ibid. 119). Instead, the radical critique argues that interviews can be no more than "methodically constructed social product(s) that (emerge) from (their) reflexive communicative processes" (ibid. 119), thus cutting them off from any other context of meaning. While this critique is aimed at the "stubbornly . . . romantic" notion "of the experiential as the authentic" (Silverman, 2000: 823), it is only able to make its point by adopting a simple realist account of experience as stable, given, and prediscursive. In this study, however, I adopt the view that conversations, as a means for entering discursively into other times and places in respondents' lives (in other words, for entering into their experiences via the experience of the interview/conversation), are valid and fruitful means both of working reflexively and for writing evocatively (Atkinson, 1996: 10–11). What is important is to be aware of the positionings implicit in conducting interviews, or conversations, in and through which stories are told (Walkerdine *et al.*, 2002: 187).

Observation

The third key issue to be addressed is to query what is meant by "observation." Observation has long been regarded as an important component of fieldwork in "natural" settings, especially during the traditional and modernist phases of qualitative research (Denzin and Lincoln, 1994; Angrosino and Mays de Perez, 2000) when, as I have indicated earlier, claims to textual authority rested on first person accounts of having "been there." Given the postmodernist critique of assumptions underlying studies of society and culture, attention has been drawn to the locatedness of the ethnographer within the research project and this has prompted Angrosino and Mays de Perez (2000: 690) to reconceptualize observation from being a "data collection technique" to "a context" in which members of social settings "interact in dialogic fashion" with researchers accepted into those settings.

The issue of the place of observation in fieldwork is also dealt with by Delamont (2002, 2004).[22] Describing it as her "favourite kind of data collection" (2004: 130), she speaks of "doing observation" (ibid. 134) as "a matter of systematic, principled, reflexive decision-making," referring in passing to looking and watching. In this study I will draw attention to observation in the sense of watching as discussed by Fordham (1996), and to inadvertently seeing things and people, but much less to systematically looking in the sense of setting out to see some predetermined category. Observation will in fact be difficult to disentangle from hearing and listening, so much is it part of the field context of research, as Delamont (2002) appears to suggest (pp. 134–37).

It is this sense of a constitutive ethnographic gaze that I wish to emphasize. To the observer, what another is experiencing may be thought of as behavior, or action: what is seen is the person having (an) experience. The ethnographer, just like the "other" in the ethnographic encounter, may therefore be present as a witness at the constitution of the "other's" experience, or may participate in its constitution, or may even help reconstitute it discursively in memory. The "other" may agree to share, or recall, such experiences in a later discursive context, but in the telling it may be subject to censorship, repression, embellishment, or any of the many possible interpretive maneuvers of which Delamont (2002, 2004) is so concerned. Equally, the "other" may be unwilling or unable to articulate some or all of the experience (MacLure *et al.*, 2010), or it may seem that such experience has become indistinguishable from temporal flow, merely received and recalled by the consciousness of one who, to all intents and purposes, presents him- or herself as a unified, coherent self.

ETHICAL ISSUES AND THEIR IMPLICATIONS

In framing my research as an ethnographic study of the ways boys' experiences and subjectivities at Hillside High School were discursively constructed, my interest was no longer in boys as an undifferentiated mass. Instead, I was interested in two sorts of students: boys in the middle school who were regarded by staff as representing the values of the school in academic achievement, behavior, and extra-curricular endeavors, and second, those who were disaffected and probably not enjoying school; boys who were doing poorly academically – boys who might reasonably be expected to be among those who would perform poorly in the final year state-wide exams up to four years later and who in every way seemed to be the very boys about whom the question "what about the boys?" was asked. My interest was focused to a large extent on this latter group who were emerging early in their high school years in terms of the school's policies and day-to-day practices as problematic. By Year 8, or at about 13 or 14 years of age after one year at high school, teachers were beginning to identify such boys who in their own ways were beginning to identify themselves. In relying on the day-to-day processes of the school I was seeking to answer the question "what about the boys?" by asking "which boys?" in a way that resonated with my experience and the experience of other teachers. In this way it might be possible, I thought, to note the effects of "institutional practices and discourses . . . on the shaping of biographies" while avoiding "generalized and unsituated discussions about the productive power of discourses" (McLeod, 2000b: 503–4). As well as the kinds of students I have outlined, I also intended to interview as many of their teachers as I could.

Before the ethnographic work could start, permission was sought and granted from the relevant educational administrators and the school's Principal. This aspect of entry to an institutional research site, together with related discussion of the ethics of the project, is all too often glossed over in ethnographies related to schools and schooling (e.g., Mac an Ghaill, 1994; Yon, 2000; Gonick, 2003) as if it has no place in the overall project. As I will show, however, gaining Human Ethics permission to undertake the study radically confined what I could expect to do. The major stumbling block was over the issue of the power I represented in relation to students I might wish to observe and interview and the possible ethical issues arising from my teaching and coordination of them. This was resolved by the requirement that I not observe or interview any student I taught or coordinated, immediately ensuring that what in one sense was thoroughly familiar would now become new, challenging, and strange as I sought research participants who were entirely unknown to me.

This requirement was to force me to seek out, among others, boys with no apparent affection for teachers or the school and ask if they would be willing to participate in the study, a daunting enough prospect for a teacher/researcher who would at the same time represent just such teachers as the ones these boys regularly confronted. I would also, of course, have to get parents' and students' informed consent before interviews began and ensure the confidentiality of names and material disclosed, but it was conceded by the Ethics Committee with which I was negotiating that if I held a group interview, the confidentiality of views aired and members' identities could not be guaranteed. In the mean time, further restrictions were added. I was not to withdraw students from class to interview them and interviews were not to take more than half an hour or take place more than once a month. I was also to notify parents in writing before any such interviews took place. From the school's point of view (and as an ethical requirement), I could not be absolved from retaining at least some of my duty of care, so I would need to tell participants that I would be bound to disclose to the school's administration anything that I might be told relating to a student's welfare; anything, for example, related to drugs, weapons, violence, or vandalism. Participants could, of course, withdraw from the study at any time. None did. As a final requirement, after some negotiation, I was able to satisfy the Ethics Committee that if, after being interviewed, any boy felt distressed about whatever we discussed, he could go to the school's welfare staff or the school's nurse for support. For my part, after months of negotiation and not without some desperation, I indicated that should I feel the need to share the burden of my knowledge I would approach the school's chaplain for support.

Very little appears to have been written about the degree to which research designs (at least at the doctoral level) are ultimately the result of negotiation with university Ethics Committees (Walford, 2002). Of more immediate importance, however, was the question of just what sort of ethnography was possible given the restrictions under which I was expected to work. Obviously, participant observation of a more or less classical kind (Woods, 1986: 36ff) was out of the question, but I could still observe from a distance, listen, and overhear, talk casually and interview individuals and small groups. I have also drawn on a variety of formal school documents such as annual reports, teacher handbooks, year level day books, records of suspension, school reports, and teachers' memos to further contextualize my observations. To a large extent I have had to be a "fly on the wall" (Roman, 1993: 282), unobtrusive and inconspicuous, and in drafting the written account of this work I have had to acknowledge the extent to which my ethnographic data – the narratives of experience – have been textually and collaboratively produced (Mishler, 1986; Silverman, 1998: 127). I determined early that I would not observe classes my participants were in as my presence would undoubtedly influence their behavior as well as the actions of other students and staff, as my mere proximity did on two occasions which I will mention in Chapters 6 and 7. I would instead rely in the first instance on the school's procedures for producing information (such as teachers' reports of a student's behavior), and also seek a range of teachers' accounts of what happened in their classes as well as asking subjects to discuss their experiences of the same classes. My resulting diary entries and audiotape transcripts represent the students' experiences of the material conditions of daily life in the school as mediated through the interviews.

The effect of the conditions under which I was to work in the field very soon took me by surprise. While both physically and visibly present to all, and more or less as familiar as ever, I became a stranger to myself.[23] I would have to identify and approach potential subjects who were essentially unknown to me and to whom I, also, was relatively unknown: the insider was rapidly becoming an outsider. Simply to ask some potential subjects if they were interested in taking part in the study would inevitably position them as students who were seen to be disaffected and whose behavior and academic achievement were somehow known to this figure of authority from the middle school, and might therefore result in refusal to participate, or even indignation and confrontation. How would I avoid, or deal with that? In overcoming this problem, as I hope will become clear, the outsider that I was, was also becoming an insider in so far as the students who did not know me, or who knew me only as a figure of authority, began to see me in a different light. The issues of trust, rapport, and possible overidentification with the boys who were the subjects of the study will be taken up in later chapters.

EXPERIENCE

As mentioned earlier, this book is concerned in a general sense with boys' experience of their schooling. If this is understood as the experience of "being schooled" then it is also very much concerned with boys' experience of themselves at school and as boys. Before moving on to a discussion of how ethnography might contribute to an understanding of this domain of experience, the very idea of experience needs further discussion.[24]

To the casual observer another's experience may be thought of in terms of behavior, or action.[25] In this formulation, behavior, not experience, can be observed: what is observed is the person having (an) experience. At the same time, the observer has the experience of observing, and the "other" experiences being observed.[26] The sense in which "experience" is being used here is essentially prediscursive: that is, it is being used descriptively in an everyday sense that requires one to suspend one's awareness of the constitutive power of discourse. In doing so it appears to claim a linguistic neutrality, but it may be argued also that such a suspension of awareness emphasizes a certain discursive distance from the constitutive field of power relations such that one may speak of persons and individuals who might acknowledge a stable, unified self, rather than of potentially nonunitary, decentered subjects and subjectivities. This is the domain of prediscursive experience even if it is thought of as socially constructed: experience, in Edward Said's memorable phrase quoted by Britzman (1995), as "the great original" (p. 229), the foundation upon which authorial and theoretical certainties have so often been asserted. On the other hand, if the surveillance of the observer is acknowledged as discursively mediated, then the experience of each may be said to be discursively constituted even as it is constructed socially.[27]

Studies of the social frequently gloss the notion of experience in references to the everyday in the way I have suggested earlier. Experience in this sense is said to be "of" something and available to a reflective subject. For example, my discussion of myself earlier – of my experience – may be understood as an account of this type: an account by a prediscursive sovereign subject recounting his experience of being a teacher, or, alternatively, as a representation of innumerable discursive encounters within which the terms I have used became intelligible. On the one hand, experience may be thought of as socially constructed by unitary subjects, and on the other it may be thought of as an effect of discursive practices which position and constitute their subjects as discontinuous, fractured and diverse – even contradictory (Britzman, 1995: 229). According to the former view, experience may be so inscribed in another's identity as to render that identity self-evident, or foundational – that is, to essentialize it – whereas in the latter case, experience is above all of being subjectivated – of being brought into being as a subject: of being made aware of oneself as a subject of a particular kind. It is this distinction, I will suggest, that opens the very possibility of an ethnographic study of the discursive constitution of experience as distinct from an understanding of experience as self-evident and unexamined.

Throughout this study I will adopt the view proposed by Joan Scott (1992), and suggested earlier, that experience is discursively produced. Taking up the question of the relationship of identity to experience, Scott asks "How can we write about identity without essentialising it?" (Scott, 1992: 33). That is to say, how can we write about experience without taking the categories of identity (e.g., schoolboy, teacher), to be self-evident, unequivocal, pre-existing, unitary, and in some sense foundational? Scott's answer is clear: "It is not individuals who have experience, but subjects who are constituted through experience" (Scott, 1992: 25–26). Such a view clearly acknowledges the productive power of discourse and suggests that attributions of prediscursive experience can never constitute an unquestioned, privileged "origin of knowing," as that would merely reproduce, rather than contest, ideological systems and received categories of representation (ibid. 22; 25).[28] To take experience for granted in this way – merely as something endured, or as the way things are – is potentially, as Youdell argues (2006a: 33), to reproduce "abiding educational inequalities and exclusions" and allow inequitable processes and "sedimented" meanings to remain unchallenged.

The implications for ethnographic research, relying primarily as they do on the researcher's claim to authority on the basis of experience (by having entered as a participant observer into another's life-world) are therefore potentially destabilizing. Such claims to authorial certainty appear to ignore the researcher's constitutive role in producing such knowledge in the experience of the ethnographic encounter (Britzman, 1995: 230). In this context, Scott's argument, that experience should be understood as the process by which subjectivity is discursively constituted, is compelling. It avoids naturalizing categories and thus avoids foreclosing on their interrogation; it acknowledges that such experience cannot be ontologically foundational, and above all, it acknowledges that by locating experience within discursive practices its very intelligibility is opened to scrutiny (see Davies *et al.*, 2001).

Scott's observation that "Subjects are constructed discursively, experience is a linguistic event" (Scott, 1992: 34) may therefore be amplified by Butler's notion of the performative, especially in relation to bodily dispositions. Given this framework, therefore, my intention is to scrutinize the discourses within which the experience of schooling arises in order, as Spivak says, to "make visible the assignment of subject positions" (in Scott, 1992: 33), or, following Youdell, to identify the ways discursive performatives are deployed in acts of designation.

AN ETHNOGRAPHY OF EXPERIENCE?

The core of anthropology, if not of ethnography more generally, has always in a sense been the analysis of experience (Bruner, 1986: 15). For Victor Turner, the notion of experience was of something "lived through" (ibid. 3); a sense of being-in-the-world entailing consciousness of experience understood not only as sense data or cognition, but also as feelings and expectations. In Edward Bruner's words, "Lived experience . . . as thought and desire, as word and image, is the primary reality" (ibid. 5). Put this way, as I have indicated, experience is conceived of as prediscursive. Gaining access to that experience, as I have said, is at the core of the project of ethnography as traditionally conceived in terms of participant observation, just as in this study it is my aim to gain access to experience constituted discursively prior to my intervention. Therefore I will assume that by appealing to memory in situations that are themselves discursively negotiated, experience as I understand it may be accessed retrospectively not so much by giving voice to subjects as by provoking or allowing subjectivities to find their voice(s). In other words, the individual becomes a surrogate for the already discursively constituted subject; a surrogate of himself as already constituted as a boy of a certain kind. Thus "participant observation" becomes a matter of seeking and listening to and watching the selves that boys take themselves to be.

SUMMARY

Given the conceptual framework arising from the theoretical influences discussed earlier, and the questions I have posed that give expression to that framework, this study has three broad aims. The first is to undertake an ethnographic study which allows us to better understand what it is to be a young teenage boy (of a certain kind) at school; the second focuses on an account of the study as a work in progress, and the third is to regard the problem of writing the ethnography as no less important or central than the work involved in ethnographic encounters.

The literature on why it seems so many boys are struggling at school shows that the problems these boys and their teachers are confronting are more or less common to a variety of educational settings; the problems I could see around me were happening in an environment that was little different from others in Britain, Europe, North America, and elsewhere (Epstein et al., 1998; Gordon et al., 2000; Francis and Skelton, 2001; Foster et al., 2001; Croxford et al., 2003; Jones and Myhill, 2004; Lahelma, 2005; Weaver-Hightower, 2003; 2009). As the issue of gender equity in relation to access and achievement is so prominent in the literature, however, it seemed important to ask "which boys?" in order to disaggregate the analytically unuseful category of "boys" and to let the pedagogical processes of the school answer that question in a way that created a space for an ethnographic study.

The fundamental issue as I saw it early in my research was to illustrate just how boys' experience of their schooling was discursively constructed in the context of the school in order to move beyond, or avoid repeating, the issue of outcomes and backlash implied in the question "what about the boys?" Merely giving voice to boys and teachers as they negotiated their relationships from day to day seemed doomed, yet again, to replicate the tendency to apprehend boys merely in prediscursive terms. In this light, Epstein's query, namely to understand "how boys experience themselves as boys" at school (Epstein, 1998b: 107), seemed especially pertinent. The reflexivity implicit in this framing suggests both that subjects be able to regard themselves as objects (Butler, 1997b: 103), and that the discursive practices that make this possible are identified. It is true that many more or less ethnographic studies have been undertaken in which boys have been asked to discuss their experiences, especially in relation to issues of masculinity, resistance and race (e.g., Willis, 1977; Mac an Ghaill, 1988, 1994; Connell, 2000), and they do claim to give voice to boys in their selection of evidence, but the local discourses and constitutive practices I wished to access (and which I will discuss in later chapters), have until recently been ignored (see McLeod, 2000b; Reay, 2002). Furthermore, in conceiving of the subjects of this research as multiply situated and as exemplifying multiple subjectivities I have had to confront my own dispersed subjectivity in seeking to resolve the problem of situating myself in relation to the participants in this study.

The research undertaken here will therefore address what I think are two gaps in accounts of boys at school: first, an account of the discursive production of experience and selfhood (thus drawing attention to the absence of a sense of the subjectivity of boys in school settings), and second, an ethnographic account of the context within which experiences and subjectivities are constituted. To this end I have focused on two groups of boys in the middle school: those who appear disengaged and disaffected with school, and those who are regarded by teachers as exemplars of the values of the school. As will become apparent, this pre-discursive characterization is far too precise and exclusive and suggestive of a binary; such identities are more often blurred and contradictory – even indistinct.

The structure of the book is as follows. In Part 1 I consider how best to undertake an ethnography of experience. In this Chapter I have identified the issue of subjectivity and its relation to experience and set out my approach to an ethnographic study of boys' experiences of their schooling. In Chapter 2 I will review the ways boys and their schooling have been framed in public debates in Australia, noting especially the ways in which boys' experiences and achievements have been characterized in populist accounts as well as in academic studies and official inquiries. It will be clear that the resilience of populist representations of boys generally and disaffected boys in particular should not be underestimated in so far as these have influenced policy. It will also be clear that even by asking "which boys?" feminist and profeminist accounts have done little more than compete for influence in gender policy initiatives, whereas to some extent perpetuating the figure of the challenging, sexist, boorish schoolboy. In Chapters 3 and 4, I will evaluate ethnographic studies of schooling (of both boys and girls, but principally of boys), and argue that modernist assumptions entrenched in dominant research processes and styles of writing have largely overlooked students' experiences by giving primacy to studies of institutional and administrative processes. Recent attempts to adopt a poststructuralist research agenda, however, have tended to open the question of student experience in relation to the forming of masculinities and femininities, often in relation to race. Following these examples, this study is intended to contribute an analysis of the discursive production of those boys who inhabit the "what about the boys?" debate.

Part 2 comprises the ethnographic chapters. In Chapter 5 I discuss three discourses dominating daily life at Hillside High School and introduce the notions of the normative and the pathological schools. I also introduce the first of the participants in the research. In the tradition of anthropologically informed ethnography, I tell my own arrival story at the school and contrast it with the arrival story of Kevin. The arrival of students at school in the literature has been entirely overlooked; their repeated daily presence in school, in spite of concern for truancy, has simply been taken for granted. Chapter 6 introduces George whose experiences of the school cast him almost as the definitive disaffected schoolboy whose identity and subjectivity clearly implicate the dominant discourses of the normative school. Chapter 7 moves to a discussion of the discursive construction of "selves" that George and other boys regarded as troublesome become aware of. In this chapter I show how these boys deal with issues of loss and grief in a context that at first sight suggests an implacable and uncaring school which may alternatively be seen to be caring but constrained within the intelligible limits of its dominant normative discourses. In Chapter 8, I turn to the question of embodiment, or the imprint of the normative school on the subjects of this study as they are meticulously disciplined in day-to-day practices of subjectification, at the same time touching on gender issues as they relate to ethnicity and care of the body. Finally, in Chapter 9 I locate the experiences of boys not regarded as disaffected in relation to the experiences of the "disaffected" research participants and illustrate the discursive transformation of one boy – George – from disaffection to accommodation with the normative school. This will show that the notion that one "chooses" one's subject position within a discourse is a modernist fallacy and that subjectification is, or can be, a painful and even traumatic experience. Chapter 10 reflects on the ethnographic work undertaken and draws some conclusions regarding the future of gender equity policies in Australian education. Finally, several questions are posed that challenge the ethical basis of mass schooling's expectation of conformity. This is followed by a brief epilogue.

2 The Schoolboy as Object of Study

> There is such a thing as "deep masculinity," which is latent in a young man and able to be developed and nurtured to fullness . . . it relates to the core aspects of being male – the chemistry, the nature and the complementarity to women that is inbuilt in being male in every cell of your body.
>
> (Biddulph, 2002: 27)

INTRODUCTION

In this chapter I undertake a review of how schoolboys have been represented in a variety of sources both within and outside the academy with reference to the claims made by competing discourses in Australia. On the one hand, writers I shall designate as essentialist hold that many (perhaps all) schoolboys are suffering because schools ignore what is referred to as their core masculinity in ways I discuss later in the chapter. On the other hand, feminist and profeminist writers tend to argue that in so far as there are problems posed by disaffected boys, they are the consequence of the construction of an oppositional, hegemonic masculinity which creates problems not only for girls and women but also for other boys and teachers generally. Influential, large-scale (frequently statistical) studies of final year achievement and ongoing concerns for equity have provided a context within which the debate about failing boys has been conducted, and which has provoked the important question, "which boys?" Throughout this chapter I have attempted to retain a sense of the adversarial nature of this debate, acknowledging the rhetorical success of the essentialist side in positing the figure of the disaffected, failing schoolboy and the challenge this poses for those working from within constructionist and discursive paradigms.

OPENING ARGUMENTS

The framing of the question, "what about the boys?" has been heard by some feminists and profeminists in the academy in Australia as evidence of a backlash against girls' apparent gains during an era of gender equity policies in their favor. Lingard and Douglas (1999), for example, claim that this backlash has been driven from the mythopoetic men's rights perspective (pp. 12, 58; Mills and Lingard, 1997), sustained by such "backlash blockbusters" as Robert Bly's *Iron John* (1991) and more locally by the work of Steve Biddulph (1994, 1997) among others. In this chapter I will sketch the terrain on which this debate has been played out. The conceptual and theoretical high ground has been occupied by those feminist and profeminist writers whose deconstruction of the question at the center of the debate has led to its reformulation as "which boys?" From their perspective, the low ground has been settled by others who argue that all boys have needs that are in many ways fundamentally different from those of girls, and who therefore problematize the issue of schoolboy masculinity in terms of biological and psychological essentialism and systemic neglect. The two camps,[1] conceptually, theoretically, and politically distinct, have engaged in a sometimes bitter debate in which the prize has been access to the centers of policy formulation during a period of neoliberal hegemony at state and national levels (Lingard, 2003; Hayes and Lingard, 2003; O'Donovan, 2006; Lingard et al., 2009).

As I will show, this debate hinges primarily on the way gender is conceptualized. On the one hand, those who privilege biological and psychological characteristics also privilege a unitary, sexed, and gendered subject whose capacity for rationality is limited only by his bodily and neurological biochemistry posited in a developmental framework. With few exceptions, their contempt for a social constructionist understanding of gender, which may be said to characterize the feminist and profeminist positions, is a hallmark of their theoretical stance. Following from this, any account of boys' underachievement or disaffection with schooling in Australia is understood as the result of systemic incompetence, indifference, neglect – or at worst, feminist intransigence – as a result of which, they claim, gender equity policies should be framed in terms of fixing injured boys. On the other hand, feminist and profeminist readings of boys' achievements and behaviors tend to draw attention to a range of contexts within which gender is constructed relationally – such as class, ethnicity, dis/ability, or indigeneity – in order to illustrate the relative disadvantage of girls in spite of whatever difficulties some boys face either in school or in the search for employment after school. Gender equity policy development in these terms, then, tends to be a matter of confronting hegemonic masculinity in order to build a more caring, humane, and less patriarchal society (Kenway, 1995b; Kenway, 1996; Kenway et al., 1997).

Against a background of various policy initiatives to which I will refer shortly, the popular press and those in the academy on either side have continued to engage in a largely adversarial public debate – essentially over the nature and direction of gender equity policies in Australia –

which has been conducted in terms of the plight of boys at school. While the aim of this chapter is partly to analyze the discourses sustaining the debate, it is also to throw light on the ways schoolboys have been textually constructed. It will become apparent that arising from populist and academic rhetoric, a certain image, or stereotype, has now firmly entered the public imagination in Australia: that of the failing, or underachieving schoolboy, disruptive, demanding, damaged – a threat to other boys, girls, and teachers alike, and not least to himself.[2]

A VIEW FROM THE HIGH GROUND

Before referring in more detail to the policy context within which the debate has been carried out since the early 1990s in Australia, I will briefly discuss the dominant discourses that have sustained the debate from a profeminist perspective. Lingard and Douglas (1999: 132–33), for example, characterize the position of Biddulph (1994, 1997) and the men's rights movement as one of "recuperative masculinity" (a "male repair" agenda), regarding all boys as homogeneous and in need of more male teachers, more active modes of learning, the involvement of fathers, intergenerational male guidance for boys and a reaffirmation of (largely unquestioned) masculine identities. The profeminist position which Lingard and Douglas represent, on the other hand, regards this as no more than an attempt to revivify "the competitive and emotionally stultifying demands of hegemonic masculinity (which would inevitably) reproduce the need for unequal relations of social power and privilege amongst males themselves and more obviously between males and females" (Lingard and Douglas, 1999: 134). The more desirable alternative, in their view, is premised on a belief in the moral, political, and social priority of achieving "socially just and equitable relations between men and women, boys and girls" (ibid. 134), a goal which, as we shall see, is also claimed by proponents of men's and boys' rights. According to Lingard and Douglas, however, it is their stance of "presumptive equality . . . which simply equates females and males as equivalent but different populations . . . neglecting the power differentials between them" (ibid. 2–3) that separates the two camps. Given this assumption, recuperative masculinists argue that gender equity programs have benefited women and girls at the expense of men and boys; hence, they ask, "what about the boys?"

The recuperative masculinist position has been sharply rebutted not only by Lingard and Douglas but also by others in Australia (Kenway and Willis, 1997; Gilbert and Gilbert, 1998; Lingard et al., 2009). Kenway and Willis (1997) investigated the practice of gender reform in schools and pointed to "the conventional and dominant meanings of success, knowledge, power, emotion and responsibility" (p. 207) against which feminists and those charged with implementing equal opportunity objectives in schools had to contend in order to get teachers and students to understand them in more humane, less masculinist ways. To their dismay, teachers frequently naturalized the behavior of boys – even when it could be legitimately described as harassment – and infantilized both boys and girls in their attempts to implement gender reform policies (ibid. 202–04). Even more worrying, in their view, has been the tendency among many male teachers to become emotionally defensive about their own gendered identities to the extent that the equity imperative in gender equity policies becomes fatally compromised in some schools. Likewise, Gilbert and Gilbert (1998) point to the way the "what about the boys?" question is framed in terms of this opposition and the implication of blame, and confront the essentialist stance of Biddulph in particular, noting (as we shall see), that "unfortunately, (his ideas) are the currency of much public debate in the area" (p. 45). This tone of regret and even belligerence on the profeminist side is frequently aimed at the media's role in representing the recuperative masculinist position in simplistic (essentialist) terms while ignoring feminist poststructuralism's emphasis on the discursive construction of meaning, power, and identity (Kenway and Willis, 1997: xix; 47; Gilbert and Gilbert, 1998: 3–6). Kenway and Willis (1997), for example, state that as a result of media reports of student academic achievements in the final year of schooling in Australia, Britain, and the United States and parts of Europe in the mid-1990s, "The boys' story has become gender reform's biggest dilemma," (p. 47) whereas Connell (2000) refers to the so-called "deep masculine" popularized by men's movement prozelytizers such as Robert Bly (1991) and "pop psychologists" such as Biddulph as being "as stereotyped as anything in Hollywood . . ." (p. 5). Indeed, Lingard and Douglas make frequent reference to McCarthy's notion of the popular media's "bardic function" of "speaking back to certain sections of the community, including the recuperative men's movement, the tunes they want to hear" (McCarthy, 1998: 83). Thus one can speak of a populist discourse in terms of its wide audience appeal via the popular press with its epistemological roots in biology, psychology and the "psy" sciences generally (Rose, 1996, 1999) aided by a burgeoning ethic of self-help in the wider society which resonates with the newly ascendant neo-liberal subject.

In the course of this chapter I shall review the populist case through the writings and quoted comments of its main proponents in Australia in the context of a range of initiatives and responses from the academy and from government. It will be clear also that governmental responses have been framed very much in terms of the populist discourse and that any attempt to dismiss it as merely reactionary and obstructive underestimates the resilience of the image of the at-risk schoolboy and the discursive regime that sustains it, as well as its strategic significance in the politics of the conservative backlash against successive gender equity policies. In addition, the populist framing of the issue of boys in education will be seen to be deeply flawed from a poststructuralist point of view by its psychological and biological essentialism and its persistent and inevitable reification of the boy as modernist subject: unitary, rational, uniquely positioned, personally responsible for making meaning and conceptually separate from and prior to the social world and its discursive (and constitutive) practices.

THE POLICY CONTEXT – INQUIRIES AND REPORTS

State and Federal concern for gender equity in education in Australia since at least the mid-1980s has revealed an uneasy relationship between sources of responsibility for policy initiatives and management. The education of girls was the focus of attention in the *National Policy on the Education of girls in Australian Schools* (Commonwealth Schools Commission, 1987) in an attempt to address inequities in participation, outcomes and postschool pathways, but by 1994 a national strategy for equity was beginning to be framed in more gender inclusive terms. As part of this, a Gender Equity Taskforce of MCEETYA[3] gathered information early in 1995 in response to growing concern among a wide spectrum of the community about gender issues in education arising from the administration of the *National Action Plan for the Education of Girls*. Its report, while focusing in part on growing concern for boys, sought to clarify the relationship of socially constructed gender to disadvantage in terms of educational outcomes, health, pathways to work and family life (MCEETYA, 1995: 3).

The framing of gender equity issues in the report of the Gender Equity Taskforce is notable for its emphasis on the relational and constructed nature of gender and for its rejection of any "backlash" argument against alleged gains by girls in previous policies. In adopting a constructionist view of gender the report acknowledges a variety of masculinities, some of which, it argues, promote values that are destructive to boys and girls, men and women. By adopting this position the report implicitly acknowledges difference within the category of gender and links it to socioeconomic status, ethnicity, indigeneity, and a range of rural–urban locations. The resulting policy document, *Gender Equity: A Framework for Australian Schools* (Gender Equity Taskforce, 1997), while including specific reference to boys, is described by Lingard and Douglas (1999) as a compromise, "the result of a policy tussle" between feminists and profeminists on the one hand, and their opponents, which at least "located girls' and boys' issues within a gender equity framework" (pp. 168; 53; 102–3).

At much the same time as the initiatives referred to earlier, Richard Teese and associates, in their 1993 report into equity issues arising out of final year examinations in Australian States, recommended the development of a regional model for identifying areas that could be targeted to improve student outcomes. If adopted, such a model would acknowledge variation within, as well as between areas, and help formulate the important questions, "which groups?" and "which areas?" (Teese et al., 1993: 2–7; 60–61). Thus the *Gender Equity* framework (1997) and this report were both beginning to acknowledge difference – within the category of gender, as well as regionally – as a basis for differentiating between boys in a way that could potentially lead to more nuanced policy distinctions and more equitable targeting of gendered and regional disadvantage.

The question of difference, however, and the relative weight to be given to evidence of girls' rather than boys' disadvantage proved to be fatal to feminist and profeminist advocates. For example, it proved to be crucial in determining the outcome of a report instigated by the New South Wales Department of Education (O'Doherty, 1994) which noted the "special difficulties" faced by boys, and while it aimed to separate issues of boys' "genuine educational disadvantage" from concerns of a "backlash" against advances made by girls, it argued that "the problems of boys are real and . . . demand system-wide solutions" to complement strategies for addressing problems experienced by girls (O'Doherty, 1994: 1). In relation to girls, boys were found to have lower retention rates to Year 12, poorer academic outcomes, overwhelmingly greater behavioral problems, poorer communication skills, lower self-esteem, to be overrepresented in programs for students with learning difficulties (especially literacy), to be insensitive to sexism, were reluctant to be seen to excel except at sport, lacked dispute resolution skills, tended to resolve disputes by fighting and to suffer from the absence of appropriate role models in the media (and in the home, in some cases), as well as in primary classrooms where there were so few male teachers (O'Doherty, 1994: 3–4; 15ff).[4]

This was indeed the picture of deficit and failure made familiar at professional development conferences, in the popular press and to some extent among teachers at Hillside High School, but whereas the tendency at these sites was to offer explanations in terms of biology and psychology, O'Doherty, like participants in the 1995 Gender Equity Taskforce initiative referred to earlier, framed his report's understanding of gender in social constructionist terms. Thus he acknowledged that values implicit in assumptions about gender require clarification to avoid the debilitating consequences of attempts to live up to stereotyped images of a singular "femininity" or "masculinity." The power of such stereotypes, especially of what the report refers to as "the dominant masculine stereotype," was said by O'Doherty to account for attempts by boys to live up to an unattainable image that prevents expression of "their true natures and create(s) barriers against their education and life opportunities" not only to their cost, but to the cost of other boys and men, girls and women (ibid. 4). Accordingly, this report proposed that New South Wales formulate a Gender Equity Strategy that would include programs for boys, for girls and for both boys and girls, rather than only for boys or girls. While these recommendations were never implemented, they clearly prefigure the settlement in the *Gender Equity* (1997) policy document.

O'Doherty's report undoubtedly contributed significantly to the representation of the disaffected schoolboy that was to become embedded in populist accounts of his plight, as I will show, but with the report *Who Wins at School?* (Teese et al., 1995), the question which has so polarized those engaged in gender equity debates in Australia – the question of "which boys?" – began to be formulated in response to the prevailing notion of "boys" as an undifferentiated category. This question was to become emblematic of the feminist and profeminist position in relation to gender equity in education in Australia and perhaps achieved its fullest expression in the report for the Commonwealth Department of Education, Training and Youth Affairs by Collins et al. (2000). Although their aims were somewhat different, each drew on statistical trends in participation and performance in the final years of school throughout Australia and revealed considerable discrepancies in the ways girls and boys use the secondary school. According to Teese et al. (1995), upper secondary education had moved from an elite system preparing a minority of young people for university to a mass system serving most young people for vastly more opportunities in postschool pathways. By the mid-1990s, girls' higher school completion rates, increased participation in once "masculine" subjects (such as Chemistry and Mathematics), and success relative to boys in other subjects were celebrated as measures of increased equity, but as Teese *et al.* argued, "it would be wrong to say that girls now rule in the classroom" (Teese *et al.*, 1995: 107). Structural changes in the Australian economy and in labor markets in recent decades have impacted differently on boys and girls in ways to which schools, parents and students have been slow to adapt. Girls' vocational alternatives, considered broadly, continue to be focused on the service sector of the economy rather than on manufacturing and construction, requiring them to make different use of school than boys (Kenway, 2000). By the same token, Teese *et al.* found boys continued to choose senior school subjects with little regard to their ability and as if structural changes in the economy were making no difference to traditional male postschool pathways. In the case of both boys and girls, as Teese *et al.* argue, it is the content of senior school courses chosen and the quality of achievement in those courses that determines a student's ability to make the most of emerging career opportunities. Not surprisingly, similar trends have appeared elsewhere (Francis, 2000; Francis and Skelton, 2005).

Populist accounts of the "boys' problem" in schools, as I will show, not only draw attention to girls' increased participation and success in senior levels and in once "masculine" subjects, but tend to ignore important subtleties and variations within boys' and girls' achievements. Teese *et al.*, however, show that girls are not as likely as boys to study the highest level Maths or Physics (subjects that can offer access to high prestige and high income careers), and that boys still outperform girls at the highest levels in spite of there being no evidence that girls are any less capable than boys. Girls underenrol in those subjects leading to what were once "male" only careers, perhaps reflecting perceptions of their talent, curriculum choices offered, self-image in the classroom and family expectations. On the other hand, girls have tended to outperform boys in the humanities curriculum in modern languages, English Literature, and some histories and continue to do so at a time when the humanities are in decline and perceived as vocationally irrelevant in some quarters. It is precisely these achievements and the gains girls have made in maths and science that are seized on by populist commentators to highlight boys' low achievements in the middle and lower ends of the spectrum of higher school assessment.

Closer inspection, however, shows just how girls and boys are differentially disadvantaged in this representation of the gains made by girls. Teese *et al.*'s evidence showed that girls tend to choose senior school subjects that are on the whole less structured and less mutually supporting than subjects chosen by boys. Business Studies, Human Development, Biology, and humanities subjects have less vocational emphasis than Maths, Chemistry and Physics, more diffuse outcomes and less reliable assessment. Furthermore, boys as a group were thought to benefit more from the modes of assessment used in subjects occupying the upper levels of the curriculum hierarchy than were girls who were thought to be favored by assessment tools used in middle and lower reaches of the curriculum hierarchy (Teese *et al.*, 1995: 108).

Such generalizations, of course, tend to hide socioeconomic and other cultural expressions of advantage and disadvantage. For example, students from high socioeconomic backgrounds tend to be less disadvantaged in terms of achievement than those from lower socioeconomic backgrounds, but the effect is not uniform (Teese *et al.*, 1995: 109). Working-class girls enrol less and do worse in Maths than girls from higher socioeconomic backgrounds, whereas working-class boys are less likely to take Maths and Physics than other boys and if they do they tend to fail them (and English), at higher rates. These same working-class boys (especially those in rural areas), also tend to overenrol in Maths and Physics and not to enrol in Literature, History, or modern languages, with predictable and dire consequences.

These trends lead Teese *et al.* to characterize the experience of many girls and boys in terms of relative disadvantage, but it is the *combination* of outcomes for many boys that has captured popular attention. Teese *et al.* conclude that boys' "school careers, on the whole, seem to be less successful, to terminate earlier, to be characterized by failure at an earlier point in time, and to be more frequently accompanied by motivational and behavioural problems" than girls' (Teese *et al.*, 1995: 108).

Furthermore, boys tend to be less well integrated into the curriculum, to dislike school more and to view school more narrowly and instrumentally than girls. Boys tend to resist the study of English and to be naively attached to the perceived hierarchy of subjects, so much so that in spite of higher rates of enrolment in Maths than girls they are overrepresented in the lowest levels of achievement. To reverse this trend (and to develop their "interior life"), they argue, boys will have to do better at English and perhaps the humanities where the ability to communicate is so centrally important (Teese *et al.*, 1995: 109).

By focusing on socioeconomic and cultural determinants of performance, the answer to the question they pose in the title of their publication (who wins at school?), is answered, at least rhetorically, by asking "Which boys, which girls?" (see Teese *et al.*, 1997). Such an answer radically undermines the assumption that there are or ought to be winners in any narrow class-based or gender-oriented sense in the evaluation of curriculum outcomes, and more fundamentally, dismisses the claim that the issue can be decided independently of this question. Moreover, it is precisely by foregrounding the notion of difference within gendered categories implied in the question and by suggesting that many girls remain in need of gender equity resources that the public debate has been fuelled.

Teese *et al.*'s concern with final-year outcomes, while important in setting the parameters for informed debate concerning educational achievement in terms of credentials, nevertheless ignored the early and middle years of schooling, an omission covered to some extent by O'Doherty's and other reports. For example, Collins *et al.* (1996), drawing on the perceptions of nearly 9,000 Year 6 and Year 10 students of the way gender was experienced at their schools found that both boys and girls were subject to sex-based harassment (mainly by boys); that bullying was rife; that disruptive behavior was common – again, mostly by boys; that access to school resources was frequently monopolized by boys; that gender boundaries in relation to subject choices seemed to be maintained and that boys tended to participate in nonsporting extracurricular activities far less than girls. While this added to the view of boys' coercive presence in schools, Slade and Trent (2000) set out "to provide an overview of what secondary school aged boys are saying about the phenomena of declining retention and achievement, and how their educational outcomes might be improved" (p. 201).[5]

Whereas Collins *et al.* (1996) had explicitly not asked their participants about their own experiences, but rather their perceptions of what was going on around them, Slade and Trent interviewed 600 boys in Years 9 and 11 in 60 schools in South Australia about their experience of school.[6] The authors' overwhelming impression was that these boys believed that adults in education were not listening to them, that the biggest hindrance to achievement in and enjoyment of schooling was poor teaching and that for many boys the personal sacrifices involved in staying on to the final year of school were not worth the "hazy promise" of future rewards (Slade and Trent, 2000: 214–15). They went on to argue that on the basis of the boys' experiences, the problems of retention and achievement cannot be remedied by "fixing up the boys" and that it is misconceived as a gender equity issue (pp. 216–17). To the boys, "mucking up" in class, being labelled as a "problem," putting up with what they regarded as bad teaching and being treated as a juvenile could all be remedied by good teaching, whether by men or women, and they disputed the view that boys generally believed it was "cool to be a fool." On the whole, as Slade and Trent conclude, for many boys education is simply "an unpleasant experience" (ibid. 228).[7]

A further report by Collins *et al.* (2000) at much the same time, however, and funded by the same Commonwealth Department, inquired into "patterns of males' and females' educational participation and performance at school and their initial destinations after leaving school" (p. 1) and sought to locate the key factors influencing the disadvantages arising from such patterns. This report, like that by Teese *et al.*, drew on gross statistical data of final year performance in a number of subjects in several States, a detailed literature review and the testimony of experts and concluded that "concern about gender patterns of participation, performance and outcomes is justified because certain differences do convert into certain disadvantages . . ." (ibid. 5). Furthermore, the authors recommended that the Commonwealth "incorporate a 'which boys, which girls?' approach (into) policy development in relation to educational performance and outcomes (in order to) refocus the public debate away from the 'boy versus girl' approach" (ibid. 9; 15; Ch. 3).

Collins *et al.*'s report, coming as it did shortly after the establishment of a House of Representatives inquiry into the education of boys and just prior to its collection of evidence, once again put the case for gender equity based on an understanding of the socially constructed nature of gender (ibid. 91–92). As I have indicated earlier, and as will become clear in the following section, proponents of a more essentialist understanding of gender, together with sections of the popular press, waged a campaign apparently on behalf of all boys against those espousing a "which boys?" view. For example, headlines such as "The Trouble with Boys"[8] not only highlighted the virulence of the gender policy debate, appearing to favor those on the side of an essentialist understanding of gender, but in at least one case suggested that Collins *et al.*'s (2000) report had been "poorly received," "buried" and "extensively rewritten" as a result of its poor reception by its funding body (Arndt, 2000a).[9] This was perhaps the clearest expression of the so-called "gender wars" into which policy debates had been dragged by the popular press.

The Committee of the House of Representatives set up in March, 2000, at the instigation of a conservative (Liberal Party) federal Minister for Education to investigate the issue of boys' education, as I have indicated, unleashed a backlash against gender equity policies that appeared to privilege girls at the expense of boys in which the role of the media was anything but benign (Lingard, 2003: 48–49).[10] Neither O'Doherty in New South Wales, nor the nationally binding *Gender Equity* framework, had delivered a boys-only gender policy. Now a Standing Committee set up by a conservative national government was to give prominence to measurable indicators of boys' "under-achievement and disengagement from learning" (Commonwealth of Australia, 2002: xv). Not surprisingly, its report presented a generalized picture of low achievement and high rates of suspension and expulsion among boys. It clearly supported the notion that boys had been disadvantaged relative to girls in senior schooling in the recent past and given the image of failing and disruptive boys it produced, dismissed the focus suggested by Teese *et al.* on "which boys and which girls?" Instead, the report argued "that for almost every socio-economic group, boys are underachieving compared to girls (especially in) the most disadvantaged socio-economic groups" (ibid. xvii) and urged the identification of strategies to redress the situation many boys found themselves in (ibid. xviii; 42; 169). It also targeted the 1997 *Gender Equity* policy document, arguing that it focused on girls' needs at the expense of boys, rather than recognizing boys' and girls' "joint and separate educational needs" (ibid. 2). Of particular concern were boys' poor literacy, factors affecting school retention and early leaving, truancy, the paucity of male role models among teachers (especially in primary schools), ill-advised subject choices in the senior school, boys' low achievement relative to girls and postschool consequences of disengagement from school.

The House of Representatives report proposed a series of recommendations for overcoming the sense of disengagement many boys had expressed to witnesses at the inquiry and for producing literate, numerate, and socially and emotionally connected students for entry into a changing labor market. Particular attention was drawn to difficulties experienced by boys and girls in the middle school (roughly Years 8 to 10), and schools were urged to consider restructuring their middle schools and work towards improving student–teacher relationships, discipline, and welfare management and pedagogy (ibid. Recommendation 14 and pp. 129–51). This focus on attitudes to behavior and relationships in the middle school was already a feature of the popular and populist image of the problems boys were said to be having (e.g., early leaving), and was noted by Ludowyke and Scanlon (1997) in Victoria when they observed that "A degree of attitudinal disengagement from schooling can develop across the 5–8 years, however the disruptive and anti-learning behaviours which most manifest this disengagement, tend to peak around Year 9" (p. 15). Various expressions of this disengagement were quoted anecdotally to the House of Representatives inquiry, whereas Ludowyke and Scanlon also highlighted the role of peer groups in "maintaining an oppositional anti-learning culture amongst boys" (1997: 15) to the extent that many placed little or no value on learning and made classes difficult for teachers and other students. Further confirmation of this antilearning culture was expressed in a report to the Department of Education, Employment and Training (DEET) in Victoria while the House of Representatives inquiry was in progress (DEET, 2001). The report noted that in relation to the middle school, girls were outperforming boys in English and Maths, were doing more homework, were reported for misbehavior and suspended much less often than boys, expressed more positive attitudes to school and were more "connected" to school processes and values than boys. While some of these differences were marginal (e.g., on average "boys and girls alike are generally positive about school and their own experience of it"), it was still the case that "boys are more likely than girls to feel disaffected and/or alienated from school and . . . to engage in attention-seeking, disruptive and/or anti-social behaviour at school" (ibid. 11).

It is clear from the reports referred to earlier that regardless of whatever weighting is given to either socioeconomic variables or gender in explaining variations in attitudes to school and school achievement, there has been a broad consensus that some boys are experiencing difficulty at school on a daily basis, and that at the same time, other students and teachers are also drawn into this vortex of disaffection and disengagement. For example, whereas much of the evidence before the House of Representatives inquiry tended to be based on large-scale studies of statistical data allowing virtually no detailed understanding of the daily lived experience of being schooled, the inquiry also took evidence from school principals and others who tended to repeat the by now stereotyped image of the disaffected schoolboy revealed by O'Doherty (1994) and to some extent by Ludowyke and Scanlon (1997), ignoring the rather more nuanced findings of Slade and Trent (2000). Teese *et al.* (1995), however, while dependent on gross statistical data, recognized significant internal variations in their sources that suggested most generalizations concealed important exceptions, but as shown earlier, the House of Representatives Standing Committee retained a less subtle perspective. In doing so it not only reflected the prevailing impression of the disaffected schoolboy; it effectively polarized gender equity policy initiatives in the immediate future within a discourse of putative equality. In the next section I discuss the populist rhetoric that had so effectively sustained this discourse and which the House of Representatives inquiry found so persuasive in opposition to feminist and profeminist theorizing of gender equity in education in Australia by 2002.

THE SCHOOLBOY AS VICTIM: POPULIST ORIGINS

By March 2000 when the House of Representatives inquiry into the education of boys was set up, boys' education had become an issue in the popular press and among a range of psychologists, therapists, educational researchers and academics, as well as parents, for a variety of reasons. There was clearly no single issue but rather a cluster of issues, given that schoolboys ranged in age from about 5 years (prep.) to 17 or 18 years in Year 12, but there did seem to be a common, disturbing image of the failing, troubled, disengaged schoolboy, which illustrated the nexus of problems around him. In this section I want to investigate this populist image of the schoolboy and show how the discourse of failure and disadvantage which it represents has been linked not only to adult masculinity as an expression of a contemporary crisis in parenting, but also to the school (and family), as sites of both its origin and its solution.

This image is derived partly from a reaction to feminist politics since at least the 1970s in which a range of approaches and frameworks has been used to theorize gender (Brod, 1987; Clatterbaugh, 1990; Brod and Kaufman, 1994; Kimmel, 1995). One consequence of this reaction has been to acknowledge multiple masculinities rather than reassert heteronormativity, but a further consequence has been a biologically essentialist response by opponents that is particularly antagonistic to a feminist politics and which provides the context for the rest of this chapter. For the moment, it is sufficient to note that this development has created a space within which local populist initiatives have flourished, characterized not only by a conceptualization of gender which I will argue is deficient, but by an equally "simplistic conceptualization of boys as a homogeneous group whose interests are set against those of girls" (Martino and Meyenn, 2001: x) and who, as a result, have been characterized in Australia and elsewhere as the "new disadvantaged" (Epstein *et al.*, 1998).

The writers I will discuss here are linked in so far as they argue that boys have been disadvantaged relative to girls in terms of system-wide equity policies as well as structural features and pedagogy within individual schools, but they also make the strategic point that any solution to the dilemma facing boys and schools should not be at the expense of girls, whose recent advances are applauded. Nevertheless, they represent what I have referred to earlier, following Lingard and Douglas (1999: 158–60), as the recuperative masculinist position. The specific contention of these writers is that recent gender equity policies have ignored boys who, as a result are, or appear to be, falling behind in achievement and causing difficulties for themselves, for other students and for teachers. What they claim they most want to see, and to help bring about, is a change in the ways boys and men relate to girls and women, a desire premised on the belief that like femininity, masculinity has needs, but that unlike recent policies aimed at improving gender equity for girls, schools, and educational systems have neglected boys' needs to the point that their "real natures" have been stifled and as a society we have been left with the "problem" of boys in schools. In putting their case, however, these writers argue from, or depend on, a medico-biological position which essentializes gender and retains elements of a "nature-nurture" framing in which boys and girls are conditioned by sex-role socialization to the exclusion of any insights from recent sociology and social psychology or indeed from feminist or profeminist points of view (Browne and Fletcher, 1995; Biddulph, 2002; Biddulph, 1997). In spite of claims to the contrary, the tenor of their argument is explicitly anti-feminist and together with its dependence on the notion of biologically determined but unmet "needs" constitutes a "backlash" against recent gender equity policies (Lingard and Douglas, 1999; Kenway and Willis, 1997) and positions boys as beneficiaries of a "competing victim syndrome" at the expense of girls (Cox, 1995: 304).

The tone of their concern is made clear in the first issue of the *Boys in Schools Bulletin* of 1997.[11] Subtitled *"Practical Initiatives Addressing Boys' Needs,"* its founding editors, Rollo Browne and Richard Fletcher,[12] observed that by 1997 many schools had begun to address "boys' needs" and that the journal would support efforts being made by vanguard teachers and schools. After two years of presentations and workshops for teachers around Australia, they looked forward to a concerted effort by educators to influence and modify boys' behavior, preferably with the help of fathers.

In the journal's first article, Browne focused on boys and the middle school (Browne, 1997). He argued that secondary schools were failing in attempts to bring about "behaviour change" in boys and that a negative peer culture was rampant where schools were structured around subject faculties. Year 7 students, after a primary school experience with one or very few teachers, were suddenly expected to cope with 12–14 new teachers. From then on the problem worsened until "issues of masculinity, peer relations and behavior [sic]" were so entrenched at Year 9 and above that "one-off programs" to address the issues would be doomed to failure. "Under these circumstances (he argued), the peer group becomes entrenched around a 'cool to be a fool', school refuser ethic in Year 7, while the problem compounds in following years as students begin engaging in power struggles with teachers" (ibid. 2). In successive editions, stories of how schools recognized and confronted this construction of the problem were given prominence with special emphasis on the role fathers could play in reading programs and as mentors, especially in primary schools.

The importance attributed by Fletcher and Browne to the relationship of schooling to parenting, and especially of schooling to the role fathers could play in bringing up boys can hardly be overstated. From the mid-1980s parenting manuals and courses in parenting proliferated as family breakdown, divorce, and a range of adolescent pathologies combined to create a climate of concern, if not outright fear, demanding solutions.[13] Partly in response to these concerns, the *Boys in Schools Bulletin* sought to bring fathers and schools together to mentor masculinity and in the process show boys that reading was not just for girls,[14] but more than that, the *Bulletin's* themes reflected its host Project's concerns beyond education in matters of juvenile justice, cancer screening, suicide, and the role of men in the community. The range of pathologies said to afflict males became something of a mantra in the popular press and among populist writers as boys in schools were conflated with pathologized older youth and young men.[15] A pathway from innocence to trauma, violence, and suffering is implied in statistical summaries of the causes of injury and death among young men and a role is suggested for the school in helping to reverse the trends.[16]

Among these statistics, those relating to youth suicide and dangerous risk-taking behavior have been crucially important in delineating the image of the young male at risk in his guise as more or less reluctant school student. Youth and cultural studies have also proliferated around the figures of teenage boys and girls outside the confines of the school but it is the achievement of populist authors in particular to have linked the figure of the middle-school boy so closely to indicators of various pathologies. Among those to whom Browne and Fletcher turn for justification and philosophical support is Steve Biddulph[17] who opens his 1997 book, *Raising Boys,* with a story about a car accident he witnessed in which a 17-year-old boy driver and his four passengers were seriously injured as a result of the boy's failure to assess the traffic conditions. As he looks on, Biddulph is aware of the fire, rescue, police, and ambulance men [sic] "(working) in teams, calmly dealing with the situation." He goes on: "Maleness was everywhere – inexperience and risk on the one side; competence, caring and steadiness on the other . . . It kind of summed up for me the male situation" which he outlines in the following terms:

> Boys are often adrift in life, failing at school, awkward in relationships, at risk for [sic] violence, alcohol and drugs, and so on. The differences start early – visit any pre-school and see for yourself. The girls work together happily; the boys 'hoon' around like Indians around a wagon train. They annoy the girls and fight with each other.
>
> In primary school the boys' work is often sloppy and inferior. By the time they reach grade three, most boys don't read books any more. They speak in one word sentences: "Huh?" "Awwyeah!" In high school they don't join in with debating, concerts, councils or any non-sport activity. They pretend not to care about anything, and that "it's cool to be a fool."
>
> (Biddulph, 1997: 1–2)

This passage typifies Biddulph's rhetorical devices: a vivid appeal to personal experience (whether his or the reader's), cartoon-like images, gross generalizations, the suggestion of a developmental profile and differences between genders portrayed as predetermined and fundamental. His sole authority for boys' alleged failure to take on debating, concerts or leadership positions is a single article (Ireland, 1995) in Browne and Fletcher's widely read *Boys in Schools* (1995) that preceded the *Boys in Schools Bulletin*, to which Biddulph contributed the Foreword. In it he noted the "narrow role" that industrial society has given men and boys and lamented the messages boys were bound to receive: "that being male is somehow intrinsically dirty, dangerous and inferior" (Biddulph, 1995: viii–ix).[18]

What links Biddulph to some extent to Browne, Fletcher and others I will discuss later in this section is his conceptualization of gender and the hint in the text aforementioned that somehow the Industrial Revolution separated men from an arcadia in which they had been able to be what these authors believe men truly are. I will return to this particular theme in Biddulph later on. For the moment, what is important is his theorizing of gender in which the phrase "Social Construction of Gender" is dismissed as a "'buzzword' term." He explains:

> This is probably a wonderful and enlightening theory. I cannot say, as I have always fallen asleep at lectures on the subject . . . The problem with "Social Construction theory" lies in what people take it to mean. That is, that gender is purely socially shaped, starting with a blank slate.
> (Biddulph, 1995: ix–x)[19]

His response to this "oversimplification" is to emphasize biochemical differences between males and females, such as hormonal drives, and posit these differences as fundamental, allowing him to argue that boys' and men's "needs" derive from these differences: "It's time we honoured and put a positive value on the *unique qualities* of boys . . . We must redouble our efforts to liberate women and girls, and also start changing the *male of the species* or all gains will be lost" (Biddulph, 1995: x; my emphasis). This emphasis underlies Biddulph's writings and presentations to parents and others; for example, the notion of the "true nature of boys" pervades *Raising Boys* (1997: 3; 42) as do the "three stages of boyhood," "timeless and universal" though not clockwork in appearance (ibid. Ch. 2). By the time a boy ("the average boy"), is in middle school, Biddulph's account has his testosterone at 800 times toddlers' levels with a brain that has developed more slowly than a girl's, 30 per cent more muscle bulk than the average girl and "more red blood cells (the original red-blooded boy!)" (ibid. 33). Earlier, in grade 1, his fine motor skills were six months behind girls' so he was less able to handle pencils and scissors and he "(needed) far more movement and activity than a seat at a desk (afforded)" (Biddulph, 1995: x). It is these biologically determined differences, according to Biddulph (regardless of individual variations), that have too often been ignored in schools "So (boys) are immediately disadvantaged. For some, their careers as problem learners are set in motion" (ibid. x).[20]

It is clear that for Biddulph, schools are important sites where gender-as-given may be neglected or affirmed and where the consequences of its neglect can be dire, whereas for Browne and Fletcher, schools are sites where gender is actively constructed, but by agents whose behaviors are nevertheless deeply biologically grounded. In the view of all three, boys have too often been victims, or losers, in the ways schools have dealt with them by ignoring or overlooking their needs, whether biological or social (Browne, 1995; Browne and Fletcher, 1995: 4). Biddulph (1997) explains this as the outcome of a recent "anti-male" (p. 61) or "feminist" era (p. 22) in which not only have "boys' natures" not been catered for, but in which men have become profoundly unhappy and disconnected from their essential selves (ibid. 6–8; 27; 126). "The gender debate (he writes), raged for 30 years, often fruitlessly, before we woke up to the fact that *men are not winners*"; and again, "Nor are we women, as late twentieth-century ideologies have tried to foist on us" (ibid. 5, 9; his emphasis).[21]

For Biddulph, the situation is already dire. Drawing on his claim to have worked with teachers in many countries he observes:

> Everywhere I hear the same message: boys don't live up to their potential. They don't have any aspirations. They get aggressive. They think it's "cool to be a fool". The girls are getting ahead. The boys are losing the plot.
>
> (Biddulph, 1994: 126).

While he salutes girls' achievements, the solution to boys' ailments is to be found in the implementation of policies to address the relative absence of men in schools, at the same time addressing the crisis men are facing in the wider society. Thus, in a passage hinting more at sex-role socialization than discursive construction, he writes: "To learn to be the gender you are, you probably need thousands of hours of interaction with older, more mentally equipped members *of your own gender* (but) same sex deprivation is the normal experience of millions of boys" (Biddulph, 1994: 13–14; his emphasis). Given his essentialist understanding of gender, this construction of the discontents of masculinity allows Biddulph to conflate boys' problems at school with men's problems in the wider society and to locate the crux of the problem in men's alienation from their "true nature." Returning to his theme, he writes: "In nature, all development follows a laid-down sequence. In a man's development, the sequence has been forgotten and the process largely left to chance" (Biddulph, 2002: 15). As a result,

> We have to reforge a chain that was broken, a chain by which men through the ages learned to be men (because) in a break with eternal tradition, boys began being raised by women (without) the sweetness of male teaching from committed older men.
>
> (ibid. 28–29)

Here Biddulph highlights the demise of the ways gender has been acquired, or enhanced, by the learning of roles. The result is "father-hunger," or "the deep biological need for strong, humorous, hairy, wild, tender, sweaty, caring, intelligent masculine input . . . now widely seen as the most important concept in male psychology" (ibid. 29–30).[22]

For Biddulph, the solution is clear: just as men in western societies have lost their way in the modern world, so boys are doomed to lose their way unless their essential maleness can be honored and validated. This means addressing the *"inadvertent femininity of schools,"* (where women teachers predominate), by getting more male teachers back into primary schools, implementing "more boyish modes of learning," developing gender equity programs for boys and, more generally, finding ways to initiate boys into manhood (Biddulph, 2002: 129; his emphasis).[23] This sense of initiation, or rite of passage, is for Biddulph the healing balm that can mend the fractured institutions of contemporary society and allow boys and men to make the changes that feminism has demanded and which now the Men's Movement can help bring about (Kimmel, 1995).[24]

Here Biddulph's theorizing of boys' and men's problems becomes frankly mystical:

> One way to understand the meaning of initiation is to say that it is 'a journey to meet the Wild Man . . . He is both a being that is *in* men and yet also has independent life . . . All masculine confidence, of the inner kind, arises in the domain of the Wild Man.
> (Biddulph, 2002: 190; original emphasis).

This is the role he wants to see male teachers and fathers fulfilling; bringing cohorts of boys through to young manhood and in the process finishing what he claims the Women's Movement started but could never finish. Men and society would be changed for the better and the violated imperatives of biological determinism would be mended. A key device in Biddulph's rhetoric throughout his publications is a constant resort to the image of a whole and better past where "The old initiators . . . took boys into the desert and taught them one-to-one about life-and-death concerns. Their graduation ceremonies were powerful and significant events for the young men" (Biddulph, 2002: 131).[25] Mentoring thus takes on a primordial dimension for both fathers and teachers in this construction. It has been taken up by a number of boys' schools in New Zealand and Australia and Year 9 programs that offer outdoor education experiences are also at least partly premised on this notion of a rite of passage.[26]

MOBILIZING THE SCHOOLBOY AS VICTIM

Up to this point I have shown how an essentialist understanding of gender with overtones of sex-role socialization in Biddulph's writings has been taken up by Fletcher and Browne to help legitimize and frame the moral panic surrounding the figure of the schoolboy as victim. It must be admitted that this is something of an all-purpose image, arousing fear in parents as they contemplate their son's future, or a desire among some teachers and principals to redress what they see as the outcome of an unjust state of affairs. It can be used both as symptom of educational and societal failure to address alleged inequities in gender policies and as justification for a range of interventions to redress these imbalances. I now want to move on to an account of how this figure and the discourses sustaining it have been mobilized in debates concerning boys and their schooling in the popular domain in Australia.

It is necessary first of all to characterize this image once again. This is the schoolboy who has been disadvantaged relative to girls by his slower brain development, his lesser auditory processing skills by age four, his shorter attention spans (leading to inattentiveness and noncompliance), his worse verbal reasoning skills (associated with a tendency to resort to anger and violence to resolve disputes), an inability to sit for long periods and a relatively high susceptibility to ADD and ADHD.[27] He is said to be disadvantaged by a feminized curriculum and a lack of male teachers, especially in primary school, and by inappropriate or "girl-friendly" means of assessment throughout his schooling. His disengagement and antagonism are said to peak around Years 8 to 10 by which time he has learnt to repress his feelings and emotions. In Years 11 and 12, should he get that far, his propensity for over-enrolling in Maths and sciences, regardless of aptitude, may well disadvantage him at a time of rapid structural change in the economy when other subject choices may have been more appropriate.

The discourse of boys' special needs that envelops this image has its adherents among those who disparage the "which boys?" approach to the question of how best to target gender equity policies. As I have indicated earlier, this discourse does not allow for exceptions on the grounds of boys' specifically male bio-chemistry. Such views were widely canvassed (often by implication), during the period in which the House of Representatives Inquiry collected evidence. For example, Richard Fletcher argued "... we have underestimated how important the physical is. That goes to the heart of teaching styles and learning styles ..." (*The Bulletin*, 5 June 2001), and again:

> The trouble with the 'which boys' approach is that it puts the burden of reform squarely onto the most disadvantaged boys. Because it links the problem to being Aboriginal or poor, it suggests that the rest of the boys – middle-class white boys, for example – have no problems. I get just as many concerned calls from parents with sons at elite private schools.
>
> (*The Age*, 16 June 2001)

While not favoring one specific cause of boys' poor school performance, such as socioeconomic status, and admitting that boys' disenchantment with school can occur regardless of single-sex classes, Fletcher rests his case ultimately on an understanding of gender that gives primacy to the biological and in particular the neurological.[28] This is a view shared to some extent also by Dr Ken Rowe[29] who argues that boys' underachievement has long been obvious as they "(struggle) with the high levels of verbal reasoning and written communication skills required in school curriculum and assessment" (*The Age*, 3 November 2000), but rather than see the cause solely in terms of socioeconomic status or gender as a biological datum, Rowe argues that what is decisive, given boys' relative disability in verbal reasoning, is the quality of teaching.[30] In this sense he believes boys have special needs arising from their biology, as the following comment shows:

> The main difference between boys and girls is that boys' attention span is not nearly so great. There is a lot of neuro-psychological research going into this but we have no answers, only a whole range of theories ranging from the genetic to the macho conditioning of sex-role stereotypes. There is also evidence that males mature more slowly than females.
>
> (*The Sunday Age*, 2 July 1995).

How these differences are acknowledged in schools and whether or not the subsequent "needs" are addressed has provoked considerable debate around the question of the "feminised curriculum." Proponents regard the emphasis on reading, verbal reasoning, note-taking at desks for long periods, extended written assessment, the choice of texts and themes in English, teaching styles and the preponderance of women teachers as indicators of a regrettably "feminised" curriculum. In opposition to this view, Teese regards it as symptomatic of an antifeminist backlash after progress made by girls in recent decades. Commenting in support of Ludowyke and Scanlon's report (1997), he observed: "The redneck backlash against feminism really has only one subject to pin all its hopes on – that's English. If you move out of English, the gender picture tends to be adverse to girls" (*The Age*, 23 August 1997), a view he repeated while the House of Representatives Inquiry collected evidence. As the leading defender of the "which boys?" approach, Teese continued to justify his view publicly on the grounds that socioeconomic status contributes most to differences in levels of achievement "because . . . the cognitive and cultural demands that learning places on the resources of families" affect both boys and girls. Subsequent disparities in boys' and girls' achievements in year 12, he argued, have more to do with boys' resort to a gender stereotype of themselves as good at Maths and sciences, whereas girls resorted to a similar stereotype in relation to English, languages, and the humanities (*The

Age, 8 February 2000). In this way, Teese continued to argue the case he had consistently put since at least 1995: "The things that we need to do for some boys are the same things we need to do to assist low-achieving girls" (*The Age*, 8 July 1997).

The argument that boys do not have special needs, however, has not been universally accepted, as I have shown. For example, one attempt to explain why boys' performance in literacy and English in New South Wales seemed to be increasingly worse than girls' focused on the link between socioeconomic status and school achievement (Buckingham, 1999).[31] Given that because boys of low socioeconomic status were achieving less well than girls of similar status, it was argued that there must be some environmental factor at work not explained by biological differences, socialization, teaching styles, and curricula. Buckingham argues that because a major predictor of low socioeconomic status is sole parenthood, and because the vast majority of single-parent families are headed by mothers, this association with boys' low achievement should not be ignored. While Fletcher and Browne see some merit in the finding, they regard the absence of male mentors in the formative years as crucial, when female teachers, regardless of skill and experience, are left to model the enjoyment of reading as a desirable value.[32] An extreme expression of this view is put by Dr Peter West: "The people I know who are working successfully with boys are grappling with their masculinity and working positively with their masculinity. They're teaching English in a masculine kind of way . . . It's not soft and soggy" (*The Age*, 8 February 2000). West's concept of masculinity draws largely on the primacy given to biology by Biddulph but he also accommodates a constructionist position, drawing on Connell, although his is a limited conception of what social constructionism has to offer: "It means that masculinity is made by society rather than in the male and female body (and therefore) emphasizes nurture, rather than nature" (West, 2002a: 18). He clearly gives priority to an essentialist understanding of sex/gender, however, which in his view provides the material basis of reality which social processes may then obscure, leaving parents and teachers to cope with the potential distortions of perception. Thus he writes that "The issue of reality versus perception is important when we look at boys at school, in which many females are found" (West, 2002a: 19), which, for West and others, is the nub of the problem.[33] In his view, the absence of men in schools is linked directly to a decline in discipline and increasing disengagement, mirroring an equivalent failure in parenting and a rise in single-parent families headed by mothers. For example, in 1995 he said "The teaching profession is increasingly female, especially in primary school . . . Most children from broken families are living with their mothers and the boys from these families often have no meaningful men in their lives" (*The Age*, 2 July 1995).

Again, in 2004, echoing Biddulph, he observed that "Boys' energy was once validated and channelled by fathers, schools, policemen and churches.

But today, society struggles in vain to contain boys' restless energy. Many boys grow up underfathered, and schools have become a no-man's land" (*The Age*, 3 May 2004). The issue is exacerbated, according to West, by "a gender industry set up with girls as the focus, and feminism as the guiding doctrine" to the detriment of boys' welfare (*The Age*, 27 June 1995). What schoolboys need, according to this view, is an increase in the number of male teachers who know how to engage with boys' masculinity, a solution which independent all-boys schools are best able to implement, according to West, as they can openly seek male teachers for this role.[34] Until this can be done in state schools, and given the preponderance of female teachers (especially in primary schools), West asks "I wonder if boys' behaviour is being judged by people who don't understand how and why boys act as they do. As so many teachers are female, male behaviour is often measured by a female ruler" (West, 2000: 38).[35]

The solution he favors, as do Fletcher and Browne, is to bring more men into the teaching profession as mentors, either by offering male-only scholarships or by engaging fathers in their sons' education. As part of a drive to create "boy-friendly" schools, West argues that "We need males in schools who can work with boys' energy, not punish them or suspend or expel them for being boisterous" (*The Age*, 3 May 2004), a view shared in part by Michael Carr-Gregg.[36] Drawing on the work of West, Fletcher, Browne, and others, he observes that "The bulk of boys are completely and utterly devoid of a mentor figure who will enable them to go through adolescence and come out as a psychologically mature man" (*The Age*, 23 July 1996) and urges schools to do more "to stem the spiralling rates of suicide, depression and self-mutilation among young Australian men" (*Herald-Sun*, 23 July 1996). While not decrying the work of female teachers, Carr-Gregg (who also believes boys have "distinctive needs"), regards male teachers as role models in a sense that female teachers cannot be, but importantly he notes that such teachers should not be "trapped in outmoded male behavior, such as an inability to display emotion," or "confrontationalistic chest-beating stuff" (*Herald-Sun*, 23 July 1996). The sense of gender as vaguely socially constructed shared by Carr-Gregg, Fletcher, and Browne is hinted at here and is echoed in West's quirky observation that "Values are caught, not taught, so boys learn masculinity by watching it enacted" such as in "(the) jokey and blokey banter between men and boys . . ." (*The Age*, 3 May 2004).[37] Given that schools are important "masculinising institutions and cultures," however, the implications of an uncritical resort to such practices are that hegemonic masculinity may be valorized and the implementation of gender equity policies may be subverted (Kenway and Willis, 1997: 128; Francis, 2008).

Few, if any other Australian commentators, have done as much as Peter West to articulate the image of the schoolboy as victim: of poor fathering, of the absence of a father, of predominantly female teachers, of inappropriate styles of teaching and assessment, of curricula insensitive to boys' interests and of disappearing rites of passage into adulthood. It is an image of abandonment and despair; of high rates of youth suicide and associated pathologies; in sum, of wilful neglect. Commenting on "The female world of the school," West (2002a) writes: "any balanced person would have to admit we have a problem" (p. 15). To the boys, he claims, school looks like:

- Lots of women teachers, but few men teachers
- Signs that say 'girls can do anything' (but not boys)
- Teachers influenced by feminism who deliberately encourage girls to achieve (but who deliberately encourages boys?)
- A curriculum which is very verbal and rewards students with high levels of verbal skills (more girls than boys)
- Girls appearing to get the best marks and the prizes on Speech Day, apart from sport (West, 2002a: 98).

Finding themselves in an environment where "teachers prefer girls to boys, and girls on average are performing better than boys", West lists what he regards as the consequences – a composite image of the schoolboy as uninterested, failing, confrontational, and distressed to the point of depression. They behave badly, are likely to be given low marks, are often sent out of classrooms, are suspended from school more than girls, reject schools' humanist values, have low self-esteem because of their schoolwork, see school as a waste of time and ultimately seek refuge in sport and low-status, low-paid jobs (ibid. 102; 2002b).

With clear and predictable ideas about how to motivate boys and raise their achievements and self-esteem, West undertook an inquiry into "Best Practice in Boys' Education" for The King's School, Parramatta, New South Wales, an elite private boys' school. The study was to report on "how best to help boys achieve" (Hawkes, 2001a: 1)[38] and was premised on the validity of the range of data referred to earlier in constructing the figure of the schoolboy as victim: the "cool to be a fool" culture, the feminization of the curriculum, the "Growing dominance of the teaching profession by females," a recent and justified emphasis on the needs of girls, declining job prospects for boys with poor communication skills and questionable assessment techniques (Hawkes, 2001a: 3–4). At the same time, Hawkes developed the findings of the report into a full-blown defence of the need, advocated by Biddulph, West, Fletcher, Pollack, and others, for a concerted effort to improve the parenting and education of boys (Hawkes, 2001b).

Independent boys' school principals, such as Hawkes, have been quick to adopt this response to the figure of the schoolboy at risk. For example, the head of Scotch College, Melbourne (another elite private boys' school), told the House of Representatives Inquiry that "Boys and girls are not the same creatures . . . They learn differently and any policies that embrace boys' education must start from that point."[39] These were values widely shared by other principals of independent schools that potentially had much to gain from the Inquiry. They can be seen in comments by the head of the Junior School at Brighton Grammar, Melbourne, by the head of Melbourne Grammar[40] and by the Principal of Southwood Boys' Grammar School and its sister school, Tintern Girls' Grammar School, who observed that "boys and girls learn slightly differently and have slightly different needs," thus justifying "parallel education" in single-sex schools.[41]

The debate over the desirability of single-sex schools as against coeducational schools is beyond the scope of this account, but it should be acknowledged that many in the independent/private school sector have adapted the discourse of the underachieving and disadvantaged boy to justify their function in the educational system at large. In recent times a considerable movement of students from state schools in Victoria to independent girls', boys' and coeducational schools has taken place for a variety of reasons against the background of this debate. Within this discursive regime, the following statements by Rowe are typical. Commenting on the higher tertiary entrance scores achieved by students in single-sex settings as against coeducational settings, he was reported as saying that even allowing for differing abilities, and in spite of his belief that teacher quality was the major factor affecting students' outcomes, "Boys and girls in single-sex settings were . . . likely to be better behaved in the classroom and to find their curriculum relevant and teachers responsive . . ." He claimed:

> coeducational settings are limited in their capacity to accommodate the large differences in cognitive, social and developmental growth rates of girls and boys between the ages of 12 and 16 . . . Two-thirds of the teacher's time in a coeducational environment, regardless of the gender of the teacher, is spent managing either the ego-tripping behaviour of the boys or the very aggressive, assertive behaviours of the girls, which means less time is spent on task . . . So the girls have to deal with pretty juvenile, male macho kind of behaviours
>
> (*The Age*, 23 June 2001).[42]

The issue of the relevance of the curriculum to the biologically driven figure of the adolescent male once again emerges as a crucial element in the discourse of the schoolboy as victim. Boys' natures, it is said, are not catered for; they have to sit still, learn passively, read and write when they would rather be active and engaged in a variety of short, clearly defined tasks, preferably with right or wrong answers, possibly with computers and stimulated by tales of action and "blood and guts" (West, 2002a:

125). Nowhere is this said to be more evident than in the use and study of language. West asks, "When I go to the USA or the UK or almost anywhere, why do boys say they hate English?" (ibid. 121). Given his understanding of gender, and given that many boys have reading difficulties early in life and continue to fall behind girls' attainments in literacy, West develops the argument that boys' interests, especially in the middle school, are simply not being addressed in appropriate ways: they don't read, they don't enjoy reading, they don't listen as well as girls and they don't express themselves as easily or as clearly. In the wider society, boys and their parents can see that analytical skills in Maths and the sciences are highly valued, whereas subjects requiring empathy and reflection appear not to be. Therefore:

> Boys see English is seen as a female subject . . . It is about personal identity and feelings. Primary teachers are overwhelmingly female, as are most English teachers. Boys are rarely good at presenting assignments, and lose out to girls for this reason. Boys prefer a focus on action, or adventures, or on stories, rather than characterization and empathy.
>
> (West, 2001: 28).

West draws on the work of Rowe and conversations with boys in classes he has visited to substantiate this argument (West, 2002a: 10–12; 98–99) in which references to teachers are mostly to women. What is important here is not so much an implied lack of achievement on the part of boys as the way their experience is represented. A favored example from a 13-year-old boy is the following quotation from Rowe repeated in several texts:

> My English teacher wants me to write about my feelings, my History teacher wants me to give my opinions, and my Science teacher wants me to write on my views about the environment! I don't know what my feelings, opinions and views are, and I can't write about them. Anyway, they're none of their business! I hate school!! I only wish I could write about the things I'm interested in like sport and military aircraft.
>
> (West, 2002a: 10–11, quoting Rowe)

Whether this was originally written or spoken is not known, but its fluency and cogency cannot be denied. What concerns West, however, is the question of what interests boys of this or any age and whether and how schools are responding. Just what these interests might be is made clear in the following passages:

> Typical boys can do many things: take on part-time work, learn to drive a car, learn to use farm machinery, cope with various crises on

the family farm. And they do all this while they are struggling with an onrush of testosterone.

(ibid. 94)

He goes on:

> They are often interested in playing computer games. Boys like to play with cars when they are kids, lie under cars when they are teenagers, drive fast cars when they are get their licences, watch each other race cars when they are older. Most boys love activity: jumping into puddles, running around, leaping off fences, climbing trees. Boys love making a lot of noise; they love loud music and rock bands. Boys are interested in sex.
>
> (ibid. 109–10)

This resort to typicality rounds out the image of boyhood so essential to the recuperative agenda: the active, unreflective, verbally challenged, presumably heterosexual boy nursing the wounds of an underfathered childhood, now antagonistic to a feminized curriculum and female teachers at school and likely to attempt subjects in the final years of schooling on the basis of an assumed hierarchy of relevance to a masculinized (and increasingly mythologized), working life. It is an image precariously balanced between the likeable rogue – the "rough diamond" – and the hectoring, sexist, "macho" delinquent; in either case an image, at the very least, of alienation.

CONCLUSION

In this chapter I have sketched some of the conceptual terrain on which feminist and profeminist responses to the essentialist claims of recuperative masculinist writers have been made. Between the two camps, the statistical analyses of Teese *et al.* (1995) have established an increasingly dated series of benchmark observations that have been used in more or less nuanced readings to support each case in concert with a variety of interview-based evidence. Given the prominence of the question, "what about the boys?" Teese *et al.,* Lingard and Douglas, and Collins *et al.* in particular seek to disaggregate the data and ask "which boys?" thus not only acknowledging difference but also opening the possibility of inquiry into structural features of society (Lingard and Douglas, 1999: 111; 132; Collins *et al.,* 2000). Against this position, the House of Representatives Standing Committee on Education and Training, while acknowledging diversity among boys, ultimately incorporated into its recommendations the views of those commentators who relied on essentialist understandings to frame recuperative masculinity. Furthermore, the conception (advocated by feminist and profeminist writers), of masculinity/ies as relationally constructed in gendered environments in which girls continue to be disadvantaged, was shown to have little support among policy makers beyond the academy. Instead, the claims of those advocating a so-called deep, essential, masculine self, lost in contemporary society and in need of repair, have been privileged in policy development.

It is beyond the scope of this chapter to further explain why this should have happened, but some remarks are pertinent in view of what is at stake. In her submission to the New South Wales Inquiry into Boys' Education, Jane Kenway pointed to the link between gender and education:

> To put it simply most feminists want boys and men to change so that they cause less problems for girls and women and themselves, so the sexes can live alongside each other in a safe, secure, stable, respectful, harmonious way and in relationships of mutual life-enhancing respect.
>
> (O'Doherty, 1994: 23)

Achieving this with gender equity policies in schools has been found to be exceptionally difficult, not least because of the emotional demands made on boys and male teachers by such policies (Kenway and Willis, 1997; Keddie, 2010). Discourses of dominant and hegemonic masculinities have been found to be remarkably resilient and have provoked sceptical – even hostile – responses to claims made in the recuperative canon.[43] For example, Kenway and Willis (1997), commenting on boys as the "new disadvantaged," write: "'Strutting and fretting' at the center of the gender reform stage in the mid-1990s is the 'under-achieving boy'" (p. 47), whereas Gilbert (1998) refers scathingly to the "Poor boys, lost boys, damaged boys, under-fathered boys" (p. 19).[44] What is at issue here is precisely the nature, origin, and function of this image: feminist poststructuralism's advocacy of difference, discursive positioning and multiple, even contradictory subjectivities, can offer no recognizable alternative. Instead, as Gilbert and Gilbert (1998) argue, we need to focus on the experiences boys have: "we need to see how boys experience masculinities in our culture" (p. 52). But just as they acknowledge that the school as an institution is not a neutral background in the construction of gender (Gilbert and Gilbert, 1998: 114), so "experience" should not be understood, as I argued in Chapter 1, merely as a seamless, taken-for-granted context easily mistaken for the passage of time. While gender has been theorized at length, in the context of such debates "experience" remains relatively undertheorized. For example, frequent exhortations to return to the experience of boys in O'Doherty (1994) and Slade and Trent (2000) and those writers I have regarded as populist, suggest it is understood in a prediscursive, everyday sense as apprehended by sovereign subjects. As I indicated in Chapter 1, however, experience will be understood here as discursively constructed, and hence contested and contingent, a position Gilbert and Gilbert (1998) come close to endorsing in suggesting a way forward: "The starting point for boys' work . . . must be through a critical assessment of lived masculinity – and through a thoughtful and informed consideration of how schooling and masculinity intersect" (p. 25). Similarly, Kenway and Willis (1997), in writing of "males' ways of being" and the question of "what it means to be a boy or a girl at school," (pp. 133; 135) advocate feminist poststructuralist insights emphasizing the relational and discursive dimensions of experience.

In this chapter I have discussed how the failing, disaffected schoolboy has come to occupy a privileged place in the public imagination in Australia. The populist discourse of essentialism, appealing as it does to parents in need of advice on parenting and schools seeking to affirm or recuperate a sense of core masculinity (or, alternatively, avoid harming it), together with sufficient statistical evidence to sustain an image of declining male achievement in the final year of schooling, has succeeded in determining the direction of recent gender equity policy. At the same time, a more nuanced approach from feminist and profeminist writers has questioned the extent and nature of boys' alleged declining achievement and urged that policy makers ask "which boys?" thus differentiating between boys in a way inimical to essentialist epistemology. A feature of this debate, however, has been the way populist writers have appeared to draw on boys' experiences while their opponents have not, or at least have minimized attention to the context in which boys' disaffection has arisen. As set out in Chapter 1, my concern is very much with the nature of boys' experience of their schooling and of themselves, and given that ethnography is an appropriate means for understanding experience, in the next chapter I will explore how and to what extent ethnographies of schooling have contributed to an understanding of these issues and to the construction of the failing, disaffected, resistant schoolboy.

3 Writing the Schoolboy

INTRODUCTION

My intention in this chapter is twofold. First, it is to engage with a range of educational ethnographies that in one way or another deal with youth (in particular, schoolboys aged about 13 to 16 years), in order to discuss the ways in which they have been imagined and constructed textually. Second, it is to locate those constructions within the range of epistemologies and practices that have characterized educational ethnography as a genre since the 1970s. Given the vast literature available, I have given priority to studies that more or less exemplify the development of ethnography leaving to one side debate over the aptness of particular conceptualizations of the way it has changed (Delamont and Atkinson, 1980; Denzin and Lincoln, 1994, 2000; Denzin, 1997; Atkinson et al., 1999). This has entailed some analysis of changing research paradigms, touching on early structural–functionalist studies[1] and those driven by a commitment to symbolic interactionism which, according to Hargreaves (1978: 7) led to "a stampede to schools and classrooms." A brief excursus on neomarxist and other critical approaches to social and cultural studies is undertaken before moving on to feminist critiques of ethnographies of "youth" and, more recently, to disputes between those favoring modernist over postmodernist theoretical frameworks in researching relations between the school, achievement, gender, and ethnicity. The studies I have chosen are drawn from British, American, Scandinavian, and Australian research.

In commenting on these studies, I will refer to changing relations between their substantive content, research methods, and theoretical frameworks, the place given to the experience of the researcher in conducting the research and to the ethnography as text. I have been guided to some extent by Atkinson's contention that plausibility and authority are constructed by the textual practices of ethnographers (Atkinson, 1991, 1996), and by Coffey's assertion (1999: 10; 2) that a sense of the presence of "the researcher self" – "the ethnographic self" – in the work of doing ethnography in the field and in writing ethnographic texts has been crucial in deconstructing both the distinction between observer and observed and the grounds of authorial claims to truth.

EARLY MODERNIST STUDIES

To some extent the title of this section is contentious as no single text exemplifies the range of characteristics that could be identified in any narrow sense as modernist. "(M)ainstream and modernist . . . ethnography (writes Britzman [1995]), depends upon the rationality and stability of writers and readers and upon noncontradictory subjects who say what they mean and mean what they say" (p. 230). Certainly such studies, at least those from Denzin and Lincoln's (1994, 2000) modernist phase, will illustrate a distinction between observer and observed in which the maintenance of distance and a general air of surveillance and authorial superiority sit more or less uneasily with claims to have achieved rapport with significant insiders. Study designs may have been developed in such a way as to attempt to minimize the effect of the researcher on the researched and the written product may reflect this disembodied gaze, the subjects of the research usually being presented one-dimensionally and frequently of secondary importance to the ostensible object of the study.[2]

My examples will be drawn from what MacLure (2003: 78) describes as "a trilogy of 'classic' ethnographies of secondary schooling," namely texts by D. Hargreaves (1967), Lacey (1970) and Ball (1981)[3] with passing reference to Lambart (1976, 1982). As I will show, in each case the ethnographer remained a shadowy and relatively distant figure for whom issues of reflexivity were only dimly perceived, whereas attempts to explain substantive issues relied heavily on a structural–functionalist or symbolic–interactionist paradigm. In the following analysis, I will locate each study within its epistemological context in order to suggest both the possibilities and the limitations that ultimately led to particular textual constructions of schoolboys.

In their review of qualitative research traditions, Atkinson et al. (1988) point out that by 1988 symbolic interactionism had influenced "a very great deal of the qualitative research on education in Britain" (p. 235). Among those most influenced by symbolic interactionism, according to Atkinson et al. (1988), were Hargreaves, Lacey, and Lambart. Although working largely as sociologists, they were also very much the products of social anthropology as it developed under Max Gluckman and colleagues at Manchester by the early 1960s, focusing attention on small-scale settings such as factories, schools, and classrooms (Delamont and Atkinson, 1980: 140; Atkinson et al., 1988: 234–35; Lacey, 1981). While important but short-lived, Gluckman's influence led to intensive participant observation[4] focused on a variety of concerns common to social anthropology at the time: for example, custom and its relation to conflict; the place of ceremonial, or ritual, in industrial settings; issues of class, gender, and race on the shop floor and their relations to structures of power, and conflict resolution (Frankenberg, 1982). In particular, Gluckman deeply respected empirical studies that aimed to link "grounded fieldwork . . . to broader theoretical questions" (Lacey, 1982: 166), was skeptical of overly mechanistic and deterministic theories and preferred studies to be guided by a clear, central research problem rather than "the supposed analogue of a natural science hypothesis" (Frankenberg, 1982: 27).

As a result of Gluckman's conviction that a study of the particular, if linked appropriately to sociological theory could illuminate the general, a series of studies was undertaken which "were intended to focus on problems deriving from the contact and conflict within modern society between different cultures, for example middle-class and working-class, adult and adolescent cultures" (Lambart, 1982: 208). Consequently, David Hargreaves' *Social Relations in a Secondary* School (1967), Colin Lacey's *Hightown Grammar* (1966, 1970) and Audrey Lambart's work on Mereside Grammar School for Girls (1976, 1982) all emerged from this initiative (Lacey, 1966: 262).

As Atkinson *et al*. (1988) point out, Manchester was only one of several sources of qualitative research developing in Britain in the 1960s and 1970s, all adopting a symbolic interactionist approach in varying degrees of sophistication. While such an influence was undoubtedly congenial to its practitioners, these early educational ethnographies were also concerned, as I have indicated, to link the "micro" with the "macro" at a time when the liberal humanist conception of the function of education was under constant legislative revision. Such attention to the purpose and provision of education in Britain would escalate in the Thatcher years as "humanistic communitarianism" and neomarxist approaches attempted to refocus the role of education in a time of industrial decline, high youth unemployment, and racial tension (Hargreaves, 1981). Furthermore, as Hargreaves pointed out, for those laboring in the field of qualitative educational research at the time, successful attempts to link micro and macro analyses would have to be grounded in ethnographic work informed by symbolic interactionism which, by definition, "(got) close to human phenomena" (Hargreaves, 1978: 18–19; 13). As Hargreaves comments, the contribution of symbolic interactionism (which he linked to phenomenology) had helped "to put real men [sic] back into the abstract theoretical writing of much structural-functionalism . . . man must be studied in his natural habitat" (Hargreaves, 1978: 13). While such a view obviously echoed the spirit of sociological inquiry as it had developed in Chicago under Robert Park and successors (Atkinson, 1991: 1996), it also followed directly from the interests and methods of social anthropology at Manchester as its practitioners began to turn away from the study of colonial societies.

In addition to a commitment to participant observation as it had developed in social anthropology and urban sociology, some at least, of the

Manchester researchers were intent on framing their research in terms of a critique of contemporary British society. Lacey, for example, was intent on pursuing his "deepest concerns about society" (Lacey, 1976: 64) which he referred to well after the publication of his opus[5] in terms of a broadly leftist critique of "the underachievement of working-class children in grammar schools" (Lacey, 1976: 66; Lacey, 1982: 168). The Manchester studies, he wrote, were "concerned with the relation between schooling viewed as a social process and social structure" (Lacey, 1976: 63), and his particular intention, predating his study, was "to promote those sorts of intervention that would lead towards an egalitarian society" (ibid. 64), but as I will show, his ethnographic writing betrayed none of this fervor. At first confined to grammar schools, the Manchester project helped to foreground "meritocratic" versus "egalitarian" educational philosophies (ibid. 83), a debate further enlivened when Hargreaves entered the team to study a secondary modern school.[6]

A little of the importance of this distinction to Lacey is revealed in the way he introduces the reader to his text. "Though I am presenting a case study of one school (he writes), its significance is not confined to the particularistic concerns of one school. It extends to general problems in sociology and education" (Lacey, 1970: xi). He goes on "The school is viewed as a social system which is nevertheless embedded in a wider society. It is a socializing organization which is an 'integral part of the process of social mobility' and 'an intrinsic part of community life'" (ibid. x).

His aim is to "lay bare the social mechanisms within the school" that might explain the poor performance of working-class boys in grammar schools and because such mechanisms "are in part the result of pressures emanating from society," he expected the same pressures to afflict the proposed new comprehensive system which had been designed to "provide an organizational framework more likely to achieve equal educational opportunity for all sections of the community" (ibid. xi–xii). In contrast, Hargreaves takes a more prosaic approach to his task, stating his aim as: "to provide an analysis of the school as a dynamic system of social relations through an intensive study of interaction processes and day-to-day behaviour within the school" (Hargreaves, 1967: vii).

Such a conceptual framework implies an input–output model of process and structure of the type Lacey criticized for its overly strong "social determinism" and its failure to "(indicate) how the school system or individual teachers can change in order to modify (such effects)" as the underachievement of working-class children (Lacey, 1976: 68–69). Hargreaves, however, elaborated as follows:

> The aim of the study is to describe the structure and unintended consequences of selected aspects of human behaviour and organization in the school. It is through the examination of the conflicts and

deleterious effects of human action and school organization that our understanding of the social system of the school can be advanced.

(Hargreaves, 1967: x)

Thus a conceptual priority is accorded the notion of the school as a social system together with an implied structural-functionalist framework of analysis. The study of boys *as boys* is not on the agenda: the substantive focus is the workings of the school understood as a social system in a society where educational opportunity is mediated by both class and gender. The boys in this study are essentially no more than elements in a system whose function is under review.

Trained in social psychology and with three years' teaching experience in a grammar school, Hargreaves "entered the school as a participant observer . . . with the intention of examining the behaviour and attitudes of the boys in the school and their relationships with the teachers and one another" (Hargreaves, 1967: ix). Lacey, likewise, with a brief teaching background, sought to immerse himself in the school, or

> the system in order to be able to feel, recognize and describe the constraints of the various roles within the school and be able to put together a descriptive model or series of models of the processes that (he) recognised. The idea was to describe the system from a number of perspectives.
>
> (Lacey, 1976: 69)

As with Hargreaves, the study of boys and their experiences was not his prime focus, nor was the identification and understanding of the impact of streaming practices on students and teachers his major concern, although it was seen at the time as his major finding. To Lacey, schools as "socialising" organizations were "particularly sensitive to changes in the structure of (their) parent society. (They) have become major stratifying devices within society. The qualifications they distribute have been likened to tickets for the journey through life . . ." (Lacey, 1970: 186; also xi). Given parental concerns for their sons' achievement and the status attached to grammar schools at the time, the implications of Lacey's identification of what he called "differentiation" (by the school of the student body) and the resulting "polarisation" (of student attitudes to the school) – "the major processes within the school" (ibid. xv) – are discussed in the most restrained and muted tones. In the context of contemporary national social and economic changes mentioned earlier, and parental anxiety about their sons' future employment, and given the fact that among their sons a distinct "anti-group sub-culture, reacting against the dominant school values" was observed (ibid. xv), Lacey concludes that his analysis "throws doubt upon the feasibility of 'equality of opportunity' in a stratified society" (ibid. xvi; also 193), implying that the new

Comprehensives were a last-ditch attempt at reforming society as a whole (ibid. xii).

Hargreaves' study, as I have indicated, illustrates a rather different set of commitments.[7] As he saw it, his task was both "social psychological and micro-sociological in orientation" (Hargreaves, 1967: x) and he revealed a concern for the study design on this basis: "Differences in individual psychology, such as personality factors, have been excluded and many sociological variables receive scant attention" (ibid. x). This, to Hargreaves, was a severe limitation of what participant observation might achieve. To him it was "a relatively unstructured research procedure ... fraught with difficulties and dangers" and so only "exploratory in nature" (ibid. x). Indeed, he writes, "no specific hypotheses derived from current theories are tested," but as if to counter this, he makes the following commitment: "At the same time an attempt has been made to find ways in which (the processes he observes) can be measured and subjected to statistical analysis" (ibid. x). It is clear that Hargreaves is working well within a standard research paradigm of his day which required the social psychologist to investigate behavior by questionnaire and/or measurement and to maintain a high degree of "objectivity" and distance from his subjects, a research protocol made all the more difficult in this case by his intention to participate in and observe the daily life of the school and to write at least partly on the basis of this interaction.

Like Lacey, Hargreaves found that the student body was riven by two subcultures: those in the two higher streams who more or less adopted the school's (i.e., the teachers') values, which he called the "academic" subculture, and an opposing group who did not, which he called the "delinquescent" subculture (Hargreaves, 1967: 162). By "delinquescent," he meant that the group held "values (that) are negatively oriented towards the school, and in the direction of delinquent values, though not of course being synonymous with delinquency" (ibid. 162).

Throughout his work, Hargreaves draws on the language of social science available to him at the time as if its theories and terms were value free and could remain uncontested. He writes of a certain kind of boy in either subculture as a "role-model" (ibid. 180); "status frustration" and "status deprivation" become symptoms of lower stream failure to "internalise" the school values; and he characterizes the "normative structure" of each form in terms of the academic-delinquescent continuum, all the time couching his findings and observations in the restrained, tentative style so admired in the conservative academy and to which Lacey also submitted. For example, here Hargreaves reflects on his attempt to explain the formation of the two subcultures in the school:

> Most attempts at explanation in social science are beset by the multiplicity of inter-connections of the variables the researcher wishes to assess. Nor can one easily conduct experiments with human

> beings... In studying the social process within a school, the researcher has to rely predominantly on observation and record and questionnaire data, rather than on experiments, to substantiate his [sic] hypotheses. The variables at work are almost infinite, and the assessment of the contribution of any one variable becomes exceedingly difficult. In this study many of the key variables have been totally neglected; those that have been treated... are inter-related in such a complex way... that the analysis of the process of subcultural differentiation soon leads to dangerous and unconfirmed speculation.
>
> (ibid. 164).

This is not merely an aside on the limitations of his methodology in which Hargreaves exhibits a scientistic concern for the specification of dependent and independent variables in causal explanation. Here he is tentatively acknowledging that what he has found in the school is a reflection of expressions of differentiation evident in the wider society. The final cautionary reflection concerning inferences based on the study poses a dilemma, the solution to which would take Hargreaves well beyond his data and methodological paradigm into the realm of social critique in a way that was less troubling to Lacey, as I will indicate later on. Locating the school within the "larger social system," Hargreaves drew attention to the stratified nature of British (and American) society, in which "human beings are differentially ranked as superior or inferior relative to one another in certain respects" (ibid. 164). In such a society, he goes on, the primacy of "the Protestant ethic" has ensured that "the key value of our society is *achievement*: man is saved by his [sic] individual works and strivings. We exist on the myth of equality of opportunity to achieve" (ibid. 165).

Hargreaves' liberal humanist theoretical stance cannot do without the system metaphor and its concern to specify the functions of its parts. Here the notions of norm, socialization, and conformity and its opposite, deviance, are never far from the surface as the following steps in his argument demonstrate:

> If one of the key values of our society is achievement, then the school becomes a central focus and means by which individuals can achieve. Its stress on academic achievement, which is a major determinant of future occupation, represents an embodiment of these social values.
>
> (ibid. 165)

In a stratified society, however, in which the middle class has appropriated the "Protestant ethic": "The working class may not be able to attain these goals, due to their restricted access to the means, but many of them accept the validity of the values though they may sometimes appear to reject them" (ibid. 165).

It is now a small step in his argument to pathologize those who challenge, or reject, these middle-class values, and this he does in the ringing tones of a law-like statement: "When peer group and home influences are consistent, subcultural differentiation is considerably facilitated. When peer group and home conflict, the pupil is faced with a problem of adjustment" (ibid. 168).

Hargreaves is now able to introduce the concept of deviance as if the term were value free: antiacademic boys in the high streams are "deviant from the group norm" as are academically oriented boys in the low-achieving streams, making the job of their teacher doubly difficult. Not only is the problem of discipline to be faced, he argues, but "To the teacher, it is the high status boys in the low streams who are deviant yet it is in fact these very boys who are most integrated on the peer group level" (ibid. 171).

As a result, Hargreaves reaches a conclusion highly contentious at the time: that because of streaming, "the school can be regarded as a generating factor of delinquency" (ibid. 173), but this is soon followed by a return to the caution that marked the presentation of his aims and his discussion of the research design and procedure:

> To make generalizations from this research about secondary schools in general would be both pretentious and dangerous . . . (It has been) a descriptive analysis, with supportive statistical evidence, of the structure of social relations in one school. I have tried to confine myself to this "objective" task and to exclude value judgements on the school organization or on individual persons.
>
> (ibid. 182)

But as I hope I have shown, such objectivity has been far from achieved. Behind the mask of third person presentation and the occasional authorial "we," this is one of the few times Hargreaves emerges in the first person to discuss both teachers' value judgments (e.g., about "difficult" boys, the advisability of retaining streaming, academic achievement in single parent families, sport and "ability" and the removal of "undesirable" students from excursions), and the school administration's values evident in the allocation of teachers to forms, the structure of the timetable and corporal punishment. Furthermore, a founding privilege is given to the notion of structure within which the subjects of the study stand for little more than components within a more or less functional system.

STORIES FROM THE FIELD

Embedded within their broad theoretical concerns and their cautious, measured presentation and analysis of data, Lacey and Hargreaves can be seen to have warmed to their tasks as they mingled with staff and students in their respective schools. Given the way they framed their research, it was more or less inevitable that they should ultimately have something to say about boys and that teachers should be men.[8] This "discovery" of boys (as distinct from "working-class children," "pupils," or "students")[9] and their worlds emerges in vignettes and stories even more than in carefully chosen quotations from interviews. Lacey, in particular, was anxious not to open himself to accusations of bias in his choice of illustrative examples:

> The case studies which are presented exemplify, in an exhaustive manner, the combinations of factors represented in the paradigm (involving factors linked to the school, the home and the community). A strictly enforced procedure for the selection of the case studies is used to prevent the distortion caused by "apt illustration."
>
> (Lacey, 1970: xvi)

The procedure referred to[10] perhaps indicates a tension between a commitment to an analytical framework favoring the "micro," which at the same time might "counteract the tendency to make 'apt illustration' from fieldwork notes" (Lacey, 1976: 67). Lacey regarded this tendency as both "an implied criticism of much social anthropological writing" (ibid. 67) and a reply to potential accusations of bias.[11] It also reflects an interpretivist stance on his part in relation to issues of "distance," the requirement to be in some sense an "outsider," and "objectivity." From the start Lacey was

> disinclined to go along with the notion of "objectivity" . . . I saw it as my job to develop views of the system from a number of points of view – those of the parent, the teacher and the child (in order to) illustrate the dynamics of the system.
>
> (ibid. 67)

Participant observation for Lacey was therefore a balancing act in which he constantly monitored his relations with and distance from teachers, students, and parents. More often than not, plain observation together with interviews, questionnaires, and the occasional use of students' reflective essays provided the material for his writing. A feature of Lacey's text is the third person distance he keeps from the interactions he observes and is part of, a distance aided by his pursuit of a series of models of "the dynamics of the system" frequently supported by the presentation of data in sociograms. The words of the boys are rarely more than briefly edited quotations, but staffroom gossip is quoted at greater length as (occasionally) are the words of parents. The text is enlivened, however, by the use of vignettes and short stories illustrating incidents he witnessed and presented as a prologue to a moral, or to a formal social scientific conclusion.[12] Thus, for example, after starting with an impressionistic list of what happens when "the highly selected first-year population meets" (Lacey, 1970: 53) for the first time, he moves on to two incidents concerning some of these boys he witnessed early in his study. On being asked to read, we learn that one boy distinguished himself by reading nervously, giggling, and mispronouncing words, but also that he "wiped his face with a huge white handkerchief . . . blew his nose loudly" and continued to mop his brow and blow his nose (ibid. 53–54). Thus, "This short incident, one of several during the day, served to remind (the student) of his structural position in the class" (ibid. 54). Such passages inevitably lead into his construction of what he refers to as a model of "the passage of pupils through the grammar school" (ibid. 57ff), namely the differentiation/polarization model referred to earlier.

Rather longer stories appear in Lacey's analysis of parental involvement in the school's decision whether to place their sons in an express stream or not. Here, Lacey observes the workings of middle-class parents' (frequently mothers') linguistic resources as they make their appeals more successfully than working-class parents (mothers). Given his ideological commitment, Lacey not surprisingly resorts to a core metaphor when writing of this outcome. Socioeconomic classes as represented by families are described as "competing teams" in which parents are the "coach" and the pupil is the "competitor" (ibid. 125). The outcome of the deployment of family resources in disputes with the school must lead to "defeat" for one family or another (usually working-class) in this thinly veiled microcosm of class conflict and social reproduction (ibid. 152; Lacey, 1982: 174).

Given the sense of distance Lacey conveys in his text we learn very little of the lives of the proschool boys beyond their willingness to do homework, answer questions in class and have short hair. In comparison, it is clear that the "anti-group" boys exerted a far greater impact on Lacey's powers of participation and observation. In the broader academic context of growing interest in the emergence of subcultures and the concept of adolescence Lacey makes brief and relatively colourful asides concerning this group. For example:

> The content of the anti-group culture . . . may range from a folk music CND group in a minor public school to a delinquent sub-culture at a secondary modern school in an old urban area (Lacey, 1970: 57).
>
> (Two of these) boys are now regarded as bullies and "tough eggs" who . . . would rather be hooligans and have a good time than be nice little boys. They are aggressive, loud-mouthed and feared by many who are successful in terms of dominant school norms (ibid. 65).
>
> By the middle of the third year (this group) had extended their activities from collecting pop records to sporting Beatle haircuts and

attending coffee bars and dance clubs in the town centre at night (ibid. 71).

It is clear that in his fieldwork Lacey was drawn to this group and he reported later that a small number of the anti-group boys in a fifth-year class "provided without doubt the most stimulating and entertaining discussions I enjoyed in the school. The discussions had a life of their own" (Lacey, 1976: 73). Boys from this group clearly challenged his teaching role as he later reported (ibid. 73–74), and the antigroup's presentation of themselves in terms of subcultural fashion and activities outside the school frustrated many teachers as snippets of staffroom discussions show.

The distance Lacey found he needed to keep strategically as a researcher is perhaps explained by his conviction that it was essential for teachers (and for him), to develop a "teacher persona" (Lacey, 1970: 174ff) which can only have served to increase or maintain the distance conventionally expected of the ethnographer (Delamont and Atkinson, 1995). Again, stories with accompanying morals illustrate this point, and he later wrote revealingly that: "It was only through the creation of a second 'me' that I could survive" (Lacey, 1976: 77). Staff who had managed this transformation, he noted, were "delighted" when they saw themselves "taken off" in the sixth-form review.[13] Clearly, such a mask implies a kind of deception which a more reflexive awareness of the ethnographic task might not condone, although in his encounters with boys struggling to cope with the normative school the reader may see through his "teacher persona."[14] As I will show, the resort, or use of this sort of distance was to become far less common in the work of Willis, Walker, Mac an Ghaill, and others.

Hargreaves' text is in some respects similar to Lacey's in that he maintains a third person distance throughout, interspersed with colourful and finely observed stories of incidents and individuals. The balance implied in this distinction clearly interested Hargreaves when he wrote that "When man writes about man [sic] his terms seem very subjective and value-loaded ... (This) analysis of Lumley School has been written as objectively as possible" (Hargreaves, 1967: x). His text, however, leans far more heavily on the words of his informants than Lacey's: "Wherever possible the boys speak for themselves ... (but) all the quotations cannot be taken at their face value" (ibid. xi). Nevertheless, the text is replete with boys' opinions and observations (e.g., ibid. 88–89; 101–02) with little editorial comment or indeed awareness of his editorial role. Like Lacey, his identification of an antischool group led him into their world after a shaky start in which he reveals rather more about his past than Lacey did (ibid. 85).[15] This attachment was strategically useful and enters the text frequently, culminating in an incident in which, although trying as a researcher to avoid intervening in actual arguments and incidents, he took the side of the "delinquent group" against staff and Headmaster (ibid. 138–39). In this and similar stories, Hargreaves generally dispenses with the moral or social scientific conclusion, and, unlike Lacey, his illustrative stories occasionally end with first person reflections (e.g., ibid. 132; 138). Again, in contrast to Lacey, whose "self" hardly emerges until his article six years after the publication of *Hightown Grammar*, Hargreaves opens up to the reader in his Appendix, indicating some of the many ethical dilemmas he faced.[16]

Following directly from Lacey's and Hargreaves' interest in the reform of secondary education in Britain, Stephen Ball investigated a coeducational comprehensive school (Ball: 1981).[17] He found that educational and administrative processes within the school had created a polarization of students into subcultures similar to those found previously by Hargreaves (in the secondary modern) and Lacey (in the grammar school). Like them, he also asked "how one can study the social mechanisms operating within a school and employ such knowledge to explain the disappointing performance of working-class pupils" (ibid. xv), but unlike them he employed "a combination of interactionist and structuralist perspectives (to investigate) the definition and social construction of pupils' identities and their school careers" in the context of "structural constraints and social determinants" (ibid. xvi–xvii).[18] This explicit interest in pupils' identities can be seen as a significant move towards making boys into a "textual phenomenon" outside the realm of fictional literature (Harari, 1980: 46) and within the burgeoning genre of educational ethnography.

Like Lacey and Hargreaves, Ball's participant observation, mere observation (or noticing) and use of questionnaires and sociometric analysis provided him with a wealth of ethnographic data which he exploited in his writing in terms of third person and, frequently, first person narrative. Ball is present in his text in a way that the other two writers are so often not (e.g., ibid. 77; 85 and chapter 7 especially),[19] but the absence of any detailed discussion of methodological issues is remarkable (Sharp, 1981: 280).[20] What is even more noticeable and ultimately more interesting, however, is that Ball's interest in "adolescent culture" and its links to the school enables him to focus on students' experience of schooling in a way that the other two authors did not, or at least not to the same degree. Thus he writes: "we know little as yet about the ways in which pupils, especially those aged between fourteen and sixteen, make sense of school as part of their whole life-world" (Ball, 1981: 109), and he reveals this link via student diaries, essays, and interviews (Ball, 1985: 38). In their world, by the third year of secondary school, he noted that

> the management of the self in terms of the trends of the pop media does come to contribute to the relative popularity and status of pupils ... The evolution of the social structure of the form group is one

concomitant aspect of the increasing importance of independent social life activities and the adolescent sub-cultures.

(Ball, 1981: 115)

In a passage notable for its intensity and sense of revelation, Ball recognizes that "the creation of a conception of self for the pupil . . . is very different from the child-based conception of the pupil of earlier generations" (ibid. 117) and in this new environment he provides a view of schooling from the students' point of view.[21] Those in the upper levels of the school who were regarded by teachers as failures, he writes, "had ceased to be participants in any real sense in the micro-cultural world of schooling . . . they had come to see the school as an alien institution" (ibid. 118–19).

Ball's emphasis on students' experience is occasionally more expansive than either Lacey's or Hargreaves' brief references and signals an awareness of the individual student that did not fit easily into their research designs. Lacey, for example, reports a story of a boy who wanted to leave soon after he turned 15. On being asked why, he replied: "I hate all teachers." Lacey comments that the teachers found

> the remark . . . amusing, because it was so categorical and unreasonable . . . It seemed non-sensical to lump (the teachers) all together. What we forgot was that the boy's experience of us *as teachers* did not contain anything like this variability. Just as *he* was viewed by most of the teachers as rather lazy, poorly behaved and lacking in strength of character, so he felt that *all* teachers disliked him, were unfair to him and made his life miserable.
>
> (Lacey, 1970: 180; his emphasis).

Likewise, Ball, commenting on a girl of whom the staff had a low opinion, notes that on being asked if there were any teachers in the school that she liked, replied "I hate all the teachers in the whole school . . . They're horrible, it's a rubbishy prison" (Ball, 1981: 56). While it is clear that both student and teacher experiences underpin all three works so far discussed, each author manages to ignore or bypass the lived intensity of this experience as revealed in these brief passages, although as I have mentioned earlier, Lacey did reveal moments of distress and suffering some boys experienced. In general, however, they reduce experience to behavior and regard behavior as evidence of some form of process within a larger institutional, social, and historical matrix in their pursuit of theoretical structural and functional insights. Nevertheless, in these texts a sense of startled awareness is becoming apparent in vignettes of pupils who might be more complex and interesting – and gendered – than an ethnographic study of an educational system at work might suggest.

CULTURAL STUDIES, EXPERIENCE, AND GENDER

For Paul Willis, the pursuit of understanding the everyday – of what he referred to time and again in terms such as "the profane air of the real cultural world" – was no simple matter (Willis, 1981: 218). Adopting a radical Marxist critique of the social and cultural worlds of Thatcherite Britain he challenged the complacent view of the social democratic settlement in education which posited not only "the prospect of individual human development as well as the prospect of greater social equality" but also that failure at school "was the fault of education's recipients, their early childhood experience or their surrounding culture" (Willis, 1983: 108–09; Aronowitz, 1981).

Working within the newly developing cultural studies perspective,[22] Willis abandoned any view of social processes involving more or less autonomous individuals in favor of a shared, communitarian understanding:

> I . . . see society . . . as a structured whole within which individuals and groups live under differing degrees of domination, expressing *and reproducing* in different degrees through symbolic patterns and cultural practices a sense of *positionality* within and perhaps resistance to the hidden, misunderstood or unseen overarching structures which limit their field of choices and help to constitute them in the first place.
>
> (Willis, 1978: 193; his emphasis)

Experience, in this view, could therefore be investigated in terms of "the subjective dimension of what is *shared*" (Willis, 1978: 193; his emphasis), thus allowing for a notion of social experience,[23] and in this context it was axiomatic for Willis that qualitative methods, especially ethnography (understood as participant observation), had a crucial role to play (Willis, 1977: 3).[24] In a later elaboration of his position, he discussed this sharing in terms of social agents' creativity in producing such cultural forms as working-class youth's resistant identity and ultimately working-class culture, designated by him as cultural production as distinct from social reproduction (Willis, 1983). Researching such a process therefore required of the ethnographer, he argued, a particular commitment to question the apparently real and natural (i.e., not to investigate working-class pupils' educational failure in terms of early childhood experience or family dysfunction), by becoming reflexively aware of the research encounter with the subject of the research, thus entering critically into the subjects' world of meanings. Not to do so would, in his view, only produce what he called "layers of 'blank' data" (Willis, 1980: 94). Thus, for Willis, maintaining a certain conceptual distance from relatively conservative sources of theory while justifying radical social critique as ethical, represented a crisis of both method and commitment for the participant observer (Willis, 1978, 1980). This in turn was to lay the basis for subsequent criticisms of his apparent failure to avoid overidentification with the values of his research subjects, referred to ever after, as he did, as "lads."

This sense of deep ideological commitment and ebullience mark the text of Willis' *Learning to Labour* (1977).[25] In it he reports on his study of 12 working-class "lads" linked by friendship and shared opposition to schooling near the end of their compulsory education and into the first six months of their working lives.[26] His abandonment of any conventional sense of "objectivity" (in contrast to Hargreaves, for example), is implied from the start:

> The difficult thing to explain about how middle class kids get middle class jobs is why others let them. The difficult thing to explain about how working class kids get working class jobs is why they let themselves . . . The primary aim of this book is to cast some light on this surprising process.
>
> (Willis, 1977: 1)

In producing his text, Willis' particular innovation was to report on his ethnographic work first, apparently unadorned by exegesis, followed by a theoretical discussion of its implications for cultural formation and social reproduction. This textual innovation has been widely commented on. As a result of his particular sort of ethnographic involvement with "the lads," Willis was able to argue that their resistance to schooling was both culturally constructive and rational. The small group of boys, he argued, belonged to a class-structured society which prepared members of their class for manual, or working-class jobs which amounted to, and were experienced as, "subordinate roles in Western capitalism" (Willis, 1977: 3). It is this experience of subordination, he argues, that allows working-class boys the opportunity to affirm and appropriate their existence as a form of resistance. In Willis' terms, they penetrate (or see through) "the really determining conditions of existence of the working class" (ibid. 3) and come to understand a truth about themselves and Western capitalism that is "superior to those official versions of their reality which are proffered through the school and various state agencies" (ibid. 3). The result, in Willis' terms, is a cultural form he names and celebrates as "the working class counter-school culture," but for him there is "tragedy and . . . contradiction" in this. All too often such forms of penetration, or resistance, he argues, are rendered ineffective by dominant ideological processes within the school (such as vocational guidance and attempts to inculcate a conscientiously studious ethic), and beyond it in the working-class culture where "patriarchal male domination and sexism" are reproduced (ibid. 3).

As Willis demonstrates, the school is the site, or milieu, where this transformative learning takes place, but it is clearly not an intended outcome of any school policy or pedagogic process. This leads him to refer to "the profound, unintended and contradictory importance of the institution of the school" (ibid. 146) where the lads' counter-school culture informally defeats aspects of the dominant ideology stressing individualism. In contrast to Hargreaves' assertion that the necessary condition for academic success, or achievement, is individualism, Willis observes that by rejecting the school, the lads are rejecting individualism, a process mutually supported by such "profoundly naturalised divisions" as sexism and patriarchy that permeate working-class culture (ibid. 147).

Clearly, Hargreaves' delinquescents and Lacey's and Ball's antischool subcultural groups – the working-class boys teachers despaired of as oppositional and "undesirables" – were precisely those recognized widely and conventionally in official reports, as Willis observed, because of their indiscipline and truancy. Whereas for Hargreaves the tragedy was that the school was failing to develop the full potential of its students, and was thus failing to deliver the benefits of education in a liberal democratic state, for Willis the tragedy was that the counter-school culture could be so easily defeated as social reproduction in a capitalist state triumphed.

As mentioned earlier, Willis' book has been widely discussed in terms of its textual innovation. Commenting on the so-called textual turn in ethnography, George Marcus reviewed forms of experimental writing in interpretive anthropology, focusing on the ways certain ethnographic texts "take account of the manner in which world-historical political economy constructs their subjects" (Marcus, 1986: 168, fn. 5). Willis' text, while remaining "well within realist conventions" (ibid. 168, fn. 5) is presented as an exemplar of such innovation. In this text, the larger social order is represented by little more than an invocation of Marxist theory which operates as a framing narrative against which the everyday experiences of the 12 working-class boys are presented. By splitting his text into "Ethnography" and "Analysis," Marcus argues that Willis represents ethnography in the first part merely as method (participant-observation) with the mundane reporting of data, while the analysis purports to represent Willis as bearer of a truth not of his making. Referring to the split text, Marcus writes:

> this constructive division . . . frames a legitimated, autonomous analytic voice through which Willis can develop a theoretical discourse in a language to which he is accustomed, while relying on reference back to the ethnography section as a suggestion that it is not really his voice, but a mediation of what is embodied in the ethnography of the lads, conceived, significantly, as verbatim interview transcripts. So, we might say that the representation of working class experience is not at all Willis' primary goal; rather, Willis develops

ethnographic representations of working class experience to refer to it in a way that serves his theoretical exposition.

(ibid. 184)

Thus Marcus represents Willis the ethnographer as Willis "the midwife . . . who delivers and articulates what is vernacularly expressed in working class lives" (ibid. 180; 181), namely that the most powerful critique of capitalism "(lies) embedded in the everyday conditions and talk of ethnographic subjects" (ibid. 180) whose "strategic position in Marxist theory" is thereby confirmed (ibid. 181). For Marcus, the epistemological issue is whether and how Willis has translated "the orality of the subjects into the literacy of the ethnographer (or, in other words, whether) he has in fact authentically spoken for the lads" (ibid. 185) in such a way as ultimately to confirm the authority of his account for middle-class readers.[27]

A further critique has been offered by Ricca Edmondson (1984). In a passage quoted at length by Atkinson (1991: 102) and Skeggs (1992: 182), she draws attention to the rhetorical advantage Willis is able to gain in the reader's mind by representing his subjects in such a way as to elicit "a certain personal response" based on a feeling of "sympathy" for their situation and for their points of view (Edmondson, 1984: 42). Thus the lads are represented as potential victims in a "tragedy" yet seem marvellously able to avert it with humour and insight. Any disapprobation the reader might show towards the lads, who in a sense have already been textualized in public discourse as vulgar and oppositional, is therefore likely to be dissipated by this emphasis on the innocuous. Only later is the reader introduced to their sexism and racism. Furthermore, as Edmondson shows, the sociological use of examples in *Learning to Labour* gives significance to the "exceptionally telling but highly unrepresentative" example (ibid. 45) in order to achieve sympathetic and effective communication with the reader in a way, as I have indicated, that Lacey regarded with suspicion. With the help of such forceful yet arguably unrepresentative examples, Willis repeatedly allows the reader to draw conclusions without his apparent intervention via theory in the text (ibid. 45; 48–50). Such "rhetorical induction" based on "actual types," claims Edmondson, is emblematic of Willis' self-conscious awareness of rhetorical devices and strategies, an observation suggested also by Marcus in noting Willis' shrewd avoidance of the hermeneutic critique of his claim to have "in fact authentically spoken for the lads" (Marcus, 1986: 185).

Marcus' assertion, referred to earlier, "that the representation of working class experience is not at all Willis' primary goal," raises questions about the sufficiency of the experiences Willis adduces in the context of such a "strategically situated ethnography" (Marcus, 1986: 173)[28] to amount to a plausible explanation of the boys' attitudes and behavior. On the one hand, the reader is introduced to boys who appear textually more whole and alive than in the texts previously mentioned (especially in their vernacular language), while on the other, claims are made about the working class and working-class culture that elide any reference to the presence or agency of working-class girls and women. This absence is at the core of feminist critiques of *Learning to Labour* and of other texts as I will mention later on.

Nevertheless, in presenting his "lads" via extended quotations, Willis reveals through their language a good deal of the subtlety of their (pre-discursive) experience of the everyday as well as their attitudes to it, but the conditions in which this language was elicited are not made clear and he has been criticized for appearing to have identified too closely with "his chosen twelve" (Hammersley and Atkinson, 1995: 111–12; Skeggs, 1992: 192). As Edmondson points out, such linguistic representation of the vernacular justifies their being called "lads": "the term 'schoolboys' would be ridiculous" (Edmondson, 1984: 58). It is nevertheless the case that in Willis' text, the boys are palpably present in a way not evident in the other texts I have discussed, a feat also achieved with remarkable intensity by James Walker (1988) in his treatment of the schoolboys who are the subjects of his *Louts and Legends*.

Walker's ethnographic work took place in a Sydney (Australia) inner-city, all-boys school where the majority left at the end of Year 10 rather than go on to prepare for a State-wide competitive examination in their final year. The 39 boys he researched for five years through their final years at school and into the workforce lived in a mixed commercial and industrial environment and their ethnicity reflected the ethnic diversity of the area. His study, unlike Willis', is notable for the variety of contexts in which he observed and mixed with the boys,[29] but for Walker it is the school understood as a site for producing "differences, (in) social class, gender, ethnicity, post-secondary education and other sources of social status and economic power" (Walker, 1988: 4) that is pivotal in the boys' lives. Walker's aim was to investigate "the dynamics of specific youth cultures in their relations to formal schooling and the transition from school to employment, unemployment or further study' (ibid. 6) in a range of local settings in order to assess how such youth cultures might make and sustain "differences between people" (ibid. 6; 30–31), or what he refers to as "intercultural articulation." Beyond this theoretical frame and throughout the years of rapport with the "Stokey boys" his study demanded, Walker's presence in his text is unambiguous but restrained as he strives both to tell the boys' stories and allow the voices of 12 of his subjects to be heard (ibid. 173–74).

In emphasizing the individual and the choices the individual makes, Walker set out to oppose what he saw as the main weakness of the correspondence theory of social reproduction which posited a clear relationship between the power and authority structures of schools and similar structures in the wider society inhibiting radical social transformation.

Instead, he argued for a "more dynamic account of how schools contribute to (students') destinies" (ibid. 4). His focus, therefore, is on the kinds of response students make in opposition to the institutional authority of the school. He is particularly scathing of "resistance theory" (after Willis), which sought explanation in terms of "counter-school cultures, devised from wider working class antagonism to intellectual things and to 'mental labour' (connected to) the macho manualist culture of the shop-floor (and) passed on to boys through older males, particularly fathers, in family and neighbourhood" (ibid. 5). Although not addressed directly, Willis' study (among others) is clearly the target. Willis' working-class lads' explanation of their rejection of bourgeois values embedded in their schooling allows only one destiny in Walker's terms: "the bottom of the hierarchy" (ibid. 5), with no hint of redemption in terms of their being able to "penetrate" the ideology of contemporary class capitalism.[30]

In Walker's view, the alternative to accepting Willis' "cultural formation" explanation of opposition to schooling entails a focus on people's practices in daily life, which, on the face of it, puts him squarely in line with Willis and his focus on praxis. To Walker, such practices are "culture in action," revealing the link between persons and contexts where social classes, genders, and ethnic groups become differentiated. Such a focus on practice, or "behavioural disposition," he argues, will ensure a more dynamic and differentiated account of the relations between students and school than correspondence theory allows (ibid. 30), hence the prominence given throughout to the boys' decision-making and agency as individuals.

His conclusion – that the sort of bipolar model of pro- and antischool youth cultures found by Hargreaves, Lacey, Ball, and Willis – could not be empirically substantiated in his study, reflects the contradictions he found in the responses of individual students to the variety of settings in which they participated. The footballers, for example, are not at all monocultural in origin and not all bound to reject academic values in favor of the status accorded successful footballers in their working-class culture, whereas among the Greek boys, some shunned academic success and some did not; some played soccer whereas others played Rugby League, hovering in the vicinity of assimilation to the dominant "Aussie," or Anglo-Celtic culture. Walker's critics, however, take issue with his insistence on seeing "practice" merely as culture in action, Skeggs arguing that by doing so he fails to deal adequately with power. By not distinguishing between structure and the individual, she argues, Walker offers no analysis of the processes of institutionalization that legitimate and reproduce such forms of oppression as sexism and racism, so eloquently revealed in the testimony of the boys (Skeggs, 1989: 485; see e.g., Walker, 1988: 105–08). This is a serious criticism, amounting to a defence of one version of the social reproduction thesis. Willis' privileging of a neomarxist theoretical frame made a case for the reproduction of class relations[31] but in so doing he was criticized, as the following section will show, for failing to address the lads' sexism. Walker, likewise, is criticized for ignoring the boys' racism and their hegemonic (and therefore oppressive), masculinity.

FEMINIST RESPONSES

Early feminist responses to Willis' ethnographic work and text can be located within a broader attack on what was seen as a tendency among male cultural theorists and sociologists to theorize culture on the basis of evidence culled from all-male or largely male environments, thus ignoring the culture of femininity in all its class and ethnic complexity (e.g., Wolpe, 1988a).[32] Even before *Learning to Labour* was published, McRobbie and Garber (1977) took issue with what they saw as the glib and dismissive representation of girls (when they were mentioned at all), in Willis' Ph.D. thesis dealing with "motor-bike boys." In a passage that in many ways prefigures the tone of later feminist readings of masculinist texts[33] they asked (in part):

> Is this, simply, a typical and dismissive treatment of girls reflecting the natural rapport between masculine researcher and his male correspondents? Or is it that the researcher ... finds it difficult not to take ... boys' attitudes to and evaluation of girls seriously, reflects it in his descriptive language and even adopts it as a perspective himself, within the context of the research situation?
> (McRobbie and Garber, 1977: 210)

Thus, in response to the silences and marginalization of girls' and women's experiences, and in the patriarchal appropriation of terms such as "youth culture," a feminist reading of cultural studies and educational ethnographies emerged. Skeggs' response to *Louts and Legends*, for example, is exceptionally perceptive:

> whilst there is a whole confessional and advisory discourse associated with "older sisters" ensconced within the culture of femininity there is no male equivalent ... Whereas links can be established with young women through the experience of shared oppression, such as sexual harassment, which cuts across class differences, the male ethnographer is located in the position of collusion in the maintenance and reproduction of oppression through masculinity; not to collude would be likely to end any rapport that had been established. What does this tell us about the gendering of the research process? Is there a male equivalent to the feminist researcher?
> (Skeggs, 1989: 484–85)

Commenting on the misogyny of Willis' subjects and his failure to question their language, McRobbie observes that "What Willis fails to confront . . . is the violence underpinning such imagery and evident in one lad's description of sexual intercourse as having 'a good maul on her'" (McRobbie, 1980: 41). Here McRobbie has identified the unexamined "discourse of disrespect" lodged in Willis' demonstration of "how gender . . . articulates with class" (Skeggs, 1992: 182) and which she attributes to the "absence of self" in texts such as Willis' (McRobbie, 1980: 39). It is precisely the absence of such reflexivity, as I will show, that later educational ethnographies would take great pains to address.

One text from the time that encapsulates much of the feminist critique of gender blind educational ethnography is Lyn Davies' (1984) *Pupil Power. Deviance and Gender in School.* Taking the concept of "pupil deviance," Davies sets out to "(see) whether boys' and girls' deviance was quantitatively or qualitatively different, and (to consider) which sociological perspective(s) on deviance would best inform any difference found" (ibid. 4). Her notion of deviance and normality rests on who has the power to alter the course of events in a school setting and the example she gives is of a pupil who "'cheeks' a teacher into reaction, however punitive" (ibid. 3), thus exercising power over events in the classroom. Her expectation is that there will be gendered differences in how such power struggles occur and in teacher–pupil responses.

In carrying out her ethnography over two years in a comprehensive high school with a large working-class intake, Davies was led by teachers' concerns to focus on a group of girls she called (in the vernacular of the time), "wenches." She also relied "on an implicit notion of the 'normal' girl, who (was) by nature more 'immune' to delinquency, less affected by social circumstances than boys" (ibid. 148), and by her use of the notion of "scripts" to suggest repertoires of language culturally available to both teachers and pupils. These scripts to some extent circumscribe the range of possible interactions and (although she does not use the term), subject positions, available to teachers and students. Among her many findings, Davies argues that girls are not only subject to different rules from boys, but to different definitions of rule breaking where double standards apply in teachers' interpretation of rules because of their "normative expectations for female behaviour" (ibid. 138). Thus students noticed teachers imposed different punishments on boys and girls for what they perceived to be the same behavior, while male teachers were often unable to accept the ways the wenches' responses were so challenging and so resistant to change, generally preferring to deal with boys than with the wenches and their friends (ibid. 74).

Davies' discussion of this difference is central to her thesis. In her view, Hargreaves' emphasis on how streaming could explain boys' "delinquescent" response to compulsory schooling is insufficient to explain how and why the girls responded as they did. The key for Davies was to be found in the sort of status working-class girls might seek when opposing the school's academic aims. Whereas Willis' lads and to some extent Hargreaves' boys were denied, and denied themselves, academic success, they also expected to find manual work after their compulsory schooling. The wenches, however, for reasons touched on earlier, were denied (and denied themselves), access not only to academic and sporting success in the school but were also cut off from femininity as they understood it. As Davies argues, while it is difficult to generalize the "'focal concerns' of female class culture" (ibid. 171), the mental/manual dyad seems not to have been as salient for many girls in her study as it was for boys. These working-class girls in particular, she argues, experienced hugely frustrating contradictions in the patriarchal world of the school, let alone in the broader society, where they were expected to negotiate expectations of:

> being sexually attractive but not promiscuous; managing the transition from girl to wife to mother while maintaining femininity; acting out a subservient role yet having to be "caring", with the responsibility that that implies; (and) being financially dependent, yet often working to maintain the family.
>
> (ibid. 171)

Here, then, in the wenches' experience, as McRobbie and others had foretold, was a whole new terrain of research possibilities that had lain hidden in terms such as "pupil," "student," "youth culture," and "working class," a terrain that Davies recognized was in urgent need of remapping:

> *Learning to Labour* was hailed as radical and innovative, and became the sacred text for many a conference; yet a clue to the inherently conservative sexism in Willis' interpretations is the way he periodically claims all sorts of astonishing things to be "profoundly masculine" – the use of humour, taking the initiative, the ethos of the factory, doing unexpected or amusing things . . . (This demonstrates a pressing need) for empirical work on females which will "bring women back in" and counter the absurd and arrogant notion that it is only males who are interesting, amusing and active.
>
> (ibid. 172)

To do so, as she shows, is to reveal how complex, creative, and inventive are girls' individual responses and how inadequate is any explanation of them in terms of the more collective processes of subcultures (ibid. 114; 128; 171ff). Yet there was little about which to be optimistic, as she observed:

> Just as working class boys may in the end confirm their position in the wage labour structure by rejecting the avenues to mobility school

offers, resistant girls may increasingly close off during their school careers any other options than factory work or the dole followed by early marriage. School becomes doubly irrelevant both for marriage and job prospects.

(ibid. 120)

Davies' concern to help bring about a more humane and equitable experience of schooling under these circumstances by granting more power to students (especially working-class girls), was a position not far removed from Hargreaves' hopes for low-achieving boys. Here, in a further swipe at Willis, the framing narrative offered by the notions of subculture and "cultural formation" is cast aside.

A further attempt to "make girls 'visible'" (Wolpe, 1988a: 140; 137) in educational ethnography is Anne Marie Wolpe's *Within School Walls*.[34] Based on a 10-year longitudinal ethnographic study in a working-class London comprehensive, Wolpe investigated "processes . . . which contribute to the . . . fixing of female gender identities at the micro level of the classroom" (ibid. 6). While acknowledging that Willis' challenge to earlier economic reductionist theories of social reproduction had led to interest in the importance of agency, it had been left to feminist researchers, she argues, to locate the experience of women and girls within studies of the education system (Wolpe, 1988b). In doing so, Wolpe aimed to bridge the gap between "the macro level of structure (and) the micro level of interpersonal relationships" (Wolpe, 1988a: 5) but in so doing she revealed a skepticism towards the epistemological outcome of participant observation that recalls Lacey's concerns over "apt illustration." In criticizing certain feminist studies of educational settings that she claims resulted in a stereotypical view of boys and their impact on girls and teachers, she drew attention to the ethnographic use of examples – "exampling" – defined as "'the practice of fitting out an already formulated theory with supporting evidence'" (Furlong and Hamilton [1986] quoted in Wolpe, 1988b: 144; see also Wolpe, 1988a: 37–38; 45). Indeed, Wolpe's text is scrupulous in its attempt to avoid "exampling" in such a way as to stereotype girls' agency in classrooms and she praises Davies for her achievement in this respect (Wolpe, 1988b: 151), arguing for contextualized studies that take account of the experience of the individual subject in all its specificity. In seeking to bridge the macro/micro gulf referred to earlier, however, Wolpe's text uses verbatim accounts sparingly and is largely a third-person account of observations from her fieldwork through a feminist and Foucauldian theoretical lens. Given her intention to make extensive use of the experiential accounts of her subjects, especially girls, her determination to avoid "exampling" leads to a somewhat anaemic text.

THE THEME OF IDENTITY

In their framing of ethnographic preoccupations and styles, Denzin and Lincoln (1994, 2000) report that by the mid-1980s a "crisis of representation" had become apparent over the so-called textual turn in ethnography. In *Writing Culture* (Clifford and Marcus, 1986), for example, the authors had argued for a more reflexive approach to research and writing, "(calling) into question the issues of gender, class and race" (Denzin and Lincoln, 1994: 9–10). As I have shown, these issues were already being addressed with varying degrees of insight and success in British educational ethnographies, just as they were in American studies, as I will show.

This concern for reflexivity and ethnographic authority can be seen in feminist critiques not only of ethnography (Behar and Gordon, 1985) but more specifically of Willis' and Walker's texts for their uncritical incorporation of their subjects' sexism and racism. These issues were precisely the concerns of Mairtin Mac an Ghaill in his studies of boys' and young men's sense of their gendered and racialized identities in their teenage years at school (Mac an Ghaill, 1988, 1989a, 1989b, 1991a, 1991b, 1994, 1996a, 1996b; Haywood and Mac an Ghaill, 1996, 1997, 1998; Redman and Mac an Ghaill, 1996). Like Davies, he found much to criticize in the work of "white male academics' one-dimensional representations of white working-class masculinities (for underplaying) the gendered and sexual relative power of heterosexual male students' social and discursive practices" (Mac an Ghaill, 1994: 172).[35] Recalling Skeggs' (1989) critique of Walker's study, mentioned earlier, he further elaborated his position by pointing to values implicit in the very possibility of rapport between ethnographer and subject: "Male ethnographers of young men's schooling (he wrote), have systematically failed to acknowledge the implicit male knowledges, understandings and desires that we share with male research participants' schooling biographies" (Mac an Ghaill, 1994: 174). Clearly, Mac an Ghaill was positioning himself in the role of "male equivalent to the feminist researcher" (Skeggs, 1989: 485; Haywood and Mac an Ghaill, 1998: 133) by taking on a project that aimed "to explore the processes involved in the interplay between schooling, masculinities and sexualities" (Mac an Ghaill, 1994: 3). The use of the plural terms signifies not only an acceptance that "(m)asculinity is not a unified discourse" (Gilbert and Gilbert, 1998: 49), but also a denial of the assumption of the uniquely positioned subject of modernist discourse such as was implied in the texts of Hargreaves, Lacey, Ball, and Willis. Thus Mac an Ghaill (1994) commits himself to examining "the way in which dominant definitions of masculinity are affirmed within schools" (p. 4) and what it means to individuals whose sense of their masculinity is not so affirmed – who become "other" to the dominant norm. Inevitably, therefore, the focus of Mac an Ghaill's study becomes "oppressed groups" such as the gay male students whose subjectivities he so sensitively reveals in *The Making of Men* (1994).

The origins of this study, however, were not as clear-cut as I have suggested. Initially, his research design "over-emphasised gender reproduction, with particular reference to male students' future social, occupational and domestic destinies" (Mac an Ghaill, 1994: 2), but discussions with young gay students in the school "highlighted the need . . . to make male heterosexuality problematic" (ibid. 173), a reflexive turn that prompted him to rethink his understanding of how masculinities came to be affirmed, if not formed, in the school setting. As a result he revised his study design but retained his concern with examining how social relationships helped to shape masculine identities. Mac an Ghaill was beginning to see schools as "sites for the production of sex/gender subjectivities" where male heterosexuality could be seen to be "a dominant but unstable sexual category" (ibid. 2).

Clearly, therefore, his fieldwork would (and did) involve a good deal of participation in the lives of his research subjects as he attempted to understand boys' experiences in terms of meanings located in the interactions of which they were a part.[36] By entering into the "school microcultures" of management, teachers, and students, he could see how masculinities and femininities were mediated and lived, and it became increasingly clear to him that Parnell School – and possibly schools in general – are "deeply gendered and heterosexual regimes (where) relations of domination and subordination within and across microcultures" are constructed (ibid. 4).

It is clear that Mac an Ghaill adopts a radically different epistemology from Willis, for example, and that while there is no sense of a master narrative structuring his understanding, a conceptual privilege is afforded gender and difference. Feminist research, he argued, had contributed to the deconstruction of overly functionalist approaches to social reproduction and resistance theory generated by white male academics in their earlier studies of white working-class masculinities in which it was assumed "that teachers and students (were) unitary subjects occupying predictable power positions" (ibid. 172). This tendency can be seen also in the theoretical shift away from studies of sex-role socialization in the work of Connell and associates in Australia (Connell, 1985; Kessler *et al.*, 1985; Connell, 1989; Connell, 2001), largely prompted by the proliferation of radical critiques of gender. To Mac an Ghaill, the social democratic settlement of 1960s and 1970s Britain, with its curriculum focus on equality of opportunity, had failed to create a more egalitarian society. The fundamental organizing principles of modern schooling systems, he argued, were now to be seen in "the dialectical relationship between class, 'race,' gender and sexual mechanisms of control" as well as ethnicity, sexuality and disability (Mac an Ghaill, 1994: 171–72).

In order to enter as a researcher into "the material power relations of domination and subordination" (ibid. 172) that emanate from the organizing principles of state schooling mentioned earlier, while at the same time avoiding what he sees as the tendency of some theorizing to become unnecessarily obscure (ibid. 2), Mac an Ghaill sought an approach that would retain a sense of "the concrete material conditions of the research participants" while remaining sensitive to first person singular accounts of young people's developing sex/gender identities.[37] And yet for all that, Mac an Ghaill couches his analysis in terms of ideal or representative types of boys, justifying this conceptual and textual move in terms of sampling, the very issue that had so concerned Lacey and Wolpe and that had informed Edmondson's critique of Willis' work.[38] Nevertheless, participant observation became the core methodology of his study, and as his text reveals, it was centrally important to him to foreground "the key methodological and ethical question of participants' social relations with (him)," unlike earlier male ethnographers (ibid. 173). Thus for Mac an Ghaill, reflexivity is not so much an issue of self-revelation in establishing one's position in relation to the study as of one's practice in *doing* the study: of one's relations with the subjects of one's research as the bearers of knowledge and experience, *and* of one's privileged position in representing that knowledge and experience (Skeggs, 1998). In this context, as Skeggs observes, Mac an Ghaill's subjects "are not just ciphers from which subject positions can be read off; rather, they are active in producing the meaning of the positions they . . . inhabit" (ibid. 2). Throughout his text, this sense of agency emerges as a result both of his modernist epistemology tinged with poststructural concerns and of his reflexively dynamic relationship with his subjects – teachers as well as boys. As a result, a sense of plausibility and authenticity emerges from the extensive use of transcripts, recalling Walker's achievement in *Louts and Legends*[39] rather than Willis' similarly extensive but widely contested use of what his lads had to say.

It is in such texts as *The Making of Men* and, for example, *Young, Gifted and Black* (Mac an Ghaill, 1988), and *Framing Dropouts* (Fine, 1991), that authors position themselves in their writing as participants in the making of meaning, whether in articulating black students' "experience of a 'different reality'" (Mac an Ghaill, 1988: 155) from white students, for example, or in exposing how students complicit in maintaining a heteronormative hegemony in a school environment do so. In entering their texts as critics of both a social and cultural *status quo* and of what they see as epistemological inadequacies, Mac an Ghaill and Fine draw attention not only to how the experience of difference comes about and is contested, but also to how the institutionalization of difference can lead to "the promise of equal opportunity (being) subverted . . . by the guarantee of unequal outcomes" (Fine, 1991: 26).

POSTMODERN ETHNOGRAPHIES OF SCHOOLING

The question of whether and how poststructuralist ethnographies of schooling might be possible (Lather, 1991; Skeggs, 1991; Britzman, 1995; Kenway, 1995c) has been answered in recent years by a proliferation of such studies of schoolgirls (e.g., Hey, 1997; Davies et al., 2001; Davies et al., 2006; Youdell, 2010) and of studies dealing with both boys and girls (e.g., Fordham, 1996; Gonick, 2003; Tsolidis, 2006; Youdell, 2006b; Nayak and Kehily, 2008).[40] In contrast, substantive examples dealing principally, or only, with teenage boys at school are far less common, although as I have indicated, the work of Mac an Ghaill provides a clear exception. In both instances mentioned earlier, the impetus has come largely from those adopting a feminist (or profeminist) poststructuralist epistemology.

The principal characteristic of the works mentioned earlier may be found in their attempts to disrupt the humanist foundations of contemporary education and schooling (St Pierre, 2000; Hey, 2006b; Felski, 1995). They clearly question the humanist subject of schooling as "normal" or "natural" and in particular challenge what is claimed to be inherent or innate in that subject: agency, will, reason, and autonomy. There is throughout an attempt to critique this subject in the belief that any subject is the effect of discursive constitution (or interpellation), requiring not only an openness to the dispersal of subjectivity among the subject positions made possible by subjectification, but also a different view of agency from that accompanying the humanist subject. In doing so, these authors attempt (in varying degrees) to make visible the constitutive force of discursive practices by drawing attention to relations of power that bring something new into existence and that at the same time make possible a multiplicity of narratives with which to make "meanings, conventions and truths" (Laws and Davies, 2000: 206; Davies, 2006; Youdell, 2006c).

But this concern to both do and write poststructural ethnography in relation to schools and school students has also disrupted the notion of what it is to do ethnography at all and in particular what it is to claim to know and to represent others. As I indicated earlier, in reconceptualizing the task of ethnography from understanding and entering into the world of unitary, noncontradictory subjects to destabilizing the fictive truths of such worlds, and revealing how so much more and "other" is being constituted, the authority of empiricism and of claims based on "being there" have terminally undermined earlier certainties (Britzman, 1995). Thus the notion of reflexive practice has raised questions about the nature of participation in others' worlds: of "interviewing" (Scheurich, 1995), of observing (Fordham, 1996), and of achieving plausibility and coherence in writing while representing "the various experiences, voices and differences of (others) without reconstituting normatively fixed categories and identities" (Gonick, 2003: 56; Jackson and Mazzei, 2009). In working towards these ends, the very notion of an ethnographic "site" has come to incorporate a similar sense of dispersal to that of the dispersed subjectivity of research participants. This is particularly the case for ethnographies dealing with experience which, as I have indicated, has come to be understood as constructed and unstable – "lived as disorderly, discontinuous and chaotic" (Britzman, 1995: 233) – rather than as a seamless, self-evident possession of unitary subjects (Davies *et al.*, 2001: 168).

An awareness of poststructuralist concerns such as these has helped produce deeply reflexive texts in which the issues I have mentioned earlier have come to be central. I refer in particular to a tendency towards a deeply reflexive account of research in which the distance between observer and observed has been all but obliterated, the ethical problem of representing the "other" is foregrounded and "fieldwork and writing blur into one another" (Denzin and Lincoln, 1994: 10; Hey: 1997), all responses to a postmodern disquiet with authorial certainty.

For example, in *Blacked Out: Dilemmas of Race, Identity, and Success at Capital High*, Signithia Fordham (1996) reported on the results of her involvement in a public school community in Washington DC over four years. She writes: "I made a special effort to get at the community's indigenous definitions and understandings of success" (Fordham, 1996: 28) in an educational and social context marginalizing African-American adolescents and their families through discourses of exclusion which "(constructed) Black people as Other" and expected their "acquiescence to privileged-class social norms . . ." (ibid. 10).

There are two aspects of Fordham's text to which I want to draw particular attention. First, as an African-American herself, her fieldwork was felt and experienced in a deeply personal and embodied way (Coffey, 1999: 69). This is linked in her text to a pervasive reflexivity in which she confronts the problem of how to represent her subjects who, as she observes, have been so grievously misrepresented in terms of curricular and broader dominant social discourses. A central feature of her ethnography, therefore, is to reveal the "multiple responses" of Black students to their "fraudulent representation" in anthropological and other texts as they resist and try to create "an acceptable Black Self" (Fordham, 1996: 4), in some ways not unlike the students Wexler (1992) describes who wanted to "(become) someone" – to gain an identity they could be proud of.[41]

What sets Fordham's text apart is her approach to participant observation, or more particularly, to "observation," a term she dismisses as merely a polite substitute for what could be more truthfully described as "watching." This distinction is fundamental to her project as she argues that watching is the source of imaging, of representation: "it compels us to see those who differ from us as "Other" (ibid. 1). To Fordham, watching implies surveillance rather than merely noticing, and is an essential prerequisite to writing. To represent the "Other," therefore, involves watching, or "a kind of violence imposed on the watched" which compels the reader to see the "Other" in a particular way (ibid. 1). For Fordham this is both a representational and an ethical issue as she is acutely aware that such images are not neutral, and that such representations can "both construct and dehumanize (an) 'Other' (while enhancing) the power of certain segments of a multiethnic, multiracial society" (ibid. 5; 341).[42]

This sense of personal crisis and engagement sets Fordham's text apart. In trying to balance her own requirement not to do violence by watching while at the same time minimizing the potential for violence in representing her subjects, she refers to her "split selfhood" and to her "multiple subjectivities" (ibid. 4; 337–38; 340) while striving not to give a central place in her text to her own presence. In framing the response of underachieving students to their schooling as one of resistance, Fordham gives considerable priority to their words and challenges the reader to understand their actions as no less instructive than those of Willis' lads. The problem she poses, in a passage echoing Willis' (1977) framing of his concern, is how to understand "why African-American students born and reared since the passage of civil-rights legislation resist the academy's silent but powerful message to achieve academic success and in the process become a dominant Other" (Fordham, 1996: 37).

A similar sensitivity to participant observation is seen in Gordon *et al.* (2000). Like Fordham's, their text exemplifies a profound sense of the researchers' embeddedness in the ethnographic process (e.g., in comments on their self-consciously embodied presence among 13 to 14 year-olds), recalling Coffey's argument "that fieldwork is personal, emotional and identity *work*" (Coffey, 1999: 1; her emphasis), and like Fordham, they were intent on not erasing either their or their participants' subjectivities in the text they produced as attested by the frequent use of field notes detailing observations incorporating the voices of students and teachers.[43]

Finally, in Marnina Gonick's *Between Femininities* (2003), one of the most taken for granted tropes of any ethnography – the notion of arrival – is reformulated. Leaving aside any "conventional story of gaining entrance to the research site," she goes on: ". . . the entry I am referring to here is not simply into the school per se, but an entry into a realm far more elusive: the imaginary terrain of the girls" (ibid. p. 7). Here, in theorizing, researching, and representing the experience of others one sees the profound difficulties in doing, as well as the possibilities in writing, a poststructuralist account of experience in the context of schooling.

CONCLUSION

In spite of their very real differences in epistemological and substantive concerns, the authors discussed in this chapter reveal an interesting similarity in their approach to ethnography conceived not as a single invariant method (e.g., the increasingly contested idea of participant observation), but as a range of means for potentially understanding social contexts and situated meanings. Their texts reveal that the widespread ontological priority given to lived experience, and the centrality of language in studies of socially situated meaning, have remained foundational. As Britzman (1995), quoted earlier in this chapter noted, research participants have tended to remain "noncontradictory subjects," saying what they mean and meaning what they say. Feminist and poststructuralist critiques, however, have questioned the unreflective, prediscursive assumption of a foundational experience and drawn attention to its discursive and performative constitution. In doing so, they have drawn attention not only to the constructedness of the ethnographic encounter in the field, but also to the discursive and performative constitution of subjectivity and hence to the significance of the textualization of identities. This particular development is seen, in varying degrees, in post-Willis ethnographies, as I have shown, but its sustained application to the investigation of the subjectivities of adolescent boys at school is yet to be realized.

In referring to how these authors actually went about their work I have been prompted by what seem to be two contradictory positions in relation to ethnographic procedure: on the one hand, Skeggs' (1989) critique of Walker's work in which she castigates male ethnographers for not making clear the investment she claims they share with their male subjects in the oppression of others, and on the other, the standard advice that as an ethnographer one should constantly ensure that one is a stranger to the research site. If the latter is to prevail in order to avoid the charge of partiality then the former demand for full disclosure seems to indicate that the research context can never be sufficiently unknown, or made sufficiently strange, to prevent familiarity – even overfamiliarity – with subjects and some subject positions. Clearly, if one is to be an outsider in an unfamiliar environment within one's own culture (broadly conceived), then the "strangeness" that is said to ensure one's critical distance from research subjects cannot be achieved if one's gender causes one to be in all essential respects an insider, no matter how alternative, or unique, the context. In the end, this distinction can really only be a matter of degree as both researcher and researched inevitably share some understandings of the focus of the research and of the presence of the researcher. Without this there could be no trust or rapport, conditions which have their basis in the negation of difference, or strangeness, at least as much as in the affirmation of sameness, even to the point of collusion.[44]

In this review, not only does Willis' text represent a watershed in the ethnography of schooling, but so also does the feminist critique of it and all that came before it. In the aftermath, and in the wider context of poststructural critiques of the postmodern world (in art, literature, architecture, social research, and so on), textual and epistemological privilege has moved in the direction of a social ethic demanding the affirmation of difference in specific local and historical contexts, and the grounds for certainty, once provided by the safety net of master narratives have, at least for the time being, been removed.

For all the threat, or promise, of change in ethnographers' textual practices since the "textual turn," the "crisis of representation," and "the death of the subject," ethnographies of schooling – at least those dealing to some extent with boys – have not broken far out of the realist and modernist mould mentioned earlier in this chapter. Ethnography, as Coffey (1999) points out is identity work for both researcher and subject, but equally, it must also be written, and that involves a certain textualization of the subject and, in more reflexive mode, of the researcher. Authorial claims to authority based on notions of objectivity and having "been there" have been deconstructed and replaced by appeals to plausibility arising from increased sensitivity to reflexivity in fieldwork and writing. But as I have shown, albeit selectively, these moves have taken place in studies that have not only deconstructed the sovereign author and, in some cases, gender; they have taken place increasingly in studies in which no conceptual priority has been given either to boys or to girls. Where once boys were present almost by definition in studies of schooling (as in the studies by Ball, Hargreaves, and Lacey), and where later, raising the visibility of girls was the core project (as in the work of McRobbie, Davies, Wolpe, and Skeggs), more recently concern for boys, as I have shown, has been framed in terms of achievement (Francis, 2000; Francis and Skelton, 2005), which, it could be argued, is very much where it was in those earlier studies. The challenge to understand schoolboys as other than sovereign, unified subjects, concerned more or less with racialized and gendered identities as well as with achievement, in spite of contributions by Mac an Ghaill, still remains a significant challenge which I hope to address in the remaining chapters.

4 Observing Participation

THE SETTING

The research upon which this book is based was undertaken at Hillside High School,[1] a coeducational secondary school in one of the more leafy suburbs of Melbourne, Australia. The word "leafy" signifies a middle class, relatively affluent, well-established suburban population. During my time at the school, student numbers more than doubled as the student body diversified from being largely Anglo-Celtic, through a period of southern European influx to, more recently, taking in students from east and south-east Asia. Over 40 nationalities are represented.

The main reason for the persistent and increasing demand for places in the school is the school's record of achievement in the VCE (Victorian Certificate of Education). Among nonselective state schools in Melbourne, Hillside, located close to a number of well-established private schools, has a reputation for academic excellence offering an alternative for parents seeking a prestigious education for their children. The school's administration comprises a Principal, several Assistant Principals and teacher-managers of junior (Years 7 and 8), middle (Years 9 and 10) and senior (Years 11 and 12) subschools. Within each subschool there are five or six year-level coordinators and staff generally teach across the whole school. The formal curriculum is built around compulsory core subjects from Years 7 to10 plus a choice of a limited number of elective subjects. Thereafter, students undertake the VCE during years 11 and 12.

Among the ancillary staff, Hillside has a nurse and a welfare staff including a chaplain, a social worker, and two psychologists. Students are routinely offered the help of these staff if they are identified as being in need of help for a range of matters such as family break-up, bereavement, isolation, anger management, or any severe behavioral problem. There is also a careers guidance teacher who provides a service not only to senior students planning tertiary education but also to middle school students leaving, for whatever reason, in Years 9 or 10.

GETTING STARTED

Having acquired the necessary bureaucratic and school-based approval for this study, I contemplated beginning fieldwork. As mentioned in Chapter 1, my focus would lie principally, but not exclusively, with boys in Years 8 to 10 (aged approximately 13 to 16 years), identified by teachers as difficult to deal with, poor achievers, disruptive, and/or as poorly motivated – all terms typically used by teachers in their day-to-day work.

Given that I was not to include any boy I currently taught or coordinated, I approached coordinators at years 8 and 10 and asked them who, in their year levels, might fit these descriptions. I also asked who could be described as "good" students – enthusiastic, reliable, role models; those who might be nominated for awards at the annual Speech Night. During this process I asked about specific students, unknown to me, who seemed to fit these descriptions. I notified parents through the weekly school bulletin that I was undertaking this study and spoke to year level assemblies outlining my interest in boys who were not enjoying school and asked for volunteers to discuss their experiences with me. Not surprisingly there were none.

Armed with a short list of names from Year 8 coordinators, I began to approach some of the boys to ask if they would be willing to take part in this study. This was a laborios process and will be dealt with in some detail in Chapter 5. Once boys who agreed to take part provided consent forms from parents and themselves, I began to organize occasions when I could interview, or talk with, each boy individually. This usually took place in a quiet room over lunchtime where we could talk undisturbed and I could record the discussion on audiotape. All participants agreed to be recorded and I subsequently transcribed all such interviews. As I will discuss in Chapter 5, progress in recruiting participants was slow at first. After a year I had recruited a number of boys known to each other and group discussions were held from time to time which were also transcribed. Among this group were two boys I had taught in Year 8 the year before but whom I no longer taught. They were the only participants with whom I had had any prior contact. This procedure continued throughout the second year and I briefly revived our meetings during the first 10 weeks of school the following year. I had anticipated that from time to time, participants might withdraw from the process or be added to it, but as it happened none wished to withdraw and several were added along the way.

I also spoke to teachers at the start of each year in staff meetings to outline my research proposal and to foreshadow any approaches I might make to them. During those two years I had conversations with as many of the boys' teachers as was practicable in order to hear other accounts of narratives given by the boys, not in any sense to verify what I had heard already, but rather expecting to confirm their resort to dominant discourses within the formal, or normative, school. Also, as a teacher in the school I was constantly in contact with other coordinators and teachers and was present at innumerable discussions about individual students and incidents that occurred from time to time.

Procedures Adopted

The interviews I conducted with the boys are better described as conversations. They were at all times open-ended and their content depended on what had been happening in the year level and in the boys' lives and on what they were prepared to talk about. All were told in the first interview that I would have to disclose any matters relating to the possession of drugs or weapons at school as well as threats of violence or acts of vandalism relating to the school, and that whatever was discussed outside these parameters would remain confidential. It was up to them what they wanted to tell me. As it happened, no disclosures were made that were not already known to school authorities. I also maintained a fieldwork diary throughout this period.

As well as open-ended interviews, or conversations, and my immersion in the administrative and teaching processes of the school, I observed the boys in various ways. I watched as they sat in assemblies or mingled at various sites around the school, I recognized them from time to time as we passed and nodded, or spoke briefly, and I simply noticed, often inadvertently, as one or other of them came into view or had dealings with other students or teachers.

I determined early not to sit in on any of the classes of which my research participants were members (as I have said), for two reasons. First, it would undoubtedly have altered the dynamics of the classes. I did not want to influence teachers at work, nor did I want to either incite or constrain any behavior on the part of the boys. I was prepared to settle for a retrospective account of their experiences in class just as I would have to regarding other aspects of their lives presented at our meetings. In doing so it was important to understand that memories of such experience were not to be confused with the origins of those memories as the original experience was constituted.[2] At the same time, the experience of being subjectivated as a participant in the research also needed to be understood as constituting yet another experiential datum in which I, too, was implicated. Second, to have sat in on their classes would have compromised the confidentiality I was ethically obliged to grant them. At no time did I disclose to any teacher who I might be talking about; rather, I would approach a teacher and direct our conversation to who in their classes might fit the descriptions given earlier and then let our conversation focus on types of conduct, or even on instances involving this or that boy. Nor did I discuss any of my participants with other students – boys or girls – as it was *their* experiences as they were recalled and not others' experiences *of them* (except in the case of teachers) that concerned me – even given that experience is understood to be arrived at discursively and may have involved them – and in any event I wished to preserve the boys' anonymity. Interestingly, as will become clear in Chapter 9, some of the "good" boys turned our conversations to some of the disaffected boys by name in their classes whereas none of the disaffected boys ever mentioned the names of any of the "good" boys.

Documentary and Other Sources

In seeking to locate my observations and daily interactions in the wider context of the school, I drew on a variety of local documentary sources, most of which concerned either specific students or year levels, or school-wide policy. The dominant discourses of the school, for example, might be disclosed in speeches or conversations but also in a variety of formal documents from photographs to prospectuses, reports of curriculum developments, the school magazine, newsletters, and teacher handbooks. Accounts of student behavior could be located in conversations and in written documents. For example, teachers dealing with misbehavior would frequently write a description of what happened and deposit it with year level coordinators who might then ask students to write their own version and discuss discrepancies if the matter was judged to be serious enough. Such memos would form an archive in addition to the year level day books in which a more or less complete (often quite incomplete) outline of coordinators' work and what was happening among students at the year level was kept.

I also had very occasional discussions with some of the parents of the boys who took part, typically but not exclusively at or near the end of the study. Their perspectives were useful in so far as they were discursively active in helping constitute or challenge the ways their sons were positioned in and subjectivated by the dominant discourses of the school. Finally, the physical presence of the boys could not be ignored. In their appearance, their disposition, the way they walked, talked, and sat and in their voices and faces, as much as in their words, was to be found a fleeting archive of practices of accommodation, of resistance, and ultimately even of defeat.

PARTICIPATING AND OBSERVING: GAINING RAPPORT

Teacher-researchers such as myself can hardly fail to notice the paucity of discussion in others' school ethnographies of issues related to power and the ethics of gaining informed consent of minors, the selection of participants, the teacher's duty of care, and access to students beyond the school site.[3] To take the last of these, I have already mentioned, for example, how Mac an Ghaill's work took him, as a practising teacher, "from almost complete observation in many school/college activities, such as interaction with teachers, to almost complete participation in leisure activities, including hanging around the park and cafes, playing football and cricket, listening to music, attending parties," as well as allowing students access to his home (Mac an Ghaill, 1988: 8, 13). The issue of possible overidentification with subjects appears not to be problematized, but in *The Making of Men* (1994) Mac an Ghaill develops further this "emancipatory research method . . . (emphasizing) collaboration, reciprocity and reflexivity" (Haywood and Mac an Ghaill, 1998: 128; Mac an Ghaill, 1994: 5). Similarly, in her study of girls' friendships, Hey (although not a teacher), engaged with her subjects in a variety of places from classrooms to playing fields, bike shed, a cemetery, a café, shops, and school canteen to visits to one another's homes (Hey, 1997: 47–48).[4] What is significant in each case is that each recognized that their research experience was "(indivisible) from the material collected" (ibid. 39). In Hey's case, this experience resulted in her feeling "'lost', literally as well as metaphorically . . . 'down among the women' . . . somewhere between childhood and adulthood" (ibid. 38).

To each of these authors, a critical awareness of the social relations of ethnography has entered significantly into their practice and their writing. In the previous chapter I drew attention to how earlier male ethnographers were committed to versions of objectivity in their research and writing while occasionally attempting to deal with, or add on, a sense of the visceral nature of the lived experience of their subjects. Hargreaves, Lacey, and Ball, for example, all taught in the schools where they did their ethnographic work. It is instructive to note how they dealt with their awareness of the conflicts involved and the politics of gaining rapport. As Lacey notes:

> I was . . . quite unable to shed my adult status during the research period, but I *was* able to shed my teacher status, and when I did I became aware of the increased flow of information about matters that had been taboo for me as a member of staff.
>
> (1970: 177)

Similarly, Hargreaves (1967) drew attention to this "role conflict" in relation both to the teachers he worked with and the pupils, coming slowly to the conclusion that "To participate and observe involves to some extent shedding the teacher-role, since participation means accepting in some degree a normal role within the school situation" (p. 205). He had not

> foreseen that the assumption of a teacher-role, whilst facilitating . . . relations with the staff, would necessarily inhibit . . . relations with the pupils. A choice had to be made and (as a result, he) decided

to abandon (his) carefully nurtured teacher-role to improve relationships with the boys.

(ibid. 204)

In developing this awareness, both Lacey and Hargreaves mention how social encounters subsequently extended to, for example, pupil visits to Lacey's home (Lacey, 1970: 153) and in Hargreaves' case, turning a blind eye to pupils smoking, joining in "youth clubs, beat clubs and the billiard hall" and being offered stolen goods (Hargreaves, 1967: 202–04).

What is notable about these and similar accounts of participant observation in school ethnographies is the gradual awareness of the ethnographer's constitutive role in developing knowledge, as well as the cost for the teacher-researcher of developing rapport. For Hargreaves, it meant parting from school staff and appearing to side with the boys in order to achieve a researcher self. For both Hargreaves and Lacey, it also entailed a degree of mistrust in relation to appropriate social scientific procedures and hence of their "findings." For Mac an Ghaill, however, writing from the vantage point of a poststructuralist sensibility, the issue had become "the key methodological and ethical question of participants' social relations with (male ethnographers)" (Mac an Ghaill, 1994: 173) and was therefore central to and indivisible from the task of doing and writing ethnography. And in my case, as I have already mentioned, juggling teacher and researcher roles led to a sense of dissociation from being a teacher that was crucially important for gaining rapport with the subjects of my research, as it was for all the writers I have mentioned.

FROM DOING TO WRITING

Throughout anthropology from the mid-1980s a profound sense of crisis over the issue of representation occurred which led to earlier epistemological certainties being discarded in favor of more experimental, "messy," polyvocal texts (Denzin and Lincoln, 1994; Marcus, 1994; Atkinson, 1996: 22; 142). In later chapters I will draw on the work of authors who have struggled with these issues, but here I will note that the concern with textuality that Atkinson advocates converges with postmodern and feminist calls for reflexivity in the research process.

> (We) need to acknowledge (he writes), the extent to which our selves and our methods are thoroughly implicated in the processes of research and discovery . . . (but we) must avoid the contemporary fashion for narratives of personal experience as the source for an uncontaminated personal voice.
> (Atkinson, 1996; 143; also Jackson and Mazzei, 2009; Hammersley and Atkinson, 1995; Abraham, 1995; Ruby, 1982)

Clearly, Atkinson has in mind a different conception of experience than I have in this work, but his larger point is well made: language is never neutral, to which I would add that experience is never unmediated. As Amanda Coffey notes, the conventional view of ethnographic practice as the observation and analysis of others has given way to an awareness that "the ethnographer is simultaneously involved in biographical work of their own" (Coffey, 1999: 115) and that this is often recorded in private notes and journals.[5] The particular issue I take up in this study in relation to the way it has been written, however, concerns what Coffey (1999) refers to as the relationship between "narratives of the field and the self" (p. 118). Traditionally, or conventionally, some confession of the self has entered into an epilogue, appendix, lecture, or short paper, but texts that have confronted the positionality of the self in representing "otherness" have engaged my imagination and attention far more (Coffey, 1999: 125; 143).[6] In this context, in his inimitable way, Hammersley (2006b) criticizes an increasingly common focus on, and ways of writing about, "micro-ethnography," by asking "why anyone would go to the trouble of engaging in ethnographic fieldwork. Why not just write fiction in the manner of novelists or short story writers?" (ibid. p.8). The move to "so-called 'experimental' ethnographic texts," he writes, is dangerously likely to "(redefine) ethnography as a form of imaginative literature (amounting to) an abandonment of the task of inquiry" (ibid. 10). On the other hand, perhaps it will expand the ethnographic project.

The task I have set myself here, however, is to avoid filtering out the vitality and affect so often evident in the way participants in this study recounted their experiences in our ethnographic encounters, and retain a sense of story. As I indicated in Chapter 3, this absence has been the lament of writers who have remarked on the tone of disengagement in certain ethnographic monographs and the removal to appendices or later work of any vestige of engagement in the field. In what follows I hope to retain as much of that vitality as possible as I describe, or evoke, how experience emerges discursively and performatively (Tyler, 1986; Tedlock, 2000). It is assumed from the start, as I have said already, that to arrive at such an understanding ethnographically is to enter into the experience of another in retrospect by participating in the memory work of creating a story about that experience that is itself a further experience within which the former and primary object of my interest lies.

AFTERWORD AND PROLOGUE

So far I have discussed the theoretical sources that have influenced this study and outlined the procedures I intended to, and in fact did, adopt, but between the plan and the execution another story began to unfold. In the daily life of middle-school classes and especially of coordinators, it seemed that huge amounts of time and energy were put into dealing with boys (and a few girls), who were clearly disaffected and reluctant to conform to the school's norms. Among these students were the boys who had been identified for me as potential participants in my study and I found myself giving far more time to them than to the "good" boys so that, perhaps not surprisingly, my research became far more concerned with the "lads"[7] than the others. As Francis (2000) remarked of her experience researching gender and achievement in schools, "I feel sure I am not the only researcher to have found (laddish) incidents amusing and exciting" (p. 57). Taking a longer view of this tendency in British research, Delamont observed:

> Researchers have had a love affair, or love-hate fascination, with the anti-school, proletarian "heroes" of the rough, male, working class for a century, chronicling their failure, deviance and resistance. We would not, of course, want to face teaching them directly, but we have loved studying them, being around them, writing about them, building our careers upon them . . . We need to reassess our own ambivalences to these "lads."
>
> (Delamont, 1999: 14).

Indeed, to anticipate the later stages of this study, this fascination with what has come to be called resistance and "laddishness" can be found clearly in Hargreaves' (1968) asides (especially his intervention on the side of a student against a school administration), Lacey's (1970) liking for an "anti-school" group of boys, Willis' (1977) apparent identification with his "lads," Ball's (1981) concern for students alienated from a comprehensive school and Walker's (1988) identification with the boys in his study, to which could be added, for example, studies by Aggleton (1987), Connell (1989), and Martino (1999). In addition, as all these authors have found, "the researcher needs to be liked by his or her respondents" (Mac an Ghaill (1998: 137), for without this two-way acceptance of one another the likelihood of rapport, upon which our projects depend, is thrown into doubt.

Part II
That Unstable Construct

> To heighten the detours of experience and hence to gesture toward experience as an unstable construct may well agitate traditional ethnographic notions of agency and voice.
>
> (Britzman, 1995: 234–35)

5 Monday Morning

> Monday morning need not imply an endless succession of the *same* Monday mornings.
>
> (Willis, 1977: 192, original emphasis)

ARRIVING

Walking from the car park as I have done for 21 years I am aware of the arrival of other teachers and students. Boys and girls are crossing the road, lugging bags and, sometimes, musical instruments as well. Cars are parking in the crowded street outside, their doors slamming as children turn from parents to school and friends. Greetings are exchanged. The teacher on duty in the area is turning a blind eye to those who are not wearing the approved uniform.

By the time I arrive at my office – the Year 10 coordinators' office – I have already told two boys to tuck their shirts in. I don't stop as I do so, but as I pass by I ensure that they at least start to tuck them in. My day has started before I unlock the office door. Once inside there are phone messages to deal with, notices to pin up and the usual range of organizational details to be seen to. My two colleagues and I exchange greetings.

The bells ring to announce the start of the students' day. A warning bell to get them to lockers first, then a bell to go to Form assembly and seven minutes later a bell to leave for first period, but not all students have arrived on time. Already by the second bell there is a line of students at the office door to get late passes; they write their names in the "late book" while we write details on their late pass, a small, pink square of paper which they will give to their Form teacher some time during the day, assuming they don't lose it or forget. Some have notes from parents to explain their absences; most do not. They say they will get the note tomorrow. They have 24 hours to do so or this lateness will contribute to a detention: four "lates" will ensure one half-hour detention after school.

Even as period one gets under way these late students are at their lockers, clanging doors, talking, and sometimes disturbing nearby classes. We tell them to get a move on. They have 9 minutes until the bell starts period one which will end, like all periods, or classes, with a bell 49 minutes later.

I am a teacher and this has been the start of my day and my week, but I am also researching boys' experience of their schooling. The staff know. At the start of the year I gave a short talk to the assembled staff to indicate what I wanted to do, as I did the year before. I also spoke at a Year 8 assembly to let students know that I wanted to research boys' experiences and I put a note in the school newsletter for the benefit of parents.

The account I have given so far of how I entered the school today and began work has been a fiction, at least as I have recorded it so far. Of course I knew as I walked across the car park that certain students would be late – they nearly always are – and I knew that at least some would have been late because they were smoking in the park, as they do. Their smoky breath will linger as they sign the late book and when asked why they were late they will murmur, "no reason," or, "I got up late." We might briefly discuss the merits of getting up before eight o'clock rather than after, and suggest that they give up smoking, but little will change. I also know that my colleagues and I will be expected to give detentions to those students identified by the Principal or Assistant Principals, who may be somewhere in the vicinity taking the names of students not wearing the blazer as the outer garment, or not wearing the correct socks or shoes. At the same time, as we sign late passes, we will expect any student who has been put on a daily report sheet to return yesterday's report so we can check that a parent has counter-signed it before we give out another one for today. If it is not done before Form assembly we will chase it up and if they are late presenting it they will miss the assembly, with the inevitable penalty.

I will be there to deal with these students, and I will be there to take the phone call from a parent who has only just learnt that their son or daughter has not been handing in work. I will also pass on to the welfare team a teacher's concern over a student who, she has been told, has left home, and there will be incidents of bullying to mediate, but in all this, as I mentioned earlier, I will be concealing another role – that of ethnographer. I could not be more embedded in the school and its culture: I observe and I participate and I negotiate a very fine line – a boundary – between the demands and responsibilities of teaching, with all its professional, legal, and ethical implications, and the ethical and political limitations placed on me as teacher-researcher.

So my entry into the school this morning has not been as innocent as it might have seemed. I may suspect that one or more of my research subjects will be in the park smoking before school; they will almost certainly not be wearing the school uniform properly; they will not have done their homework and I will pass them in the corridor without commenting on their lateness, their uniform, or their work. They know I will often ignore them as they mingle with their friends and I may discreetly nod or say "How's it going?" if we pass in the yard, but they seem not to know that I am observing – watching – their conduct and bearing in a myriad settings. The difficulty is to see them being admonished for some indiscretion and to keep my distance – to pass no judgment, to seem not to have heard or seen at all. Not to notice the blush or the embarrassment; not to seem to hear the voices raised in anger; not to be seen to have witnessed the confrontation. They and I will talk about it in time, but for the moment the school's processes and protocols will unfold as they and their teachers and coordinators negotiate another day.

AIMS

Having briefly described the school in Chapter 4, my intention in this chapter is to outline what I take to be the key framing discourses of the administration, teachers, and students who make up the formal or normative school that is Hillside High School. In doing so, I will position myself within these discourses and their fields of power and discuss the recruitment of students for this study, concluding with one boy's account of his arrival at school. In my discussion of recruitment I will deal explicitly with the sort of physical and emotional work involved, touching on both my successes and failures. Throughout the chapter I will suggest that all who constitute this school are subject to the "normalizing gaze" and relations of "disciplinary power" (Foucault, 1991, 187: 184) inscribed in the school's dominant discourses and hence in the surveillant function of teachers. I will begin to show how the "meticulousness of regulations" and the "fussiness of inspections" subject students in particular to "infinite examination" (ibid. 140–41; 189) – a theme that will recur throughout – in which bodies and minds are produced and normalized. It is precisely this panoptic function, as I will illustrate, that the teacher-researcher has to resist in constructing a fieldworker self that will engender rapport with subjects. Finally, in Kevin's arrival story,[1] I will suggest that the normative function of such disciplinary power provides an occasion for, or a site of, resistance to its "coercive individualization," inciting individual subjects, such as Kevin, to reject such positioning and the pathologized subjectivity it entails, and to reclaim, or defend, a sense of selfhood discursively opposed to the dominant and normative discourses of the school.

DOMINANT DISCOURSES

The deliberately bland and factual profile of the school I gave in Chapter 4 is scarcely one that would be offered by the administration of Hillside

High School to parents of prospective students. Upon entering the school, one enters a discursive domain within which the institution of the school and all who comprise it are constituted (Foucault, 1970). For example, in my daily arrival I arrive, in my own mind, as a teacher, but the moment I step out into the car park I also enter into the discursive and performative practices of the school. In being recognized as one whose presence is appropriate, I am immediately designated, or interpellated, as "teacher," or "sir," a designation repeated day after day and at countless moments throughout the day as my subjectification – my "ongoing constitution in discourse" (Youdell, 2006b: 48) – is never complete.

In this section, taking up questions raised in Chapter 1, I will indicate what I take to be the school's dominant discourses,[2] namely those of excellence, community, and care. As indicated in Chapter 1, the notion of discourse is understood as a field of intelligibility comprising texts and other discursive practices (such as actions), which position and construct participants as subjects of a particular kind and which locate the school textually within its broader community. Each discourse encodes what Foucault (1983a) called "dividing practices" by which a subject is "objectivated," or, as we may say, labeled: given an identity within which he experiences division "inside himself (or) from others" (ibid. 208); for example, the "good" student and the "difficult" student. As I will show, largely on the basis of documentary evidence, teachers and students at Hillside High School are imagined and constituted as recognizable and competent within a discursive domain of unitary subject positions. I will also draw to some extent on the performative aspects of discursive practices, but will leave to later chapters an analysis of the challenges they pose to this ideal, unitary figure.

Excellence

Whether new parents perusing the school prospectus, staff members reading their handbooks or students sitting through assemblies, all encounter the textual pervasiveness of the discourse of excellence, equating with what Lather (1991) describes as "the Enlightenment project of emancipation via reason" (p. 37). Thus parents, students, and staff will read or be told that: "the school has developed a rich intellectual culture (which) manifests itself in an outstanding record of achievement based on excellence and leadership in Victorian education" (Prospectus, 2003). In publications and school assemblies, student achievements in the VCE, described as continuing "the strong tradition of outstanding results," will exemplify this discourse and honor boards will be inscribed in gold lettering with the names of students whose achievements mark them as exemplary. At Speech Night each year, a large part of the celebration of all student achievement will include speeches that reinforce the school's "outstanding reputation" based on "a long history of excellence."

The night will include a parade of prize-winners in subject areas and the dux of the previous year – his or her prizes and achievements suitably described – will be introduced for acclamation. Such achievement is ultimately summed up in a series of prized statistics: those with an ENTER[3] score of 99.0 or more, the VCE class's median ENTER score, the number gaining the maximum study score of 50 and, more often than not, the number of those achieving special awards. Furthermore, the school's VCE achievements will be subject to comparison with "like schools" and Hillside's favorable ranking will again be stressed, especially in staff meetings. References to students' academic excellence will also reach the local and major metropolitan press from time to time, further reinforcing the desired image among parents and the wider community and validating the efforts of student high achievers and their teachers.

For the rest of the student body, excellence will be celebrated throughout the year in newsletters, assemblies and in the privacy of individual results in academic studies, leadership, music performances, sporting achievements, and service to the community, and it will be celebrated again in the pages of the school magazine at the end of the year. Teachers, meanwhile, are exhorted to "extend" all students and not "teach to the middle," and students know that homework will be set and assessed and that there will be periodical tests. Examinations from Year 9 onwards in June and November will further accent the school's emphasis on academic achievement, as the student diary and year-level assemblies will also remind them.

The discourse of excellence, therefore, is endemic in newsletters, speeches, honor boards, newspapers, and in conversations between teachers from time to time as well as between teachers and students and between students and parents. It underscores musical performances and sporting events wherever they take place and it is embodied in the students who, by definition, are made manifest when clothed in the compulsory school uniform and whose identity and separateness from all that is not Hillside is thus lauded as a source of pride uniquely theirs. This is a theme to which I will return in Chapter 10.

Community

The discourse of community underscores any framing of the formal work of the school and of the relationship of families to the school. It simultaneously constructs, reinforces, and valorizes the normative school as a discursive community while excluding outsiders – even outsiders within – as "other." School charters[4] routinely construct home-school relationships in terms of expectations of parents (such as the expectation to uphold the goals of the school), and of opportunities for parental involvement in the life of the school. By upholding school goals, parents are expected, for example, to ensure that their children are properly dressed in the school uniform, assist with homework and provide their children with the appropriate learning materials. Parental involvement in the broader life of the school is constructed in terms of an ethic of giving in which time and commitment are valued as forms of contribution to the teaching and learning environment of the school. Thus parents may contribute by becoming involved in a variety of support groups (such as those of Asian parents, Greek parents, and friends of Sport or Music), by volunteering assistance in such areas as literacy and numeracy, the library or coaching sports teams, or simply by attending parent–teacher interviews or working bees. In these and similar ways, parents are recognized as partners with the administration and teachers in the education and care of their children.

The discourse of community, however, is far more pervasive than appeals to parents. In the school charter, the annual report, prospectuses, handbooks, and especially in staff meetings, the concept of the school as a community of learners is endlessly refined. Not only is the core purpose of the school said to be to enhance learning for students, but in order to achieve this and other goals set by the school charter, professional learning opportunities for staff are organized and become priorities in teacher assessment. In documents, staff meetings, and the work of staff committees, teachers are expected to undertake studies reflecting the administration's framing of their core focus on pedagogy and the resultant achievement and modeling of a learning community. Teachers may therefore be seen as role models for whom learning is a central activity in their professional lives and whose participation in such learning is evidence of their willingness to collaborate with the preferred vision of the school's culture. Such teamwork, it is argued (e.g., by the Principal in a variety of forums and publications), together with parental involvement, makes explicit the extent to which the core values and beliefs of the school community are shared.

Care

The third discourse to which I want to draw attention is what I have called the discourse of care. It is almost inconceivable that a school would not care about the welfare or academic achievements of its students, but at the same time the appeal to students' welfare and the development of their potential is foundational within the discursive formations that constitute the school. For example, the justification for asserting that the core responsibility of teachers and administrators at Hillside is to enhance student learning and prepare students for life beyond school is the claim that "(the) central mission of the school is the development of the whole person (such that he or she has) the capacity and desire for independent life-long learning" (School Charter, 2003–05). Teachers are therefore expected to have a deep understanding, revealed in their classroom work and their ongoing learning, not only of how students learn but of the "several distinct stages of personal growth and development" through which "young people pass" (Prospectus, 2003). So, for example, the school's Teacher Handbook (2004) outlines Hillside's educational policy in terms of what the administration and school community take to be essential for the education and development of young people: a commitment to a safe and enjoyable learning environment, to literacy and numeracy as forms of communication, and to understandings of the physical, cultural, social, technological, and personal worlds within which the student lives, with added emphasis on awareness of aesthetic, recreational, and vocational issues. To help achieve this and to draw attention to the focus on welfare, or well-being, the role of support staff is framed in terms of the individual's personal well-being. The school's policy, as set out in the Handbook, is "To foster the psychological well being and moral development of students, promoting such values as self-respect, self-discipline, courtesy, social interaction and co-operation, respect for other people, a general pride in achievement, and the ability to make independent, responsible decisions" (Handbook, 2004).

This formulation is mirrored in codes of conduct and in particular the staff (and support staff) codes of practice, which draw on all three of the discourses I have discussed. Thus, staff are to value and care for each member of the school community by, for example, respecting the rights of students by treating them equitably and valuing cultural and other forms of diversity; developing and maintaining positive, cooperative, and effective relationships with other staff; helping to provide a safe, secure, supportive, and harassment-free learning environment; treating each other with respect, courtesy, sensitivity, honesty, and respect; working cooperatively with the administration and communicating effectively. More specifically, teachers are expected to value the learning needs of all students by promoting excellence and high self-esteem; by challenging and supporting students in an emotionally safe environment; by adopting a range of teaching styles which cater for differences in ways students learn; by developing student-centered approaches to teaching and learning to empower students to take an active, creative, and responsible role in their learning; by developing strategies that explicitly teach skills of thinking, cooperative learning, social skills, and metacognition and by establishing and communicating achievable expectations to students. They should also use a range of assessment methods, keep accurate records and report to parents, students, and school staff as appropriate (School Charter, 2003–05). The teacher's duty of care is inscribed in every facet of teachers' work, illustrating how, as Foucault (1980) observed, the Enlightenment project of emancipation via reason becomes a field of power-knowledge characterized by increasingly normative surveillance and regulation.

In such ways not only are teachers (and by implication, students), constructed textually, but so are they also in the meticulous and minute technologies by which students, in particular, become describable (Foucault, 1991; Youdell, 2006b: 37) and which will be the subject of comment in later chapters. Such prescriptions and techniques become both the content and context of countless staffroom conversations, meeting agendas and the thousands of interactions that daily constitute the work of the school.

TEACHERS

In a trivial sense it is clear who the teachers are and who are the students in any school, but my aim here is to suggest how any teacher (or any student), is discursively constructed at Hillside High School by examining the linguistic repertoires and other textual resources conventionally used within the discursive environment of the school. The overwhelming impression is that "teachers," as emblematic of the normative school community, are conceived of as unitary identities.

Teachers at Hillside, like any teachers in Victoria, are typically subject to State government codes of conduct as determined by Ministers of Education and their officers. Thus, they are expected to be adequately trained and aware of their obligations as public sector employees. Within the school, as I indicated earlier, teachers are presented, and present themselves, as professional, caring, adults. Teachers new to the school may be introduced at assemblies, and all teachers will introduce themselves to new classes at the beginning of the school year, in ways that stress these qualities. More particularly, teachers will be expected to adhere to role descriptions set out in Staff Handbooks which stress their responsibility for maintaining good classroom management and for participating in their own professional development and annual review. In terms of teaching, they will be expected to attend class well prepared and to develop and sustain "a positive relationship with each student, giving positive recognition where possible" (Staff Procedures Handbook, 1997), ensuring that students remain motivated as a result of courtesy, humor, and acceptance. The image of the teacher as facilitator and gentle leader unfolds in advice to be punctual, to ensure that the "tone" of the class is appropriate, to have a classroom management plan in mind, to greet students and wait for them to become attentive, to encourage participation, not to talk over noise, not to make elaborate threats, to avoid creating an "emotional atmosphere," to avoid standing or sitting for long periods at the front of the class, to follow up homework, to dismiss the class in an orderly fashion and to leave the room tidy and ready for another class. In the event of disruption caused by a student, the teacher is advised to make eye contact, to call the student by name when mildly correcting him or her, to perhaps have a one-to-one discussion, to isolate the student within the room and follow up privately or even to send the offending student from the room to a level coordinator or Assistant Principal in the company of a reliable student. Textually, such teachers are ungendered, but in performing their tasks, they daily negotiate gendered identities under the gaze of students already acknowledged in other ways as girls or boys.

This list, of course, is far from complete, but it does elaborate, to some extent, the primacy given to pedagogy in the discourse of excellence referred to earlier. Whether in the class, on excursions, supervising sport or other extracurricular activities, or on yard duty, teachers at Hillside will also be constantly monitoring student behavior and assessing the need for intervention in order to ensure that the school is safe, caring, and supportive. In such matters, the capacity of teachers to ethically and professionally evaluate their own decisions is mirrored in their accountability to the broader school community, including administrators and parents. To this unitary figure, of whom is expected at the very least, competence, care, and right judgment – in a word, "professionalism" – the threat of instability is ever present.

STUDENTS

Students, likewise, are constructed in policy documents as genderless (except in relation to school uniform policy, as I will mention later on), and as the subject of the school's (and parents') pastoral and pedagogic responsibilities. Their rights, as determined by the school, are paramount. They are to "be treated fairly and equally, regardless of physical, intellectual, sexual, racial, cultural or religious difference"; to feel safe and free from harassment; to be able to work and play without interference in a "reasonable learning environment"; to have access to an appropriate curriculum; to be informed of their educational progress and "to express concerns and be heard, where appropriate" (Handbook, 2004). On the other hand, they are to behave responsibly at all times and respect school property and the school environment; not interfere with the learning of fellow students; be punctual and attend regularly; work consistently and complete set tasks; ensure that communication with parents takes place and be aware of and abide by the school's welfare and discipline policy (Handbook, 2004). Clearly, in proposing the normative student, this discourse is also positing an "other" who transgresses and threatens; one who in being identified displaces the unitary ideal by revealing "the student" to be "a site of discursive power and contestation" (MacLure, 2003: 19).

It is in the detail of school and classroom rules, however, that the figure of the student becomes more clearly defined. In the classroom the student is expected to be punctual, bring the required materials, be orderly, follow directions the first time given, work consistently, listen to and respect the opinions of others, not talk over others, and not bring food or drink to class. At the level of the normative, institutional school, a vast range of proscriptions and prescriptions govern behavior. The first rule, again, is to follow directions the first time given, and thereafter procedures for arriving late, leaving early, what to do in case of illness, where, how, and when to move through the school, where to be at recess and lunch times, what to do in case of emergencies, when to enter the buildings and so on are set out in Handbooks and the student diary and are discussed from time to time in class and assemblies. The rules also make clear what students may not bring into the school: alcohol, drugs, illicit substances, weapons, radios, ipods, electronic games, mobile phones, chewing gum, and so on; that they must not interfere with school property, not carry bags to classrooms, and not invite or encourage "non-members of the school community" onto the school grounds (Handbook, 2004).

But it is in the matter of the compulsory school uniform that the textual and the rhetoric of embodiment come together most clearly. Students are enjoined to wear the correct school uniform (which varies between summer and winter), and, especially in the case of sport, to wear it correctly. A note from home is expected if a student's uniform is incomplete or not worn at all, in which case a special pass will be issued by a coordinator. Failure to adhere to this rule will mean that a student will be barred from attending an excursion or sporting event. Boys and girls alike are told in class and assemblies how to present themselves in the uniform, and their school diaries and Handbooks contain these detailed instructions. For example, shirts must be tucked in; a watch may be worn, but no jewellery, although a single plain sleeper or plain small gold stud may be worn if ears are pierced; the blazer is the only outer garment permitted to be worn to and from school and on school occasions, except on days of extreme heat; T-shirts and skivvies are not to be worn visibly beneath shirts; make-up and nail polish are not to be worn; prescribed shoes only (with flat heels) are acceptable; extreme hair styles and coloring are unacceptable; boys are to be clean shaven; and for girls, skirt length is monitored and a choice of four colors of hair ribbon is offered (Handbook, 2004; Student Diary, 2003–06; Prospectus, 2003). Such a policy clearly requires the support of parents and is justified as promoting a sense of identity and pride in belonging to Hillside; a sense of ownership of the school; a sense of equality between students and a commitment to the expectation of high standards of achievement and performance.

In daily observation, it is clear that the vast majority of students wear the uniform at least in part, if not in its entirety, as it should be worn. As I have indicated, those who do not are mildly admonished and those who arrive dressed in casual clothes will be sent home to change once parents have been informed. Excursion groups appear neatly in uniform and whenever there is a subschool assembly in the school hall, students who do not own, or do not have a blazer with them, will be seen often frantically arranging to wear blazers belonging to others. Those who are wrongly attired will be given detentions. On stage, student leaders and those called up to be awarded prizes or congratulated for their achievements will wear the uniform to perfection, along with the academically gowned members of the Principal class. The climax of the school year will be Speech Night during which the staff will ascend the stage in academic procession, colorfully gowned, and the student body will appear as near to perfectly dressed in the uniform as possible. Parents will glow with approval.

BEGINNING FIELDWORK

It is one thing to enter the school daily as a teacher; it is quite another to enter it as a teacher-researcher. With the permission of the relevant education authorities, the Principal and school council, and, as I have mentioned, by informing the staff and parents of my intentions, I began a period of what is conventionally described as participant observation. I participated as usual, I observed, and given the ethical constraints imposed on this study I began the quest to recruit participants among staff and students. My primary concern was to let staff and students know what I was doing while at the same time preserving the anonymity of anyone who wished to take part. I thought it important, therefore, to avoid any possibility of staff or students engineering discussions or behaviors that would be reported to me by the other during the course of the research. Given this approach, I soon found myself becoming clandestine rather than merely unobtrusive in order not to be seen to be recruiting participants. The work of crafting my researcher self that Coffey (1999) draws attention to had begun.

Although I say I went about my participation in the life of the school as usual, the ethical constraint not to research any student I currently taught or coordinated pushed me in a direction that was immediately challenging, if not strange and unfamiliar. Delamont and Atkinson (1995) in particular urge ethnographers to make the familiar strange, and in my position as teacher researcher this was, at least at first, a constant concern. Coffey, however, has challenged this prescription, arguing that sustaining the "duality of observed and observer" sets up the process of ethnographic discovery as a prolonged attempt to pass from outsider/stranger to knower/participant such that "(the) fieldworker ... purposely divests him/herself of knowledge and personhood in order to achieve eventual understanding" (Coffey, 1999: 20). To Coffey, this "simultaneous mortification of the self in order to achieve (ethnographic discovery)" (ibid. 20) is anathema. In her view, fieldwork is a constant projection of one's self into the fieldwork situation such that one's "own sense of personhood ... engages with the personalities, histories and subjectivities of others present in the field. Our own subjective personality (she writes) is part of the research and is negotiated within the field. Ethnographers are not outsiders looking in" (ibid. 57). To do ethnography in Coffey's terms, therefore, is to recognize "the interpersonal and emotional craft work (that is integral to) the philosophy and practice of ethnographic work" (ibid. 57). One is in the position of having to manage one's relationships in the field as much in terms of one's emotional commitments, she argues, as of one's rational pursuit of knowledge. Furthermore, as a participant in the lives of others, and dependent on rapport for their responses, not only must one actively and reflectively produce a "fieldwork persona" (ibid. 66), but one must constantly negotiate and craft a "fieldwork body" (ibid. 65) acceptable to others in the field. Thus, in Coffey's terms, the physical and emotional *work* of fieldwork – the reflective crafting of the fieldworker's presence – denies prescriptions that stress the strategic need to maintain or (re)create "distance, marginality and estrangement" (ibid. 21) in favor of recognizing the epistemological and personal significance of the relational engagement that is fieldwork (ibid. 158–59).[5] With this in mind I went in search of participants.

The "I" that I am to myself is "him" or "he" or Mr Whelen, or even "sir," to others. As a level coordinator of Years 9 or 10 I had duties that defined me in terms that set me apart from other teachers who were not coordinators and which defined me in the eyes of students as a figure of some authority and influence. For example, as coordinators, my colleagues and I organized students into form groups, organized weekly level assemblies, monitored student progress, phoned parents of students we had found guilty of misdemeanors and perhaps called them in for interviews, arranged meetings with teachers to discuss certain students, kept the subschool head and Assistant Principal informed of issues, compiled records of interviews with parents and students, supervised attendance, checked truancy, supervised report writing, assisted in the planning of curriculum, advised the year level promotions committee, organized examinations, approved excursions and camps, liaised with welfare staff and monitored student use of the sick bay. From time to time we also supervised the suspension of students whose behavior had contravened the limits of what was deemed acceptable. Students "in trouble" with teachers, whether for relatively minor infringements or not, therefore experienced coordinators as upholders of the school's discipline and welfare policy, and in this capacity my colleagues and I might be seen by students to be figures of authority, perhaps needing careful negotiation, able to punish and not to be trifled with. Alternatively, we might be seen by the most recalcitrant among them as no more than "paper tigers." Far more common, however, were our roles as mediator in disputes (whether between students and staff or between students), and as counselor to troubled students. In these roles students might discern a certain sense of care, of tact and of support – or not – as the case may be. It scarcely needs pointing out how the effects of disciplinary power distributed throughout these and countless other discursive practices constitute both who we can be as teachers and who can be students.

Thus, when I set out to recruit subjects for this research I went encumbered with whatever personae these responsibilities and my reputation gave me.

RECRUITING SUBJECTS

The principal aim of this study, as I explained in Chapter 1, was to inquire into boys' experience of their schooling where experience is understood as discursively produced. My interest was not in boys as a mass, and certainly not in groups of ideal types such as "the lads," "swots," "poofters," or "New Enterprisers" (Willis, 1977; Connell: 1989; Martino: 1999; Mac an Ghaill, 1994) defined heuristically by the researcher. Instead, and arising out of my experiences as a level coordinator, I was interested in two sorts of students daily acknowledged by the teachers: those exemplifying the values of the school in academic achievement, behavior and extracurricular activities, and those who were disaffected, challenging, and failing. Given the way the "which boys?" debate has been conducted, as I intimated in Chapter 2, my research interest was focused to a large extent on this latter group whose presence was becoming increasingly visible by the middle of Year 8. In grounding my definitions in the day-to-day processes of the school I was beginning to answer the question "which boys?" in the context of widespread concern about boys' achievements and behaviors in a way that resonated with my experience and the experience of other teachers around me.

George was the first Year 8 boy I recruited. The first time I spoke to George was at the school House athletics carnival. My job was to patrol the boundary beyond the athletics field, moving among the groups of students and keeping an eye out for anything untoward, especially anyone climbing the fence to leave, or escape. On one such sortie I came across George – and I only knew him by sight at the time – because he was somehow the center of attention among a group of Year 8 students. He was large for a Year 8 boy – solid, his bulk enhanced by baggy "homeboy" jeans and a voluminous bag slung across his back. He was loud and swore constantly as if he were singing a "rap" song, but most of all he was moving among his friends, grabbing or hugging them one at a time and kneeing them more or less gently in the groin. It seemed to be a lot of fun judging by the loudness of their mock pain and the general air of lightheartedness. Nevertheless, I walked up to him, had a few words with him about what he was doing, reminded him that there were no such things as play-fights at the school and told him to stop it. What I retain most clearly from this encounter is his surprised and rather challenging look as he took in what I had said. He was, perhaps only momentarily deflated, and I have no doubt it all started again as soon as I moved on.

At some point after this I asked his year level coordinator who this boy was and was told firmly that he was a thug – one who terrorized other students and spoiled lessons for teachers and students alike. Teachers, it seemed, were none too fond of George, yet he was precisely the sort of student I hoped would become part of my study.

The restriction that I not research any boy I taught or coordinated was to force me to identify (among others), boys such as George with no apparent affection for teachers or the school and ask if they would be willing to participate in the study, a daunting enough prospect for one who would at the same time be just such a teacher as those they regularly confronted. Furthermore, as mentioned in Chapter 1, significant limitations had been imposed on the ethnographic work I could expect to do.

Recruitment was painfully slow in the first year, although I was completely taken by surprise when the first boy I approached – one in Year 10 who was consistently unwilling to do any schoolwork and who was frequently suspended for disrupting classes or endangering the safety of others – agreed straight away.[6] My approach to George during recess time in the schoolyard was met with a similar reply, although his first words were "Am I in trouble?" It seemed that my initial approach and very brief outline of the research emphasizing my concern for those who were having difficulties with school was in fact being heard as a non-threatening attempt to understand their experience, but it was a carefully crafted approach. I walked up to George slowly, trying to appear as though it was no more than an accidental encounter. We stood apart at a conversational distance, as other students thronged the area, my hands in pockets, appearing casual, and my voice bearing none of the hallmarks of authority. I recalled the way I had leant against a locker bank in order to talk with the other boy in Year 10, and which seemed at the time to be so essential to the creation of a self that would counter whatever other image I might have had in their eyes.[7]

One boy I was particularly concerned to bring into the study featured in many discussions by coordinators. I will call him X. At first he said he would think about it, but that is where the matter stopped. Throughout my fieldwork I built up a picture, or story, of what was happening among my participants and in their year level as a whole, and it became clear that X and another boy who also declined to take part in the study – call him Z – were key players in the year's dramas. One day, in order to organize a meeting with Z, I located his class just before a lesson started and asked his teacher if I could see him outside the room for a minute, whereupon X shouted "Don't tell him anything!" Regardless of why I was there, in an instant, and very publicly, I was positioned as an outsider, a figure of authority, someone to be opposed. Luckily, Z appeared unmoved, but the incident was followed by the teacher bringing X out to me to deal with in my capacity as a coordinator. This was only one of two such incidents to potentially dislocate my fieldworker self from my role as teacher and coordinator, and I was able to quietly reassure X that I was not asking about him, that he had had a chance to be part of the study but had declined and that whatever I was discussing was not his business.

I mention these details for two reasons. First, such incidents constitute much of the daily life of some students and teachers and out of these contested moments come memories of particular experiences. In talking with students I would be doing just this: asking them to talk about the moments that constituted not only their experience but that in some way were also constitutive of their subjectivities. Second, I expected to find that all participants in the study gave considerable priority daily to experiences in the informal school setting (Gordon and Lahelma, 1996; Gordon et al., 2000) as distinct from the classroom and academic achievement. This is hardly surprising, but it needs to be emphasized that the formal, normative school and its requirements can be experienced as an imposition, a kind of intrusion into the projects, preoccupations and desires that make up a student's daily life. This is not something I, as a teacher-researcher, was in a position to participate in, although I might observe it in part (or watch it unfold), and together with my decision not to sit in on subjects' classes it underlines the fragmentary and ultimately textual nature of my data.

With the help of Year 8 coordinators I was also given the names of boys who were thought to be "good" students and two agreed to join the study immediately. I had chosen them from among a daunting list of others when I had time to locate them, but from the start their responses (although they were unknown to each other), were equally plain and matter-of-fact, as my field notes suggest:

> Arjay and Jake came in easily. Both described as good, model students, parents signed quickly as did the boys. Arjay . . . was quiet, tentative and it showed me just how difficult it could be to get such students to reflect on their taken-for-granted world of daily experience. This was also the case for Jake who speaks easily but not very reflectively about himself.
>
> (Fieldnotes, 25.11.2003)

Over the following year, each suggested friends who might join and who indeed did, so that by the second half of 2004 there were two friendship groups clustered around Arjay and Jake, none of whom cropped up in discussions with coordinators as problem students. George, on the other hand, was unable to bring X and other friends into the study, but my frustration in not being able to persuade several disaffected boys who did not know me was relieved when, in the second year of fieldwork, two boys I had taught the year before – Robbo and Gerster – were now free to take part. It was again clear in discussions with them and in seeking parental permission for all participants to take part, that the focus on boys who were not enjoying school was a crucial determinant in their decision to be part of the study, but in their cases both they and their parents had, in a sense, come to know me the year before, though not without some considerable difficulty in class. By all accounts, their notoriety had moved on with them.

As I have already pointed out, however, this was not the case with X, nor was it the case with Z who, after saying he would think about it, later told me "It's not going to happen." Blunt refusal such as this, which left me exposed as dependent, and which may have briefly empowered those who refused, was luckily not a common response. For example, among those I was advised to approach was Kevin, a friend or acquaintance of George, Robbo, and Gerster, who I first encountered sauntering along a corridor during class time. There were just the two of us and I greeted him and introduced myself, asking if he knew who I was while outlining the research and emphasizing my concern for boys who were having a hard time. My fieldnotes record the encounter:

> His nick-name is Schnapper . . . and he was immediately open to the suggestion. I arranged to meet his parents, which I did . . . They were encouraging because they wanted to see him more settled at school. Indeed, they had bought into a sort of self-help form of therapeutic guidance and offered to send me details in case we could use the material at school . . . Kevin took his time signing his form – several requests . . . before it was done, but he was always airily cheerful – always "gunna" do it – and I think it was finally a bit of a hurdle for him to commit himself.
>
> (Fieldnotes, 23.11.03)

At the other extreme and by far the most difficult to persuade among those who ultimately did take part, was Otto:

> Not often at school, and said to be quite anti-. There is clearly a group of Year 8 boys whom the Year 8 office despairs of . . . because of their threatening physicality and disruptiveness, who see it as a matter of solidarity not to let me in, even though one of their key members (George) has been talking to me for months. Evidently we have each maintained the necessary discretion as Z and X seem to have no idea of his involvement.
>
> (Fieldnotes, 23.11.03)

After months of prevarication, Otto came into the study once I had spoken to his mother who knew me from earlier acquaintance through teaching her other children and especially from coaching Otto's older brother in football.

By the time I withdrew from the field after two years, 10 boys all from the same year level were involved in the study. The five "good" students were two separate groups of friends, while the other five, described as difficult or disaffected and including George, Kevin, Robbo, Gerster, and Otto comprised one group, all known to each other more or less well.

MONDAY MORNING REVISITED[8]

It is no simple matter to go to school. It is not the same as attending school.[9] It is about waking up, about getting ready, about thoughts connected to homework done or not done, tests prepared for or not, about facing the uniform and getting into it and then actually making your way to school. Above all, out on the street, it is about interpellation – about being "hailed" both as "student" and as a student of this or that school.[10] It can be done alone or with friends, on foot or on a bike, in a car or bus, and it is ultimately about arriving: greeting others, being greeted and recognized, accepting the discipline of bell times and adopting the attitude of a "student" embodied in the policies and expectations of those who constitute the formal, or normative school. Facing school – facing others, looking ahead to the structured day – is the prologue to all that transpires thereafter.[11] On Monday morning, as I arrived, somewhere out there were the boys who took part in this study. For example, here is Kevin talking about getting to school:[12]

JW: Kevin, I understand you're on detention at the moment.
K: Yep.
JW: What was that for?
K: Um, being late to school.
JW: Being late?
K: Mm.
JW: Funnily enough I looked through and you've got heaps of detention for that.
K: Ah yeh, hh.
JW: I looked through the records yesterday in the Year 9 office just before we were going to talk and I've got, you, you've got, you're the champion latecomer in Year 9 I think. I think in term 1 you had 21 late days, you got 4 detentions, and so far in term 2 in ten school days up to yesterday you had seven lates. So, um, tell me about this business of getting to school. What's making you late?
K: Um, the hour that we have to come to school. Leaving.
JW: Well, what's that?
K: It's too early.
JW: Too early in the day?

K: Mm. Like at primary school we used to rock up at nine o'clock. I'd be at school, on time, every day.
JW: Mm.
K: Mm? But now we've got to oh I dunno. What time do we have to get to school?
JW: Well it pays to be here by eight thirty.
K: Yeh.
JW: but your Form assembly's not till about eight fifty.
K: Eight fifty.
JW: Mm.
K: Mm.
JW: Eight fifty-two I think it is . . . So you're not there on time?
K: No.
JW: Do you walk?
K: Ah yeh I walk.

Two months before, at the start of Year 9 during a conversation in which Kevin discussed problems he had with several teachers, I had asked:

JW: . . . so basically you, you're happy to get up, come to school?
K: Yeh. Get up, get up, that's the real problem.
JW: What's the problem there?
K: Oh, adjusting from the school holidays, getting up at eleven in the morning back to eight.

Having reminded Kevin of this, I went on:

JW: Well the school holidays are well behind us.
K: Oh, we just got back into school, how many weeks are we into the term sir?
JW: This is the beginning of the third week.
K: Yeh.
JW: But you look at your 21 lates in term one. That covers
K: Mm.
JW: weeks. So what I'd like, the reason I'm asking is because, you know, when you get up in the morning do you look forward to coming to school or not?
K: . . . Not really.

This was our second unstructured interview, or conversation. We are relaxed, together in a room at school with the tape recorder. It is lunchtime. Kevin's use of "sir" is habitual and perhaps reflects his Year 7 enrolment in a Catholic boys' school he was pleased to leave in order to come to Hillside. I am prodding, listening.

JW: No, that's, that's the thing I w-I want to know. Yeh. So you don't really look forward to coming to school.
K: Mm.
JW: Right. An', and, between us, what we want to do is try and talk about what is, right? I mean, I haven't got a magic wand.
K: Mhm.
JW: I'm not going to make it better, but I want to know from your point of view: when you get up in the morning, and you see the uniform there, you know you've got to get in it
K: Mhm.
JW: you know you've got to walk that short distance to school, what's going through here? (Pointing to my head).
K: Um, ah, I dunno.
JW: You dunno . . . You must be thinking ah, what do you think, things like, "Do I have to?"
K: Have you ever seen that movie "Looking for Alibrandi"?

Catching me quite by surprise, Kevin has begun to contextualize his response by drawing on a representation of student life he identifies with drawn from his Year 9 English syllabus[13] and in the process position himself as bearer of privileged knowledge. More than that, he has begun to construct an account of himself that will position him as in a sense typical and would throw into doubt the plausibility of my having positioned him as deviant with respect to the normative expectation of students. The interrogative privilege that was mine briefly passes to Kevin as we attempt to return to common ground (Clark, 1996). I admit to being a "cultural dope." We go on:

JW: No, I haven't.
K: Have you read the book?
JW: No.
K: No. It's about, she's the vice-captain of this school
JW: Right.
K: St. Martha's, I dunno, I guess it's the equivalent to say (here Kevin mentions private girls' schools) . . . an' um, . . . in Sydney
JW: Right.
K: and it, it goes about like she's in Year 11 or 12 and it talks about all the, the issues with HSC which is I think our VCE
JW: Yep.
K: and um just like coping with it and how . . . how, how everything is based on life
JW: Mm.
K: just like the VCE thing. Why should it be?
JW: Yep, yep . . . so you're saying to me
K: and, and at such an early age, like we've got er, like we've got exams in Year 9

JW: Yeh.
K: and when I don't pass these exams I've got to stay down, right? Correct?

I try to avoid overly correcting him and suggest he checks with the Year 9 office. We go on:

JW: What you're saying is that you think that there's a percentage that's going to count later on
K: Yeh.
JW: and the mid-year exams contribute to that.
K: Mm.
JW: Well tell me how you see all this. Do you see this as a big hurdle?
K: Yeh, huge.
JW: Huge hurdle . . . in which the exams are a key component?
K: Mm.
JW: But, but I'm talking to you about getting to school every day.
K: Yeh.
JW: There's no exams every day.
K: No.
JW: So what's, what's the hurdle every day?
K: It's not a hurdle, it's just . . . like getting to school
JW: Yeh.
K: isn't a hurdle.
JW: Well what is?
K: I don't know.
JW: I'm guessing.
K: Like
JW: Because you must be leaving for school very late to get here so late.
K: No, I left about 8.40 this morning.
JW: That doesn't leave you much time, does it?
K: I only live ten minutes away.
JW: Yeh.
K: I got here at 8.57.
JW: Late.
K: Mm.
JW: Ahm, well, so, so what's the holdup? Is it getting out of the house that's the holdup?
K: Um.
JW: Do you stop off for a smoke . . . ?
K: Yeh I do stop for a smoke, yeh.
JW: You wouldn't be alone there.
K: No, oh well I'm not, um . . . Yeh that 'n . . . ge- . . . getting ready for school, finding the uniform in the morning, having a shower,

JW: Right.
K: all that sort of thing.
JW: Do you get help for that or are you pretty much on your own?
K: No, mum's usually still in bed . . .
JW: Right, does anyone wake you up?
K: Yeh yeh.
JW: Right, so your family is sort of urging you to get off.
K: Oh yeh well kind of.
JW: A bit?
K: Well, I get up because of my phone. It goes off, got an alarm on it.
JW: Oh I see, right, right.
K: And um, set off the alarm and I get up.
JW: Right, right. So, by the time you get to school
K: Mm.
JW: you've, ah, are you ready to dive into period one, or are you
K: Yeh . . . theoretically I'm ready, yeh.
JW: But how do you approach it, I mean are you really thinking, you know, it's just another day? This is, this is.
K: To be honest like yeh I just rock up to class and play it by ear, see how it goes, really.
JW: Yeh, yeh.
K: Like I don't really think about anything when I go to school.
JW: But you're late so often, say you've been sort of late out of home, had a smoke on the way, it's just another day
K: Yeh.
JW: and I'm not really looking forward to it and why should life be based on school
K: Mm.
JW: and there are exams coming up
K: Yep.
JW: and they're a hurdle, yeh?
K: Basically in a nutshell.
JW: In a nutshell, OK, good. OK, that's fine.
K: Which is what every kid faces I guess
JW: Right.
K: but I just end up being late to school.

This is Kevin's story – or even our story – in which each of us is perhaps crafting a self we will think is adequate to our task. Caught up within the multilayered framing discourses of the school, Kevin is working his way towards a construction of himself in the context of a conversation that is itself taking place within the limits of his already discursively constituted identity as disaffected, disorderly, and challenging and mine as teacher, authority figure, and now researcher. It is only three weeks before midyear exams and he is only too well aware of his fractured and tentative attendance and, as it happens, his randomly completed class work. In spite of being described by teachers as disaffected, however, he reads voraciously and has finished his Year 9 novel in three days, appropriating much of the anguish it deals with. In the delicate business of developing rapport, he knows I will not mention his smoking to others: it is old news and our discussion is a sign of his trust in me. "To be honest" he says, and I believe him. In the work this passage represents, I have been trying to avoid any hint of censure so as to gain and strengthen rapport while Kevin finds a way of talking about how and why he arrives at school as he does.

A moment of revelation comes, after a pause, when Kevin admits to "Not really" looking forward to coming to school. Seeing my difficulty in trying to provoke this admission, Kevin seizes the initiative, positioning me as one not sufficiently credentialed to understand his difficulty. As the initiative returns to me, the problem he has identified as a barrier to a willing engagement with school, and thus to a timely arrival, is described in a strong voice as "huge." Not until the issue of smoking on the way to school is broached, however, does Kevin reflect on the matter of physically presenting himself as a student of the school. Now dressed in uniform and walking to school, generally alone and well after others, he is "theoretically" ready for the school day, but as he says this I overlook whatever meaning this cue may have for him.[14] Not yet ready to admit what he has been smoking, Kevin once again takes the discursive initiative, constructing a sense of impending arrival: "I just rock up to class and play it by ear, see how it goes, really."

This is a boy speaking from an already subjectified position, as I am. Foucault is not interested in either of us as individuals, but with our subjectification and what we do when we speak. Each of us in our own way is struggling to come to terms with the discourses within which we have become subjected in relations of power that constitute the very boundaries of our possible experience and of our mutual linguistic intelligibility (Butler, 1997a: 41; Davies, 1997: 272). Furthermore, each of us in our own way is struggling to "refuse what we are" (Foucault, 1983a: 216). In order for me to study Kevin and others like him described as "difficult," I must refuse "the type of individualization (with which I am) linked to the state" (ibid. 216). In order for Kevin to refuse his designation, he, too, is beginning to refuse "(the) kind of individuality which has been imposed on (him)" (ibid. 216) not only by the school but also by the gaze of all who see him make his way to school. Each of us is therefore exercising a kind of (linguistic) agency in an effort to "hail" some other sense of self into being – to make ourselves into subjects of another sort – for whom a sense of self, no matter how illusory or how briefly, is congenial, recognizable to the other, and, for our purposes, more authentic. In putting on the uniform and stepping out into the world, Kevin has announced himself as already subjectivated, but in dawdling and stopping to smoke, he contests the power of the gaze that has constituted him. He will do all that he can to ignore the "Hey, you!" moment he loathes, for in refusing to be designated by others he appropriates the act of designation to himself. Such moments of self-recognition, as Kevin indicates in his indifference to the normative school, may be shot through with loathing for his imminent "submission to subjectivity" (Foucault, 1983a: 213) – for who and what he is thought to be and thus at what arrival at school may seem to confirm.

6 George

INTRODUCTION

In the last chapter I began to hint at the parallel existence of two schools or two communities within the formal institution of Hillside High School: what might be called the normative school constituted largely by the dominant discourses of the administration, and the pathological school, arising out of the binaries implied in the dominant discourses and confirmed to some extent in the refusals that began to emerge in Kevin's arrival story. In this chapter I want to further investigate the experience of particular boys such as Kevin who, in being regarded as troublesome by teachers, daily seek and construct discursive spaces of their own within and against the disciplinary apparatus of the normative school. More specifically, taking up Epstein's challenge, the purpose of this chapter is to examine how one boy experiences himself as a schoolboy, or, following Walkerdine *et al.* (2001), to examine how he lives his subjectivity, inhabiting the discursive spaces accorded him. It will concern George who has just turned 14 shortly after the start of Year 8.

FIRST SEMESTER

When I first noticed George at the athletics carnival it was early in Year 8. It was not until mid-June of that year that he became one of my subjects, still known to me only by reputation. Two days earlier, a meeting of his teachers had discussed a litany of concerns. Within a fortnight of school commencing in late January, George had pushed a boy in the corridor as a result of a "punching game." Within weeks he was spoken to by a coordinator about "nipple gripping" another boy and subsequently about "chopping" yet another boy in the ribs. Throughout this time he was repeatedly late to class at the start of the day even though he was at school well before Form assembly. He had been sent out of more than one class and his progress report, written by the end of first term (approximately 10 weeks into the school year), revealed his academic work and behavior were cause for concern in almost every subject. George had missed detentions, argued about being on detention and been reprimanded for not wearing his uniform correctly – his shirt was often not tucked in. Furthermore, a number of parents had complained about George's impact on his class and were asking that their children be moved to other classes. Teachers noted that George rarely brought the right equipment to class and that he was often late and disruptive as a result. Then early in term two during a lesson he threw a plastic floppy disk cover that injured a boy's eye and was identified as having thrown an egg at other students out of school. As a result of all this, George's father had been contacted, and George was referred to the school chaplain to talk about his behavior and suspended for two days. Upon returning, he signed a contract in which he promised not to talk back to teachers or "give them a smart comment"; to listen to teachers; to try to improve his attitude towards teachers and, when being reprimanded (as it was expected he would be), he promised, in his words, "not to turn around and smirk at . . . friends (not that I do that anyway)."

Within a short time, however, George was said to have brought offensive material to class, intimidated students and threatened a boy two years older. The issue, as coordinators and his teachers saw it at the midyear meeting I attended, was how to get George to modify his behavior and at the same time minimize his impact on others both in and out of class. It seemed George had ignored his contract entirely, so the immediate solution was to suspend him for three more days for "(behaving) in a way as to constitute a danger to the health of a student (and for) consistently (behaving) in a manner that interferes with the educational opportunities of any other student or students" (Department of School Education (Victoria), Discipline Procedures, 1994).

Such was George's situation when I first interviewed him in midyear. Upon his return from the three-day suspension, he was removed from class for eight days following complaints of bullying. The sketch I have given of his behavior is no doubt incomplete and certainly lacks any reference to friends in his year level or persons or events in his life outside school. In this extract from his first interview, when we were very much strangers to one another, George admits to liking school and wants to go through to the end of Year 12 and then on to TAFE[1] College:

JW: . . . How would you describe the way you feel about school?
G: Um, well, I enjoy school . . . ahm . . . There are classes that I don't like and there are classes that I enjoy . . . very well. Ahm, when I like . . . I like them, but if I had a choice to be here or at a TAFE I'd choose a TAFE.
JW: Why's that?
G: Ahm, because I can start . . . so I can start getting . . . like used to what my work patterns . . . patterns would be like and that

JW: Right ... Um, what sort of work do you have in mind, then?
G: Um. I wouldn't mind going into a trade. Like a carpenter or ... a yeh, something to use my hands
JW: Uh huh.
G: ... and being outside like instead of an office job

In a highly academic school, George has begun to adopt the discourse of excellence in so far as he sees himself attempting the final, publicly certificated years of school, but at the same time he clearly imagines and hopes for a future in which his manual skills will bring him satisfaction. In the rarely acknowledged hierarchy of subjects in the school, George is beginning to suspect that those he likes will count for little in the end. This raises the question, for me, of his approach to, and work habits in, more academic subjects:

JW: So it's a bit of a, bit of a chore, bit of a problem for you to ... do the ... the way we work?
G: Um ... well, not really. I mean ... yeh (self-conscious smile).

Given that George says that he likes school, the question of what it is like for him to be in class and to know he does not cope well opens a space for reflection on his response to teachers and subjects:

JW: Is it the subject matter or the teacher?
G: Um ... prob'bly a bit of both. So ... But, yeh, I mean with Maths I don't particularly enjoy Maths, but like, I like the teacher, Miss Smith, I like her ... I like her personality and that, so perhaps I ... yeh
JW: What sort of things don't you like?
G: Um, well, like subject-wise? Or? Anything?
JW: Anything.
G: Like Maths and English, I mean, I have to know them, so like, I'm taking an interest in them, but like if I didn't ... really ... like ... you didn't really have to have Maths or English, then I wouldn't like be that interested in it because you know the main factors in your life is Maths and English and I'm trying to work a little bit harder on them ... but um like Geography and History, I don't really enjoy, um
JW: Because you don't see any relevance, is that what you're saying?
G: Yeh, that's right. Well that's sometimes I just turn off, right ... and um, yeh, it's ah ... just that. Doesn't interest me, and ... yeh. But, like in, like last year in Year 7 when we had Woodwork for one semester I *loved* [his emphasis] it
JW: Yeh.
G: because I got to work with my hands and I could make things an'

that, and um, Art I enjoy. I um . . . and Graphics I quite like and Home Economics, that's, that's good, an' um . . . .

George clearly experiences enjoyment in Woodwork, Graphics, and Home Economics (as his progress report showed), tolerates Maths and English and dislikes History and Geography, but he makes a distinction between the teacher and the subject:

JW: What about, what about the way teachers talk to you, the way teachers . . . .
G: Ahm, well, some teachers, like, like sometimes which (?) kids . . . when they um, like they are in the one class because of a certain teacher, or (?) like a certain teacher because of the class or, something like that, but like with me like, if the teacher is like nice, and like in a like . . . say if you like muck around for like the first time you meet her you might muck around a little bit like talk here and there and, like, she might not let you off, like let you off with a little bit, but if you keep on doing it, fair enough . . . tell the kid off, but um, if like a teacher first time like this year when I was in my Maths class, Mr Brown, um, you know we were talking a bit and he allowed that, like yeh, he'd let you talk but he, like once you go a bit too far that's when he'd say stop, and that's when like . . . that type of teacher I like, type of teacher like that, but some teachers . . . yeh, they just shout an'(go?) y' know, speak once, yer straight in trouble. So . . .
JW: So how do you feel when they when the teacher does like behaves like that themselves?
G: Like strict an' that? Um, well I'd be . . . I'd sort of like because I . . . say, sort of a thing like "Monkey said, monkey says, monkey do" . . . like the teacher tells you not to do it like you can't really like, can't really help yourself so you start talking a bit, or, yeh . . . but if the teacher says you know, you can talk a little bit, then, like I've noticed it myself, like, where teacher said not to talk at all I talk, and then if the teacher says you can talk a bit I don't really talk, so . . . yeh, and um . . .

Here, in response to a question about "teachers," George constructs his answer in terms of a hypothetical situation in which, having met a teacher for the first time, he ascribes femininity to the teacher who "might not let you off" for mucking around and talking, whereas he was instantly able to draw on a concrete example of being let off by recalling his first meeting with Mr Brown. In the case of the hypothetical woman teacher, George admitted that "if you keep on doing it" then it was "fair enough (to) tell the kid off," suggesting a sense of fair play that is immediately contradicted in his allusion to Mr Brown's refusal or failure to do just that when he says "that type of teacher I like . . . ." Here, it seems, George is inadvertently constructing women teachers as potentially unwilling, or unable, to tolerate a student going "a bit too far." As it happened, only three of his eleven teachers were male, two of whom (in manual subjects), had found his academic progress ten weeks into the year to be "Good" and his behavior to be "Consistently positive." At the other extreme, six of the women who taught him, and Mr Brown, found his academic progress to be less than satisfactory whereas only three (and Mr Brown) found his behavior to be a matter of concern, the other four regarding it as "Satisfactory." George may well like Mr Brown, but the latter's assessment of his behavior and achievement, as with many of his other teachers, together with concerns expressed in meetings by coordinators and George's record of behavior out of class, place him at odds with the discourses of excellence and community and test the normative school's capacity to adequately care for him.

Throughout these exchanges, George's experience in the general sense of the temporal flux of events is evident. He enjoys, or dislikes, or tolerates; he talks in class when he should not and he copes with teachers. As this exchange took place at midyear, soon after he had returned from his three day suspension, he may well have been uncharacteristically reflective and he certainly spoke from the position of one who knew he was thought of by teachers and coordinators as thuggish and disruptive, quite apart from being identified by me as precisely this sort of student – the sort of student I wished to talk to. For my part, I was concerned to establish a rapport that would ensure further cooperation, for example, by not passing judgment and by maintaining an inquiring tone. In particular, George's habit of ending a thought with "yeh" and with constantly fracturing his sentence construction with "like" revealed a rhetorical style that required complicity on my part in so far as the sense of a sentence often had to be inferred. When I adopted this style myself (". . . when the teacher does like behaves like that"), my complicity was acknowledged in the tone of his response leading to a momentary reflection on both his behavior and experience. George seemed quite at ease, so I asked how he might account for his constantly getting into trouble:

JW: Do you get . . . do you think you get into trouble . . . um . . . because of relationships with other kids, or because of relationships with teachers?

G: Um . . . like again, a bit of both, sort of. It's like (?) last year when I first got suspended that was because I was in a fight and with a kid, a kid obviously, and um, it was basically because he was being, like, teasing my family like that and . . . not . . . saying good stuff about my family, and . . . I went a bit angry and annoyed with that, so, I, hit him, and then, like about a week passed and that, and then we all got into a big fight and the teacher, not the teacher but

the student that were, the students that were arguing and that and then like even if the teacher's nice or whatever, you have to suspend them because of, you have got into a fight and that, so . . . yeh, the times like, there're times I've been like to the teachers, like rude to the teachers and I've got suspended.
JW: What've you said or done that's rude?
G: Um, well we s . . . like not recently, like a few weeks ago um, Miss Jago was um was had different shoes on, like I had, I didn't have the right black shoes, I had the runner, runners that were black shoes, and um, I had them on and she said to take them off and I said "But they're the same" so I talked back and ah the way I talked back wasn't good, or it wasn't in a nice way, sort of snapped, at her, and um, which wasn't, right, but I know that, and um, yeh, then I got suspended, from that, like, sort of like being a little bit smart the way I reacted back to her so, yeh, that's all.

In recalling both instances, George accepts the consequences of fighting or of being rude in so far as the protocols for establishing a safe and respectful learning environment are invoked, but he also abridges his story by glossing over details not only of what happened, but of what was felt. In his focus on the exchange with Miss Jago, his coordinator, he reveals a capacity for empathy and seems aware that in this moment he is trapped in a subject position which confirms, yet again, his being constituted as oppositional and difficult. This sort of exchange, as I have indicated, was by no means unique: George was almost daily positioned as oppositional in discussions with coordinators and in teachers' reports, and yet having said he likes school and wants to go through to year 12, how will it be possible for George to manage that?

JW: . . . do you see yourself going right through to the end of school here, or . . .
G: Yeh . . .
JW: Right through to Year 12?
G: Yeh, I want to go all the way to Year 12 . . .
[. . .]
JW: Right. OK. How are you going to manage that if you . . . if you've got these, you know, if you snap occasionally or you, you get yourself suspended?
G: Yeh, oh well (chuckles) I haven't quite thought that . . .
JW: I'm only asking because, um, you told me you liked school
G: Yeh.
JW: um, but, you know, there's still a fair bit of it in front of you.
G: Yeh.
JW: Have you thought about getting through all that?
G: Um, well . . . well I want to go all the way to Year 12, right, but,

like it depends on my behaviourwise, like if I keep on playing up, well then, I, I won't probably ever make it to Year 12.

The puzzle for George, as he seems to acknowledge – given his propensity for being suspended – is to work out how he might get through to the end of Year 8, let alone Year 12, after which he could enter the vocational course he wants. To fail in that enterprise would be, I suspect, not merely to create a sense of uncertainty about his future, but would, in the short term, destabilize precisely what he sees as the foundation of his liking school – friendship[2] – as the following exchange reveals:

JW: What's the best part about school?
G: Um . . . the best part about school . . . like, it's just, like you get to make friends like, y' know, like if you didn't like say if there was no school, you wouldn't really make friends, or some people would, but, like there are some people who might be shy or something, you know they're not going to go up to a stranger and say, introduce themselves and that, but at school it gives you the opportunity to make friends, you know, like go on camps and then you become, know each other more and all so it gives you that opportunity to make friendships and, yeh, you can be friends for, for ever, or however you like, an' but um . . . they might, they are the opportunities like, there are hundreds of others an' that . . . (chuckles) . . . I don't know, like, a lot more, but um none that spring to mind.

Certainly none to do with schoolwork and learning; but in thinking this have I unwittingly resorted to a discourse I have tried, as teacher-researcher, to discard? After all, how could the best part about school be being hailed as a bully or as disruptive? How could the best thing about school be detentions, or being suspended, or failing in class-work, or enduring confrontations with teachers? Perhaps in some way yet to be revealed by George or the other boys it is indeed possible, but then perhaps also in being subjected by those authorized to regulate minds and bodies, speech and actions, the more painful discursive incursions by the normative school are countered most successfully from within the sanctuary of the peer group.

SECOND SEMESTER

When next I spoke to George I asked him to verify the reasons for his suspensions earlier in the year. According to him, the first two-day suspension was for "nipple crippling" and he'd forgotten what the three-day suspension was for. By then the midyear reports had been given to students to take home and I asked him what his had been like. Unlike the equivalent report in Year 7, when he had failed four subjects, this time George was happy to have failed only two. Other incidents, such as his failure to attend detentions, were briefly discussed, and it was clear that this caused him no concern: they had started because he had been late to school as a result of staying up past midnight playing computer games, and to miss one detention meant he then had to do two, and so on as they accumulated.

What began to emerge, however, was detail of George's enjoyment of school in the company of friends. This is a theme that became clear in discussions with other boys identified by coordinators as not unlike George and to which I will refer later on, but in the mean time I will confine my observations to George and what is perhaps better understood as "getting into trouble."

FRIENDS

On being asked what the "nipple crippling/gripping" which had led to suspension was all about, George had this to say:

G: Um, well, there was, like with the punching.
JW: Yeh.
G: Um, like with the punching, like, there used to be between all our, all us friends, right, the guys that we hang around with um a punching game, right?
JW: Yeh.
G: Called "punch for punch"
JW: Yeh.
G: an' you'd punch each other until one just gave up
JW: Yeh.
G: an' we played that amongst ourselves. We wouldn't go up to someone we don't know. Like
JW: Yeh.
G: smack 'em, an' then we were playing that and then the teachers didn't like that, so they said to stop, so we stopped, but a few people kept on playing an' then, we all got into trouble, an' then um, yeh, that's for the punching an' things. An', for the nipple cripple, I done that to a friend an' then, they said I done it to somebody else, which . . .
JW: What does that make people do?
G: Scared.
JW: Oh right.
G: Yeh . . . but not like . . . when you nip . . .
JW: Yeh.
G: What does that do?

JW: Yeh.
G: Oh, just like . . . like, give someone a nipple cripple and it's like it stings
JW: Yeh.
G: a bit.

Here George is describing a game that might be played in class, in the corridors or in the playground and which his coordinators and teachers would routinely stop, usually with the observation that there was no such thing as "play fighting" – it was simply fighting – but to George and his friends (at least one of whom had declined to join the study), this was clearly a means of marking the group's identity, consolidating friendships, and performing what their teachers so often referred to scathingly as their customary machismo.

For example, on being asked how he had responded to the first-term progress report which was so damning, and how his father responded to it, he recalled his relationship with friends:

G: Well, I mean, some, like, like in Greek I know I muck around because . . . it's just habit because I'm with all my friends an' that, and um, so, yeh, I can't help it. Like I, I mean I know I can help it but it's like it just comes an' that, so yeh I muck around 'n that so I know for Greek that that's right, and um yeh just for like History an' that, all the other ones . . . Like with History I muck around a bit but not as much as she says I does an' that . . .

Here George has chosen to refer to an elective class composed almost exclusively of Greek-Australian students from a range of other Form groups. He and his male friends in particular are in their element in Greek, but his academic progress is dismal. He admits to similar behavior in Music. On the other hand, History is studied in his Form group, along with the other core subjects, and here George is rather more isolated. Walking past such a class one might see him sitting half facing the teacher at the front, half oriented to others around him, engaged in some sort of repartee with the teacher who has seated him near the front where (in this case) she might believe that he can be managed at close quarters while keeping an eye on the rest of the class beyond him. George's ready smile in such circumstances, his habit of engaging anyone in chatter, and his sprawling, expansive posture at his desk, all contribute to a presence none of his teachers can ignore. His English teacher, Miss Dillon, gave the following description of the class at work:

Teacher (Miss Dillon): [. . .] Every girl in that class is a very beautifully behaved girl and there wouldn't be one of them who's not really

	good at their work, or at least average and very good. You've got all these girls who are quite passive
JW:	Mm.
T:	and that, that I find a real problem because there's a wealth of intelligence there
JW:	Yeh.
T:	but they sit through this group of boys who dominate because they and, these boys are I have not found them really ever to be rude to me, but there's a repartee that goes on between a group of them. There's a little comment made and it'll be re-they'll be replied to and it'll be back and forth chatter and perhaps a little bit of verbal bullying or . . . A lot of it's done in fun
JW:	Mm.
T:	in a way
JW:	Mm.
T:	ah, but very hard to quieten down
JW:	Mm.
T:	this this group, I'd say about six or so.
JW:	Mm.
T:	So it's a great imbalance in the kinds of students and the result it has is that the girls . . . I can imagine having these girls on their own and you'd get a wonderful response from them [. . .]

In such classes, friends are not essential for "mucking around" but as by definition it is so interactive they certainly help, and in George's case they contribute to an impression held by many teachers that there is a hard core of boys – many but not exclusively Greek-Australian – who constitute a problem which began in Year 7. When being allocated to Form groups, coordinators attempt to break up such friendship groups, but in elective subjects such as languages other than English, Art, Graphics, Woodwork, Metalwork, Home Economics, Music, and Sport it is usual for students to reconstitute themselves in friendship groups and for reports of challenging behavior to become relatively common. For example, in a Metalwork lesson George was described as throwing small pieces of wax and a mini basketball around the room, calling out and talking while instructions were given, and annoying the teacher and other students in the process. He completed no work at all. At this time in second semester, Year 8, George had been given a daily progress report to hand to the teacher at the start of each lesson. The idea of such reports was to help coordinators monitor behavior and class work and to provide examples when discussing issues with parents. Each teacher would comment on aspects of George's work and behavior and return it at the end of the period. At the end of the day, George was to show the report to coordinators for their comment, briefly discuss his behavior, take the report home to have it signed by a parent and return it before first period the following day when he would collect another until some improvement was noted and sustained. As might be expected, such students often failed to follow the instructions, avoiding the judgment of coordinators before going home, losing the report, not getting parents to sign, or "forgetting" to return it the next day and so not picking up another.

In such ways the surveillant function of the normative school reached down into the minutiae of lessons. For example, two days before the incident in Metalwork, George's daily report revealed he had not completed homework in English, his Geography fieldwork was overdue, behavior in History and Maths was satisfactory, and in Science, rather than work, he had spent his time studying for a test, thus falling behind. Furthermore, he had not brought his school diary to class so he could not record homework in the prescribed way and nor could his teacher write a communication directly to a parent. Two days later, all was well in English, his behavior and attitude in Maths were described as "Awesome!" but in Music he had been "talkative." Nevertheless, his coordinator was well pleased.

Such improvement in any student was usually short-lived and George was no exception. In classes of up to 28 students, it must have occurred to George that not all were behaving like him, and that teachers responded differently to others. The following exchange on this theme was prompted by his Art report:

JW: It says here you're often behind in Art, or ah, you need to concentrate, or ah, little work is being done . . . Do you actually . . . like, when you get in class an' you see some kids, sort of getting into it, an' it might be girls, or it might be some of the boys, but some kids just get into it . . . what's going through your mind? . . . You don't

G: Like, you said, when you see them working

JW: Yeh.

G: an' that?

JW: Yeh.

G: Oh, like, when I see them working it's like you know an' if I'm talking to someone 'n I see people working I say to myself, y' know "I should be really doing that instead of talking", so I might, do my work for about y' know five or ten minutes[3]

JW: Mm.

G: an' then get sidetracked an' start talking to an' that . . . my friends . . . in the class 'n that . . . so . . . yeh.

JW: Yep, yep.

G: So, we give

JW: Concentration?

G: Mm, well the concentration doesn't last for long.

With no reference to any particular subject, George avoids a potential sense of isolation by drawing on his own particular discourse of friendship. Through it he is constituted as sociable and supportive, but caught up in the school's discursive formations as a student, and given the question, "What's going through your mind?" he confesses: "I say to myself y' know I should be really doing that instead of talking . . ." This is the sentiment he might express to a concerned parent or to a coordinator or teacher trying to cajole him into trying harder, but here, in this context, there is no pedagogic consequence, and, as far as I can ensure, no hint of criticism. This is George confessing, reflecting on himself as he has been required to do so often when in trouble, as he goes on to do at first in relation to concentration and then in relation to pure enjoyment:

G: Like, it depends what, um, thing, like, it depends what um lesson it is
JW: Yeh.
G: like, if it's Maths or History or, I mean Maths I, I know I have to do, and History or Geography or something like that, along those patterns, I don't, my attention span doesn't last long 'cause it's not like I don't feel. Like I don't really feel interested in it, but with stuff like Needlework an' um Home Economics we done last semester now what we're doing, um, Ceramics, you know I love doing those things, like with my hands an' that so I'm, I'm very interested in doing it. It's like with Metalwork, y' know we're making rings 'n that, that's why I've got it on (showing me a ring he made) 'cause I took it home. Um, we're makin' rings, an' the first week when we started doin' it we Miss Webster showed everyone how to do it, an' a few people didn't know what to do an' that an' I was like, not teaching them but I was helping them how to do it an' it's like some people didn't know how to solder gaps together so I done that an' I helped them out with it an' then pop it in the acid an' then make it round an' that
JW: Mm.
G: so I helped them in doin' that an' that an' I really enjoyed doin' that an' the same with Home Economics I help people an' in Graphics I help people a bit
JW: Mm.
G: so, an' yeh. An' now we're doing um Ceramics, yeh . . .

George's construction of himself in this exchange emphasizes the joy of manual dexterity and pride in technical knowledge. George the disrespectful, the bully, the disorganized here admits liking Needlework, and in spite of the throwing incident in Metalwork wears his creation – a ring – with pride (although coordinators will tell him to take it off as it signifies a weapon should a fight arise). Above all, George is proud of his ability to help others and, by implication, of others' willingness to acknowledge his help.

The satisfaction George experiences in manual subjects, however, is starkly contrasted with his experiences in core subjects as he has already admitted. In the following exchange I attempt to seek a discursive context in which to try to come closer to the circumstances in which his experience might arise;

JW: [. . .] I, I'm just trying to get a bit of a feel for . . . what it's like when a teacher goes off, like when a teacher sends you out because you obviously, you know, you're obviously doing well and concentrating in some of those areas but in other areas it, it just seems to go wrong.
G: Mm.
JW: I just don't know where that, where it comes from. Does it come from the teacher, or does it come from you?
G: Ahm
JW: Can, you, can you remember anything specif-that the teacher's actually said to you
G: Like
JW: as they're throwing you out, or as they're going off at you?
G: Um, well there's, sometimes with Mrs Dingle when she sends me out she goes "You're mucking around, too much, get out," or something like that, an' um, yeh, so, ah, that's basically what they say.
JW: Mm.
G: But um, Mrs, like, if it's me or the teacher it's probably a bit of both, like sometimes if the teacher's not like, y' know, like um with Miss Smith now, she, with when she goes to ahm, how do I say it right because to explain the work, right, sometimes she might not say it a way that I understand, right an' like, not that I feel embarrassed or shy or something like I don't, I don't feel right to put my hand up and say, "Miss can you say that again" just in case . . .
JW: That's interesting.
G: Yeh, so I, yeh. So I don't really ask, I just like to look on with someone else.
JW: Why wouldn't you put you hand up? Be honest.
G: I don' I don' . . . just . . . if I put my hand up an' say "Can you do it again" just like worry about people saying "Oh, you, like you dumb arse" or something like that
JW: Yeh.
G: but instead of doing that
JW: Mm.
G: sit there an' do nothin'.[4]

In such moments in class, George experiences a certain indignity and responds in silence, conscious of being positioned as academically inept. In this sense, silence becomes subterfuge and resistance to positioning, but it is hardly a safe refuge. A mere question, the collection of homework, the promise of a test – all will find him out, and the fun he has with friends will likewise constitute an offence.

JW: [. . .] What about, say when [your coordinators are] speaking to you, do you . . . do you um . . . Well they must be telling you they must be saying you know "You've gone too far" or something, you've, "You're going to get suspended"

G: Yep.

JW: How do you respond to that? What do you think and how do you talk to them about it?

G: Well, if like they say to me I, I'm going to get suspended for something, an' say that something is I haven't, say that something I've been suspended for I haven't done an' I know I haven't done, like, something, I don't know how it happens, but something inside me, just like goes, not nuts, but just says you know, why am I getting (?) for something I haven't done or something I haven't you know

JW: But the teacher's convinced you've done it.

G: Yeh, an the teacher's convinced I've done it, but um, yeh. Oh something. One time with the nipple crippling, when I got suspended, I don't know who I done it to, right? An' I knew I didn't do it to anyone apart from my friend Jim, right, an' my friend Jim we're the best friends in the class an' that, anywhere wherever we are, where we are, an' you know he gave me one like that an' that was it, we started laughing about it, an' I know it wasn't him an' then they said I'd nipple crippled someone and . . . I and I asked them you know, who did I nipple cripple, and, they go, "Oh, we're not allowed to tell you" an' then yeh . . . it doesn't give you much information to say it I've done it or not, an' when I asked them, like, how come you can't tell me, Miss Jago said "Because that person's afraid you're going to bash them an' will do something"

JW: Yeh.

G: an' so I mean I know that people think I mean I know I've thought that when I've dobbed something in.

JW: Yeh.

G: But like I'm not that kind of person who you find out who they are an' then you know you go bashin' them or, you know I wouldn't even go near 'em after that just in case they think I want to do somethin' to them an' they go to the coordinators. Yeh, oh, when the teachers say that to me I just get a little bit angry an' then . . .

JW: So how, what do you do when you get angry? Do you tell them to piss off, or . . .

138 *That Unstable Construct*

G: Oh, (?) once I like close the door an' like I've gone (?) slam to myself
JW: Bash the lockers, kick the walls?
G: Um, well, last year when I, yeh I kicked the locker and I dented one of them
JW: Did you?
G: lockers a bit of back in so
JW: Yeh.
G: um . . .
JW: This year?
G: Oh this year, I mean I basically when I've been told I've been in trouble just before school's about to finish or at lunchtime
JW: Yeh.
G: so that way if I'm on my way home my dad picks me up I just go straight home an' just punch the wall or something.
JW: Yeh.
G: Yeh, there's a wall with lots of holes in it, lots of holes
JW: (chuckles)
G: in the garage.

It is clear from George's account that he experiences a range of emotions, all socially and discursively constructed on a daily basis, and that getting into trouble, which he and a number of his friends do almost continuously, can be thought of not only as resistance to the normative school but at the same time as submission to the normative school's disciplinary technology of confession: there seems to be no escape. In a strictly Foucauldian sense, George is a prisoner of the panoptic technology of the school.

IDENTITY

Midway through his second year at High School, George has clearly been labelled by teachers and coordinators as argumentative, physical, threatening, a bully – even violent. To some students he is undoubtedly someone to be avoided, but on the other hand, George experiences himself and is experienced by others as a friend. This touches on the question of how, and more importantly, who, has the authority to control and identify individuals and groups, an essentially political question. As an issue of interpellation it arose in Butler's (1997a) account of the illocutionary force of performatives in Chapter 1. According to George Marcus, "the modernist problem" (Marcus, 1992: 311) in anthropological and ethnographic research turns on the question of "how collective and individual identities are negotiated" in the context of "culture as lived *local* experience (ibid. original emphasis). In the late twentieth century, he notes, the ethnographic enterprise increasingly came to describe culture "at the level of experience" (ibid. 311) and thus became concerned with studies of the "self," whereas earlier, realist narratives had been more concerned with structure and function within the familiar and uncontested tropes of community and subculture upon which they depended. This point was made earlier in Chapter 3.

As I have begun to show in relation to Kevin and George, identity is contested terrain. At the very least it is relational – "a constant process of becoming" (MacLure, 2003: 19) – subject to constant revision and renegotiation, ensuring that the self of one who is subjected is also elusive, multiple, and unsettled – one might almost say troubled (Lather, 1991: 118; Dormer and Davies, 2001: 5).[5] This became increasingly clear as the question of George's identity was played out in an equally discontinuous, phantasmatic drama throughout Year 8, unscripted but none the less real for all that.[6]

As the second half of Year 8 wore on, George's identity was confirmed over and again by episodes of behavior that allowed the surveillant power of the normative school, vested in teachers, to label him. This was not so much a matter of negotiating identity as of contesting it, and to the extent that George did contest the opinion teachers and coordinators had of him, it could be said that he was complicit in substantiating it. As I will show in the next chapter, "getting into trouble" may require precisely this complicity in speaking and acting from subject positions produced (or hailed), by the dominant discourses of the school.

From midway through Year 8, George's position as a student in the school became increasingly tenuous. By the end of Term three a survey of students' perception of bullying had identified George as a major offender. He was alleged to have kicked one student in the groin and to have wrestled with a student on the floor before a class started. Together with his father and head of subschool, George was brought before the school Principal and warned of imminent expulsion. He was then suspended for five days, bringing his total for the year to 10, and upon returning was to report twice daily to the head of subschool. As a further condition of enrolment he was to be professionally assessed by a counsellor.

For most of the final term, and as the end of the school year approached, there had been few reported incidents concerning George and he thought he had begun to improve:

G: Um, second half of the year, well I've picked up a bit like . . . um. I picked up a bit with my ah in class, like not mucking around so much, not like trying to sit around with my friends, like, I still sit with my friends sometimes, an' um, yeh, like putting more effort into my work.

He was now able to recount his success in a Maths test and report that he had studied at home, something that, he said, he never used to do. He enjoyed this success:

G: [...] I feel better when I, I feel good when I pass a test like you know I can do this thing, and even when I do my work in class I usually finish in front of everybody else ... so I've got a bit of spare time at the end so I speak with my friends that have finished or whatever.

But there had been problems. Only two weeks before, George had told his coordinator, Miss Jago, to "'F' off" (as it was recorded), resulting in a day's suspension rather than the threatened expulsion. Given his history so far this year I asked how he thought others saw him:

G: Um, because of my size, an' like 'cause I'm loud an' things like that people see me as sort of (attempts pronunciation) ah can't even, intimidating? That's the word
JW: Yeh, mm.
G: intimidating, and, yeh, like I've got, for instance [...]

Here George recounted a story of a fight in a football game outside school as a result of which he believed he was punished for being bigger than his opponent. At about 170 centimeters tall, and weighing around 110 kilograms, George presented a formidable physical presence for a 14-year-old, and undoubtedly his sheer proximity could be intimidating to students and teachers alike.

In spite of these difficulties, George continued to enjoy school ("I enjoy coming to school because I get to see my friends an' you know an' things like that") and even to support the climax of the year, Speech Night. It was no doubt in George's interests to both sound and be supportive in the presence of those who policed him, and he may even have thought of me in those terms, but it seemed to me at the time that he simply wanted to talk. Speech Night involved two months of singing practice for the Junior school which meant that on occasion classes were cancelled and students were cajoled and encouraged to learn the songs and were all expected to attend, as a choir of about 600, on the night. For George, this was an occasion to encourage friends to attend, and, as I learned subsequently, it was also an occasion on which they could plan to stay out virtually all night, not that George told me at the time:

JW: How did you, what did you think about all the training for that?
G: Yeh (?) With that I enjoy those kind of things like you know I had friends saying oh you know "I'm not goin' to go" an' things like that. I said "What are you goin' to do at home, just sit on the computer?"

George on Himself

By this stage of the school year, certainly among Year 8 students and their teachers, and given that it was his second year in the school, it is fair to say that George was one of several boys who could be described as notorious. The disciplinary apparatus of the school had produced numerous reports from teachers, students, and parents of George's behavior. His teachers had discussed him at length, he had been offered and accepted welfare support via the chaplain and he had had his reading and perceptual abilities assessed professionally outside the school.

As a result of confrontations with teachers, coordinators, and the head of his subschool, George, like any other student in trouble, was expected to tell what he had done or said and to reflect on its impact on others. As part of this process, he would be expected to write his version of events. For example, early in the year he had written: "I wouldn't care if it happend [sic] to me. I decked a person."[7] In these moments he was being brought inexorably under the gaze of the normative school and would be positioned as one who had a confession to make. Thus, in the contract he had signed in second term, George had had to admit that he talked over teachers, that he made "smart" comments, that he needed to improve his attitude to teachers and that he involved friends in these misdemeanors to the extent that teachers and other students were disadvantaged. As I indicated earlier, George challenged this last observation while accepting the overall picture it offered, but was required to agree to the following statement inserted at the insistence of the administration in order to confirm his ongoing enrolment: "I may not be all I could be at this point of my life but I will try and be the best I can be." With these words conjured from the discourse of care, George's subordination and further subjection were effectively ensured.

In contrast to the identity constructed in these processes of subjectification and techniques of normalization, George had revealed pride in another identity of which the normative school seemed oblivious. His willingness and ability to offer help in Metalwork, as he saw it, allowed him to present a benign and authoritative image which gave him great satisfaction. Furthermore, his preparation for and participation in Speech Night were undertaken willingly, even if by that time of the year he was on notice of expulsion if he failed to conform to normative expectations, but as I have indicated, George was thinking ahead to the opportunity the night gave for exploits after the main event. In this context George's capacity for supporting friends was a source of pride. For example X, who, as I have mentioned, had refused to participate in the study, and others, informed George they were not going, but George had other ideas:

G: [. . .] Well I told my friends [that they would be at home playing on the computer] and I got my friend . . . to come. He said he wasn't going to show up to the practice . . . Do you know what I mean? And he came for that and things and that, you know. (I got?) a few in my class to come
JW: Mm.
G: an', yeh. I, I enjoy those kind of things. I enjoy going out

JW: Mm.
G: you know, so yeh.

A further example which illustrates how George's friendship was crucial to his sense of self emerged in discussions about a friend who was routinely described by coordinators as a "school refuser" – one who stayed away for long periods as a matter of course. In the following account, George tells how he went out of his way to try to ensure the daily arrival of his friend:

JW: [. . .] Do you know why he stays away?
G: Um, well me and X we were just before we were meant to come to school like this was last term and me and X were to go and get him and bring him to school 'cause what his dad arranged with me is that I go to him go to his house every morning and take him bring him to school and I can't do that every morning you know wake him up early (?) and things like that. I mean I done it for like a number of weeks like two or three weeks and . . . every morning I'd go there, wake him up, he'd still be asleep at like eight o'clock.
JW: Yeh.
G: I'd say "[. . .], get up" and he'd say "Nah I don't want to go to school." An' I'd have to physically pick him up, chuck his clothes on him, say "Get, go in the shower"
JW: Yeh.
G: "Get your clothes on"
JW: Yeh.
G: and (?) all about an hour
JW: Yeh.
G: an' after about two weeks I kind of got sick of it so, you know, I don't need this
JW: Yeh.
G: 'cause it was getting me, pretty ugly, as well, 'cause
JW: Yeh.
G: not getting anything.
JW: Yeh.
G: (?) me and X went to go and get him an' he said "No" an' I said "If you don't come, I'll take your phone and I'll break it and I'll bring it back to you in pieces" and he goes "You won't do that" so I broke his phone, broke it, and gave it back to him in pieces
JW: (chuckles)
G: an' I said "I done it" [. . .]

Teachers on George

Teachers' and coordinators' opinions of George have constituted much of this chapter. At the midyear meeting of teachers to which I referred earlier, however, and in spite of the suspension that followed, a more subtle impression was being conveyed. On the one hand, teachers had clearly wanted the administration to confront and deal with George's behavior, but a number of teachers present described George as pleasant enough one-to-one, but troublesome and disorganized in class. For example, George's Maths support teacher was particularly effusive about him, observing almost at once, with a smile, "If ever there was a boy in a man's body . . ." George was among a small number of students who struggled in Maths and English who could either be helped in class by a support teacher, or removed from class to be helped in a smaller group. In a later interview, this teacher remarked that most of these students in Years 7 to 9 were boys and that there were more than she could usefully deal with. In the initial stages of the process of identifying students in need of extra help, she remarked that students preferred to be with their peers and not withdrawn from class, but among themselves and with her a certain acceptance soon prevailed:

JW: What sort of things did they say to you about the difference it made?
Teacher: . . . Um, "Oh Miss, ah, when we're in class, um, th-th-we don't like asking questions because the kids know that we're dumb and we are silly like you know we feel a bit awkward asking questions because the other kids know we're dumb but when we're with you it doesn't matter because, you know we are anyway" . . . "We're the vegie, we, we're the vegie Maths."

Afraid of being called a "dumb arse" by other students, as he had said, George could to some extent avoid any stigma within this small group and among some of his friends. Ms Finlay, the teacher, found that as a mother of several boys she "knew things about boys that age and . . . knew the games, the movies and so we could build a rapport." Nevertheless, she commented without prompting that they could misbehave or drift off task in her class "like George who really has, very little interest in . . . school. He just, doesn't care." In spite of this she expressed undoubted affection for him, acknowledging a sense of frustration she thought all in the "remedial" group must be experiencing. Looking back on her class with George she told of how:

Teacher: . . . I've seen him just sit there I mean he'll do anything.
JW: Mm.
T: He'll, he'll take somebody's diary and have a look through it
JW: Mm.
T: and and because he's George, with some degree of power, um,

	the others, but nice enough with it, you know the others just allow him to do it.
JW:	Mm.
T:	He'll . . . you know, sit 'n, sit 'n doodle, sit 'n look at the cars in the back of his own Planner, draw on his Planner. I've seen him disintegrate a hat in one lesson,
JW:	Mm.
T:	just sit there and colour it in with texta and then start peeling bits off it and
JW:	Mm.
T:	he'll do anything because he's just not interested. School is not the place for George.

His English teacher, Miss Dillon, likewise remarked on his failure to produce work in class. He would concentrate on a film so long as it was exciting, and he might offer very short "quickfire answers" to questions, but after eight months of the school year she'd "had virtually no work, written work from him this year." However, given the presence of a parent helper in class, George responded eagerly to the close attention he could not normally get in a class of 28 and "actually (produced) a whole page of writing." She went on:

T:	[. . .] the interesting thing was that having seen what he wrote this week and everyone's pleased with him, including his coordinator and so forth, I said "Well that's really good, George, that you've written that, but, you've really written about an introduction to the whole topic. Now I want you to actually describe, imagine that you were at the night club"
JW:	Mm.
T:	"and describe what took place [. . .] Oh no, no Miss. No, I done this. No. no I'm not doing it again." So once was enough even though it wasn't what we wanted [. . .] He responds to praise.
JW:	Mm.
T:	Um, he responds really well if he's given a, a practical task such as setting up the video
JW:	Mm.
T:	ah, although he may use it as a little power structure thing that he's the only one that can do that [. . .] he's quite good technically.
JW:	Yeh.
T:	One little glitch in the thing, and he can fix it
JW:	Oh yeh.
T:	um, but in other ways he's very difficult [. . .]

For these two teachers it appeared that George was a daily challenge and yet each could draw attention to redeeming features.

CONCLUSION

It is clear that George's identity was daily constituted at the intersection of competing discourses and that George himself contested normative attempts to discipline him. In terms of dominant discursive formations emanating from the administration through coordinators and teachers as well as students and some parents, George was understood as difficult, obstructive, overbearing, and even potentially dangerous. On the other hand, George's enjoyment of school, in spite of constant attempts to fashion him into a student of a certain kind, was undiminished by the end of the year and his status as friend and helper, even among some teachers, arose within an oppositional discourse, privileging an alternative sense of community arising out of friendship from which all who represented the disciplinary apparatus of the normative school were excluded.

The question of identity, however, was not confined to George. By midway through the last term of the year I was utterly frustrated by my inability to bring more boys into the study. Kevin was lingering over the return of his permission forms and two others representing boys who seemed to have no difficulty with the school were still thinking about it. More to the point, in my view, was my failure to convince two of George's close friends to take part. Z had shown slight interest, and his parents were supportive, but when he said "It's not going to happen" at a moment of confrontation with his coordinators the matter was over. As for X, who had called out to Z "Don't tell him anything!" he had been approached by George several times but to no avail. X, he said, hated "authority figures" and did not want me contacting his father. It seemed there was nothing I could do about it, but perhaps I came close during Speech Night rehearsal:

> During the morning practise I observed the junior forms and musicians go through their routines, but one incident stood out. The buses took quite some time to arrive from school and at one point a music teacher came walking up through the throng with a student in tow – it was X. She was extremely upset, claiming he had been rude to her on the bus, and I think for a moment she thought I was a Year 8 coordinator . . . She told him to wait in the backstage area where I was . . . I went over to him and asked him quietly what had happened. He was fairly glum but agreed he had said something rude to her. I said "You aren't having a good time, are you?" and he seemed meek and acquiescent for a moment. I said "This is exactly what I said I would like to talk to you about. What's it like being in your position? Look around you. No-one else is in your position. Think about it."
>
> I didn't see him again during rehearsals, but the music teacher placed herself near George in the massed singing and he had a wide

grin at some point. Again at night, there was George, large as life in the balcony and singing.

(Fieldnotes, 28.11.2003)

For some, apparently, I was irrevocably associated with normative authority. For George, it seemed, this was no problem, nor would it be when others agreed to take part in the New Year.

7 Year 9

INTRODUCTION

In Chapter 6, I offered a representation of a student – George – as he was constructed by teachers in their reports of him, and as he and I constructed him in our discussions. In a sense, of course, I was still unsure of who George was. Before me was the boy – the person, the individual – who could be said to occupy the subject positions that were George, just as I also occupied, or stood for, the subject positions that constituted the various identities that were "me." Each of us (and this would of course be true of all participants in the study), was the unstable product of our discursive interpellation, but this did not entail an unproblematic acceptance of the positions offered as if they were simply *a priori* categories (Hall, 1997: 10). Rather, it opened up possibilities for reply, negotiation, assent, or even resistance and refusal. As Hall (1997) points out, and as I mentioned in Chapter 6, it is one thing to be "hailed," but to be effectively "sutured" as a subject to a subject position requires also "that the subject invests in the position" (p. 6). At this point if the language of consciousness interposes itself – that is, the language of intention, volition, knowing, agency – it is not to suggest a reintegration of the Humanist subject but, as in the later Foucault,[1] to signal a move away from the subject as docile, disciplined body to a desiring subject seeking to regulate and fashion a self through practices recognizable in terms of Butler's notion of discursive and performative agency.

The focus of this chapter will therefore be on the notion of "the self." Here, the "self" is not to be confused with the person, or individual, nor is it to be thought of as a fixed identity or whole, coherent subject, regardless of situation and context. Instead, the "self" is understood to be socially and discursively emergent. Thus, as I have reiterated throughout, subjects are positioned in competing and simultaneous discourses in such a way that identity and selfhood are experienced as fragmented, contradictory, and contested.

The notion of crafting oneself – or one's selves – situationally and interactively, therefore, implies that identities cannot be bounded entities, expressing essential, or distinctive attributes such as "real," inner feelings. Identity in this sense is therefore not something fixed, but rather "negotiated, open, shifting, ambiguous, the result of culturally available meanings and the open-ended, power laden enactments of those meanings in everyday situations" (Kondo, 1990: 24).

This, as I indicated at the end of Chapter 6, applied with equal force to me and to my relations with those who took part in this research just as it does to the crafting of this text. Participation in the field becomes a matter of inserting oneself into contexts and processes, adopting subject positions in discourses and practices which are always already in operation, and negotiating between "Self" and "Other" in unstable fields of power. Ultimately, however, participation and observation give way to memory and reconstruction as the ethnographic text is created.[2]

It is thus that in "language and narrative conventions (as Kondo observes, that) . . . the most striking insights into the simultaneously creative and disciplinary production of 'selves'" (ibid. 26) becomes apparent, and it is here that the unity and coherence of the "whole" (Cartesian, rational) subject is most vulnerable. The way is opened for the subject to become "a site for the play of difference, a site for the play of shifting and potentially conflicting meanings" (ibid. 36) and it is precisely into this fluid environment that those who took part in this study, especially the boys, daily struggle with the hegemonic and totalizing discourses of the normative school while at the same time attempting to assert themselves as whole and comprehensible in ways that subvert that power. This chapter will show how these boys take up, manipulate, contest, and refuse subject positions in discursive formations of their own as the school attempts to make them into subjects of a certain kind in assemblies, classrooms, and in examinations.

PROCEDURE

In this chapter it will be necessary to write about experience in two registers: first, in terms of the ethnographic present tense in order to establish a more or less invariant context in the everyday world of the subjects of this study, and second, in terms of a chronological unfolding of specific mundane events in their lives. Thus a relatively static and generalized narrative will function to support an account of specific experiences as they uniquely constitute a domain in which identity and a sense of selfhood are contested among the boys.

ASSEMBLIES

Each school day starts with a Form assembly. Should Kevin and George arrive on time they would put their bags in their lockers in the corridor allocated to Year 9, take their books and materials for periods one and two and make their way to their Form rooms for the brief assembly. There the Form teacher will "take the roll" which has been collected by a roll monitor (usually a Form captain), noting absences, and read the daily bulletin to the class. Latecomers will be expected to show late passes collected from level coordinators' offices before they are registered as present. Occasionally there will be interruptions from messengers or students collecting money for various causes. Early in the year, Form teachers oversee the election of Form captains, subject to approval by coordinators. After seven minutes a bell will end the assembly and students will have two minutes to get to whichever room they have been allocated for period one.

It is, of course, a great deal messier than this. Kevin and George are likely to have been encountered dawdling and urged to hurry and not be late. Teachers shepherding students through the grounds and coordinators patrolling the corridors will almost certainly have told them to tuck their shirts in. In the minutes before Form assembly, corridors throughout the school will be shoulder to shoulder with 1,800 students milling around lockers, jostling and greeting one another. In the Year 9 corridor, boys and girls will greet one another volubly and ostentatiously. George and friends greet with a ritual handshake, starting with a "high five," loudly affirming their friendship and some boys and girls greet with a hug and a brief kiss. Coordinators will do what they can to abbreviate these gestures and move them on to Form assembly where Form teachers will be more or less successful in establishing enough quiet for proceedings to take place. Many students will continue their greetings while another student reads the bulletin and the Form teacher deals with latecomers who have to be sent away for a late pass.

Once a week the Year level will have its own assembly held in a theatrette capable of holding all 300 students in Year 9. Here Form teachers mark their rolls while coordinators convey normative expectations to the students, outline procedures (such as at exam time), and occasionally introduce guest speakers. More often than not the Form assembly will go well past the time allotted for it and cut period one short. In the first year level assembly for the year, coordinators reminded students of school rules banning makeup and excessive jewellery, the need to collect late passes early, the prohibition on eating in corridors and their responsibility not to hang around in corridors between lessons. This pattern is repeated weekly with occasional variations. For example, before Form captains are elected, students who nominate will have to give a brief speech at Level assembly outlining why students should vote for them.

This assembly is also a great deal messier than the description given earlier. Students will enter the tiered theatrette when permitted after they have been to their lockers and as they do so *en masse*, coordinators will watch for violations of the uniform code. Girls will be asked to take off pendant earrings and boys will be told to tuck in their shirts. No food will be allowed in and latecomers will have to leave their bags outside. The three coordinators will stand at the front of the assembly maintaining order with the aid of a microphone and the implied threat of detentions. They are watching the students who are watching them watch the students . . . Those who were late will be let in and lined up to hear messages while their late passes are written out and class rolls amended. Those without adequate excuses will be given a detention after school for half an hour on a predetermined week-day. George and Kevin will often be found among them.

Once a term there will be a school assembly. As it is impossible for the whole school to be accommodated as one body on the site, each sub-school will have its own assembly. Students are notified several weeks in advance as these assemblies take place during lesson time and last about 50 minutes. All students must wear correct uniform including the school blazer. They are ushered into the school hall by teachers whose lessons have been cancelled because of the assembly, and by the coordinators, and marshalled into rows of seats, Year 9 at the front, Year 10 behind them; boys on one side, girls on the other. An Assistant Principal on stage at a microphone establishes an atmosphere of quiet, if not respect, among the more than 600 students and then they are directed to stand quietly while the official party enters. The school Principal and Assistant Principals in black academic gowns lead student leaders and any visiting speakers onto the stage where they stand in front of their chairs while a teacher leads the Assembly in singing the school song and national anthem. Singing is accompanied by piano and the words are projected onto a screen. After the school song, which extols the virtues of their school, students are asked to sit quietly and proceedings begin. Usually, school captains and other senior student leaders act as masters of ceremony, introducing the Principal and other speakers, and often they also have well prepared speeches to make. Applause follows each speech as well as introductions to visiting speakers, and may be especially loud after presentations to high achievers in State or nation-wide academic competitions or for sporting achievements. Finally, a music ensemble or soloist will perform to loud applause as the period bell rings, usually for morning recess or lunchtime. Students are then directed to stand and the official party leaves the stage, after which students will be dismissed row by row in an orderly manner.

Of all the technologies of surveillance available to the school, perhaps none enacts the principle of panopticism more faithfully than the assembly. Certainly, in class rooms it is still possible to speak of a front where the teacher's desk is found, and students sit at desks in rows before the teacher or in a U-shaped formation, again in front of the teacher, and teachers more often than not stand before their students (or walk around the room), engaging them eye to eye. In the grounds, before, during, and after school, teachers "on duty" look and evaluate everything they see.

It is in assemblies, however, especially the subschool assembly and the one whole-school assembly for the year, Speech Night, that the school stops, and one sees in them rituals of reflexivity, or "moments of self-commentary" (Meyerhof and Ruby, 1982: 17) in which the normative school performs itself for all to see, urging all members of the community to act on themselves in thought, word, and deed. Speeches spelling out the virtues of values such as tolerance, respect, and resilience, faultless musical performances and the public award of prizes all enact stories about incidents and students that, whether metaphorically or literally, illustrate the most fundamental concerns of the administration. In these moments, the normative school performs stories about itself.[3]

But of course the experience of the subschool assembly is so much messier, more varied, and more contested than I have indicated earlier. As the doors open and students file into the hall, the space is filled with the sounds of chairs scraping the floor, students calling out, and teachers sorting out the occasional pushing and shoving.[4] I position myself well behind Year 9 students so that I will not be called on to discipline any of the subjects of this study and, if possible, so that I can watch them. Eighteen teachers, eyes scanning the students, remain standing around the margins of the hall and down the central aisle as the students are seated. There are no problems as the official party enters and an Assistant Principal congratulates the students on the way they have sung the school song. This ploy is designed to encourage a compliant and cooperative student body, but closer to the floor teachers have been wandering past the rows of students (especially the boys), encouraging them to sing, to stand up straight and to take their hands out of their pockets as they sing. New student leaders are introduced to much applause and some cat-calls as teachers' eyes scan the student body looking for culprits. In a joint speech, the new boy and girl Captains and Vice-Captains exhort students to become ever more studious and to involve themselves in school activities such as debating and the many clubs and to take advantage of the many leadership opportunities offered: they and the other student leaders did and they have no regrets. Now is the time to set goals for this year and for the senior school that lies ahead. The Principal then outlines the school's newly refined approach to curriculum – "a community growing together through learning" – and focuses on what he will refer to as one of the four key "pillars" of the curriculum – "learning to live together." This, he says, will be the theme for Term 1, and in an address covering the tragic effects of devastation felt around the world after natural disasters, weaves in references to how Australians have given aid generously to make the point that generosity can create harmony among nations as well as among one's peers. Students applaud as he is followed by the chaplain. In a power-point presentation featuring the relative proportions of the world's major religions and Australia's population in relation to those of other continents, he urges students to contribute generously to appeals for good causes, ending by saying: "Work with passion, excel and contribute." Finally, the musical item, drowned momentarily by the period bell, draws much applause and students are asked to stand as the official party leaves the stage. The Assistant Principal then tells students to be seated and comments on their behavior during the assembly. Coordinators, who have withdrawn several boys from the assembly for talking or kicking the seat in front of them, will be asked to take other students aside and give detentions for various misdemeanors, and at last the middle school is dismissed as rows of students converge on the doors to an abbreviated morning recess.

In the first subschool assembly of the year, George seemed preoccupied with others around him, as was Kevin. Several others who would later join the study were among seven Year 9 boys (including George and Kevin), given detentions at the Principal's direction for misbehavior during the assembly. Already by the third week of the school year, these boys were establishing themselves as disruptive and disaffected, carrying on reputations gained in the previous two years. For example, in less than fourteen school days, Kevin had been late to school seven times; had given a teacher a false name when late to class (but, as the teacher said, "to his credit" had later admitted it); had walked off instead of staying to discuss this matter when asked to; was found to be very agitated and swearing in class by one teacher, and with other students had been late to Maths after wandering around the school, allegedly unable to find his class. George, too, had been late to class more than once; was suspected of having been involved, with X, in the "disappearance of two muffins" from the canteen and had already truanted by day two of the Term.

By midyear the topic of assemblies had come up in our discussions. Kevin and George had now been joined by Gerster whom I had taught the previous year.

JW:	Change the subject again. Assemblies.
Kevin:	Yeh fine I love assemblies.
George:	I don't think they should go for longer.
Kevin:	Yeh longer.
Gerster:	Remember in Year 7 we got a whole period for assemblies?[5] It was mad.[6]
All:	Yeh.
George:	We miss out on a few, oh you got extended (?)
JW:	Do you, do you ever remember anything said in assemblies?
Kevin:	Not really. You sort of listen
Gerster:	Oh generally I don't.
George:	In the morning like you know
JW:	But I mean school assemblies.
George:	it's been an hour since you've been awake – oh like

JW:	School assemblies too. (?) Any sort, any sort but Year 9 assemblies you know how (?)
George:	Oh yeh.
Kevin:	I don't think we've had one this year. Have we had one?
JW:	Yeh, two or three, yeh. Had a couple.
Kevin:	See, I don't even remember being there (chuckles).
George:	Oh no I remember the one where we I the only reason I remember it because I (?) this in general assembly I just sit there, mucking around with a mate or something (?) you just sit there
Kevin:	You'll play snake on the phone. That's cool
George:	Yeh. Right (chuckles)
Kevin:	Yeh oh yeh I wouldn't bring a phone to school
George:	An' um, you know you just sit there an' you just look around for an hour or so an' then the only thing, for me, remembering that we had one is the singing. I remember now we were always mucking loud, singing (Laughter, especially Kevin)
Kevin:	Ugh! Love doing that bit
George:	Like you get a whisper round people (Whispers: "Sing loud sing loud" you know) 'n stuff like that so you know because the fun part of you're tapping
Gerster:	You tap people in front of you on the shoulder and stuff
Kevin:	And when your shoes are wet one day there was like a whole a whole assembly just rubbing their feet on (Laughs, especially George)
Kevin:	Took (the Assistant Principal) like five minutes to get hold of everyone.
JW:	So these are the these are the fun things?
All:	Yeh.
Gerster:	Remember on Speech Night how me and you were coughing?
George:	Heh.
Kevin:	Yeh I heard that started coughing (chuckles).
George:	Who started that, you know?
JW:	So you all attended Speech Night?
All:	Yeh.
JW:	I know you were there (to George).
George:	I love going there.
Kevin:	I was on stage for the whole thing.
JW:	On the stage.
Kevin:	Yeh I was looking hot that night.
Gerster:	George kept saying "Did my breath smell?" and he kept breathing in my face all night and it was just oh man!
George:	(Laughing) It was, I had, it was 'cause I didn't know if you have a lot of chewies, like, sort of, somehow makes your breath smell bad, and I had like a lot so my breath wouldn't 'a

	smelled bad. [. . .] (Acting out): my breath smell bad? God like. Mrs Green sat next to us
Kevin:	She's a nut case.
George:	and like, she was like "Something smells like oh sh-" (?) yeh that's about it . . . Yeh.
Gerster:	Yeh Speech Nights are (?)
George:	I love Sp-I love stuff like that you know where you're with all your mates
JW:	Mm.
George:	an' stuff.
Kevin:	The best part of Speech Night was going out after it in the city. I reckon that's best.
JW:	And that's about eleven o'clock at night.
Kevin:	Yeh.
JW:	Onwards.
Kevin:	Oh well.
George:	I didn't get home till about six, seven in the morning.

There are three observations I would make about this encounter. In the first place, when remembered, relived or re-enacted, experience can seem utterly discontinuous – even momentary – set within the flux of time. This should not surprise. If experience is socially constructed and lived through, then in a sense persons have experiences. If, however, experience is an effect of discursive positioning and discourses are encountered discontinuously, then experience, like subjectivity, is discontinuous. To be positioned in this way is to experience one's subjectivity more or less fleetingly, but such experience is none the less embodied and potentially available to memory. Thus these boys who are subject to the normative gaze of teachers in the playground, corridors, classrooms, and assemblies, in their own ways deconstruct the hegemonic disciplinary apparatus of the school through their discourse of friendship and fun and render the normative judgments of the school more or less ineffective.

Second, there is a subtext evident in Kevin's contribution. Whereas George's trust in me is securely placed, Kevin is still unsure. "I love assemblies," he says, with more than a hint of sarcasm, perhaps to see if I would defend them, and having apparently forgotten his misdemeanors in the assembly described earlier. Again, when he mentioned having a mobile phone (which contravened school rules), he was quick to pretend mock innocence: "I wouldn't bring a phone to school." On this day he seems to want to test my ethnographer self, probing for any vestige of authority as rapport is tentatively established.

Finally, the sheer exuberance of the group should not escape comment. They are well known to each other and here, when permitted to speak in their own words (although George checks himself when describing the smell), they carry the conversation on together with little interruption from me – in fact I was little more than an observer in the latter part. Selected events from seven months before were recalled with remarkable clarity and it might be objected that they were fabricating a story, which in a discursive sense they were, though I would say not for my entertainment or to mislead me. They may also have been exaggerating the fun they referred to, or the risks they might have taken or even the actions they claim to have participated in, yet in so far as I am concerned to locate their experiences in their discursive repertoire, the truth of their recollections is not at issue.

THE EVERYDAY

Kevin

By the midyear exams in Year 9, Kevin's lateness to school had become chronic. For example, by the end of Term one he had supplied only one note for 21 absences. This, and other acts such as deliberately tripping another boy in a Physical Education class and repeated teacher reports of misbehavior resulted in detentions, both after school and at lunch time, at least some of which he simply did not attend. In class he sat with others described by teachers as disruptive and was thought to be affecting other students adversely. In one incident another boy had landed a "spitball"[7] on him. He brought this to the teacher's attention at the start of the class and when told it would be dealt with as soon as the lesson was under way, replied "F***!" and later ignored the teacher's directions in an attempt to sort the matter out. Work was not being done and he was well behind in all subjects requiring homework although he was seen to listen occasionally while teachers talked. The correct materials were often not brought to class and sometimes he would read a novel rather than do Maths or Science. The consensus among teachers was that he showed no respect, being reported as swearing aggressively on several occasions in Form assembly and class, spitting, and saying "F*** this!" or "F*** you!" while pushing and shoving. During the midyear exams he was directed to stay back after school for detention and his cigarettes were confiscated. For this he would have to watch a video explaining the dangers of smoking.

An account such as this, based on teachers' reports and the Year 9 Day Book in which coordinators noted incidents briefly, omits the visceral intensity of students' and teachers' experiences. Indeed, in reporting Kevin's speech, female teachers uniformly referred to the word "f –" and, in signifying their distaste, often referred to it in speech as "the 'f' word." Coordinators and teachers also sought explanations and causes for confrontational behavior, such as alleging Kevin was "an attention seeker" and although intelligent, was disorganized. In fact, Kevin was discreetly being constructed in terms of a welfare narrative within the discourse of care, as was the case whenever the support of the school's psychologists, chaplain and other welfare staff was sought. The locus of concern shifted to the family and even Kevin's eating habits became the subject of comment. Kevin's experience at this time, therefore, arose not only in countless confrontations with teachers, in the crucible of care as welfare staff probed and offered support, and in the company of friends, but included the knowledge that an interview with his mother had been organized with a view to trying to prepare him for the career path of his choice. As a result he was allowed to drop a senior Music elective and it became clear that what he really wanted was to become a chef and go to a TAFE college as soon as he could leave school. As part of this settlement he was moved to another Form for second semester, leaving behind a number of friends and joining his new Form with something of a reputation.

George

By midyear, teachers had reported George for a number of incidents. He was occasionally late to school and was sometimes late to class, rarely bringing all books and materials required. He was involved in a pushing incident in a corridor, was alleged to have stolen another student's property and was suspected of involvement in a fight involving students after school. His failure to wear the correct sports uniform in Physical Education classes became an issue and on one occasion, taking offence at a comment by the teacher, told him to "f*** off, f***ing wanker!" and then, in the teacher's view, proceeded to stand over him. In other classes he was said to be talkative and was sometimes sent to the coordinators or given lunchtime detentions. His gold necklace and cross, which he wore against school rules, also became an issue as did his playing with a mobile phone in class. During the midyear exams he was absent for the Maths exam. Finally, he was suspended for two days for punching a student who he mistakenly thought had hit him.

Again, this brief outline of George's experience omits the intensity of interactions and hardly suggests the emotional investment in clashes at all. George's father was contacted at various times in an effort to contain George's behavior, and then after an incident involving X and George, which caused a female teacher to feel threatened, his future at the school was put in question. At a meeting between the Principal, an Assistant Principal, and George's parents it was decided that the school's curriculum was inappropriate for him and that to avoid expulsion, he would have to agree to abide by a contract for the rest of the year (as he had had to do in Year 8), and accept help from the school's welfare staff. He would also be given careers counselling. Like Kevin, George was also being constructed in terms of a welfare narrative which mobilized the discourse of care and its associated disciplinary technologies.

Gerster

Gerster was occasionally late to school and appeared to teachers to be able, but poorly motivated. He was elected as the male Form captain but remained more or less on probation. On one occasion he was put out of class and even from the corridor continued to distract others. During this incident, when told he was setting a poor example as a Form captain, he remarked that teachers can be badly behaved as well and further baited the teacher. He was also thought to be involved in teasing some students and was given lunchtime detentions. On the whole, his class work was satisfactory but confrontations continued with a small number of teachers.

In the infinite regress of detail surrounding these boys' lives, not to mention those of their friends and the multitude around them, these were the sorts of incidents that distressed the normative school. In their responses, administrators, coordinators, and teachers sought to locate causes in terms of the psyche in which crises, extremes, and the language of interiority were privileged. The preferred mode of intervention beyond talk and detentions was for the professional management of the psyche, whether by psychologists or the chaplain, supported by careers counselling or, in extreme cases, by medical intervention. Thus the student was taken out of the hands of coordinators and classroom teachers into a private world of care to which few were privy.

In a year level of over 300 students – more than half of them boys – the incidents I have recorded make up only a minute fraction of what they were living through. Events at home clearly had consequences at school, but at least as important were the myriad other interactions going on around them in class, in the corridors and in the school grounds. In the following section I will recount two such events that were inextricably meshed with their experience at school and which had immediate and lasting consequences.

GRIEF

Three months before the end of Year 8, George's grandmother was found to be terminally ill. No significant change was noted by teachers in George's behavior in the remainder of the year but it had begun to prey on his mind, as it did throughout the first half of Year 9. Her death and funeral immediately after the midyear exams culminated in George's mourning in terms of his Orthodox religious beliefs by not shaving, initially for 40 days, but then for a further two months during which he reluctantly trimmed his facial hair. Once again, coordinators were called upon to manage this infringement of school rules, but George was obdurate. Coming on top of the incident in which the teacher felt threatened,

George was now constantly enmeshed in interviews with coordinators, having to explain and justify not only his appearance but also his apparently threatening behavior. The outcome, as mentioned earlier, was the meeting in which he was told the terms on which he would be allowed to stay until the end of the year.

As a result of his grandmother's death, George, together with Kevin and several other boys were admitted into a program for managing grief and loss run by the school chaplain. Fortnightly meetings of the group were held in the following months during which George began to appear to me to be noticeably less ebullient. He wore his uniform correctly and seemed less cheerful, more preoccupied. He was under no illusions about his future in the school: at 15 he knew there was no place for him there next year.

The populist construction of disaffected schoolboys reviewed in Chapter 2 makes much of their alleged inability to come to terms with emotionality, either their own or others'. Sometimes coded as emotional literacy, such accounts emphasize a resistance to expressing emotion, either because it involves a form of language not yet learnt or because of a tendency among boys to regulate their masculinity in terms of stereotypical and hegemonic values that deny any gendered validity to the expression of emotions (Reichert: 2001; Martino: 2001). While it may be argued that emotions are mental states, they may nevertheless be understood as enacted and constructed socially through language (Burr: 1998). Thus George, Kevin, and Gerster had no difficulty showing happiness, confusion, anger, and even meekness in our discussions and in encounters with teachers, but occasions and contexts for showing grief were far more rare. In George's case, the illness and death of his grandmother provided both the occasion and the context.

About two months after her death our discussion moved to her illness and decline:

JW: [. . .] obviously that was upsetting
G: Yep.
JW: and um how did, when you came back to school um basically two weeks after her death . . . um, were you still carrying that with you or not?
G: Um, still am, now
JW: Mm.
G: and um, yeh. Well I didn't really cope . . . that well with it. It was, she was like a mother to me as well.
JW: Was she?
G: And um, yeh like I didn't really want . . . 'cause when I came, like when she passed away I had some friends with me, that night at the hospital like a few days later who I met up with and I went out with them to get it off my mind and stuff

JW: Mm.

G: and just those two friends, were really like, comforting and like you know "Don't worry about it" thing and both of them come to this school [...] and um, they were really helping me out through it and then when it came to the funeral – like helped me out with the funeral like set up with stuff like the hall, so it wasn't really that, I wasn't really thinking about it that much 'cause um, it was a bit harder 'cause I had everyone saying you know "Sorry" and then you'd think about it

JW: Mm.

G: and, yeh   sort of like that yeh.

George has clearly been able to show deep emotion with friends in the context of broad family grief and he had no inhibitions about discussing it with me two months later (perhaps with the benefit of the chaplain's intervention), but he had told no teachers of her illness during first term and made no mention of her death until after his suspension for punching a boy near the end of Term 2. The subsequent discussion with Principals and parents concerning his future coincided with this crisis.

JW: Do you know or do you understand why they wanted to . . . expel you?

G: Um. . . . .(chuckles) I was just told, like, behaviour, and yeh . . . 'cause I've been suspended so many times through my school life that yeh.

JW: So how do you feel about that?

G: Um . . . well it sort of came at the wrong time also 'cause with my grandma and . . . I think if, my grandma, hadn't passed away and, before this was starting to happen it wouldn't have hit me as hard, but because it hit me while my grandma passed away while she was sick, it, it mounted on the stress, that I had

JW: Mm.

G: and um, and the teachers some like 'cause they started accusing, they started to accuse me, accusing me of harassing (a girl), by laughing at her.

Here the accumulation of crises hints at the way George has been positioned as recalcitrant while enduring, or living through, his grief. Returning to school for semester two, coordinators noticed a change in him straight away, but did he?

JW: Have you noticed any change in yourself?

G: Um.

JW: It's a big thing for a Year 9 boy to be put in this position of being you know to think about going out at the end of the year. Have you

G: Yeh.
JW: how, h-how do bear, up, with that? How do you carry that along with you?
G: Um . . . try not to think about, heh.
JW: You try not to think about it.
G: Yeh but obviously you can't help that because yeh but um . . . I'm not really sure, I . . . yeh just gradually try not to think about it and like, just lay back, and do my work and not get into so much trouble . . . as I used to you know.

During this time, George and his parents investigated alternative schools and the issue of the facial hair dragged on.

JW: Been told to shave?
G: Yeh that's 'cause a part of my contract but, 'cause, with, my grandma passing, it's, sort of out of respect and stuff to not shave for forty days.
JW: Is it?
G: Yeh, and I didn't shave for forty days but, sort of a little thing in our family, we wanted to take it to the three month, right? And like, obviously I (might not want?) to shave
JW: Mm.
G: like not for all of it to come off, but, like a little bit of facial hair
JW: Mm.
G: and like even if I keep it trimmed or whatever so I have a little facial hair for out of respect
JW: Mm.
G: because normally for us you're not really meant to shave, at all, but I'm sha-but I just want to.

The coordinators, however, insisted that he shave it off:

G: [. . .] So they told me to shave it all off. So I shaved it all off and, I was pretty annoyed that I had to shave it all off 'cause I wanted it out of respect for my grandmother
JW: Mm.
G: and um, [. . .] now it's starting to grow back and um, again they want me to shave it off but there's only a week left out of that three month.
JW: Oh right.
G: So he-I want to ask (the coordinator) I know he'll say "No" but . . . um if I can just keep it till then next week and then I'll shave it off 'cause I want it out of respect [. . .]

Looking back over the year, it was clear where George's priorities lay:

G: [. . .] we've been with my grandma, you know just trying to get
JW: Mm.
G: most of the time that we can with her that she had left
JW: Mm.
G: and I, I knew I had work to do and I knew I had assignments to do as well
JW: Mm.
G: but . . . for me, they they didn't know because I wanted to be with my grandma, wanted to spend time with her, and stuff like that, and, and s-after school we (?) I wanted to stay with my grandma [. . .] because we had an idea when like the doctors had an idea but the idea was more later but she you know she went closer
JW: Yeh.
G: before she was ready or whatever
JW: Yeh.
G: and . . . it dad felt like saying to (the Principal) like, wouldn't care about the schoolwork at the moment because, we had, something more important than that
JW: Mm, mm.
G: but if we say that to (the Principal) he's just going to think that we can't even tell, we we couldn't really tell any of the teachers or whatever because they'd probably just think, "Oh" you know, "he's only just saying that as a" . . . as a excuse or whatever but . . . me and dad didn't really . . . not not care but like didn't really take any notice of what the teachers and stuff were saying because we wanted to spend time [. . .] and I wanted to spend time with my grandma which was like a mum to me so . . .
JW: Mm.
G: I didn't care what the school said had to say about it.
JW: Mm.
G: I put family before anything else, so
JW: Mm.
G: Yeh.
JW: So that, you're telling me that was pretty much your concern all through the first half of the year.
G: That, that was basically my whole concern for the whole year.
JW: The whole year.
G: This whole year
JW: Mm.
G: and a bit of last year because we started to find out but . . . yeh.

Clearly George regards himself – positions himself, and is no doubt positioned by family members – as dutiful and loving grandson and son in a discourse of Greek Orthodoxy, revealing contradictions and tensions between it and the discourses that constitute and sustain the normative school. Furthermore, in not wanting to appear to be seeking sympathy nothing had been said to teachers and so emotions aroused in George were confined to family and close friends. I was only the second teacher he told after the event, and in two discussions prior to that there had been no indication of what was taking place in the family. Now, however, he was prepared to talk and admit his feelings. Seeing grief in other family members he observed casually: "I'm just there by myself and think about it and you know have a little cry to myself and stuff, and um yeh . . . ."

LOSS

In Term three, having been moved to a new Form (which he disliked), Kevin's confrontations with teachers and coordinators came to a head. During this time he went to live with Gerster's family and had little contact with his own. He was periodically absent, flouting rules regarding late arrival, but joined the chaplain's group dealing with loss and talked with other counsellors. He was reported as being disruptive in Form assemblies and classes, on one occasion jumping in and out of the windows during a detention. His beanie,[8] which he wore constantly in contravention of the uniform policy, became a focus for coordinators' attention and he refused to hand it over in a number of confrontations until threatened with the Principal's intervention. He was removed from class for three days internal suspension (as there was no parental home for him to stay at), failed to attend detentions after school and refused to hand over a "water bomb"[9] more than once. Then at the end of term he interrupted a year level assembly.

I was not present at this assembly and will reconstruct it through the words of a coordinator and students who were there. The immediate cause of Kevin's intervention, according to him, was the removal from school (by his parents), of X, the close friend of Kevin, George, and Gerster who had steadfastly refused to join them in this study. According to the coordinator, Kevin arrived on time and asked her if he could give a farewell speech for a mate who was leaving. Some weeks before, a group of students had rehearsed and performed a farewell for a friend leaving school, and now Kevin wanted to do the same. As there had been no parental notification of X's departure, the coordinator declined Kevin's request, adding that if she received definite news of X's departure Kevin could prepare a farewell and it would be considered. At this, Kevin "stormed off and sat down . . . he was . . . angry." The assembly went ahead and at the end Kevin stood up, "said his piece" and, pointing down from where he stood in the tiered seats to coordinators at the front, said accusingly "It's all their fault!" As students were leaving, an Assistant Principal took him from the assembly and subsequently he was suspended, or, in the words of the coordinator, "eventually really didn't come back."

Asked whether this outburst was out of character for Kevin, the coordinator indicated surprise that it had happened after speaking to her because "(she) had built up quite a reasonable relationship" with him, a fact acknowledged by welfare staff. They had, as she said in reference to his family situation, "literally shared the box of tissues." Almost immediately, she recalled, Kevin's demeanor seemed to indicate that he knew he had "blown it . . . I think he realised then that he'd actually bitten the hand that fed him . . . ." Later, as he was being led by coordinators to the front of the school to be taken home, he noticed me glance up from my desk and seemed embarrassed, even sorrowful, somehow trapped.

Two months later I asked Gerster, George, and Robbo (15, Anglo-Australian and openly defiant), to recall major incidents throughout the year. Kevin's last stand in assembly was instantly recalled in the broader context of their mutual friend, X, having left the school.

JW: [. . .] What are the big stories this year in Year 9?
Gerster: Oh X leaving.
G: Mm [. . .] That was a shock. He come to school one day, like one day you're talking to him and the next day like "Hey, I'm going (away)" and that.
Gerster: Yeh. Yeh I remember that. I like he rung me up like during the night [. . .] he's like "Oh I'm going (away)" and I thought this is another crap X story and you know and anyway he comes over and he's like all upset and everything and like shit an' then an' then I went to school the next day with him, school kicked us out (chuckles).

They had come, out of uniform, with their friend to help him collect his things, but had been told to leave. In George's words, the coordinators "were being tight arses that day [. . .] when X came to get all his stuff." Robbo recalled the assembly:

R: [. . .] then Schnapper stood up in assembly [. . .] and goes "Ah oh I'd just like to draw your attention that X's gone" [. . .] And then he goes "If you want to blame anyone blame them," pointing at the coordinators
JW: Weren't you there?
G: No, I wasn't there. I missed it.
R: Oh it was so funny
G: I walk in and like . . . oh OK, everyone's gone a bit funny. I walked in you know I thought I had something stuck on my back or something like [. . .] I was late for assembly. I walked in and like OK shit (chuckles).

R: Oh it was so funny.
JW: I've never seen a thing like that before.
R: No, no (I haven't either?) [. . .] it was funny (laughter, especially George).

What was immediately clear was that the boys missed their friend and they believed that somehow the school in the persons of their coordinators was to blame for X's leaving. Speculation concerning reasons for his departure lie outside the terms of this study, but what can be said is that the boys who were the subjects of this study were just some of the 180 or so boys in Year 9 who constituted a tumultuous throng and that their experiences, while not common to all, were, in an everyday sense, in no way unique. Over the course of this group interview, in a torrent of stories about their lives out of, as much as in school, their empathy and support for each other and for X and other friends was constantly illustrated. More than that, Gerster later revealed how bereft he was at his friend's departure as he truanted for days at a time, not seeing any point in attending. In this and later discussions these boys made it clear that the school had failed to recognize their sense of loss, had failed them in not recognizing what they saw as a need to publicly express their loss and had punished Kevin as well as them not only by imposing due process implacably but by seeming to be so indifferent.

TROUBLE AND FUN

The last of the boys regarded by coordinators as disaffected to join the study (Otto), did so towards the end of Year 9. He had been absent for long periods earlier in the year and while his mother was eager for him to participate, it had taken three months for him to finally commit. By the end of first term in Year 10 we had met only once and in a group discussion with Robbo and Gerster, who were by now used to our meetings, his tentativeness in answering questions was occasionally made very clear. For example, after a detailed discussion of a recent event which led to his suspension, he alone of all the boys in the study turned my questions back on me:

O: Can I ask you something? Why out of everyone did you choose us three?
JW: Because it well it was in the initial thing I said to you. I was looking for boys who probably weren't enjoying school . . . who were probably having difficulties.
Robbo: I'm having a *great time* (his emphasis).
JW: Yeh that's the thing, that surprises me but probably having the diffic-

Robbo:	No I'm not.
JW:	I mean if you get suspended or you, you know you're in trouble or you're sent out, then, you know, your work's probably pretty ordinary, or you know you (?)
O:	(? Never said anything like that?).
JW:	So that
O:	You get the impression that
JW:	They're the sort of boys
O:	But you get the impression when somebody gets suspended they're not enjoying school
JW:	Yeh, well I would have thought that, but what I'm finding is that a lot of you actually enjoy school because it's where your mates are and it's a
Robbo:	That's pretty much right.
JW:	social set-up
O:	Yeh it is.
JW:	But it's the other side, it's the official side, it's the learning side, the behaviour side that is often going wrong. I'm interested to hear why that is
Robbo:	*I hate this school!* (with great emphasis).
O:	Not a bad answer, Mr Whelen.

Otto's insistence on getting a credible answer that did not in any way cast aspersions on him and the other boys had opened a space for Robbo to suddenly and emphatically interject after earlier suggesting sarcastically what he felt about the school ("I'm having a *great time*"). In amongst the bravado and bonhomie, Robbo had asserted a sense of selfhood as if it were a refuge, a safe but hidden place from which to speak. George had done the same when speaking of his grief as had Kevin when he hijacked the assembly. It was also something that happened once rapport was established in discussions, especially group discussions, but rarely at the same level of emotional intensity. In contrast, their constant and unrelenting positioning by teachers as combative, disaffected, and difficult conferred on them an identity they rejected in often bitter encounters.

The bitterness – even hatred – displayed on such occasions contrasted remarkably with the enjoyment the boys said they sometimes found in being so positioned and certainly in retrospect they not only found much that amused them but revealed how their discourse of friendship was so mutually supportive and so profoundly important in constituting subjectivities.[10]

Just prior to George and Kevin's crises at the end of second term, after the midyear exams, Kevin mentioned that because one of his teachers liked him he was doing "alright" in that subject. Our discussion with George and Gerster took up his comment:

JW:	How can you tell if a teacher likes you?
G:	They pay more attention towards yuh. Like say 'cause in Woodwork Mr Edwards, you know he helps me out
K:	He's mad
G:	an' everything, right. An' see if I ask Miss, ah... say Mr Smith, you know, he goes, his answers are basically, "Yes," "No," (said very deadpan) there's no explanation.
All:	(sounds of agreement).
Gerster:	Yeh, I think teachers can pay a lot of attention towards you if you are a troublemaker.
K:	Yeh (stifled laugh).
JW:	Sort of works both ways doesn't it?
Gerster:	Mm, not, but not that way. Respect (?)
K:	Not that we respect them or anything, so
JW:	Well... sorry, work on that. You know, you get, you get attention from teachers so you say he likes you or she likes you, ah or you don't get much, she doesn't like you but um you also get attention for
Gerster:	Being disruptive.
JW:	What were you going to say, Schnapper?
K:	[...] It came on like in some respects you pay more attention to others because they're oh as much as you can say teachers like us all they don't.
JW:	Mm.
All:	(sounds of assent).
K:	You can't convince us to believe they like us.
JW:	Mm.
Gerster:	But, but you know, you got to deal with it I mean they're people exactly like, you can't expect them
K:	to like us, yeh
Gerster:	You know, as they can't expect us to like them, but (even more?), like, we'd, we'd like like them to like us sometimes. They'd like it if we liked them as well, it'd be much easier for everyone though, but, it's not how it works out a bit.
(?):	Yeh.
G:	You see, some teachers, if they know you're a troublemaker, they'll tend some like Mr what's it, Mr – oh I can't remember his name. I had him last year for Maths um, he paid more attention towards me because I was, basically the troublemaker, and he thought if he helped me, I wouldn't be talking or
JW:	Mm.
G:	or disruptive or maybe making trouble in class so he helped more, sorry, he helped me more, then some um other kids was you know they were troublemakers and they sort of knew what they were doing because I didn't know that much you

	know thought maybe if you know I paid attention towards him he won't disrupt my class or something like that. Some teacher think of it like that but some others think "Oh he's a troublemaker," you know
K:	Stick him out two minutes into the classroom
G:	Yeh.
K:	They just don't deal with it
G:	Even if you don't do anything they say, you know, if you go oh you know, drop short (?) drawing or whatever, they'll think "Oh now he's going to do it for the whole class so get out" Then you're basically out there
K:	For the rest of the lesson, just chillin'
Gerster:	It's so much better when like if you're a troublemaker or something and teachers actually give you an opportunity to like improve on yourself.
K:	They notice more.
Gerster:	Mm, and they don't, they don't like the cold shoulder like, they'll give you a chance to get better an' I've noticed like (?) some of my mates and stuff . . . yeh, yeh.

In this lengthy passage the boys show considerable insight into what goes with being positioned as disruptive: the complex, even subtle emotional probing that goes into detecting whether one is being liked or not, and the deconstruction of teachers' motives. Clearly also the boys position teachers they are thinking of as more or less naïve and transparent and exercise a degree of agency discussed earlier in terms of resistance (see Chapter 3), but which perhaps ought more usefully to be thought of as a discursive assertion of other selfhood made possible by the momentary dominance of their discourse of contempt. Indeed, their daily experience of school often seems to be an endless rehearsal or repetition of this defence of selves known only to them and their friends.

But how premeditated are such moments? Having been recently put out of class, Kevin replied:

K:	[. . .] Um . . . it's hard to explain sort of, 'cause um you know what's going to happen
JW:	Mm.
K:	but you can't really do anything about it unless you don't want to be
G:	See if you argue back with the teacher, you're just more likely to get into trouble, there's no real point arguing but some, sometimes even with me like you know teacher will say "Get out of the class" and I haven't done anything so you might
K:	Yeh so you argue your point.
G:	Then, then ah you argue your point and then you get sent

	to the coordinator and you get in more crap with the coord, more trouble with the coordinators an' when it's not even your problem.
JW:	What's it, what's it like when you get to that point, when you get to the coordinators? I've seen all of you one way or another at various times in the coordinators and
Unclear:	(?)
K:	Yeh exactly. You just think that they're dumb and they're wrong and then that justifies what you do because you know you're right.
G:	Mhm.
Gerster:	Oh, when I go to the coordinators, doesn't, I don't, I don't get stressed out or anything.
K:	Exactly, you take it on the chest.
Gerster:	Sometimes there are days when you just get in the class and you think "I don't really want to be here."
K:	Mm.
Gerster:	You just want to get kicked out.
K:	Mm.
Gerster:	(?) two minutes or whatever.
JW:	Are there many of those days? (?) [...]
K:	You sort of turn up into class and then you realise and then you know what you're going to do and you just
G:	You don't really want
K:	what the teacher's like on the day
Gerster:	Yeh on the, on the way to school you have no intention of what the day's going to be like until you actually get there
K:	Yeh.
Gerster:	and your whole experience is like, *god!* (great emphasis).
JW:	What, the first time someone tells you to tuck your shirt in, or
K:	Tuckin' your shirt in is not too bad 'cause as soon as they turn their head in the other direction they don't pay any notice of you so you just keep walking.
JW:	(chuckles)
Gerster:	Yeh, but, it just kind of, as soon as you get into working you know, *oh man!* (great emphasis).

If Kevin had some idea how he would behave in certain classes, Gerster claimed not to, but at the same time sensed the inevitability of conflict. For each boy it was a familiar path, encapsulated in a brief moment in Robbo's experience early in Year 10. At the time I was teaching across the corridor from the incident. His teacher came over to my room, thinking I was his coordinator, and, clearly upset, asked me to discipline him. As I was not his coordinator I declined and suggested she take it up with the Year 10 office. Robbo and I momentarily exchanged blank glances. He later recalled the incident in the context of hating the school:

JW:	Tell us about the time you were put out in the corridor earlier on . . . Remember earlier on? I was teaching in a class over the road, you were
R:	Oh Mrs Berkowitz, as soon as you walk in the door, "Sit over there!" "Nah." I hate how they just move you as soon as you walk into the door. I like to have my own choice about where I want to sit.
Gertster:	I used to have Mrs Berkowitz [. . .] I got sent out seven lessons in a row once, huh! [. . .]
JW:	So what did you do?
R:	Oh, she goes . . . "No wait!" Alright, I sat down orright, I remember it now. I sat down, she goes um, she's talking, and she goes "Get out!" So I get out and she goes "Nah sit back here!" an' I'm like "No you sent me out I'm going out now." I sat outside. [. . .] I'm just like "What the hell?" Just leave it, an' I don't like her [. . .]

George also recalled a composite of similar moments as a discussion turned to how the boys claimed to be able to "crack" certain teachers:

G:	But like, some teachers, they, give you – I don't know if I should say – they give you the irrits, right?
JW:	Any language you like.
K:	Oh, yeh (chuckles).
G:	Um, they like they give you the shits after a little while because say like teachers kept nagging at you like "George do this," "George do that," you know, "George write with a blue pen," "George write with a red pen"
K:	Yeh (chuckles).
G:	with your margins, stuff like that. I mean little stuff like that I can, your pens.
JW:	Mm.
G:	It's not really going to affect your education if you write in the wrong coloured pen or whatever, and little things like that can annoy someone
JW:	Mm.
G:	and I know, I know it annoys me
JW:	Mm.
G:	and you just give it back to them.
JW:	Mm.

G: Like if the teacher doesn't backchat you or not like, you know

JW: Mm.

G: if you back, backchat a teacher then they you know keep on going on with you know oh "George keep quiet" you know, "You soosh, sh, sh" then you tend to give, or I tend to it back on 'em more, but the teachers, if I backchat the teacher and the teacher just goes "Orright" and leaves it at that, or if they keep on, but if they keep going on, then I'll be right.

JW: Mm.

Gerster: I love, I love arguing sometimes.

K: Yeh I know, it's great. I'm an antagonist. [. . .]

Here all three boys illustrate how conflict creates a space in which identity is discursively constructed: certainly those teachers and coordinators who had most to do with them seemed to recognize this. Near the end of Year 9, Gerster recalled an incident that illustrated what he meant by gaining enjoyment from arguing. He began by mentioning a teacher's comments in his midyear report:

Gerster: [. . .] She said that I was pretty much, really bad, and she, doesn't like me in the class, and ah it's fair enough.

JW: Um, she's the one you get under the skin of a few times, occasionally, don't you?

Gerster: Yeh, I've gotten better but um, she's she says I'm to me I was thick in the head the other day and I'm getting annoyed at her, so I was kind of pretty bad to her next day as well, day after.

JW: What did you say?

Gerster: Oh, oh I got moved and I asked her something, and um, I didn't think it was that bad a question, I think it was about the excursion or something [. . .]

JW: Do you remember your actual words?

Gerster: Um, it was, I don't remember my actual words it was about swimming at the excursion, 'cause we were going to Port Phillip Bay

JW: Mhm.

Gerster: and she said "Are you that thick in the head that you can't understand that" or something an' I said it, I said "If you think I'm thick in the head" you know "now's the time to tell me," you know, and she's like "No, I, I don't think you're thick in the head" and I, and I'm like you know, well, you know, "You said I was in a way," yeh.

JW: So you had a talk like that in class, did you?

Gerster: Yeh.

JW:	Mm.
Gerster:	Kind of gets her worked up because all the kids start laughing, yeh.
JW:	Right, right. OK. And, and she just dealt with that, 'n let it pass?
Gerster:	Oh, well the next day, was, we both held a bit of a grudge I guess...
JW:	Give me details [...]
Gerster:	Oh, it was just like, as soon as I got into class it was like "You have to stay behind because you haven't done this notice" and I got annoyed at that because I didn't bring back the notice, which I should have brought back this morning – damn! Oh god – ah (chuckles) and so she got angry and then I got angry and then 'cause I was angry I had to stay in, and it, it was like back and forward and um she started saying how no-one wants to hear me holding up the class... all that, stuff you know like
JW:	Mm.
Gerster:	an' I'm like oh you know... I think I should have my fair say (?)
JW:	Yeh.
Gerster:	and, "You're continuing with it as well as I am so we're both holding up the class"
JW:	Right.
Gerster:	and she... was under the idea that I started the argument, yeh.
JW:	And what were the other kids doing while this was going on?
Gerster:	Oh just sitting there... sitting there.
JW:	Just watching?
Gerster:	Some were laughing.
JW:	Yeh. Mm, mm.

Robbo also described how getting into trouble could become a site in which not only might identity be constructed but how in challenging that identity a sense of selfhood might be affirmed. Knowing his reputation for being difficult, he distinguished between one teacher he thought understood him, and others:

JW:	What does a teacher have to do to show you that they understand you?
R:	Well, most teachers when they look at me an' they see a student like the way I acted they just presume that I'm that sort of person. Mr – doesn't do that.
JW:	How do you think teachers see you then?
R:	Meaning?

JW: Well you know. You say when most teachers look at you they think you're going to behave in a certain way.
R: Yeh [...]
JW: How do they look at you?
R: Like they, they think I'm going to, make trouble that lesson and I'm just sitting there waiting... you know.
JW: Is it something about reputation
R: Yeh.
JW: or something about your appearance, or what?
R: Reputation.
JW: Reputation.
R: Yeh.

Thus "reputation" emerged from relations with teachers who did not understand him. Asked to give any details he could recall about incidents in which his reputation might have been gained, he went on:

R: Like you, you know how it just starts up when you talk
JW: Yeh.
R: then it just gets worse like, then you, then I started to swear.
JW: Right.
R: Then it just got worse [...] Then I'd just go to the coordinators and it would just get worse there.

Recalling a specific incident, he continued, pausing briefly to reassure himself that I would not revert to an authority figure:

R: [...] she 'cause she used to go "You're a stupid little boy"
JW: Right.
R: and start saying all that... Am I allowed to swear?
JW: Yeh.
R: Oh well, I used to tell her to "Get f***ed. It's not right, you can't call me that."
JW: In class?
R: Yeh 'cause I got really annoyed... yeh.
JW: Right... Oh well she wouldn't have been too happy with that I guess.
R: Nuh. Well I couldn't help it [...] I just get annoyed easily.

In spite of advice from welfare staff, things were not much better for Robbo in Science, but as in Gerster's narrative earlier, Robbo could occasionally turn conflict to his advantage:

JW: And does anyone else in the class get into much trouble?
R: Depends [...] Tran does, at times.

JW: Do th-does someone get into trouble just to sort of support you? Like if you get into trouble first does someone else come in and support you?
R: Tran sometimes.
JW: See I reckon you and Gerster were a bit like that last year until it got sorted out.
R: Yeh.
JW: Well is it like that this year?
R: A little bit.
JW: Mm . . . So . . . so Tran might look at you getting into trouble and saying, say to himself
R: Helping me sort of
JW: Yeh.
R: Yeh.

In a separate interview in which he claimed to have been "out of trouble for ages," Gerster referred somewhat nostalgically to much the same *modus operandi* in getting into trouble. In his own laid back way he had been trying to "step up a bit" as he knew he would be going on to Year 12 and would possibly be the first of three brothers to gain his VCE:

JW: [. . .] Is it different, to be out of trouble?
Gerster: Yeh it's good. You kind of want to get in trouble sometimes (We both chuckle and laugh).
JW: Why's that?
Gertser: 'Cause all you mates are like getting in trouble and you're the one sitting out and you know. Everyone's relying on you to get in trouble like.
            (JW laughs; Gerster chuckles).
JW: It tests the friendship a bit, does it?
Gerster: Yeh, oh like yeh (chuckles) yeh it's good, yeh. But we all, like it's better to stay out of trouble in the end.

The change that Gerster is referring to here will be discussed in the next chapter, but for the moment what is important is his recognition that conflict is constitutive of identity and that whatever power teachers think they have in such moments may be countered or undermined by the discursive production of friendship and, if necessary, contempt.

In these excerpts it is clear that fun often comes at a price for these boys. Moments of sadness – even great sadness – of anger, frustration, and incomprehension may be countered as students attempt to construct mutual empathy and enjoyment, often at considerable cost to the teacher, but the stakes are high for the boys too. Selves are put in question; known selves are daily challenged and certainty is threatened in the fragmented and uncertain experience of selfhood in class.

EXAMINATIONS

It is by now a commonplace observation that schools perform a surveillant function for society at large, and in particular for parents and potential employers (Broadfoot, 1986). Much emphasis has been given in this chapter to the normalizing function of the school through observation, recording and the attempted imposition of techniques of subjection by way of punishment (c.f. Foucault, 1991: 178). In making its normalizing judgments and in developing a hierarchy of observation, Hillside High School reveals how "ordinary individuality – the everyday individuality of everybody – (that was once) below the threshold of description" (ibid. 191) has become the domain of a disciplinary power that aims to make the unruly tractable. Disciplinary power in the sense in which Foucault uses the term is exemplified in the examination – whether medical, psychiatric, or pedagogic – which is said to be "exercised through its invisibility; (but which) at the same time . . . imposes on those whom it subjects a principle of compulsory visibility" (ibid. 187). Thus, if the source of the validity of normalizing judgments in the school is, or appears to be, anonymous, ubiquitous, objective, or universally agreed (e.g., on the basis of credentials), then power and knowledge have coalesced in such a way as to produce examiners and those who are examined. For Foucault, the significance of the examination, therefore, can hardly be overstated:

> The examination combines the techniques of an observing hierarchy and those of a normalizing judgement. It is a normalizing gaze, a surveillance that makes it possible to qualify, to classify and to punish. It established over individuals a visibility through which one differentiates them and judges them.
>
> (Foucault, 1991; 184)[11]

It is therefore in the practices of subjection required by tests and examinations and in the records they generate (e.g., reports of progress and achievement), that an important part of the apparatus of social and institutional control is to be found (Hoskin, 1979; A. Hargreaves, 1986: 214; Ball, 1990a; Meadmore, 1997).

While testing within subjects at Hillside commences early in Year 7, formal examinations are introduced midway through Year 9 and again near the end of the year. These are meant to focus student attention on learning and to ensure preparation for testing in the senior school as well as in the final-year state-wide exams. The formal curriculum imposes a certain structure on work that must be completed before the examinations, and teachers are expected to ensure students revise their work and devise revision timetables for study at home. Time is given during Level assemblies to advise and help students organize their time and set goals and students are given a specially prepared guide to studying for exams.

Among other suggestions urging them to look after themselves, they are advised to have a quiet place where they can study; to be comfortable – not too warm or too cold; to take a 5-minute break every 20 or 30 minutes; to stay fit by eating healthy meals and getting exercise and to get enough sleep. Tips for actual revision such as reading over class notes and relevant sections of textbooks and practising writing essays within a set time are also emphasized. In spite of the care teachers are expected to take in revision and preparation, students are advised to regard the examinations as little more than "common tests," not much longer than a normal class period. Formal classes are suspended during the week in which exams are held and students, who must still wear the school uniform properly at all times, come and go depending on their exam timetable. When entering an exam room, students are expected to be quiet and, especially when doing an exam, not to communicate with one another.

On any exam day, students mill around outside their rooms noisily discussing their prospects and performing their anxiety. On being allowed to enter the rooms, bags and notes are left behind, students are ushered to desks where exam papers have been set out and soon enough, quiet descends so that all exams may start on time together.

Kevin's anxiety at the approaching midyear exams in Year 9 has been mentioned in Chapter 5. At the time, which was early in the school year, Kevin was under the impression that exam results at Year 9 had much the same consequences as those of final Year 12 exams. Drawing on his reading of *Looking for Alibrandi*, he expressed concern about how so much seemed to depend on passing exams "at such an early age," and that consequently, exams seemed to him to be a "huge" hurdle. Immediately after the midyear exams, by which time his and George's problems were entrenched, he, George and Gerster discussed their experience of the exams:

JW:	[. . .] how did you approach them, how did they go?
Gerster:	Oh. Well I approached them with um not so much care, ah I didn't put heaps into 'em, more into subjects like I wanted to do better in than others, like English, or Maths and um Science (?) Um, and I really had no intention of passing with flying colours but um every, everything else I, I did as good as I should have (?) but that's about it. What about you?
K:	Um I just thought I'd like play it by ear and um (?) so I wouldn't suggest to anyone else that they do that but um, yeh it was alright. The exams weren't really that hard, but um, you know.
JW:	Did any of you do much study? (At this point Kevin looked distinctly sheepish, something only I noticed).
K; G:	Nah.

Gerster:	Enough, like, most of my studies um like making my cheat sheet like, you know, and um, I didn't do study for Maths. That's about it.
JW:	Did you, were the exams a big hurdle for you?
Gerster:	Um . . . really stressed.
K:	Yeh, oh ah if you let them worry you it'll probably get to you but if you just sort of said "Oh well."
JW:	Sit back, relax.
K:	(chuckles) Yeh. Like I studied about ten minutes before each exam on like, some questions, and like, yeh.
JW:	Was it as big a hurdle as you thought it would be?
K; G:	Nuh.
Gerster:	I, I was thinking exams, really stressful, kind of
JW:	When did the stress really kick in?
K and G:	When it started. When you're sitting in the exams.
JW:	Yeh but you might have started studying ten minutes before but when did you get stressful long before that?
Gerster:	Um, I got, when I heard the idea of exams I thought "Oh god," you know, like . . . "This is, it's huge," but then, when I got there and sat down, like I was in the hall and there was lots of people, but um, you kind of just think, it's just like one big test.

George agreed, but did not add that he had nevertheless stayed home during the Maths exam. A month later it was clear that Kevin's approach to being examined had not changed when, on visiting his class to deliver a message to another student, I found the class doing a test, but not Kevin. He was just sitting back, grinning.

By the second semester exams later in the year, Kevin had gone, George was contemplating having to leave and Robbo thought he was on the brink of expulsion. Here George, Gerster, and Robbo discuss the end of year exams:

Gerster:	I did alright because my counsellor told me stuff to do an'
JW:	Mm.
Gerster:	I'd like . . . learn (?)
JW:	Mm, mm.
R:	Oh, I remember the . . . oh who was it, was it you that kept on like the last exam the kid that didn't have any tissues? Actually it was me!
G:	Yeh that was you!
All:	(great laughter).
R:	Yeh I remember I was sitting next to this guy (?)

G *(saying it quite deliberately, slower than usual):*	Every time we'd sit in the hall, right, everything you do in the hall, like when there's do in the hall, like when there's everyone's dead quiet, you can hear everything. All of a sudden you hear this (makes nasal inhalation noise).
All:	(great laughter).
G:	Right? I was like oh OK, fair enough, it was just a little one, an' he goes (louder noise)
All:	(laughter).
G:	Oh my god he's full of this
All:	(laughter).
G:	an' everyone would look up and like disturb 'em from thinking. I was like I had the *best* (his emphasis) answer to put into the History thing (Robbo laughs loudly).
G:	right? An' all of a sudden I could hear 'im starting up so I was
All:	(laughter)
G:	I made sure I had it in my head, and I was thinking he was going to do a big one (makes the noise) an' like c***, I forgot all my f***in'
R:	(laughing) oh yeh.
G:	I forgot all this shit I had to write down.

Gerster has let slip a reference to a counsellor his parents have hired for him outside school but his drift towards a more conscientious approach to study in no way inhibits Robbo or George or threatens to destabilize their friendship. Indeed, it appears that George also has made an effort to prepare for his History exam. Together they reconstruct a memorable moment which leads on to others:

R:	Remember when someone called Schnapper's phone?
G:	Yeh! (claps his hands).
R:	I called Schnapper's phone during um the exam an' it went off.
JW:	(chuckles).
R:	It was in the hall.
G:	No that was me as well, that was me.
R:	Yeh (laughs).
G:	I was sit-he was sitting there, like exactly where Gerster is and I'm sitting the exact same distance or whatever, I'm sitting there an' I forgot to put my phone on silent, I'm sitting there doing my test an' all of a sudden whet's 'er name walks past an 'um [. . .]
R:	Oh yeh yeh and then your phone goes *zzzzzzz*
G:	No, my phone went off like de na na (sings call tone), and I'm like
R:	Oh yeh (laughing)
G:	Oh I'm so shat off I'm like (slaps thigh).

The discussion moves to phone management during exams and George recalls another incident which led to a confrontation with a teacher wanting to take his phone:

R: Remember, remember in the Woodwork exam?
G: Mm (sings call tone) Ellie's phone went off an' the teacher thought it was mine [. . .] I was wiping my nose, I had my hand in my pocket 'cause I finished, orright?
R: An' he thought it was you.
G: An' he thought it was me an' he said "Get outside!" an' I'm like "What for?" "Get outside!" "Why do I have to get outside? I haven't done anything plus it's cold outside."
All: (laughter)
G: An' then he goes "No, get outside now!" an' I'm like alright we'll see what happens when we get outside. He goes "Give me your phone"
R: (laughs).
G: and I'm "I haven't got a phone." An' then he says "I can see it in your pocket" and I go "Oh alright" an' I pulled it out.
R: An' he tried to snatch it off you an' you've gone "Woo!" (sarcastically).
G: Yeh, no he tried to snatch it like he had it like, I'll show you, I'll just use the phone (demonstrating) right, he had it like that, like say you're about to grab it, right
JW: Mm.
G: I had an' all of a sudden I just went voom! Like that (makes snatching motion)
JW: Mm, mm.
G: an' that's when I hit myself in the head.
JW: Mm.
All: (laughter)
G: [. . .] an' then um he goes "Give me it back now. I won't take it off you" so I gave it to him an' I was about to snatch it because I didn't trust him an' he goes "Oh there's your phone rang" an' I go "No it didn't. Check, there's no missed calls on the screen."

And so the confrontation continued, and in the remembering and the telling not only is their friendship again confirmed, but the normative school's rituals and agents of surveillance are discursively constituted as sites of play. Indeed, such moments seem to illustrate how far they were from identifying with the paragons of academic achievement in their midst, how irrelevant was thought of membership of such a community and how improbable it was that they would discern any sense of care for their welfare. Looking back on the year, and given their daily confrontations with teachers and hostility to subjects they perceived as irrelevant it is doubtful that any of them had sufficient material to revise for exams, let alone revise thoroughly. None was able to show me any files of work let alone evidence of complete and thorough work, despite numerous requests. Robbo had no time for History and Geography, found Science too demanding and showed no enthusiasm for English. Gerster liked English, especially poetry, but complained about the way he was being taught, whereas Kevin enjoyed English immensely until he had to change class, and even read his first term novel in three days. George found it all difficult by midyear, but enjoyed Woodwork, as did Otto and Robbo. Otto, who had stayed away for weeks at a time early in Year 9, found all subjects too episodic and admitted he had no notes worth studying. As for how to balance the demands of study with advice on maintaining health and fitness, Robbo said he never had breakfast and Kevin (whose eating habits, as I have remarked, were a worry to welfare staff), was a heavy smoker. The idea that they should pause every 20 or 30 minutes while studying and do some exercise or have a warm drink, let alone ensure that their notes were complete, seems to have been understood as advice for someone else.

CONCLUSION

If the disciplinary and normative technologies of the school are represented in assemblies, classrooms, and examinations by buildings, spaces, reports, and above all by teachers, it certainly does not follow that the power to report, to define, to label, and to construct identities will be uncontested. In the daily interactions (or fields of power), in which identities are contextually constructed and negotiated, students have been shown to at least occasionally have the upper hand. The subject – both of the teachers but more particularly of the boys – has been shown to be a site of dispute and ambiguity, where selves are constituted creatively; sometimes desperately, sometimes violently, sometimes with humour, in often unequal contests. The question of who will prevail and precisely what is at stake hangs over the clash of discourses. For these boys the "I" and "you" of discourse are less about ascribed identity and more about selfhood – the selves they take themselves to be and represent to others. In moments of grief, loss, uncertainty, confusion or threat, friendship sustained by a discourse of contempt, as I have shown, offers validation, safe haven and for each may confirm a self of last resort.

8 The Student Body

INTRODUCTION

In this chapter I move tentatively from an admittedly disembodied view of the boys who are the subjects of this study to a recognition of their blatantly physical presence in school. This distinction has to some extent been a consequence of my focus on the analysis of discursive positioning. In a brief critique of social constructionist accounts of gender and sexuality, Connell (1995) noted that the body tends to be theorized as "a canvas to be painted, a surface to be imprinted . . ." (ibid. 50), but "(with) so much emphasis on the signifier, the signified tends to vanish" (ibid. 50–51). In other words, due largely to Cartesian dualism, he observed that "bodies (have gone) missing . . . from social theory" (ibid. 59; Burroughs and Ehrenreich, 1993), just as Judith Butler (1993; Salih with Butler, 2004) was placing the materiality of the body in question.

Whereas anthropology has long been interested in the human body, the sociology of the body is relatively recent (Watson and Cunningham-Burley, 2001: 1). On the other hand, the body has long been accepted by cultural theorists as a site of identity and resistance (Hebdidge, 1979),[1] and Haraway (1985) has conjured up striking images of possible bodies in a technologically mediated world. In spite of her subversion of what might count as nature, Connell maintains a distinction between the natural and the social in his notion of body-reflexive practices in which "bodies are objects and agents in the same process" (Connell, 2001: 18). This is especially clear in his discussion of the ways versions of masculinity are socially constituted. "The body (he writes), is inescapable in the construction of masculinity" (Connell, 1995: 56), thus allowing "meaningful bodies and embodied meanings" (ibid. 64); always already material and always sites of meaning. While it is tempting to accept this formulation, it is rather Butler's theorizing of discursive performativity, as I mentioned in Chapter 1, and which Youdell (2003, 2005, 2006a, 2006b) has illustrated so clearly, which has challenged the ontological distinction that sustains Connell's analysis. In this chapter I shall draw attention to embodied subjects, drawing further on Foucault's theorization of how bodies are marked and disciplined by discursive power, and on Butler's notion of performatives. My intention is not to regard the body as a neutral, prediscursive phenomenon but to apprehend it as it embodies ways of being in terms of the discursive, everyday world of Hillside High School (Gough, 2004: 115; Youdell, 2006b: 72).

The subjects of this study are adolescent boys developing a "heterosexual sensibility" indicative of "adolescent peer masculinity" (Connell, 1995: 123; 129). To Connell, a bodily sense of masculinity, evident in what he calls "body-reflexive practices" (ibid. 59–64), is central to adolescents' engagement with masculinities, or, as Butler (1990) observes, to their daily enactment of their masculinity.[2] Among such displays, Whitson (1990) argues, competitive sport allows the demonstration of prowess in aggression, strength, and skill and as such is not only "one of the central sites in the social production of masculinity (but is an) important requirement for status in most adolescent . . . male peer groups" (p. 19). This was confirmed to some extent by Mac an Ghaill (1994) in references to the ways some ethnically differentiated groups of students, occasionally in collaboration with teachers, constructed hierarchies of masculinity at school. But for boys who dislike or show no aptitude for sport, the alternative is "to stake their claims to masculinity" (Whitson, 1990: 19) in other ways such as academic success, physical aggression or sexual conquest (Connell, 1990: 295). In relation to academic success, so far I have shown that if learning is a subjectifying practice, George, Robbo, Otto, and Gerster refuse compliance or at most grant it grudgingly. I have also shown in part that as a subject of disciplinary power and an object of teachers' gaze, these boys' disaffection with their schooling is frequently manifest as a daily confrontational "team game" offering manifold opportunities for masculinizing practices. As such they construct a daily social reality in a forbidden zone, flouting rules and negating teachers' authority in what might be called a search for "embodied autonomy" (Gordon and Lahelma,1996: 304).

As Connell remarks, "concern with the embodiment of social relations brings sociological analysis much closer to the world of everyday experience" (Connell, 2001: 15). To speak of the gaze of teachers in this everyday world and the body-reflexive practices of students is to speak of what is most visible about the human body. In that sense it has been remarked that the visible body – the body surface – may be thought of as a literary or ethnographic text which can be read for evidence of its cultural and social construction (Burroughs and Ehrenreich, 1993). If this seems to return the psycho-biological individual to one side of the skin it nevertheless allows the social self to be located on the symbolic stage of the surface (Turner, 1993: 15; 36). Guillaumin goes further, insisting that the sexed body is entirely constructed, as opposed to given, and as such is constantly in the process of becoming – never finished – as capacities and traits are maintained and cultivated (Guillaumin,

1993: 41). For example, she draws attention to the way men have learnt, from childhood, to maximize their use of space: "Look at (their) arms and legs which extend widely on seats, chair backs, and their open – even brusque – gestures while moving about" (ibid. 50). There will be echoes of this and similar observations in this chapter. "Men manifest the weight of their person in a sort of staging of their own importance" she notes (ibid. 51), to which might be added references to voice and its volume. Furthermore, in commenting on "the playful use of the body" (p. 52), she notes that in learning to fight, many boys "learn not to fear the contact, in fact to experience it as spontaneous and natural" (ibid. 54). Thus, she observes, "the masculine body is constructed to be spontaneously in solidarity with the bodies of other men," a sort of "playful cooperation of the street" learnt and "practiced [sic] by children and adolescents" (ibid. 54).[3]

I move now from what is essentially an emphasis on behavior, action, voice, and gesture in the aforementioned remarks, to the normative school's disciplinary fetish with a discourse of appearance.

UNIFORM(ED) BODIES

Like Kevin, Robbo sometimes found it difficult to get to school on time. "You know how just after the holidays you can't wake up?" he said. Nevertheless he claimed to be on time more often than not, but was ambivalent about putting on the school uniform. Whether he resented being identified as part of the school community or was responding to the licence it gave teachers to speak to him in a certain way about school, such as how he wore his uniform, (or both), remained unclear.

JW: When you look at the uniform in the morning, and you put it on, are you happy to do that? Would you rather have no uniform, or, how do you feel?
[. . .]
R: No uniform.
JW: You don't want uniform. . . .' Cause when I've seen you in your uniform, and you look pretty scruffy (both laugh) . . . but um . . . you know I mean it seems I, I get the impression, tell me if I'm wrong, but I get the impression with your uniform you'd rather be wearing anything else.
R: Yeh.
JW: 'Cause it's you know, your coat's half off or your collar's up and your pants are halfway
R: Yeh.
JW: around your waist
R: Oh well.

JW: but ah
R: I don't wouldn't mind I don't mind wearing it but if I had a choice of wearing something else I would.
JW: Mm.

Robbo was a walking invitation to any teacher to upbraid him about the way he wore his uniform and he knew it, but was totally unconcerned. Like Kevin with his beanie or George with his facial hair or any of his idiosyncratic variations on the uniform – earrings, dyed hair, nonschool cap – Robbo, with his shirt out, coat askew and gelled and spiked hair, looked defiant. Each tended to wear his shirt out at the waist, as did the vast majority of boys, and even when it looked as though shirts were tucked in, they were often merely tucked up under the jumper with a hint of a flap hanging out discreetly over the belt at the front to one side. In this respect, Gerster, in particular looked just like any other boy, and in winter all were inclined to wear a T-shirt under their white school shirt (still often hanging out), again inviting reprimands, especially if it was visible at the neck or was black, or if any words or symbols on the front or back could be read through the shirt.

In Chapter 5 I mentioned the school's uniform and outlined many of the regulations governing its correct wearing. The justification, as I indicated, is to be found in claims to identity and affiliation in the school's prospectus, handbooks, and student planners and its appearance in photographs used more or less as marketing devices (e.g., in the school foyer and in various publications to parents and prospective parents), says much about the symbolic universe of the school. Together with the school song (still, quaintly, incorporating a motto in Latin) referred to in Chapter 6, a house system and a multitude of student leaders known as "captains" or "student representatives" to replace a redundant prefecture, all constitute an expressive order which augments and contributes to the administration of the school (Meadmore and Symes, 1996). In so far as the school uniform is a disciplinary tactic in achieving certain social and pedagogic goals it is indicative of "governmentality" in the sense used by Foucault; that is, as one of a constellation of tactics and techniques by which a population can be known and rendered docile (Foucault, 1978). Thus in its wearing students are not only subjected in terms of homilies of identity and belonging but also by their very embodiment of an ideal. Worn perfectly it validates and valorizes certain subjectivities over others (Meadmore and Symes, 1996: 212) as appearance, posture, comportment, deportment, and even hygiene become the locus of the "micro-physics of power" by which the student body is to be subjected (Foucault, 1991: 26). It is in the transgression of all that is valued in this discourse of the uniform, however, that the disciplinary regime of the school manifests itself (see Youdell, 2006a; McLeod and Yates, 2006: 55). While the school assembly and examination are prime examples of disciplinary mechanisms for administering the school, ensuring the differentiation and normalization of the student population, so also is the school uniform at a daily yet more symbolic level. Here transgression or resistance inscribed in appearance ensures a certain distinction and individuation as the relentless gaze of disciplinary power vested in teachers "compares, differentiates, homogenizes (and) excludes" (Foucault, 1991: 183). Kevin, George, Robbo, and Otto (at least while they are at school), live daily on the receiving end of these techniques.[4]

For example, in Year 8 George had been amenable to wearing the school uniform (at least in part), and in Chapter 6 he described how one indiscretion ("sort of like being a little bit smart" when he "sort of snapped"), led to suspension as a result of a coordinator's surveillance, finding that he "didn't have the right black shoes."

In his answer, by recognizing that "the way I talked back wasn't good, or it wasn't in a nice way," George rehearses the moral precepts encountered in this moment of discipline. Sanitizing his own part (by not recalling the words which weren't "nice"), George gives some credence to the notion of self-discipline and self-correction at the ethical centre of Foucault's principle of panopticism: "the vigilance of intersecting gazes" (Foucault, 1991: 217), of which mine was now but one in the context of this early discussion in which I was trying hard to avoid being positioned, or positioning myself, merely as a friendly teacher who might at any time pass judgment, or reward appropriate responses. In Chapter 9 I will return to the sense of self which moments like this reveal.

It was therefore not surprising that George should say that he was happy enough to wear the school uniform:

G: Um . . . well . . . I don't mind wearing the uniform, right, but like sometimes . . . yeh I mean I'd rather wear casual clothes, instead of the school, but um . . . like when you wear a uniform it makes the school look good an' it makes you look good instead of comin' to school you know in baggy clothes 'n big shoes 'n . . .
JW: Have you been caught out for wearing the wrong uniform?
G: Yeh.
JW: How do you feel when the school cracks down on the uniform?
G: Um . . . like sometimes if you're like wearing all your clothes like all the right clothes but you might have the wrong, well you might have a shirt underneath or you might have you know a different jumper like a sports jacket 'cause you've forgotten your other one at home, like stuff like that, like, it's a bit . . . not like stupid (?) but like it's only a jacket, or it's only a jumper or shirt or something, but if it's like you're wearing totally the wrong stuff, you know, fair enough, you have . . . you might, you'll get in trouble.

Asked if he thought the school went too far in its reaction to breeches of the uniform code, George revealed how variable that response could be and how the terrain of compromise might be negotiated:

G: Um . . . well see, there are some teachers that do and some like sort of depends on the teacher . . . There're like . . . you know, say if it was Miss Jago, like just for instance, she might let you, like she'll let you wear a shirt or, if she sees it she'll just let you do the button up, or, you know, stuff like that or if she sees you wearing a jacket she'll say "Take it off" or, or you know "Find another one from the lost property to put on" or something, but there are some like coordinators that would like (crack up?) and they'll like "Take it off", they'll make it like, wear it an' then get you into trouble, detention for it, but they won't, you know, (make you?) take it off or something, yeh.

For Gerster, in Year 9, the issue of uniform was quite straightforward. If any teacher wanted to do anything about what he wore, he would oblige:

JW: [. . .] what about the uniform? I see you wearing the wrong sort of T shirt and so on.
Gerster: Yeh.
JW: Yeh, how do you feel about uniforms and the way the staff implement the policy of the uniform?
Gerster: Oh, I'm fairly fine with it but I wear T shirts (a lot with a shirt?) an' I'm happy to take them off when teachers tell me to take them off but um, yeh, yeh, yeh I'm, yeh I'm cool with the uniform.
JW: You don't wish then that we didn't have uniform policy, or uniform?
Gerster: Oh, I think uniform's a good idea.
JW: Do you?
Gerster: Yeh. When you got no uniform you know, you just (?) you know, keep wearing too many or a you know get dirty an' stuff.

Thus, on the whole, neither Robbo, George, nor Gerster was inclined to make the issue of school uniform a site for entrenched resistance: its value was both expressive ("it makes the school look good") and instrumental (in so far as it meant one's casual clothes did not "get dirty"). Their attitude was more one of casual but persistent indifference to normatively valued appearance. In so far as the boys sought to express individual identity or reluctance to conform, they did so far more in terms of embodiment than appearance. When seated in class, a certain uprightness and alertness was generally expected by teachers, so George's sprawl (to which I have already referred in Chapter 6), was sufficient to warrant comment by his teachers. Robbo, too, could be seen sitting back, often turning around to talk or, when apprehended, make little or no effort to change his posture. In assemblies too, if the boys shuffled or bumped or slouched they might be told periodically to "sit up," and reference has already been made to the importance attached to the correct posture during the singing of the national anthem. Likewise, when being reprimanded, any tendency to slouch, or any attempt to lean against a wall when sent out of class would be met with further precepts. Again, when moving from the grounds into school after morning recess or lunchtime, these boys were invariably among the last to arrive at their lockers, refusing all entreaties to "hurry along" and then when in the corridors, further time might be taken in elaborate greetings and discussions.

Passing reference has been made to George's stance on one occasion being interpreted by a teacher as a form of intimidation and indeed, it was in standing, especially when being disciplined for some offence that the boys were most likely to have their appearance and posture commented on. At such moments tempers could be frayed and voices raised as a teacher demanded that the student "stand up straight." Otto, in particular, was thought by teachers to be intimidating, and any of the boys might be told at such times to "relax," "calm down," and lower their voice. On being put out of a class on one occasion (see Chapter 7), for example, Robbo's propensity for "talking back" and his comportment drew comment from his teacher, as he refused to stand where he had been told to. In certain instances, teachers might ignore provocation or avoid potentially fruitless confrontation, which may have been the teacher's strategy in the following example:

> I walked past (a room) when they were doing English [. . .] and while all were listening attentively to a student speaker, Otto had his leg up across the top of his desk. I'm sure the teacher knew. (Otto) saw me look in and made no attempt to move it. Others continued to look to the front.
>
> (Fieldnotes, 27.10.04)

The curriculum of the body was also implicated in the school's anti-bullying policy as well as in the formal curriculum. Given a very broad and inclusive definition of bullying, George, Otto, and Gerster were all regarded as bullies at various times during the study, usually for hitting other students but also for being physically intimidating through gestures, as well as verbally. The school's formal duty of care required teachers to ensure that it was a safe environment for all and it was a suspendable offence for any student to cause it to be unsafe, as Robbo and George had found out. The investigation by coordinators of allegations of bullying frequently led to detailed discussions of how bodies were used in clashes and to reprimands in which students (invariably boys during this study), were reminded of the distinction between appropriate and inappropriate physicality. Subjects such as Physical Education, Sport and the elective, Health Education, were all designed to counter such behavior and each gave considerable emphasis to physical as well as emotional well-being in a common psycho-biological discourse of adolescence. Students found smoking, for example, were required to view a video outlining the physical harm they were doing to themselves in the first instance rather than simply be punished with a detention. Care for the growing body was thus a particular focus of pedagogy. As far as George and Robbo were concerned, Health Education was one of the more interesting subjects:

JW: So what about ah, best things?
      [...]
G: Just sitting there and watching a video, especially in Health and you see like
R: Sex.
G: bodies and shit, like tits.
      (laughter: both talk over).

Here, if further proof were needed, is evidence of the heteronormative gender regime these boys affirm as they construct their masculinity. My response is to ask: "So the video's a good thing?" whereupon talk turns to Woodwork (which is also enjoyable), and how to pass the time when videos are boring, by texting messages on their mobile phones and even playing with "gameboys."

GIRLS

As ethnography, this study has tended to focus on the experience of schooling of a small number of disaffected boys. Inevitably their experience in a coeducational school should take account of girls, but my focus throughout was limited to boys as subjects. My principal concern has been to uncover and understand, as it were, the view from the boys while at the same time acknowledging my own part in its construction.

The cohort of which these boys were a part comprised a little over 300 students, more than half of whom were boys. In almost every class (of 25 to 28 students), boys outnumbered girls by four or five students and vastly outnumbered them in Woodwork and other manual arts subjects. Whether discussing their behavior in class, subjects they liked, subjects they disliked, teacher responses to misbehavior or actually doing class work, the boys never made references to, or comparisons with, girls and nor did I suggest that they might. When mentioning incidents that happened outside the school, however, occasional references to girls were made, but it was not until I mentioned my observations of corridor and schoolyard life that discussion moved to the place of girls in their daily lives.

I have mentioned elsewhere the loud, ostentatious greetings boys gave each other in the corridors, usually at the start of the day, and especially the stylized handshake. It might be repeated after morning recess or after lunchtime, but equally remarkable was the gushing, shrill greeting girls gave each other accompanied by hugs and kisses on the cheek. When performed in the physical limitations of a school corridor lined with hundreds of lockers and hundreds of students jostling for access there was little room for movement. At such times almost the entire student body of Year 9 was in contact with one another, some more so than others: by Year 9, greetings between boys and girls had become rather more intimate than was usual in Year 8 as George, Kevin, and Gerster confirmed:

K:	I like this topic. G? (chuckles).
Gerster:	Yeh.
K:	What annoys me is the no touching policy. Like if you could just be hugging them or something an' then you'll be like told to like shove off or something.
G:	Yeh well say if yuh, say if you like your friend is a girl or whatever (?) you just give 'em a kiss on the cheek to say hello or whatever an Mr Wilkinson comes along and Miss
K:	Yeh Mr Wilkinson's the worst about it I thought.
G:	He pulled me up once for, giving a girl a kiss on the cheek an' like, "You shouldn't do that you know you can get charged for (?)" you know, send you down to the Hillside police station, stuff like that, right.
Gerster:	Just ask her next time George.
G:	(chuckles).
JW:	You wouldn't have, you wouldn't have had that much said to you in Year 8 would you?
G:	Nuh.
JW:	You've all sort of discovered girls a bit more this year.
G:	Like Year 7 'n 8 you oh you discover girls but like, Year 9 . . . for me like Year 8 and Year 9 are sort of the parts where like you know you start kissing girls you know when you see them in the corridor. Year 7 and Year 8 I used to look at all the Year 8s and Year 9s an' *aw, kissing girls!* (his emphasis).
Gerster:	Like yeh, yeh (? chuckle) Yeh you get into Year 8 an' you're like, sweet.
G:	*Yeh I get to do this now heh, heh* (his emphasis).
K:	*I've finally reached the year (?) sick!*[5] (his emphasis).

Nine months later, after Kevin and George had left the school, Robbo, Otto, and Gerster again confirmed the persistence of this heteronormativity but now emphasized the discourse of friendship with which it was to some extent in conflict, as the following conversation shows:

JW: [. . .] I asked George and others last year about, like I see students in the corridor . . . by Year 9, um, when all friends are greeting one another.
Gerster: Oh the handshake.
R: Mm.
JW: And, and the kissing of the girls an' that.
Gerster: Yep.
JW: Now how, how are girls fitting into your school lives this year? I don't want to know about outside the school, but what about
Gerster: Oh they're, they're alright (?).
JW: What are they, do you still greet one another the same way or have you gone through a sort of kissing phase in the corridor?
R: Yeh I still greet 'em.
Gerster: Yeh, yeh I give 'em the odd (kiss?).
JW: Mm.
Gerster: Couldn't be bothered.
O: More Robbo's girlfriend than anything.

Robbo mixed with girls at lunchtime and morning recess but neither Otto nor Gerster said they did, or were seen to. As Robbo commented, "some of 'em just don't care," but the question of just how important their relations with girls were at school lingered:

JW: Are girls as much friends as boys are?
Gerster: Nah! Nah! Like, what are you getting at, are you saying like . . . are we like, are we like better mates
JW: Yeh.
Gerster: than or say is he better mates with a girl than he's better mates
JW: Yeh.
Gerster: with us
JW: Yeh.
Gerster: as a guy?
O: Nah nah we grow up like . . . our mates, our group of friends, and there's a few girls that are in that and then (? Greeks ?) yeh?
JW: Yeh.
O: and then, then you've got obviously friends at school. So what you, your main group of friends

JW:	Mm.
O:	is obviously, you know, you value them more than ones at school.
Gerster:	Yeh, I, I value my friends.
JW:	Just boys or boys and girls?
O:	Boys and girls. You've got girls that are, you know, friends of the girls as well.
Gerster:	I value my friendship with these boys more than like the girls in the school like
JW:	Yep, yeh.
Gerster:	'cause like . . . I dunno, girls are too annoying, sometimes.
R:	They scream.
O:	Yeh but they obviously get along better with their own.
Gerster:	Yeh exactly, yeh it's vice versa.
O:	You don't really relate to 'em.
R:	'cause they can talk to girls about a lot more stuff.
Gerster:	Like they talk about you know, periods and crap like that.
R:	(chuckles) Where did that come from?

There was a certain tension throughout this discussion as the boys occasionally made oblique references to mothers, sisters, and Robbo's girl friends. Gerster's declaration of mateship was said with some emphasis and there was more than a hint of pride in the way he positioned himself as independent of girls. As our discussion came to an end, the boys' banter neatly encapsulated this distinction:

JW:	What, what girls in class would you spend any time talking to?
O:	Oh, only got like, one decent one in class.
R:	Who is it?
O:	[–]
R:	She's not decent.
O:	She's alright.
R:	(?)
O:	What are you talking about?
Gerster:	She's nice.
JW:	What, what about you, Gerster?
Gerster:	Oh I'm not, really, mates with girls in my class.
JW:	So you wouldn't find yourself turning to a girl to talk to her much?
Gerster:	In my class?
JW:	Yeh.
Gerster:	Nuh.
O:	He turns to me a lot.
Gerster:	Yeh . . . we have a, heartfelt conversation every night

JW: (laughs).
Gerster: (chuckles).

Again, the discourse of friendship, at once so heteronormative, so theatrical and so binding, remained dominant and unassailable. But it was open to further distinction as the issue of ethnicity revealed.

ETHNICITY

On rainy days, lunchtime was shortened by 15 minutes so the periods after lunch were brought forward and students could be dismissed earlier at the end of the school day. Corridors and rooms, which were normally shut at lunch times, were opened and students were allocated to "wet day rooms" by year level. Teachers normally on yard duty were expected to patrol the corridors, preventing random wandering and overcrowding and ensuring that rooms were left in a suitable condition for teaching. These were usually difficult occasions. On one such wet day I encountered George and X:

JW: Talking about being with your mates now, now I noticed this the other day on the wet, wet day, right, you're all in the rooms and that and you know everyone wants to be out of the rain and you're walking up the corridor and you had a mate or two with you or something and you looked in the room and said "No wogs"[6] and then off you went again.
G: Oh.
JW: What's, tell us about that.
G: (chuckles). Oh no not because there aren't any wogs like the group that I hang out with you know I hang out with these guys (referring to Kevin and Gerster).
JW: Yeh I know.
G: and stuff like, you know
JW: But you were looking for a specific group, specific group of boys.
G: and you say "Where are the wogs?" You know everyone "Oh they're down in the corridor" (?). Now you just, like, if you say you know where are the "skips"[7]
JW: Yeh.
G: (?) that's what they're
JW: So do you have this sort of identity among yourselves? You know, do you refer to George and his mates as the wogs or do you refer to others as the skips or
 [. . .]
Gerster: Yeh I call them wogs.

192 *That Unstable Construct*

K:	Yeh skips, everyone knows it.
	[...]
K:	An' then you've got the Asians.
JW:	Do you among the kids are they, sort of ... Do these groups, really exist? I mean like you do refer to one another like that do you?
Gerster:	Outside of school and inside.
	[...]
G:	Sometimes there's some-like you know the wogs we don't tend to screw around with Asians you know, because of the name they've got, you know, they got like stuff like that [...]

There followed a detailed description of how fights start at a nightclub and in a nearby suburb when groups of ethnically identifiable boys encounter one another, and how this knowledge carries over into school.

JW:	Is that, is that like in the school too? [...]
G:	[...] Oh school, in school I haven't really noticed it.
Gerster:	There are there are a few.
Kevin:	Yeh like the hard core Asians there are a few running around with but.
Gerster:	You know like but there's not as many.
G:	No.
	[...]
K:	[...] like the majority of everyone which is where Hillside High gets its name I guess.
JW:	What name?
K:	Like
G:	Asian school.
K:	Yeh
G:	'Cause you know we've got like nineteen hundred kids or something?
JW:	Mm, mm.
G:	and I suppose 80% of that nineteen hundred is ...
JW:	Asian.
G:	Asian.
JW:	Mm.
G:	right, yeh.

The ethnic mix of the school population was referred to in Chapter 4, but here the boys' perception has inflated the figure considerably. In spite of this and the stories these boys told about themselves and the almost daily conflict with teachers, relations among students throughout the school were remarkably peaceful. It was noticeable, however, that at morning recess and lunchtime, students of Asian origin tended to mix together rather than with others, although this was far from universal. It was also noticeable that groups of Greek-Australian boys tended to "hang out" together, sometimes in the company of select Anglo-Australian or Asian-Australian boys. It was just such a group that George had been looking for on the wet day.

Indeed, friendships often crossed ethnic distinctions. In Year 8, George's close friend was Tran who by Year 9 was helping Robbo out in moments of trouble (see Chapter 7). Robbo, for his part, was prepared to help Tran out whenever he thought he was being treated unfairly. One teacher, he said, had "been racist to Tran many times. It's funny." Tran had told me this himself, but now Robbo was going into detail, saying that after returning a test, the teacher had said: "if you were Australian and you weren't born overseas you would have done better," prompting Gerster to comment:

Gerster: I don't get that, like all like, like, like, the best marks out of our class are coming from kids born overseas.
(Brief general laughter and agreement).
R: Yah [sic], (the teacher) keeps going [. . .] on about, if you're Christi-if you were born in Australia you should all, do better.
JW: Mm.
Gerster: I've heard Mrs – like crack it if kids speak in Chinese.
R: Yeh.
(Mild general laughter).
Gerster: You know, she like tells them not to speak Chinese in class.
JW: Mm.
Gerster: They should speak in English.

George identified with Tran's predicament easily. His experience of grief (described in Chapter 7), was mediated through and through by his Orthodox beliefs which had marked him out as "other" in a regime of surveillance that was ultimately determined to exclude. The gold crosses and chains that were sometimes visible around the necks of Greek-Australian boys and girls also signified difference and likewise were the cause of comment by coordinators having to impose the school's dress code. But George was no innocent in class:

G: I got told off by Mrs, by Ms, by Miss – for
R: For speaking wog.
G: Saying "edet."
R: Oh yeh I say the same in Science [. . .]
JW: For saying what?
G: "Edet." Like
R: Like a wog.

G: It's like a Greek thing like where they
JW: Oh it's a Greek word is it?
G: Yeh.
(R and G): Yeh.
G: It's like, it's on the end of everything you say like you know like "edet", like "eledet"
JW: What's he say?
G: [. . .] I've got to say it in things like "Come on edet"
JW: Mm.
G: Edet!
JW: Mm.
R: Edet!
G: Yeh, like that, right, and she started telling me off [. . .]

Clearly, George and his friends were self-consciously aware of their ethnicity at school. Students were either "wogs," "skips," or "Asians" and they generally mixed happily although certain "Greek" boys had gained a reputation among some teachers for confrontational behavior and a certain loudness. From time to time, for example, George took particular delight in calling out to friends 20 or 30 meters away, filling the space with his booming voice and attracting attention from anyone who heard him.

FIGHTS

Given the school's duty of care, threatening the safety of others and disrupting the learning environment by fighting or threatening violence, as I have indicated throughout, constituted major offences and could easily lead to suspension (as George and Robbo well knew), or even expulsion. In both individual and group discussions, George, in particular, seemed able to recall a remarkable number of occasions in which he was involved in "hitting" in one form or another, and in fact gave the impression from time to time that he remembered such occasions fondly. In Year 8, for example, he recalled kicking a locker in Year 7 and again in Year 9, in a discussion with Kevin and Gerster, recalled a fight in Year 7 with some fondness but also with a sense of injustice that he shared with Robbo, given their experience of the consequences. At the time we were discussing another fight about which George claimed to have known nothing:

G: When was this?
    [. . .]
R: You were outside. I was in there. I couldn't do anything.
G: When was this? (incredulous).

R: It was like I, if I get in a fight
G: Like remind me.
R: I get kicked out of school now
JW: Yeh.
R: 'cause they told me that last year 'cause I got in two fights last year and they go "If you get in another fight you get kicked out"
[...]
G: Oh yeh. In Year 7 you know when I got in a fight with Benny.
R: Benny, yeh.
G: I was having a good fight with him, like it was the first fight
R: Yeh, yeh, yeh (over George)
G: and someone in Year 7 and I got suspended?
R: Yeh.
G: Right. I'm still getting shit from that.
R: Still?
G: Mm.
[...]
JW: How? How does
G: Oh because, every time
R: They, they bring it upon you
G: Yeh.
R: If you get in trouble, they'll bring everything you've done
G: Yeh.
R: in the past upon you.
G: And they'll say, they say every year.

When we were having this discussion, George knew he would be leaving and although resigned to his fate was rather bitter about the way the school's administration had constructed him as violent through the accumulation of records of transgressions. To some extent he believed he had a point. Early in Year 9 when coordinators believed that a fight was going to take place during lunchtime a hurried search was made for him in the belief that he was an instigator. When found, he was taken by senior staff and questioned about it, but as he later said: "I was in detention [...] so there was no way they could pin me, pin me down for doing something or whatever." Nevertheless, by third term, George had been suspended for punching a boy.

But it was the larger fights that most tested the teachers' powers of surveillance. Although few and far between and on occasion taking place outside the school, they tended to be preceded by rumor and brought about by the intersection of events both in and beyond the school. Asked what the "big stories" had been in Year 9, I prompted Robbo, Gerster, and George to comment on a particular fight only to have them pretend innocence before launching into details of the fight George had been suspected of organizing:

R: Fight?
G: Which fight?
R: Which fight?
Gerster: Which fight?
G: Oh, the Year 10 and the Year 9 fight, I remember that, that was fun.
R: I looked on with George.
G: Or again maybe not (loud general laughter: George looked at me impishly, perhaps wondering how I would react).
         [. . .]
R: Oh that was *funny* (his emphasis).
G: That was funny.

And again George recalled when coordinators "tried to pin it on me, for starting the fight [. . .] for throwing the first punch [. . .] and I got them back for pinning it on me" by having been in detention, but it appeared from his contributions earlier that he had later joined the melee. Robbo's memory of enjoying the occasion continued:

R: Oh, it was funny, like, it was like five of them and there was like a hundred wogs just come.
JW: (chuckle) It was a Greek thing, was it?
Gerster: Yeh I was just like sitting on the oval just like chilling out, and (the coordinator) was like, "Oh I don't think we can hand out fifty suspensions in the one day" (light laughter).
R: Oh it was funny. I was just sitting on the wall.

This was merely one of several such incidents allegedly brought on by events outside the school that the boys either knew of or took part in during Year 9. On another occasion (mentioned earlier when George claimed to know nothing about it), an incident at a party had led to a brief fight during which a knife was said to have been produced. The drama surrounding this allegation and the frantic work of coordinators in defusing the situation, questioning participants and bystanders and suspending offenders, again illustrated their policing function in differentiating between students to protect the normative school.

CARE OF THE BODY

Whether through Physical Education, Sport, Health Education, assemblies, or buying food in the canteen, middle school students daily received messages through the formal curriculum, posters, and homilies about the desirability of maintaining a healthy body and mind. George's participation in Physical Education was desultory and he had trouble fitting into the sports uniform, but he had played football during Year 8 outside the school when he was 14. Given his size and weight he knew he was a formidable presence as he revealed in a discussion at the end of Year 8 (referred to briefly in Chapter 6):

JW: How do, how do you think, now, I don't know the answer to this question. How do you think people see you?
G: Um, because of my size, an' like 'cause I'm loud an' things like that people see me as sort of (attempts pronunciation) ah can't even, intimidating? That's the word,
JW: Yeh, mm.
G: intimidating, and, yeh, like I've got, for instance there was, when I was at football, 'cause I do football outside school. When the season was on I got into a bit of a fight on the field
JW: Mm.
G: and then we had a tribunal an' things like that, I, they got, the tribunal got me an' the other guy to stand up, and, like, you know, show your build and things like that, an' um, an' they gave me a week for being bigger, more intimidating than
JW: Ah yeh.
G: than
JW: Yeh, yeh. So you think that teachers, or students
G: Yeh.
JW: or generally people might see you as intimidating?
G: Yeh.

George believed that this event beyond the school's reach had somehow marked his identity within the school and he was powerless to change it, just as his observation of his Orthodox religion had set him apart. George, Kevin, Otto, Robbo, and Gerster, all clearly disaffected with school, inhabited or loitered in this indeterminate boundary zone between home and school – not gate-keepers, not escapees, not quite members – yet clearly wearing, performing, or embodying their disaffection in defiance of the normative school.

For example, Otto, who as mentioned earlier was perceived by several of his teachers as intimidating, maintained a strong, athletic physique through football training with a local team. Only Gerster among the other boys participated in sports and he was prepared to admit enjoying taking part in the annual House athletic carnival along with Otto, whereas Robbo truanted on such occasions and George simply went along with friends if they were going. Otto's attendance at school was erratic at the best of times but in Year 10, absent from class for weeks on end during the brief interschool football season, turned up for games and was even named "best on ground" in the school's newsletter, a fact later recalled with much hilarity by Robbo and Gerster.

Like all State High Schools, smoking was banned for teachers, parents, and students on the school grounds and in the buildings. Nevertheless, teachers on yard duty kept an eye out for student smokers and generally knew where they could be found. Robbo, who claimed to have given up smoking, was not among them, but Kevin, who stopped for a smoke on the way to school, usually was. As the crisis in Kevin's domestic life worsened, I asked him to discuss his smoking:

JW: In all the troubles that you've had at home . . . um . . . yeh I saw you one day and you were in the your dope beanie[8] or something or other. You, that was, you really looked as though you . . . you weren't part of the school that day . . . um, do you get . . . is it important to you, to be with the kids because you're they support you, or, help you?
K: Kids?
JW: Friends.
K: Yeh yeh . . . it's . . . it . . . with divorced parents um sometimes you you need to keep up friendship
JW: Mm.
K: links or otherwise it can be difficult and stressful like.
JW: Mm.

Again the importance of friendship was emphasized, but I had clearly not asked the question I wanted to ask. I was skirting the issue, testing our rapport.

JW: Um. . . . . .OK now we're just trying to you've said to me you've had a smoke you've had a sm-you know, the odd smoke on the way to school and that sort of thing, and um, one of the things that kids, do, from time to time is they, they get off their face with one thing or another. Um, especially if they're having the sort of problems you're having.
K: Yeh sometimes kids use that as an excuse but I've never used that. I've never relied on it. I do it purely for . . . um, the enjoyment and so forth aspects I guess.
JW: Have you had the influence of it at school? I mean have you been on your
K: Yeh.
JW: off your face at school?
K: Mm.
JW: How, how . . . has, has that affected er have you then got into trouble, or has it helped you then got into trouble, or has it helped you get through the day or what?
K: Yeh, it makes the day go a lot quicker, to tell you the truth.
JW: (chuckles).

K: Um, but teachers sort of know and they smile at you and they just sort of . . . not, I'm not telling names but they sort of know.
[. . .]
JW: So a teacher would recognize
K: Yeh yeh, some teachers do.
[. . .]
JW: Some teachers will know
K: Yeh.
JW: and they'll just leave you alone?
K: . . . Not really. Like they still pay, the same amount of attention they don't sort of catch you out, depending on the teacher they might. Like ah . . . not really sure what they'd do, it'd be up to them.
JW: Mm.
K: Um [. . .] they sort of pull you aside and say you know "What's going on?"

Here Kevin reveals how fluid is the distinction between school and not-school; between being in and being out of school. It is a powerful challenge to the school's discourse of community in so far as he admits transgressing key values and regulations governing community membership. But he was not alone. Coordinators on another occasion suspected a boy of being under the influence of alcohol. Parties the boys attended outside school frequently involved alcohol and at the end of Year 9 George, Gerster, and Robbo recalled drunken moments as well as the day one of their friends – the boy mentioned earlier – "rocked up pissed." As Gerster said, "that was like funny."

CONCLUSION

In this chapter I have reconstructed and represented a sense of the corporeal and the visceral mediated by the clothed, gendered, ethnic, youthful, and embodied subjects of this study. I have tried, moreover, to convey a sense of the positivity of embodied experience and its part in the constitution of the subjectivities of the boys. In so far as I have touched on issues of gender construction, however, I have been drawn to Swann's (2002) question, "Yes, but is it gender?" One could equally ask, "Is it ethnicity?" Is it gendered ethnicity, or ethnicized gender, or any or all of these, or more? What it is, undeniably, as I have said from the start, is performative evidence of the constitution of experience.

Throughout this work I have drawn attention to the discursive struggle over the nature and meaning of that experience. This chapter in particular has focused attention on the dialectical relationship between the body and discourse, exemplified time and again in discursive performatives.

The docile, subjected body posited by Foucault has not materialized; in its place is the contested body, stigmatized in its subjection but sustained also by oppositional technologies of selfhood.

For example, as the period of George's mourning drew to a close his coordinators spoke to him about breaches of his contract. He had arrived late to class, had no books, wore an incomplete uniform, was still unshaven and had been rude and aggressive to a coordinator. He was told the contract would be invoked at the next breach leading to instant expulsion and his father was informed. Together they met with the careers adviser and George continued to attend sessions with the chaplain. In the yard while walking past boys playing basketball one of them bumped into him and George punched him. He "accidentally" got paint on a teacher's jacket, leading to a detention, and on another occasion wandered through a detention, disrupting it. His last progress report early in the last term of Year 9 showed satisfactory progress in five subjects out of ten, with teachers commenting favorably on recent improvements in attitude and achievement in those five subjects. My fieldnotes record the impact of these events: "(George) seems larger than ever, walks slowly. Perfectly dressed in the uniform but with a neatly trimmed, short beard. Greets all friends effusively with a fairly dramatic handshake – mostly if not all Greek friends" (Fieldnotes, 27.10.2004).

A change had come over him, but in the end, with days to go before the end of the school year, in our last interview George embodied all that offended the normative school:

JW: Ah this is our last interview I suspect for the year because George's going to leave [. . .] um Gerster was crook yesterday, he's come in, he's got a bit of a beard, ah an' hasn't had a shave for a few days.
Gerster: I shaved last night actually.
All: (general laughter).
JW: And Robbo he's in his ah basic school gear, Robbo's in his PE gear. Ah, George is ah, George is in his normal gear. He's in his school gear. He's got a gold chain, he's got a gold earring in each ear, ah bracelet, silver bracelet on his right arm ah
G: Got a South Melbourne hat.
JW: South Melbourne hat, South Melbourne Hellas (George giggles). Yeh, another bracelet on his right foot, ah right (laughter) right left um left wrist
Gerster: I'm not into jewellery.
JW: (laughs) and I think he's got his black T shirt somewhere around about has he?
G: Oh nuh, I took it off [. . .].
JW: Oh right, you had it on your belt before

G: Yeh.
JW: when I saw you in class? [. . .] Yes, his shirt's unbuttoned and he has a very hairy chest.
(all laugh)

That was the last I saw of George.

9 The Aspirational Self

> What of the desires and pains of male adolescence? Where are the insecurities and anxieties?
>
> (Hey, 1997: 17)

INTRODUCTION

In this chapter I belatedly, and briefly, draw attention to boys described as "good" by their teachers; that is to say, they are regarded as good students in the sense of both achievement and behavior. Hammersley and Turner (1980) long ago pointed out that relatively little research had been carried out on students variously described as proschool or conformist and little has changed in the intervening quarter of a century. Certainly occasional references to conformist students cropped up in early educational ethnographies (Lacey, 1970; Ball, 1981) and became a particular focus for Hammersley and Turner (1980). Observing that researchers seemed to have "taken over the preoccupation of teachers with problem behaviour" (Hammersley and Turner, 1980 in Hammersley and Woods, 1984: 161), they and others began to move from a research paradigm they called "normative functionalism" (ibid. 168) to an interactionist analysis based on students' definitions of the situation. Thus Turner (1983) was able to point out that disruptive students were not disruptive all the time any more than conformist students were "good" all the time, building on Furlong's notion (1976) of an "interaction set" of students who supported one another in often disruptive dealings with teachers in much the same way as the boys I was studying.

These early studies of student adaptations to the normative school and of student perspectives tended to rely overly on such static concepts as the definition of the situation (Hammerlsey and Turner, 1980) and were carried out according to the criteria of modernist and realist ethnographic participant observation. The intention was not only to describe, but to explain developing models of student behavior grounded in the assumption of a unitary student subjectivity. For example, Davies (1984) administered a questionnaire to teachers to elicit their understanding of a "well-adjusted, reasonably successful pupil" (p. 67). Whereas most teachers in the school she studied made no distinction between the characteristics of boys and girls who fitted this description, their stereotype of a good male student was related more to achievement than to behavior (ibid. 68), leading her to observe that "(the) perfect pupil would presumably be androgynous, selecting aspects of both sex roles" (ibid. p. 68). More recently, in an investigation of student achievement, Francis (2000) found that in describing "the ideal pupil," boys tended to emphasize good behavior whereas girls tended to emphasize approaches to learning (ibid. 66–68; 155).[1]

Throughout this work, however, I have shown that boys are not simply the passive products of socialization; like men and women they are actively creating themselves, but not necessarily, as I have said earlier, as an expression of a prediscursive intention, or agency. Rather, the boys in this study are understood as having developed an awareness of themselves as schoolboys of a particular kind – that is, they know themselves as subjects – as a result of the "reiterative power of discourse to produce the phenomena that it regulates and constrains" (Butler, 1993: 2, quoted in Hall, 1997: 15), or, in Foucault's words, as "practices that systematically form the objects of which they speak" (Foucault, 1972: 49). But to say they have been produced as "effects," through and within discourse, is too neat, too clinical, too decisive (see McLeod, 2000b: 517). To the observer or analyst, such positions may be clearly delineated and fully occupied, but how and why are they "taken up"? Are the disaffected and challenging boys that this study has been so concerned with to be understood in these terms – filling those subject positions – or perhaps as more or less desperately seeking to assert themselves through and within alternative discursive formations privileging friendship and desire for experience beyond the school? Are the "good" boys to be understood any more clearly? In this thoroughly performative and intertextual domain, as Walkerdine (1993: 463) has observed, "the subject is a textual relation, not coterminous with the person at all," and yet the subjects of this study and I have confronted each other as much as persons as we have as subjects.

The awareness of self (which I mentioned in Chapter 8), in such an intertextual context, is described by Dorothy Smith (1988: 42) as "the lived moment bringing local settings under the jurisdiction of textual discourse." While Smith has in mind the constitutive force of texts promoting particular femininities, this emphasis on the discursive and textual constitution of favored norms resonates also in the school setting. If we ask how the good student is to be identified, then, as I indicated in Chapter 5 (referring to various school handbooks), and in Chapters 7 and 8 (referring to assemblies and uniforms), there is a range of textual material emanating from the school and presenting an image of the paradigm, or iconic student.[2] This student can be seen in photographs around the school, in the annual magazine, in weekly newsletters, on honor boards and trophies and in acknowledgments of past students, and is constantly to be inferred from all that is written and said about current high achievers and good citizens. As such it will be "read" by parents, visitors, and those seeking to enrol new students. The image is again foremost in the slightest comments from teachers to students in class and assemblies and is enacted above all in the most formal moments when students are "on show" – again, before parents or the general public – whether perfectly dressed for excursions, totally committed to school events such as house sports, music performances or, above all, in assemblies. There, student leaders in perfect uniforms gilded with badges, annotated pockets, and colors stand shoulder to shoulder with school principals, dispensing prizes, advocating the community's values and personifying all that the student body might aspire to: "the image and its embodied correlate" (Smith, 1988: 43).

In such moments students themselves are public texts in which favored image and moral instruction are combined to reinforce appropriate behavior. Student, family, and school are discursively united and linked to the practices and expectations of schooling as the figure of the student as most desired, most fulfilled, and most rewarded is identified in texts, embodiment, and interaction. Could it be that school rules and regulations such as those at Hillside High are among the last resting places of that body of literature once devoted to the cultivation of paradigms of behavior in manuals upholding the proper, the good, right conduct, and the polite? (ibid. 57). Is this the ethical project of student work, subsumed within discourses of excellence, community, and care and revealed through technologies of assessment, reporting, confession, and judgment? The good or amenable student will thus seek to display in body, effort, achievement, and "behaviour" all that public textual images and doctrines of right conduct authorize. The body may fail to conform and the texts of the ideal may be encountered as both alien yet familiar (as any newly enrolling student will testify), but what is ultimately at stake in this production of a self is the student's identity.

This chapter suggests the ubiquity of the image and texts of "goodness," or compliance, and discusses the difficult work of manifesting it. It may be assumed that this textually mediated discourse presupposes readers (students) competent in the skills of bringing this image into everyday practice; that the implied reader is a student willing to comply and that therefore a particular relation to self arises in which the student becomes an object to him or herself. But as shown in Chapter 2, there is widespread concern that boys do not appear to have these skills, or at least to apply them reluctantly, selectively or not at all. They might defiantly oppose the textuality of normative discourse, rejecting its calls to reflect on the self on its terms and, like George, be caught up endlessly in reports of their "permanent imperfection" (ibid. 50). As I will show, however, it is ultimately a question of whether or not these images become objects of desire, and if so of kindling, harnessing, and articulating this desire in order to bring about a particular objective – the desire to be good, to achieve or, more radically, to change.

But here I must acknowledge a difficulty as the question of representation erupts at this point. In so far as I have attempted to portray George, Kevin, Gerster, Robbo, and others – to convey a certain portrait even as they were offering self-portraits – here I have blurred the outlines, flattened the visual field and put aside the subtleties of shading and color.[3] In doing so I may have done no more than offer caricatures of the boys who started out in my mind, and were presented to me, as the "good" boys. Theirs was in some ways, as I hinted in Chapter 5, a less emphatic presence, their experience both distantly yet sometimes surprisingly closely connected to that of the "failing" and disaffected boys who claimed so much of their teachers' time, and by extension, of mine also. The question of how to represent them focuses attention on my own part in the textual construction of all who participated in this study and perhaps does so most dramatically because of the binary (good/bad) that underpins the institutional origins of the identities I sought. Such decisions, which are essentially about what to include, what to leave out and how to do it, as Hey (1997: 89) acknowledged in discussing the "editing" of one of her subjects, go to the heart of the ethics of participant observation, the quest for "truth" and the issue of power in the social relations of ethnography.

YEAR 8

Arjay

In one particular Year 8 class there were those who did get into trouble and those who didn't. It was more a question of frequency than of "either/or." Arjay tended not to get into trouble, but then again he did – occasionally. It wasn't a class that was easy to work in, but then it wasn't hard to work in either: it was "in between," he said, and having friends from Year 7 with him helped.

So in 8N there were students who misbehaved and Arjay thought that "probably" made it "hard" to work. Those kids talked too much and didn't do their work. It would start with students talking too much. Then teachers would "calmly explain" what they wanted and if students kept going then maybe teachers would raise their voices.

Arjay treated these moments as a lesson in ethics: "I guess it's like a lesson, in like, you learn that not to do these things maybe. You don't want to get in trouble with teachers." But if you don't want to get in trouble with teachers – if you do the right thing – do you get in trouble with others in the class? Arjay found he did sometimes when they called him a "nerd," but to him a nerd was "a person who's smart, does their things properly" – so it didn't faze him or others it happened to. Anyway, it didn't happen all the time and he got along with others in the class most of the time and especially with teachers. It showed in his reports, which he thought were "alright" and which his family were "pretty happy" with. For example, teachers would say he did his work but "maybe (he) should not be as disruptive, things like that."

Arjay disruptive? All he did was talk, but the comments were never unfair "because teacher (sic) actually sees everybody, like, as, what they do and you might not even know it and what they write I accept [. . .] because they know I've been doing it." Nor did his friends feel picked on or targeted by teachers, but "(t)he same boys who get into trouble, pick on different boys." It was only comments – nothing physical. They picked on kids who did their work: "boys who you know, maybe they look different." So what have you been called, Arjay? ". . . called fat, smelly." You could easily get upset over this, but really "it's not important" so you just get on with your work.

On reflection, though, perhaps "one or two" teachers did "target a couple of boys, but most of them are pretty fair." Like, "some boys do major things, they talk and teachers don't care and then another boy he says one word and she has a go at him." She has a go at him. Anyway, "there (are) some fun students, some quiet students. [. . .] we joke around maybe, have a couple of laughs [. . .] but still do our work." Phys Ed. and Maths were good, History too, but English was "too much work in so little time." And teachers were so important when liking a subject. So Arjay, what makes a good teacher? "If they're easy to talk to, easy to ask for help, not strict but outgoing and things like that. If the teacher's like strict an' all that, always angry, or things like that you don't really feel comfortable" and he'd had a few of those, especially this year.

Family commitments meant Arjay couldn't get to Speech Night. Looking back on the year, Arjay recalled "a couple" of comments from teachers that his work was really good, but what stuck in his mind was "about not maybe being disruptive." That stuck in his mind. Nevertheless, the thought of mixing with a whole new group in Year 9 was exciting.

Most of Arjay's friends had come through from Year 7 with him, including Benny. He had been happy with History, Geography, and Maths in Year 8 but had occasionally got into trouble for "probably being a bit rude or something," like talking too much, and he had been in "a play fight, once or twice." He'd found the class a bit hard to work in, what with Tran and George in it, but he'd tried to avoid the distractions. Tran could be "pretty cheeky" and "they would often um talk really loudly [. . .] or make jokes . . . about the teacher [. . .]" who was usually a woman. Benny found himself looking up and listening "but (he) would try to kind of, get back down to (his) work, but, sometimes (he) couldn't." It was worst in English when Tran and George would call out and "(make) jokes at the teacher" so that when she told them to get back to work "they would act like real offended or something [. . .] and then they would try and make an audience for the class." They would look around and try to draw you in, especially George: "He liked you to join in but he was probably happier being a clown."

Jake

Jake liked coming to school in Year 8: it was all about friends, learning and rewards. He had been "nervous" at the start of Year 7 – the move from Primary School was "a big new step" – but by the end of Year 8, aged 14 and 190 centimetres tall, he was at ease with school. He played volleyball for the junior school and had received Speech Night awards in Years 7 and 8. Jake was unsure about what these awards were for specifically, but was aware that they were given to students who exhibited attitudes and behaviors the school valued: perhaps it was for carrying out the duties of a House Captain in the junior school. In this role he would have helped senior captains and teachers organize swimming and athletics carnivals and begun to develop leadership skills. He would have shown commitment to the school.

To Jake, the best things about school were "doing well in PE 'cause I like sport [. . .] getting House Captain awards, getting awards for doing good things [. . .] and just getting congratulations from other people an' from teachers an' things."

But there was more to school than that. All those new teachers in Year 7 – that was a good thing he said

> because like you didn't have to put up with the same teacher every class and you wouldn't see him like, not every day. Some teachers you might not like for whatever reason but I'd probably think it'd be better to have different teachers for every class because they're better in that like subject..

Telling whether or not a teacher liked you was hard, but "you could sort of talk to (those who liked you) a bit more [. . .] it's easy to flow 'n talk about anything [. . .]." Well, "not really anything but you could talk about sports." On the other hand, some things about teachers were hard to take.

> (S)ome teachers like sort of might sort of start off as a bad student and you sort of know like teachers they sort of like give you a chance an' you sort of don't take that chance 'n you might take it later on an' then they don't give you the opportunity to keep going.

To keep going? "Like you try to improve yourself or they just like sort of, got your voice in their head because you've been talking often an' they blame things on you that's not always your fault." Like times Jake had been blamed for "just talking 'cause I'm a pretty loud student an' everyone knows how loud my voice is 'n it carries around the classroom."

Anyway, "once in a while you get in trouble [. . .]." In Year 7 others in his class would talk back to teachers and not stop when they were asked to. They would do "things like not following teachers' directions," but this year (Year 8), "they go a bit further with teachers 'cause they might know their limits." You'd be sitting in class and "they could just keep talking to 'em or annoying 'em every class and making fun of 'em sometimes. Just like pushing their limit." It was, he agreed, a kind of sport. Some teachers tried to ignore those students but others "like kicked 'em out."

At such moments the class would stop work – or try to go on:

> sort of like when someone gets in trouble an' teacher's yelling at 'em normally everyone stops an' sort of listens. Like when someone gets taken outside by the teacher you have to be quiet and sort of a bit, sort of like when a teacher's in a bad mood at the start of a period they're going to be in a bad mood with everyone else for that period.

When it happens

> we try to put that behind us and try to have a fun lesson every time, but, he doesn't really give us the chance to have a good lesson, like sometimes we go in there in a good mood an' he's in a bad mood and he makes us in a bad mood an' everyone's just like in a bit of a bad mood.

You just had to try to "ignore it and sort of just put it behind, and keep going."

The worst thing about school was teachers. They were "good to me but not to everyone else [. . .]. (They) sort of don't give up on like picking on someone [. . .] like Otto." You'd go into a class in a good mood and when the teacher appeared you could tell from their looks or voice what sort of mood they were in: "they might just, like, talk to someone or yell at 'em for just like talking for a second when everyone else is and you sort of like think, 'OK, someone's in a bad mood today.'" It never put Jake off school but he could see why boys like Otto could be put off coming to school. The worst he'd felt was after "trying hard at doing something and not really getting the right response back which you tried to get."

In Year 7, Jake had been in Gerster's class. In Year 8, he was in the same class as Otto.

YEAR 9

Arjay and Benny

Arjay found Year 9 "great . . . different . . . a good challenge." Work was "a step up" and there was "more homework" but he was in a class where it was pretty easy to work. He enjoyed English, especially writing stories, debating, and reading novels. History, Geography, and Commerce were "good" but Science was a lot of work and after school he generally went straight home and tried to get homework done. Most homework only took an hour or so but "a major assignment [. . .] might take [. . .] two, three hours to complete." The half-year exams had not bothered him "majorly;" he had just wanted "to get good marks" so he had "(taken his) books home, read through them, made notes (and) revised [. . .]." It had certainly helped him, as had suggestions from his parents. The half-year report had indicated he could have done better in English and Maths and his parents were pleased but teachers commented that with effort, Arjay "could be on top." Even though he seemed to be working well, he thought that if he "you know put (his) full concentration into it (he could) get it done well" – and he wanted to do well.

But it was sometimes hard to concentrate when others were noisy. If they were chatting to the person next to them the teacher might ask them to stop or move them, but Arjay had avoided having them placed next to him. Maths was "a lot of work" but unlike Year 8 "she makes sure it's done" and there was lots to do in History, Science, and English as well and homework was regularly checked. Commerce and PE were especially enjoyable. At morning recess and lunchtime, Arjay, Benny, and friends might play soccer on the oval but sometimes other kids tried to steal the ball or take over so they would move off and find a quiet place to chat.

Having positioned himself as studious and generally compliant, any reticence Arjay might have felt about revealing himself to be selectively conscientious and only occasionally disruptive was put aside in joint discussions with Benny. Looking back on Year 9 with only weeks to go before the end of the year, both agreed it had been "a good year" and Benny added: "Not too many slip ups." So Arjay, you couldn't possibly have been perfect students all year, could you? Well, "yeh of course everybody gets into trouble [. . .] you know, minor things here and there [. . .] in class sometimes, just muck around and stuff [. . .] just being loud." Benny remembered: "probably like just yelling out stuff, across the room, at friends [. . .] stuff that's not relevant to class [. . .] like about last night's television show," usually in History, and the teacher would say "Settle down [. . .] be quiet, do the work." Benny would do it again in English too, calling out to others up to five seats away, so it was no wonder, he thought, that "she didn't seem to like some students," including him. Arjay thought "most of the class" was doing it but she would single out

Benny and send him to the coordinators where he was "told to um behave (himself) more in class [. . .] 'cause it probably wouldn't be fair to like give like a detention for just talking in class." Benny reckoned he had been sent out four times and Arjay thought he'd been sent out "a couple of times [. . .] for the same reasons." Benny was sure she had favorites and was less critical in her remarks on their essays than she was on his.

Half way through the year Kevin joined the class. Benny thought he "didn't seem to get in very much trouble at all (because) "(t)he teachers kind of . . . you know, didn't mind what he was doing [. . .]. Like, if anything, he was the worst of us all." From then on, he thought, "the class got a bit disruptive [. . .] because [. . .] he just made a lot of fuss about what he was doing [. . .]." A lot of the time he'd just sit there reading a book, but then he'd argue with the teacher, mostly during English.

> (H)e often yeh in English he tried to he he tried to be a clown a lot of the time, like he would um, he would try and say this and miss and try and get people to, to, follow him or laugh at him or something

but he was "pretty good" with other teachers, especially if they were strict. Kevin never seemed to do his homework or bring the right equipment to lessons and Benny thought this had an effect on the class. "(A) lot of people in our class were, trying to, trying to become friends with him [. . .] pretty much all boys [. . .] (who) were trying to be like him, trying to get him to like them," but when it was all said and done Benny thought Kevin didn't really fit in.

Then one day in Level assembly at the end of term three Benny remembered Kevin stood up and interrupted the coordinators as they were naming students who were leaving. "(H)e just butted in" and "said something about, um 'Blame the coordinators, that X's gone' um 'It's their fault' something like that, and he got in trouble but I don't think he seemed to mind." There was some clapping but Benny thought those students "were just trying to, trying to become friends with him." Arjay "vaguely" remembered what Kevin had said too but he didn't remember any applause. In fact, by the end of the year neither Arjay nor Benny could remember any major incidents that had stood out throughout the year. Lessons, excursions, free-dress days, sports events had all passed unnoticed and there were no fights to speak of although Benny had got into a fight with one of his "fellow students" and been sent to the coordinators by a student teacher, but otherwise he'd been in "no real trouble."

As for girls, Arjay thought that in Year 7 "you'd speak more to boys (?) Most of your friends would be boys like you know every year you get more friends that are girls," and Benny agreed. Relations with girls in class, they thought, were friendly, but Benny observed that while not many girls mucked up, when they did "the teacher wouldn't see it." He'd seen it happen and thought boys got in more trouble because of their reputations: teachers "either purposely ignored it or (were) just slow to pick it up" with girls.

To Benny, this was unfair. A fair teacher "doesn't really focus on anyone, have any grudges or anything," and Arjay added, referring to one teacher, "(S)he treats everyone equally." In her class, Benny said, "no-one receives any better treatment or anything [. . .] she always knows if someone's doing something wrong [. . .]," but this was not the case with all teachers because one teacher held grudges.

> (L)ike, for example, in Science, I was talking in one, so she moved me to the front of the class [. . .] she made me stay there, for about eight lessons [. . .] like even (when) I walked in the room and she told me to go there and I hadn't done anything which I didn't find very fair [. . .] until eventually I just didn't move.

But it had still been a good year. They had enjoyed worksheets, essays, and assignments in History and apart from assessment the work in English was fine. Benny struggled in Maths and French was hard, but Arjay found Maths "enjoyable." Physical Education had been good, too, and each had enjoyed playing sport for the Middle school. They even enjoyed Speech Night rehearsals because it meant "lots of periods out of class" but the idea of mucking up during rehearsals seemed foreign to them. As Arjay remarked, "It's a bit hard to talk when you're supposed to be singing," but it was a pity to miss out on Physical Education. As for the end of year exams, Benny studied "a fair bit" over two days, working up to six hours at a time going over notes and both were happy with their results. Commenting with pride on his History results, Benny said it "just shows that . . . like if the teacher's more fair, then, like students are more motivated to work."

Neither won a Speech Night award but Benny finished the year with awards in State-wide competitions in Maths and French. Both had carried out responsibilities for clearing rubbish in corridors and the grounds and Benny had attended a student Christian group.

Jake, Harvey, and Tim

The highlight of the year for Jake was the first Maths lesson: nothing else eclipsed it. Their new teacher "was Chinese so it was a different accent and just like the way he spoke, couldn't understand him" and he couldn't pronounce all their names properly. During the lesson Jake recalled that "we got moved." It had been a good year though, all agreeing it had been "fun" and "a bludge."

The fun often happened in Maths. There was that time when the teacher told all three of them and a friend to leave the room for talking when all the time the girls were doing the same thing, so "they had to come outside of their own goodwill because we were told off but they weren't," according to Jake. "They volunteered to take themselves out [. . .] because they did exactly the same thing 'n they thought it wasn't fair that only us guys would get told off," he added. Then they were sent to the coordinators for "just mucking around." To all three, mucking around meant "Making the teachers' lot harder," or "Making it harder for teachers." "Probably nothing personal against them," added Tim, "it's just, funny, it's fun [. . .]. Just being smart, like, talk back to them [. . .]." Like the time Harvey was sent to the coordinators. Tim remembered the teacher saying "'Go to the coordinators' and you said 'No' and he kept saying it and you said 'No' and he kept saying 'Go to the coordinators,' you kept saying 'No' and we were laughing all the time." And all the time they knew they were supporting one another while the teacher "just sort of sat there sort of staring." "He'd just given up on us," said Harvey, and by the end of first term Jake thought all respect had been lost on both sides: "(We'd) pushed our boundaries." By then they believed they had a "reputation, for just mucking around," but only in Maths.

By contrast, relations with their English teacher could hardly have been friendlier. They knew he was in his early 20s and like them had been a "skater" and, they thought, still was. Skateboarding: it meant "he was probably similar to us" so they didn't muck around for him "'cause it's just a different class [. . .] different spirit." Harvey thought he respected them and they all enjoyed a sort of joking relationship with him. For example, they thought they could go up to him and ask "How's it going?" They could go "(p)retty far" with him.

Then there was History. Tim had "nothing against (the teacher)"; he was "just boring": he talks, we take notes from the board, then we talk. Jake also found him "annoying" because of "the way he teaches" and admitted being slack – even though he liked the subject matter – by avoiding doing homework, except for bigger assignments. Geography wasn't bad, though. She was "a pretty good teacher" although some of the boys tried to "give her a hard time" because they didn't like the subject. Science? Tim felt he got "picked on" for "I dunno, must have done something," like the time he was given a detention for talking when he wasn't but everyone else was. To which Jake added:

> Unfair . . . yeh . . . it happens with every teacher I'd say [. . .]. Just like, teachers not seeing everyone what happens goes on [. . .]. 'Cause like they're writing on the board and they look up and they just see, they look normally straight away to the back two rows or three rows

and that's where Jake and the others sat. The English teacher called them the "back seat toughs" so occasionally, just for fun, they'd sit in the front.

The Physical Education class was all boys until two girls joined. It was a good group with lots of "Greek guys." They stuck together "a lot" but the Asian boys only stuck together "sometimes." Everyone got along alright, thought Jake, but "(e)very now and again we have a bit of a tiff." The problem was more Year 8 Greek boys and perhaps Year 10s. There was no ethnic disharmony they could identify but Harvey thought "the Greeks fight, they stuff around a bit" and there was "no real designated Asian group, there's lots of scattered ones." Last year it was more "like the Greeks versus the Aussies" when George was in the thick of it. "They like, they like having fun," thought Tim. "They like to pick on us because we're, Australian, it's nothing [. . .] we don't take it to heart."

Girls? All agreed it was a "bit more social" now with some boys having girl friends but at the same time Harvey added there was "(n)othing much different from Year 7 really." Jake noticed

> it's mainly the girls that are having fights now [. . .]. (T)hey just sort of have these little fights and they get over it the next week [. . .]. (T)hey just sort of have these little bitch fights and just sort of go on about pointless things.

"Girls will be girls," added Harvey.

As for highlights – really major incidents – the boys could think of nothing beyond that first Maths class and the teacher's continued mispronunciations. Had they noticed X going? "No, it didn't really affect us," said Jake. And what about Kevin in the Year 9 assembly? Harvey recalled immediately: "Well that was good [. . .]. That's what he thought, what he believed [. . .]. He stood up against authority." They all clapped and cheered, especially as they recalled Kevin had talked over one of the Assistant Principals. As Tim said, "it was good what he thought because I think they were pretty good mates."

At morning recess and lunchtime they avoided the oval. It was "too far to walk" so they hung around the canteen. They couldn't be bothered walking that far to kick a football. To Jake, the oval was where the smokers went "and you think the teachers must be stupid because [. . .] the teachers know they're smoking." "But they don't go down there," added Harvey.

Looking back, Year 9 had been fun: Harvey gave it 10 out of 10, adding almost as an afterthought that he had been a class captain, but Tim, who had failed Maths in the final exams, only gave it 4. There had been "a bit of a slump," thought Jake. Just before exam time they had begun to sit apart from each other in Maths but the exam was still hard. Results in all the other subjects were good, "Bs or As," and they were looking forward to Year 10. Harvey had been a Form captain, boundary and goal umpire for football and had played football and cricket for the middle school, while Jake had once again been a House captain and played basketball for the middle school, but this year there were no Speech Night awards.

DISCUSSION

If the preceding representation of the impressions given by Arjay, Benny, Jake, Harvey, and Tim can be said to reveal, or suggest, a common discursive tendency it might perhaps be thought of as a discourse of doing well and being good. It is of course discontinuous and even fleeting, but it can be discerned in terms of desire, rhetoric, and behavior. In the case of Arjay, for example, his respect for teachers and subject matter in Year 8 is evident in his comments that "You don't want to get in trouble with teachers," that they "see everybody," that "what they write I accept" and that "they know I've been doing it." He could live with being called a "nerd" and in spite of classroom disruptions from George and others he wanted to work and do well and was hurt, or at the very least confused, by teachers' comments that he had occasionally been disruptive. He wanted to do better.

Together with his friend Benny, Arjay continued to want to work and do well in Year 9. He did his homework when it was set, and they both wanted good marks in exams for which they prepared at least adequately. Both played sport for the middle school, both entered into the spirit of Speech Night preparations and Benny entered statewide academic competitions. Both also expressed concern that the fair assessment of their work might be compromised by teachers whose motives they questioned.

In the case of Jake, the rewards offered by sport and leadership seem to have presented him with an image he could hardly refuse. As a house captain for two consecutive years his leadership skills and reliability were acknowledged with prizes at Speech Night and he particularly liked being congratulated for his effort and felt let down when hard work was not rewarded. In Year 8 he knew it was appropriate to maintain a quiet demeanor when a teacher had taken an unruly student outside, stating matter-of-factly that "we try to put that behind us."

By Year 9 Jake was doing homework selectively and was scathing of teachers he described as moody or unfair: in fact, he thought teachers didn't always see what was going on and those who didn't went down in his estimation. He and his friends were nevertheless so concerned to do well in exams that they went so far as to move away from each other and work individually in order to ensure success in Maths. These boys, who were all involved in middle school sport, were nonsmokers and were somewhat scathing of smokers among their peers but were tolerant of the more knockabout Greek-Australian boys.

All were content to wear their uniforms appropriately, Arjay believing that for those who did it, having a shirt out was probably no more than a matter of comfort. A major concern common to all was the fairness, or lack of fairness, in teachers and thus for what they thought would be the consequences for their assessment and reporting. In spite of this, all got into some sort of trouble, more especially in Year 9 when, as Jake said, they experienced a bit of a "slump," but in their evident pride in academic results and their willingness to admit to being motivated by fair and approachable teachers, their priorities were clear: they wanted to do well and, if they had to, behave, or be good.

Furthermore, Harvey, and especially Jake, had crossed a certain threshold in seeking and attaining their positions as captains. They had, however briefly and intermittently, become the image for others to aspire to. As Form captain, Harvey had been required to present a case for his elevation to this position at a year level assembly, be acceptable to coordinators and finally be awarded a captain's badge at another year level assembly. Throughout the year his reliability and trustworthiness were at stake. Jake, however, had higher goals. As House captain he had written an application for the position, undergone an interview with senior staff and, on being found to be acceptable to teachers and an Assistant Principal, be presented with his badge at junior and middle school assemblies.

DESIRE

Leadership

Among the many facets of "care" for students for which Hillside High School prided itself was its "distributed" model of leadership, by which was meant that opportunities for modelling roles, working with teachers, sharing decision making (up to a point), and showing initiative in a public domain were diffused throughout the curricular and cocurricular structures and processes of the school (Strategic Plan, 2004). From School Captains and Vice-Captains through leaders of sports, music, visual arts, theatre arts, environment, debating and House captains (in Junior, Middle, and Senior schools), through peer support leaders, language tutors, student representative council members, student ambassadors, and on to a range of committee memberships and form captains, students aspiring to leadership positions were offered opportunities, training, and support.

A cursory reading of claims made by students aspiring to be Form captains will illustrate their wishes to take up a particular subjectivity offered by the normative school. The duties[4] of Form captain may be summarized as: an expectation to support the rules of the school by example and encouragement to others; to liaise with the Form teacher and level coordinators on matters related to the Form; to liaise with individual students and groups within the Form; to perform administrative tasks as requested by teachers; and to initiate and encourage activities that would benefit the wider community through social service. In carrying out these duties, students are told they would need to demonstrate certain skills, such as a willingness to uphold school rules, take initiatives, speak on behalf of

> The position . . . which I have selected to represent the school, as House Captain and Student Representative have been chosen because of the existing skills I possess and to assist me developing those I require to further my goals. I have a gregarious nature, am a good communicator, am a creative "ideas man," work well with both fellow students and staff members. I am forthright in expressing my thoughts and beliefs. Throughout my school life I have held numerous leadership positions. Refereeing volleyball for two years I have had to control age groups from under 20s through to helping under 8s understand the rules of the game. Having coached volleyball for five years, I am now the current under 12 Age Coordinator which includes organizing 100 players into 11 teams and resolving varied problems that arise during the season. Hoping you look favorably upon my application.

Figure 9.1 Application for leadership position.

the Form, communicate clearly, and address groups up to the year level at assemblies.

In pre-election speeches to their assembled year level and in applications, students frequently claim to be willing to listen to others with grievances, to represent students' interests, to enjoy working with people, and to organize events for the Form. They also claim to be sociable and, frequently, to have had work experience or to have held similar positions involving responsibilities that had already prepared them for the serious business of being reliable, and some even link this aspiration to a career path leading to work with others, such as psychologist or social worker.

Similar claims are characteristic of those hoping to become House captains, although no public disclosure in a speech is expected: that is left to an interview. In this position, students would be expected to foster participation by others in school sport; promote House spirit; attend meetings involving the organization of activities; chair House meetings when required and address assemblies. Skills involved in communication, exerting a positive influence, displaying initiative, following instructions, and meeting deadlines are presented as benefits that successful applicants would acquire in the position. Students who apply frequently tend to claim a particular ability in sport, to be sociable and reliable, to be proactive in motivating peers, to have a proven track-record in cocurricular activities and to have had experience in a range of jobs both in and out of the school requiring leadership, and say they can produce references to support their claims. Much of this is evident, for example, in Jake's application for either senior school House captaincy or membership of the Student Representative Council. (See Figure 9.1)

It is clear that Jake constructs himself as experienced, authoritative, organized, dependable, and ambitious, all traits looked upon favorably by teachers and administrators of the normative school, and at the same time as a figure acceptable to his peers. In so far as this represents a discourse of aspiration, or self-improvement widely diffused among students, it may be said to contribute to the constitution of the paradigm student in much the same way as high grades in the discourse of academic excellence. Interestingly, Jake was not inclined to see his role in various misdemeanors in class as in any way compromising his ambitions and nor, as it turned out, were teachers. In the new school year, Jake, once again, was a House captain.

Self-Improvement

When I first encountered George in Year 8 at the House athletics carnival it was not as a participant or as a particularly interested onlooker but as a loosely affiliated member of the school community enjoying himself (albeit under some duress in having to be there at all), with friends. Others, including Jake, were organizing, recruiting, marshalling, competing, urging, and in various little ways ensuring that the carnival happened at all, but he and others who sought leadership were not alone in wanting to do well and be good. For some, desire could be mapped in terms simply of wanting to do, or be, better.

For example, by the end of Year 8 George still thought that getting as far as Year 12 was a distinct possibility, but he knew that if this were to happen he would have to make changes to the way he worked and behaved. Sitting in class, George was well aware of other students around him doing their work, and, as he admitted in Chapter 6, reflected on his inability to maintain concentration. Midway through Year 8 had he admitted thinking about it:

G: Oh, like, when I see them working it's like you know an' if I'm talking to someone 'n I see people working I say to myself, y' know I should be really doing that instead of talking, so I might, do my work for about y' know five or ten minutes an' then get sidetracked an' start talking to an' that . . . my friends . . . in the class 'n that . . . .

In moments of reflection such as this George could be critical of what he saw as a short attention span but equally he justified his inattention in terms of lack of interest (in History, Geography, and English in particular), and inability, especially in Maths. This reflexive confrontation with incomprehension led, crucially, to further introspection, such as he revealed in his reflection on his Maths teacher in Chapter 6:

G: [. . .] like with um (her) now, she, with when she goes to ahm, how do I say it right because to explain the work, right, sometimes she might not say it a way that I understand, right an' like, not that I feel embarrassed or shy or something like I don't, I don't feel right to put my hand up and say, "Miss can you say that again" just in case [. . .] So I don't really ask, I just like to look on with someone else.

JW: Why wouldn't you put your hand up? Be honest.
G: I don' I don' . . . just . . . if I put my hand up an' say "Can you do it again?" just like worry about people saying oh, you, like "You dumb arse" or some'ing like that
JW: Yeh.
G: but instead of doing that
JW: Mm.
G: sit there an' do nothin'.

Removal from the mainstream Maths class to a smaller remedial group, however, brought him some success. Looking back on the year, George reported an improvement in his Maths results with some pride, especially when reminded of his fear of being labelled a "dumb arse":

G: [. . .] I was studying at home which I never used to do, like, I said if I pass I pass, if I
JW: Yeh.
G: don't I don't, but, (if I?) pull my socks up an' so you know it's not like that any more, if I pass I pass (?) it's not like that so, I got to do my work studying, things like that.
JW: And how does that make you feel when you get the results back, and how does that make you feel when you approach another test? How, how . . . Do you feel better in yourself?
G: Yeh, like, yeh I feel better when I, I feel good when I pass a test like you know I can do this thing, and even when I finish my work in class, you know
JW: Mm.
G: (?) like, when I do my work in class I usually finish in front of everybody else
JW: Mm.
G: so I've got a bit of spare time at the end so I speak with my friends that have finished or whatever.

George thought he had indeed "picked up a little bit" throughout the year, and while acknowledging with typical understatement that "there still might be a little bit of failure," attributed any improvement to his father's prodding but more especially to pointed advice from an "uncle":

G: [. . .] I picked up a bit with my ah in class, like not mucking around so much, not like trying to sit around with my friends, like, I still

> sit with my friends sometimes, an' um, yeh, like putting more effort into my work.
>
> JW: What's brought this about?
>
> G: Um . . . just like was when we were at a family barbeque there was a er like family member relative of ours who um was sort of in the same situation like (?) being expelled things like that an' he said you know like I wasn't going to try at the first start of the year, like the first two semesters, so the first semester and ah he just said, in the second semester he put in a bit of effort and he was trying, and he was trying and all of a sudden he was passing tests
>
> JW: Mm.
>
> G: you know
>
> JW: Mm.
>
> G: doing his homework, things like that
>
> JW: Mm.
>
> G: so I says to myself, you know, "If he can do this, well I can as well" so I started to put in effort.

As earlier chapters have indicated, it is clear that whatever changes George claimed to have made to his work habits and behavior in class were short lived and often imperceptible to teachers, which he blushingly admitted at the time. When reminded of his relative's remarks early in Year 9, and asked whether he was still motivated to do better, he replied that in Maths, for example, "I don't understand, a word she's sayin'," so he just talked to others as he did in most subjects. By midyear, however, having been in and out of trouble, George mused that "there's no real point arguing with a teacher" as it usually led to being removed from class, but it was not until his grandmother's death, his mourning and the signing of his behavior contract that the will to do and be better in terms laid down by the school's administration became noticeable. George felt the discomfort:

> G: Um, it's been . . . alright, sort of a rough trot, but . . . yeh, huh . . . Schoolwise, um, it's sort of changed with school because um 'cause I've been put on a contract where I have to . . . ah obey by the rules that they've put on the contract for me to stay until the end of this year, and um it's sort of a little hard trying to keep up with those rules because you've got to remember you know if you want to muck around with your mates you can't because of certain rules and regulations you have to abide by.

Both parents and school Principal had negotiated this fragile extension of George's presence in the school during which he and his family had accepted not only the school's authority in the matter, but the school's normative assessment of him. "As soon as I slip up I'm out," he had said, so he tried to do his work, not get into trouble and "not [. . .] think about it."

During this phase of George's schooling, his involvement with the school chaplain in the small group of boys dealing with grief was designed to help him and the others express feelings and resolve their grief. It was also hoped that they would learn self-control, how to listen, how to be listened to and how to make appropriate decisions in order to avoid confrontation and deal with their sadness. Some sort of change was expected, and even though homework was rarely a priority for George at this time, his coordinators did note a change in his attitude to class-work and behavior, although George was loath to admit it. By year's end, however, having improved some grades and having begun to hand in homework, George admitted that he had been making an effort to conform, but he looked back almost with pride on his old self:

G: Um, I remember about the year . . . um, at the start of the year I was a bit of a smart arse.
JW: Mm. (George giggles)
G: Um, yeh I was a bit of a smart alec, ah um, and s' half way through the year, I went through a little bit of trouble and then I had to change school, like for next year
JW: Yeh, mm.
G: so then I changed so basically throughout the year I remember changing.

As I mentioned in Chapter 8, the change in his appearance and demeanor were obvious but so also was the absence of that old bravado, replaced in corridors and formal spaces, at least, by a new and unfamiliar moroseness. In his mind it was not a result of the chaplain's intervention; as George said: "reality hit me and said [. . .] if I don't change um . . . like my behaviour and stuff mostly it's going to upset me next year," meaning he could expect not to transfer to the vocational course he had planned.

JW: Did it really hit you like that?
G: Yeh, it hit me like *bang!* (his emphasis).
JW: Did it?
G: I woke up.
JW: I reckon, I reckon you, you walked around looking really glum, for a long time, really
G: Yeh.
JW: as if the wind had been knocked out of your sails. Did you feel like that?
G: Yeh. Felt like I . . . you know, just came to school, not to talk to any of my mates.

JW: Mm.
G: I could talk at recess and lunch and that's it
JW: Mm.
G: and yeh some of the students in my class noticed
JW: Mm.
G: and um some of the teachers noticed, and
JW: Did, did anyone say this is a good change, or
G: Oh erm, oh all the teachers said it was a good change, like you know, I was talking to (the chaplain) before and he goes um he was very impressed with the way, I changed and stuff, so
JW: But how did you feel? Did you wish you didn't have to change?
G: Oh . . . I didn't think I was that bad.
JW: Mm.
G: You know, what I was been like
JW: Mm.
G: was just bein' a bit of a smart arse for a few years but um . . . yeh, but I changed and changed for the better.
JW: Mm, mm, 'cause you said something like that last year didn't you?
G: Yeh.
JW: You got a message from a cousin?
G: Yeh.
JW: So it's, it's happened?
G: Yeh.

Whereas George, Kevin, Robbo, and Gerster had all lost a friend in dramatic circumstances, and George had lost his grandmother, Kevin lost his family. During its disintegration he expressed a degree of contempt for a parent and explained that this extended as far as teachers too:

> You sort of ah lose respect for some of your parents and you lose respect for other authorities thinking you know "my parents can't sort of tell me what to do, why should you?" [. . .] Which is probably not the greatest attitude to have but I don't know, I, can't stop it sometimes [. . .] it's automatic.

By now his parents had separated and he had been taken in for several weeks by Gerster's parents. He had also been in the same group as George with the chaplain, dealing with grief, and I asked whether he had noticed any changes in himself:

K: Ah . . . probably since I've been living at Gerster's, probably not as angry, I guess.
JW: Mm.
K: Um, not as hurtful towards my mother maybe [. . .]

JW: I was interested to hear you say that [. . .] your parents, can't tell you what to do why should you like the teachers, is that right?

K: Oh, sometimes if, your, main authority figures in your life are your parents, right?

JW: Mm.

K: Well, I lost complete respect for my mother and um if she told me to do something I don't know maybe it was rebel a rebellious attitude but I just if I didn't see the point I wouldn't do it if it was her just nagging for some stupid reason I'd just ignore her

JW: Mm.

K: and um yeh sometimes 'cause teachers sort of do that as well. If they ask me to do something and it's reasonable I'll do it. If they're just doing it for the hell of it like my mother does just saying it for their own benefit, with most of the time they don't do it they don't just say stuff to hear theirselves talk [. . .]

This was a more reflective Kevin than I had encountered before – somewhat quieter and more settled – and he readily agreed, attributing the change to his move to the new form in which he had no friends. Here he found he was able to do more work and concentrate better:

K: "[. . .] I find um 'cause I'm in a class which is a bit more academic teachers sort of um . . . it's hard to explain . . . they set work but not . . . like it's hard, it's not heaps because they know what you can do, or or or that they know they can do it they just need a certain amount of work . . . .

But such change as there may have been became irrelevant with his surgically swift removal from the school. Gerster, with whom he had been staying, evinced the pangs of conscience in little moments of reflection throughout our discussions. Aware that he had gained quite a reputation in Year 8 for misbehaving, and had been suspended in Year 7, he stated early in second term in Year 9 that so far the year had been

fairly good. I just try to step up a bit this year considering, um and, like I'm alright at my work but my um homework and study is probably not the best and I was trying to get better this year.

While the outcome of this effort had been mixed, he had come to the view, like George, that getting into trouble was "just not worth it" and framed his response in terms of the likelihood of being expelled, rather than the more desirable prospect of leaving on his own terms. In the group discussion at the end of Year 9, Gerster amused George and Robbo with his retrospective account of the year in which he was embarrassed to admit to his success in Maths:

The Aspirational Self 223

Gerster:	Um, I didn't really fail anything last semester, so um I feel like the black sheep right now.
All:	(laughter with gusto).
Gerster:	No I, I was, had my trouble handing in work like Schnapper, Kevin stayed
JW:	Mm.
Gerster:	at my house for like five weeks
JW:	Mm.
Gerster:	lived there pretty much, well actually did live there
JW:	Mm.
Gerster:	and that kind of put me back a bit, so I kind of got into his work habits
JW:	Mm.
Gerster:	which, my work habits weren't, you know, very good at the time
JW:	Mm.
Gerster:	and they weren't getting better with him staying there and um, I (dunno?) I just didn't hand much work in [. . .]
JW:	So what did you do to improve?
Gerster:	I didn't really, I studied a bit more, like, I'm not much of a studier, I kind of get a bit sidetracked like, with study
JW:	Mm.
Gerster:	like look at the TV [. . .] hear people in the kitchen downstairs and get hungry (all laugh) [. . .] and. I dunno I just studied a bit more and um then I got like [. . .] Maths average is sitting on about 80% for a while
G and R:	What!? (incredulity; their emphasis).
Gerster:	and then um I got into linear equations [. . .] I had to stop studying. Thought, I got a bit ahead of myself, I thought I was pretty set [. . .]

His improvement had also extended to Geography, a subject in which he had frequently boasted of upsetting the teacher. At a time when he, too, had begun to re-evaluate his behavior, Robbo joined Gerster in his reflections:

Gerster:	[. . .] (She) hated me, and then um she started to love me because I was being really nice, and started doing work an' (chuckle).
JW:	What did you do to be really nice?
Gerster:	Oh um, oh I dunno I just kinda
R:	Stop being a smart arse – don't disrupt the class.
Gerster:	I had to get more in, and then, and then I started to [. . .]

By the end of term three in Year 9, Robbo had moved from thinking school was tolerable to being able to admit he "(didn't) really like the school that much, really." He felt burdened by his reputation and continued to truant from time to time. A camp organized by welfare staff for a small number of students like him was planned to coincide more or less with final exams so he thought he "might not be doing them," but by term four he had noticed a change: "it just happened over the holidays. I don't really know why, I just changed . . ." But it had not been quite as straightforward as that, as Robbo admitted at the end of the year:

JW: Have you made any changes or adjustments?
R: Oh well last, last term they gave me a sheet of work to do
JW: Mm.
R: and I had to finish it to pass Year 9
JW: Mm.
R: so an' I sort of couldn't get in any trouble (if they wanted me to?) and they said, they told me if I, if I was going to fail Year 9 which I was going to if I didn't do my work
JW: Mm.
R: I wouldn't be allowed to come back here next year. I'd have to find a different school and do Year 9 there.
JW: So are you going to come back?
R: Ah yeh I passed.
JW: You passed everything.
R: So I eventually did my work and got a bit better.
JW: Fair enough. How did you feel? Did you feel like
R: Oh yeh better [. . .]

CONCLUSION

The observation that the category "schoolboy" does not signify a unitary identity is just as true, as this chapter has shown, of the signifiers "good" student and "failing," "disaffected," or "challenging" student. If there is nothing essential or unitary about any of these subjects, then to speak of them occupying such subject positions, therefore, is to put those positions in question. Investment by the boys in this study in discursively ascribed identity, as this chapter has shown, is conditional – never determined, always open to dispute. In resisting the normative observations, calibrations, and regulations of teachers (and indirectly of parents), most of these boys not only disputed, or resisted, the identities ascribed to them, but were able also to emphasize what seemed to them to be a certain authentic and unified identity, at least up to a point, both in our encounters and in their dealings with teachers.

For example, Jake was able to assert a certain confidence and authority in his discursively mediated encounters with teachers in seeking leadership positions which effectively disarmed whatever ways he had been positioned by his less enthralled Maths teacher. Whatever else he was, Jake was both a vocal critic and a leader and knew the value of academic achievement: this was the identity he wished to cultivate. Kevin, meanwhile, was indifferent to whatever reputation he had acquired from teachers. Like Robbo, Gerster, Otto, and George, his face was turned to friends and the discursive formations they sustained. Kevin still loved reading, but not for homework, and would not give up smoking, and Robbo, like Otto, was a pillar of resistance. All illustrated in countless ways what Walkerdine (1990) refers to as "a constantly erupting pathology" (p. 25). For his part, Gerster was caught somewhere between extremes but found himself validated as friend and supporter. In the case of George, however, the gradual dissolution of a sense of self and the struggle to acquire the discursive competence to appear as what had hitherto been alien to him, even with the support of welfare staff, revealed a sense of loss that the others seemed unable to contemplate.

The point at which their sense of selfhood began to give way – certainly in George's case – seems to have come about as the boys gradually accepted that as students they were required to acquiesce in mass schooling's demand that they participate in their own subjection. In Chapter 1 I drew attention to Foucault's claim that "a relation of surveillance . . . is inscribed at the heart of the practice of teaching . . . as a mechanism that is inherent to it . . ." (Foucault, 1991: 176). In this observation, Foucault is referring to the centrality of power relations in the formation of subjectivity. Lived experience, for Foucault, is the experience both of being subject *to* the discipline, or control, of others – "a form of power which makes individuals subjects" – and of being the subject *of* one's own self-discipline, or self-knowledge (Foucault, 1983a: 212; Grant, 1997: 676). The locus of power relations in the lived school experience of these boys has shifted, as this chapter has shown, from resistance to the subjectifying power of others (the experience of subjectedness), to the experience of self-surveillance; to the acceptance of the law of the school by self-regulating subjects. They have begun to act on themselves in ways that are instrumental both to themselves and to the school by accepting discursive practices that have established a certain "truth" about them and in so doing have come to manifest, however tentatively, a desire to be other than they have hitherto been.

10 Conclusion
Another New Beginning

I set out in this study to ask what it is to be a boy at school, prompted initially by Epstein's challenge to understand "how boys experience themselves as boys" at school (Epstein, 1998b: 107). My concern arose in the context of the ongoing debate in Australia and elsewhere over the question, "what about the boys?" and from my years of teaching. This question, as I have indicated, arose initially out of concern for what seemed to some to be a disturbing trend of falling achievement among boys in the final years of school together with a widespread sense of disaffection among many boys with their schooling, while at the same time girls were said not only to be doing well but to be doing so at the expense of boys. This debate about a "gender gap" in the popular press and the academy has taken place within and against what feminist and profeminist writers have characterized as a backlash against gains made by girls and, indeed women, in the last two or three decades in education, and signifies a disturbingly polarized constituency.

On the one hand, the question at the centre of the debate has been asked by those who advocate an essentialist understanding of gendered identity allied with some who are sympathetic to a nominally social constructionist account of gender. Whether arguing for a hard-line biological and psychological essentialism or not, those who do so rely, more often than not, on a prediscursive, unitary subject in which rationality and agency are understood as given. Their clashes with feminist and profeminist writers, whose work is grounded in a far more nuanced social constructionist epistemology, have produced something of a standoff in which academic inquiries and government-sponsored reports have fuelled one side or the other of the debate while at the same time each side attempts to influence gender equity policies in Australian education.

Against this framing of the issue of failing boys, concern for difference in terms of class, location, indigeneity, and ethnicity began to emerge from large-scale statistical studies of boys (and girls) at the end of their schooling. As a result it was argued that it was no longer feasible to think of all boys as undifferentiated, and that a more appropriate response would be to ask "which boys?" Which boys were in need of help and advice? Which boys in particular should society and policy makers be concerned about? Which boys was this debate really about?[1]

To Biddulph, and to those he both drew on and inspired, the answer to these questions remained "all boys". In their view, modern industrial society had produced an under-fathered boy increasingly remote from his authentic biological self and destiny, remote from traditional masculinizing rituals and caught up in a feminized curriculum and pedagogy. This figure of the boy out of time and out of place, failing and disruptive at school, in dire need of help, has attracted considerable popular and governmental support in formulating gender equity policies in Australian education and attempts have been made to accommodate him within a variety of federally funded local initiatives. While he was said, on the one hand, to exhibit all the characteristics of a testosterone-laden, psycho-biologically driven adolescent, on the other he was characterized as showing all the hallmarks of a disturbingly hegemonic and socially constructed masculinity. My daily experience of boys who could unquestionably be described as fitting the figure of concern was tempered by the thought that such boys were in some sense being produced by the school, so an early issue for me as teacher-researcher was how to bring such boys into a study of their experience of daily life at school. To do so in terms not of the school's making but in terms of a poststructuralist critique, Epstein's question became a matter of asking how boys are subjectivated at school: of asking how they become, or are made to become, or make themselves become, boys of a certain kind. What subjectivities do they acquire and how are they imagined and thought of by others? Above all, at school/in being schooled, what do they experience? At the same time, and no less important, was the issue of how to enter the debate taking place beyond the study without going over old ground and reinforcing entrenched positions.

In doing so, I have not set out to identify "poor boys" or justify boys being boys, nor have I sought to blame the school or women teachers for the experiences of the boys who took part in this study and neither have I compared girls and boys, or claimed any sort of entitlement for boys. In asking how boys experience themselves as boys at school, two broad understandings of experience opposed one another. On the one hand, a common sense understanding of experience as something one had – a possession of the sovereign individual – of the everyday world, seemed to resonate with accounts of the unitary subject, as if the object of experience were ontologically separate from, or prior to, the experiencing subject. Alternatively, a poststructuralist theorizing of discursively constituted positionality and subjectivity emphasizes their achievement in performative and discursive terms. Experience, in the sense suggested by this formulation, unfolds performatively, discursively and intertextually; like identity and the self it is constantly in a process of becoming – fluid, not fixed, achieved, not given. Thus I have tried to adopt a view of experience which might allow insight into the constitutive moments of subjectification, making visible the coming into being of experience and at the same time the possibility of its capture in thought. In this, Foucault's notions of surveillance, governmentality, subjectification, and discursive formations and Judith Butler's notion of performativity have been crucial. In characterizing the "world of discourse" within which daily life and experience at Hillside High School becomes intelligible (Foucault, 1990: 100), I have attempted, as Foucault urges, to reconstruct this discursive realm in terms of "the things said and those concealed, the enunciations required and those forbidden . . . and . . . the shifts and reutilizations of identical formulas for contrary objectives . . ." (ibid. 100). In doing so, I have, of necessity, exercised a kind of surveillance over relations between the boys in this study and the work of their teachers whose expertise in regulating the conduct of school students is so essential to governance in a liberal – and especially a neo-liberal – state with its increasingly insistent demands for personal responsibility, performativity, and accountability (Rose, 1999). It is a task, moreover, that has brought into focus the local, the present, and the particular to locate these boys' "felt sense of self" (Butler, 1990, quoted in Hey, 2006b: 444) – a sense of "who they thought they were" (Miller and Rose, 2008: 7) and of how they came to be this way, rather than who they were said to be by others.

Investigating and writing about boys and their discontents in the field of education, leaving aside purely literary accounts, and in spite of several decades of ethnographic and other large-scale and interview-based studies, has produced a relatively restricted range of accounts. Early ethnographic studies of processes happening in schools (and of students and teachers, sometimes almost by default), reflect ethnography's realist and modernist tendencies, but it is in more recent studies, prompted by poststructuralist and frequently feminist theorizing that a more reflexive, less logocentric approach has become possible. Whereas once the schoolboy was conceived of as a unitary subject, capable of rational thought and agency in studies of the structure and function of the school or the classroom, recent studies have illustrated how schools can be and are regulative and productive institutions in which the outcome of schooling is not only academic achievement (or the lack of it), but also the production of gendered, classed, and racialized subjectivities. This development is largely due to poststructuralist theorizing which has posited a nonunitary subject, discursively dispersed and standing in opposition not only to the foundational subject of essentialism but to the equally foundational humanist subject of education.

Partly arising from this observation, I took the view that in their daily interactions at school the boys in this study and their teachers were doing something other than endlessly constructing and reconstructing their gendered identities, or more simply, their various masculinities and femininities. In doing so it was not my intention to deny that gender was going on, or being done, but to acknowledge that so also were age and ethnicity. Thus I hoped to avoid the frankly Euclidian metaphor of "intersections" that is so clearly inadequate when touching on the complexity of identity and which continues to permit the analytic prioritization of one category at the expense of others. Instead, by problematizing what amounts to the experience of being constituted as this or that sort of boy at school – of being produced in discursive and performative relations of power – I have turned my attention to an epistemology denying the truth of "the" disaffected schoolboy as a foundational identity within the discourse of achievement. The figure of the disaffected boy at risk – the rhetorical achievement of biological and psychological essentialism – is erased once the subject's dispersal in discourse is recognized, leaving in its place a site of potentially boundless discursive and performative possibility. For those living within and subjected to and by the discursive realm of the school, however, the exercise of agency and power come together in the daily attempt (especially by students) to trump interpellation by asserting a sense of selfhood without which it seems there can be no experience. It is perhaps only because of the discursive and performative agency required to bring a sense of an experiencing self into being that the notion of intersecting categories of significance has come to mean anything at all.

Working within the confines of the school – present among and witness to its subjectifying practices – the question of the efficacy of an ethnographic study of what amounts to the experience of coming into being posed itself daily. The very constructedness of the ethnographic encounter and its reliance on memory has had to be acknowledged as has the "identity work" not only have I had to do but so also have the boys in this study. And beyond having "been there" (although as I have said, never having quite been where so much of the subjectification has taken place), the question of representation has been paramount. In writing, therefore, the ethnographic claim to have "been there" was a claim that in one sense I abandoned from the start only to replace it with another in which "there" amounted to moments of reflection on things seen and other moments of jointly constructed meaning which, together, might hopefully evoke a degree of plausibility.

Before finally reflecting on what I believe it means to the boys in this study to be a schoolboy, or perhaps to be a school student of any kind, the question of gender equity policy within which this study partly arose needs to be addressed. In the years immediately following the House of Representatives inquiry into boys' education in Australia, $A19.5 million was made available to fund initiatives addressing the findings of the inquiry at the level of the school, or groups of local schools. This process of the devolution of gender equity policy to local communities and the more than 200 schools that applied, had outcomes that were in many ways entirely predictable. The federal inquiry, as I have shown, proceeded on the basis of a gender binary, prioritizing an essentialized notion of masculinity which was further valorized in what passed for policy discourse of the day (Ailwood, 2003; Keddie, 2005; O'Donovan, 2006). Indeed, as Lingard and others have argued, the absence of a concerted and centrally mandated gender equity policy in Australian education after 1997, popular media throughout the period of the federal inquiry operated as a source of *de facto* gender policy in education (Lingard and Douglas, 1999; Lingard, 2003; Mills, 2003). With arguments for recuperative masculinity in the ascendency, policy once again became a site of contest in which hopes for the acceptance of a constructionist understanding of gender were left to advocates at the local level, with mixed results (Lingard, 2003; Hodgetts, 2008; Keddie, 2010). It became increasingly clear that the federal inquiry had done little to change educational structures or practices or to challenge popular notions of boyhood, masculinity, and femininity as "boy friendly" curricular and pedagogical practices were retained or reinvigorated (Martino *et al.*, 2004; Cuttance *et al.*, 2006; Mills *et al.*, 2007; Hodgetts, 2008).

Somewhat paradoxically, however, just as the federal government in Australia (whether Liberal/Conservative or Labor) has increasingly centralized its control of education policy, for example in mandating a national curriculum and nationwide measures of achievement in literacy and numeracy at key moments throughout the school years and in devising measures of school effectiveness, it has evacuated the field of gender equity policy. The discourse of policy in education is increasingly focused on measures of whole school achievement founded on assumptions of individual improvement (see Youdell, 2004). With little or no reference to gender (policies are for "students"), the feminist and profeminist agenda of hoping to change the behavior and attitudes of at least some boys with the support of a centralized gender equity policy has had to be abandoned (Hodgetts, 2008).

This call for schoolboys to change, or be changed – to become someone else – reiterates a sentiment that has been expressed by feminists and profeminists since at least 1995 in Australia and represents an impasse in the construction of gender equity policy in Australian education. With or without such a policy, attempts have been made at the curricular and pedagogic levels to challenge the gender regimes of schools, dominant expressions of masculinity, bullying, homophobia and what it means to succeed at school, just as other innovations have perhaps reinforced existing and arguably inequitable understandings of masculinity and gender relations. Just as responsibility for these changes has devolved to the school, so discourses of care, inclusivity, gender equity, and the prospect of success have become apparent in the ways both private and state schools market themselves, but at the centre of these moves is the teacher and her or his class and the practices that go on there. So far, in England and Australia, attempts to resolve issues identified around the education of boys in terms of curriculum and pedagogy have been entirely questionable in relation to teaching practices, assumptions about learning, curriculum content, and the nature of outcomes desired (Kenway and Willis, 1997; Lingard and Douglas, 1999; Lingard et al., 2009; Martino et al., 2009; Skelton and Francis, 2009). In the absence of compelling evidence, it is perhaps not surprising that policy writers in England, as Francis (2006) has noted, have continued to represent boys generally in terms of the humanist and frequently essentialist assumptions of education policy discourse as "vulnerable and disaffected . . . deserving (of) sympathy and attention" (p. 192). In the contemporary neo-liberal environment, however, failure to behave and learn and achieve in acceptable ways positions some such boys as undeserving and even beyond redemption, adopting a presence in the popular imagination as "folk devils" (ibid. 196), not unlike the image I have referred to earlier as essentialism's triumph. Youdell, (2006a) however, has shown not only how the discursive practices of schooling can operate to produce such "problem" boys ("unintelligible subjects," "impossible boys," and "impossible learners" in her critique), but also, and disturbingly, how the politics of exclusion can compromise any attempt to realize equity in education.

If the issues raised in this study are to be addressed at all, the current impasse in gender equity policies will need to be abandoned and new approaches developed. It seems entirely likely that education policy discourse will continue to be devised in terms of the subject of humanism (if not of essentialism also), and that poststructuralist insights will continue to be marginalized. In the current neo-liberal moment, however, and in the absence of policy, "problem boys" will continue to be constituted in schooling's discursive and performative practices and exposed to injunctions to govern their behavior better, to adopt techniques of reflection and confession and to perfect repertoires of conduct; in a word, to practice inhibition (Foucault, 1991: 294; Rose, 1999: 42–43; Smith, 1992). As Laws and Davies (2000) have observed, such "training in 'normality'" is "not necessarily benign" (p. 208); in fact, since there may be so many conflicting discourses for boys in school, "Managing being a boy and being a subject at the same time, can verge on the impossible" (ibid. 220). Exhortations for boys to change, therefore, and policies designed to bring about changes in behavior, attitudes, and achievement are hardly likely to alter some boys' experience of schooling any more than experience as I have understood it here is likely to be the object of educational policy.[2] Perhaps gender equity policy in education has become too narrowly focused on matters of curriculum and pedagogy; perhaps it is time to return instead to the task of how better to think what schooling and education could be, which after all, is not necessarily the sole province of policy makers (Dillabough et al., 2008). In this regard, John Dewey's (1997/1938) thought on the nature of experience in education can be read, at least in part, as an early attempt to critique the sovereign individual of Enlightenment thought and its relation to the experience of schooling.

To be a schoolboy – indeed, to be a pupil or student of any kind – is to daily wake with the knowledge that whatever other identities one has, *that* is what one is – inevitably already positioned in discursive formations (which are never purely singular), which both permit and limit what one can say and do and what can be said and done to or about one. This much is surely well known. To prepare for school – to put on a uniform and step out into the world, carrying a schoolbag – is to announce oneself to the world as already subjectivated. To be such a student is not only to be hailed as such by all who see him or her, but by virtue of being so visibly present, the student also hails him or herself into being. It is in the act of being designated by others or of appropriating the act of designation to oneself, that a subject is constituted.

Such self-recognition, however, as Kevin showed, can be shot through with ambiguity, resentment, and loathing. Why get to school early, let alone on time? What is the attraction once there? Why not stop for a smoke? Why not smoke some "choof"? Such contempt for the normative school emphasized his pathological status in the eyes of those whose job it was to encounter him and the other boys in this study. The boy who arrived affected by alcohol, the boy George tried to get to school on time and Robbo, George, Otto, and Kevin themselves in their cavalier attitudes to the wearing of the uniform and to timely arrival, all resist their interpellation as students of this school and so dispute the subjectivity it entails. To these boys, the attractions of truancy, which, as they know, might just as soon become isolation and friendless boredom, are real but ambiguous. To arrive at school, however, is to be hailed and recognized by friends within another discursive and performative context in more or less constant opposition to the dominant discourses of the school.

More than that, to arrive at school and to join one's class, as these boys knew, is to surrender, or be drawn, to a more specific interpellation by this or that teacher as rude, challenging, violent, difficult: a whole lexicon of more or less daily disapprobation awaits each of them. As Youdell (2006a, 36) says, "these subjects . . . at least at the level of the everyday or commonsense (may appear) to precede their designation (but are more properly understood as artefacts of their) performative constitution." The deployment of discursive performatives directly through the spoken word and written language (by teachers and coordinators exercising their surveillant and normalizing function), or through the apprehension of teachers' bodily habitus, or obliquely through representations of the school's dominant discourses in photographs, homilies, and narratives, all work to position these boys as oppositional and disaffected, to which they respond by deploying performatives of their own. In the absence of any authoritative written text they deploy their bodies, voice, and language by standing too close, by lounging, slouching, dawdling, fidgeting, and glaring; by swearing, speaking too loudly, or seeming to threaten and challenge; by asserting a bodily and vocal ethnicity; by not working in class, by ignoring or refusing to do homework, and in countless other ways by confirming their reputation, they are seen to be, and are reported as, "other" to the normative school. In these ways, subjects and teachers may be designated in their own discourses of friendship and contempt as boring, irrelevant, incompetent, unjust, or even as "bitch," or "c***," as George said of one male teacher, while students may be designated as "nerds" or any of a vast range of other pejorative terms. As Butler (1997a) observed of "hate speech", such illocutionary speech acts immediately produce effects, in these cases by constituting others, including teachers, as subordinate subjects who, more often than not, resist such discursive positioning.

Such a characterization may well suggest that George, Kevin, Robbo, Otto, and Gerster illustrate the sort of "laddish" behavior that British researchers in particular have identified ever since (if not before), Willis' (1977) *Learning to Labour*. Certainly they liked "mucking about" at the expense of teachers, occasionally "putting down" more conscientious students, disrupting classes from time to time, supporting one another in their antipathy to the normative expectations of the school and in some respects could be seen as beginning to presume as desirable a certain passivity in girls. On the other hand, it is questionable whether any of these boys could be said to unequivocally embody the "cool to be a fool" ethic which was central to the panic implied in the "what about the boys?" debate. It might have seemed to Arjay and Benny that George and Kevin, for example, were simply playing the fool and trying to attract attention at the expense of others like themselves, but neither George nor Kevin ever asserted outright pride in disruptive and clownish behavior and none sustained any contempt for others who enjoyed and were good at their schoolwork: indeed, they unhesitatingly acknowledged the academic superiority of others. Robbo and Otto may have hated school and ignored homework, Gerster may have looked forward to upsetting his Geography teacher, and George may have regarded History and Geography as boring and irrelevant, but each knew that successful achievement, at least in Maths and English, was essential if they were to move beyond school into desired career paths, and that a broader range of achievement was necessary if they wanted to move up into the senior school. What is more, each not only liked certain subjects but certain teachers as well, and just as teachers daily designated them as disruptive, the same teachers, and others, could and did from time to time praise and encourage them.

To a degree, much the same could be said of Jake, Hamish, and Tim and of Arjay and Benny. All wanted to go through to the end of Year 12 and all were prepared to concentrate in class, do homework and prepare for exams, but not to the exclusion of having fun, even if that meant annoying teachers and participating in various forms of disruption. In Jake's case, however, this "laddish" behavior was balanced against an open commitment to the more individualistic ethic sustaining his leadership ambitions within the terms set down by the normative school.

In the case of each boy, but perhaps more clearly in relation to George and friends, the notion of a sovereign, unitary subject as the object of the dominant discourses of the school is seen to be a vacuous fiction. Far from merely fulfilling different roles, the boys are seen to inhabit an array of subject positions within discursive formations emanating not only from the school but also from home and family as well as from among their friends. Thus, Jake is encouraged to pursue leadership ambitions and George is encouraged to stop "mucking about" and being a "dumb arse." In George's case, the dispersal of his subjectivity was laid bare in his response to his grandmother's death and to the school's response to his grief. Whereas failing and disruptive "lads" like George are so routinely taken to be unable to communicate emotions and feelings, George expressed his grief as good son, family member, dutiful grandson, and so on, discursively emphasizing his ethnicity in the process much to the confusion of teachers and administrators. Likewise, Kevin, Robbo, and Gerster grieved for the loss of a good friend, truanting and expressing their emotions in illocutionary terms suggesting a linguistic agency not sanctioned by the normative school. Very little by way of emotional expression, it seemed, was repressed, and in coping with grief and loss, with or without the pastoral intervention of the school, their fragmentary subjectivities were blatantly and even painfully disclosed.

A central tenet of this thesis is that just as gendered identities are discursively produced, so is experience. All the boys who took part in this study jointly constructed accounts of themselves with me and in doing so were encouraged to recount moments of interpellation against which I could read, or discuss with teachers, other reports of the same incidents. I was rarely "there" when such incidents took place, as I have said, so as not to influence either the boys or the teachers in any way, but I was nevertheless able to watch and overhear in other ways. I stood back. What I saw and heard, and what we later reconstructed in our own encounters clearly arose out of the constitutive power of language and other performatives. For example, in locating themselves within competing or conflicting discourses, the boys and their teachers experienced themselves, often in visceral and deeply emotional ways, as diffuse and contradictory. More specifically, in resisting the normative observations, calibrations, and regulations of teachers, most of the boys who participated in this study not only disputed the identities ascribed to them but were able to emphasize a sense of a certain authentic and unified identity, at least up to a point, sustained and confirmed discursively with friends both in our encounters and in their dealings with teachers.

This can be seen no more clearly than in the case of George. In his final weeks at the school, George was in the throes of becoming a figure acceptable to the normalizing judgments of teachers and administrators.

At last he was complicit in the production of a new subjectivity (Walkerdine *et al.*, 2001: 176), tentatively seeking a place from which to speak while facing the ethical crisis of complicity, rather in the manner of persons seeking to change class identity (Skeggs, 2004; Hey, 2006a: 302), or to assimilate. The position of subordination from which George had long been produced as a subject was now only resisted in a token way as he invested more openly in normatively acceptable appearance and approach to work only belatedly flaunting the old identity as if recognizing the futility of doing so. As I did early in the study, he, too, was becoming a stranger to himself.

Calls for boys such as George, Kevin, Robbo, Gerster, and Otto to change – to become less boorish, less intimidating, less vulgarly masculine, for example – no matter how well intentioned and justified – need to take into account just what such change requires of those from whom change is expected. Who may legitimately demand the identity work necessary for the self to act upon the self? How is such legitimacy warranted? On what grounds are such demands or expectations regarded as acceptable or desirable? What discursive and performative possibilities can there be for such change in contemporary schooling? To see George grapple with the dilemma of how and why he should change – perhaps to become "less Greek" as well as less boorish and so on – is to be left in no doubt about how difficult and how painful this reconstitution of subjectivity can be. Furthermore, to be required to make such change on the grounds of the desirability of conformity to the normative demands of discourses promising emancipation but producing instead the experience of pathology and oppression is to put in question the ethical core of mass education and the neo-liberal subject it aspires to produce.

To ask how the boys in this study experience themselves as boys at school, as I set out to do, is potentially to arrive at a somewhat static understanding. Instead, as I have shown, theirs is in varying degrees an experience of the transience of self – of contested affirmation, of fluidity, of submission, and uncertainty. Such, ultimately, and in particular, is the experience of being George, Kevin, Robbo, Gerster, and Otto.

Epilogue

When next the achievements of boys at the end of their schooling are aggregated and analyzed, the likes of George, Kevin, Robbo, and Otto will be missing. Whatever the debates, theirs and their potential contribution to the whole will have been silenced by their early departure from the education system and their stories will be marginalized. Looking back at the end of Year 10 it seemed to me that in searching out these boys as early as Year 8, we – the coordinators, teachers, and myself – had done too good a job. By about the age of 14 these boys, and others like them, had become the objects of a disciplinary system (in the Foucauldian sense), that relentlessly pursued their increasingly resistant subjectivities to the point where departure, either on their terms or the school's, was the ultimate resolution of their experience. Here, one could argue, was the ultimate failure of the school's dominant discourses in so far as no skill or achievement of theirs conformed to normative excellence, their continued presence was regarded as an affront to the community and in being removed from it, or in removing themselves, such care as they received culminated in their being positioned within a crisis of selfhood.

Otto could see it clearly at the end of what would have been Year 10 had he completed it. His departure from school had been connected to an incident with a boy two years ahead about to do his final exams. "He was probably having a great life," said Otto, now waiting on a pre-apprenticeship program at a TAFE College. Hundreds had applied and he was one of 70 to be accepted, but it hurt him, he said, that when asked for his highest level of school achievement he had to say "Year 9." Almost his last words were "I hate that school."

Appendix I
Reading Interview Transcriptions

The following procedures have been adopted in transcribing interviews:

. . .	pause to nearest second (for example, three seconds)
(?); (go?)	indistinct; probable word(s)
(?)	substantial passage indistinct
[your words are]	author's clarification
[. . .]	section of text omitted
(laughter)	author's comment
———	Name omitted
italics	to emphasize tone and/or loudness

In my transcriptions I have tried to give an idea of the way each boy fumbled for words and constructed his own particular grammatical structures. The uses of full stops and commas are in most cases the result of guess-work. The absence of a full stop at the end of a line signifies that a turn in the discussion is incomplete.

Notes

PART I BOYS IN THE FRAME

1 GETTING AT EXPERIENCE

1 The Victorian Certificate of Education undertaken over Years 11 and 12. Student results in the final year are used to calculate an overall score used in applications for university entrance. In some studies (subjects), portfolios and performances may be used.
2 "Hegemonic masculinity can be defined as the configuration of gender practice which embodies the currently acceptable answer to the problem of the legitimacy of patriarchy, which guarantees . . . the dominant position of men and the subordination of women" (Connell, 1995: 77). It is not to be thought of as invariant, but is nevertheless seen to be a successful claim to authority. The achievement and politics of hegemonic masculinity/ies have been the subject of ongoing critique: see Frank (1987), Donaldson (1993), Clatterbaugh (1998) and Phoenix and Frosh (2001). For the views of boys aged 11 to 14 and comments on hegemonic masculinity's narrowly constricting effects see Phoenix and Frosh (2001) and Frosh *et al.*, (2002).
3 Connell's critique and rejection of role theory and socialization is crucial to his theorization of gender (Connell, 1987: 191–96; Connell, 1995: 25–27). He also notes, in relation to essentialist claims, that "Arguments about gender are plagued by an assumption that what is biological or 'natural' is somehow more real than what is social" (1987: x). This will be shown to be the case in relation to essentialist claims in Chapter 3.
4 As Walkerdine (1989) observes, "there are no unitary categories 'boys' and 'girls'. . ." (p. 273).
5 Francis (2008) explores the implications for male teachers, and for teaching generally, of a variety of masculinities among teachers.
6 This brings together issues of identity, performativity, and agency. Sunderland and Litosseliti (2002) ask

> whether we are all automatically performing or constructing our gender *all the time*; if so, we are presumably also simultaneously performing other identities (e.g. our ethnicity) and at times the performance of one identity must then be privileged over that of another.
>
> (p. 27; original emphasis)

7 Connell (1995) is sceptical of what he sees as postmodernist claims "that discourse is all we can talk about in social analysis" (p. 71). His notion of

discourse is never made particularly clear and this comment suggests that he understands it in terms of what Butler (1993) refers to as "linguistic monism, whereby everything is only and always language" (p. 6).
8 Throughout this study the word "text" will refer to both talk and writing. See MacLure (2003: 106) and Sunderland and Litosseliti (2002: 12).
9
> We shall call discourse a group of statements in so far as they belong to the same discursive formation; it does not form a rhetorical or formal unity, endlessly repeatable, whose appearance or use in history might be indicated (and, if necessary, explained); it is made up of a limited number of statements for which a group of conditions of existence can be defined. Discourse in this sense is not an ideal, timeless form that also possesses a history . . . it is from beginning to end historical – a fragment of history, a unity and discontinuity in history itself, posing the problem of its own limits.
>
> (Foucault, 1972: 117)

10 In his early, "archaeological" period, when Foucault was explicating his notion of discourse, he had in mind the emergence of the human sciences, such as psychiatry, medicine, and even economics. See Foucault (1994; 1972).
11 The term "discourse" is highly contested. As MacLure (2003: 174ff) has pointed out, the "radical suspicion of reason, order and certainty as governing principles of knowledge and existence," so characteristic of poststructuralism, has drawn many writers to question the configurations of power/knowledge (discursive formations) typifying constitutive social formations and institutions (p. 178). This deconstruction has revealed how *unrelievedly textual* is the social world – to the extent "that textuality is the *condition* of truth, being, substance . . ." (p. 179; original emphasis). This is congenial with Foucault's exposition outlined earlier. Other writers, however, have developed ways of analyzing actual texts. This "(l)inguistically oriented discourse analysis takes a more micro-analytic focus, concentrating on . . . 'what people actually say and do'" (p. 182). See also Sunderland and Litosseliti (2002: 8–12), Fairclough (2003), Parker (1990), and Potter *et al.* (1990).
12 In *The Order of Things* (1994), Foucault writes "Without imagination there could be no resemblance between things" (p. 69), and in trying to grasp the discontinuous and irregular extent of discourses he writes of "a network of analogies that transcended the traditional proximities" of the classical sciences in which "isomorphisms appear to ignore the extreme diversity of the objects under consideration" (p. xi). This openness to, or discovery of, similitude enabled him to speak of the equivalence of the objects of discourse. Thus, in *Discipline and Punish* (1991), he writes: "Is it surprising that prisons resemble factories, schools, barracks, hospitals, which all resemble prisons?" (p. 228).
13 For Foucault,

> Power is everywhere; not because it embraces everything, but because it comes from everywhere . . . (P)ower is not an institution, and not a structure; neither is it a certain strength we are endowed with; it is the name that one attributes to a complex strategical situation in a particular society.
>
> (Foucault, 1990: 93)

Rather than speak of power, Foucault preferred to speak of "power relations" (1991: 27), signifying both its ubiquity and, as Butler (1997a) notes, "that contemporary power is no longer sovereign in character" (p. 74).
14 This argument has been well rehearsed by, among others, Fraser (1983), Ransom (1993), Ramazanoglu (1993), Kenway (1995a) and Francis (1999a,

2000) and is perhaps the main reason for Skeggs' (1998, 2004) and Francis' (2000) and Francis and Skelton's (2005) retention of a modernist epistemology. See also Tsolidis (2006) on refusing to take sides.
15 For Connell's contribution to the rejection of sex-role theory, see Kessler *et al.*, 1985 and Carrigan *et al.*, (1985).
16 Discourse, to Davies and Harré, is understood as "largely a conversational phenomenon" (1990: 45) including nonverbal aspects of conversations. In clarifying this they write: "discourse is to be understood as an institutional use of language and language-like sign systems . . . It is that in terms of which phenomena are made determinate . . . (It) is a multi-faceted public process through which meanings are progressively and dynamically achieved" (pp. 45–46). Such an understanding opens discursive practices to empirical analysis in a way that Connell's ambiguous approach to discourse does not.
17 Butler (1997a) adds:

> I propose that agency begins where agency wanes. The one who acts (who is not the same as the sovereign subject) acts precisely to the extent that he or she is constituted as an actor and, hence, operating within a linguistic field of enabling constraints from the outset.
>
> (p. 16)

Agency, in this sense, is therefore understood as an effect of discourse.
18 Butler (1997a) writes:

> If a performative provisionally succeeds (and I will suggest that "success" is always and only provisional), then it is not because an intention successfully governs the action of speech, but only because that action echoes prior actions, and *accumulates the force of authority through the repetition or citation of a prior and authoritative set of practices*. It is not simply that the speech act takes place *within* a practice, but that the act is itself a ritualized practice. What this means, then, is that a performative "works" to the extent that *it draws on and covers over* the constitutive conventions by which it was mobilized. In this sense, no term or statement can function performatively without the accumulating and dissimulating historicity of force.
>
> (p. 51; emphasis in original)

See also Butler (1997b: 93–94).
19 For Butler's relevance to the sociology of education, see *British Journal of Sociology of Education*, Special Issue, (2006) 27: 4.
20 Being reflexive is something of a vexed issue in ethnography. Skeggs (2002), for example, contrasts "reflexivity as a resource for authorizing oneself (*being*) and *doing* reflexivity in practice" (p. 349; original emphasis). She is scathing of the former for what she claims is its capacity to authorize the researcher at the expense of his/her subjects: "The central point . . . is how reflexivity becomes a property of the researcher's self *not* of the practice of the participants" (p. 359; original emphasis). Her discomfort with self-narration is well documented (Skeggs, 1998, 2004: 367), in contrast to Walkerdine *et al.* (2002) who typically espouse a reflexive awareness on the part of qualitative researchers not only of their own subjectivity but of the production of that subjectivity by the narratives and discourses they jointly participate in (pp. 179; 186; 194). See also Kenway and McLeod (2004).
21 MacLure (2003), for example, writes of "intimate, convivial, egalitarian field methods such as 'conversational' interview styles . . . that intentionally

curtail the authority of the academic researcher" (p. 100). Holstein and Gubrium (1995), in discussing "active" interviewing, advocate the activation, stimulation, and cultivation of a subject's "interpretive capabilities" in conversation in order "to provide an environment conducive to the production of the range and complexity of meanings that address relevant issues, and not be confined to predetermined agendas" (p. 17). Thus, "The analytic objective is not to merely describe the situated production of talk but to show how what is being said relates to the experiences and lives being studied" (pp. 79–80). That is, the incitement to converse may open access to something more than the immediate conversational encounter.

22 For example: "I believe too much educational research is reliant on interviewing"; "I do observational research, I do fieldwork, I watch, I do not believe in interviewing... I am totally out of step with the narrative/interview culture of the 1990s" (Delamont, 2004: 89–90).

23 For the gradual awareness of this phenomenon and its emergence into the text, see Tedlock (1991).

24 This is not to suggest that the notion of experience has not been incorporated into studies of education as Chapter 3 will show. See also, for example, Corrigan (1988), van Manen (1990, 1999), Eder *et al.* (1995), Ramazanoglu and Holland (1999), Schostak and Logan (2001), and Lahelma (2002).

25 Here I understand behavior as a generic term encompassing social interaction which might variously be described as performing, doing, achieving or otherwise constructing gender, or indeed ethnicity, youthfulness or any range of identities. The question for the researcher is not which one of these (or which combination of these) is going on, but what contextualized practice is being acknowledged by participants.

26 As Bruner (1986) observes, "We can have an experience but we cannot have a behaviour" (p. 5). Furthermore, following R. D. Laing, Kapferer (1986) notes that we cannot experience each other's experience, although we can share, or be present in, the situation in which that experience is had. Such a view challenges the notion of, for example, men's experience, working-class experience, and so on.

27 As MacLure (2003) puts it, "Experience is not . . . something that is natural and self-evident: it is *produced* through discursive practices" (p. 19; original emphasis). See also Pattman *et al.*, (1998: 126).

28 Dorothy Smith (2002) has adopted much the same view though with particular reference to Mikhail Bakhtin's notion of speech genres. She writes that experience should not be understood as referring to

> an authentic individual act of consciousness that gives access to a world directly known... (There) is no experience that is not already discursively structured... Any particular utterance... draws on what has been laid down in the past... and at the same time launches the genre into the future... Each next speaker or writer is in dialogue with discourse.
> (p. 42)

2 THE SCHOOLBOY AS OBJECT OF STUDY

1 For one attempt to establish a basis for renewed "mutual cooperation" between what he refers to as "practice-oriented" and "theoretically oriented" literature in this area, roughly analogous to the distinction I have drawn, see Weaver-Hightower (2003: 408). Francis (2000) and Francis and Skelton (2005) have addressed this hiatus with some success.

2 The equivalent, in almost all respects of the "lads" of British studies. For a useful review see Francis (2000, pp. 94 ff).
3 Ministerial Council on Education, Employment, Training and Youth Affairs reporting to the federal Minister for Education.
4 In a similar vein to O'Doherty's findings, a report produced for the Victorian Association of State Secondary Principals argued that "boys' performance is declining in real terms" (Ludowyke and Scanlon, 1997: 3) and that "the level of alienation of boys in the school context" was alarming (ibid. 7). Like O'Doherty, the authors took a constructionist view of gender and also distanced themselves from media coverage of gender issues in education which portrayed the educational outcomes of boys as being opposed to the educational needs (and recent gains) of girls. They also draw attention to Connell's notions of gender regime and patriarchal dividend in terms of the personal and social costs of such cultural structures and the assumptions embedded in them.
5 The study was funded by the Australian Department of Education, Employment, Training and Youth Affairs.
6 Initially the report drew on the views of 1,800 boys who completed questionnaires. See Slade (2002).
7 See also Slade (2001 and 2002). "most boys see themselves to be stuck with an unsuitable, out of date and culturally inconsistent learning environment they cannot change" (2002: x).
8 *The Age*, 17 June 2000.
9 All claims were denied by Jane Kenway, one of the authors (Arndt, 2000a).
10 See, for example, *The Age*, 23 June 2002; *The Weekend Australian*, 16–17 June, 2001; *The Sunday Age*, 27 October 2002; *The Age*, 8 May 2004.
11 The bulletin was produced by The Men and Boys Project which had been set up in 1996 as The Men's Health Project within the Family Action Centre at The University of Newcastle (*Boys in Schools Bulletin*, 1(1), 1997).
12 Rollo Browne, independent consultant to schools on boys' education; Richard Fletcher, manager of the Men and Boys program at the University of Newcastle; lecturer in health sciences; head of the Engaging Fathers project with the faculty of health at the University of Newcastle; former plumber, circus clown, and teacher (Arndt, 2004).
13 "When we see a boy born these days, we have our hearts in our mouths – how will he turn out?" (Biddulph, 1997: 2); Carr-Gregg and Shale (2002: 159ff). On parenting, see, for example, Elium and Elium (1992), referred to in Biddulph (1997); P. West, *The Age*, 29 January 2004.
14 Getting boys to enjoy reading, to develop the capacity to express themselves (emotions, feelings) and to see that men could do so emerges as a constant theme in reports from schools in the *Bulletin* and a major focus in the job of changing boys' behavior in schools.
15 For example, see Carr-Gregg and Shale (2002: high risk-taking, 50; youth suicide, 159–65); Biddulph (2002: 4) on "the statistics on men's health, happiness and survival" which he claims shows that the view that "it's a man's world . . . is a lie."
16 M. Carr-Gregg, reported in *Herald Sun*, 23 July 1996 concerning rates of suicide, depression, and self-mutilation. See also *The Age*, 28 September 1996; *The Age*, 13 April 1997; on teenage gay students, *The Age*, 29 December 1999. Issues of truancy, bullying, violence, and binge drinking are commonly discussed in this context. Carr-Gregg is a prominent Melbourne adolescent psychologist.
17 Steve Biddulph, trained as a psychologist: "Australia's best-known family therapist and parenting author" according to his publisher (Biddulph, 2002).

18 See also Pollack (1999) on "real boys," "real men," and "real fathers." "Boys today are in serious trouble" (p. xxi). Connell (2001: 5–6) includes Biddulph in his list of "pop psychologists" who "tell persuasive and entertaining stories," some of which from America "are undoubtedly faked."
19 Gilbert (1998, 20) has also drawn attention to this passage. Opposition to any notion of constructionist theorizing remains entrenched among conservative opponents of feminist and profeminist academics. For example, Jennifer Buckingham (2004), in a study for The Centre for Independent Studies, writes that

> the Association of Women Educators . . . subscribe to the theory that gender is socially constructed. This myth is inexplicably entrenched in universities, despite mounting genetic and neurological evidence supporting what the other 99% of us know – boys and girls are born different. We can guide their behaviour and shape their attitudes, but only within the parameters biology allows us.
> (p. 9)

On the other hand, Rollo Browne (1995), who is clearly sympathetic to Biddulph's position, observes that: "As a theory, the social construction of masculinity is dynamic and subtle in its complexity. Our response needs to be equally broad" (p. 229).
20 This preoccupation with the biological and neurological persists in *The Boys in Schools Bulletin* as links are made to approved styles of teaching and learning and to mentoring of boys. See Nagel (2005) and Delfos (2005).
21 In the first edition of *Manhood* (1994), chapter 3 was titled "Swimming in a Feminist Sea." By 2002 it had become "Liberation for the rest of us!"
22 "If there is no father around, then the child depends more on finding other men – at school for instance. Yet men are disappearing from the teaching profession, especially in primary schools, which creates a problem" (Biddulph, 1997: 17). Note also the more sober reflection of Formaini (1990): "The problem of the absent father is one of the most common syndromes in therapy and it often requires years of therapeutic work to bring it into full consciousness" (pp. 163–64).
23 He writes: "Unless you can connect to the inherited masculinity of generations of older men . . . (t)housands of years of masculine culture is missing for you" (Biddulph, 2002: 34).
24 A movement of men originating in America concerned to retrieve and celebrate what they see as their essential maleness (Kimmel and Kaufman, 1994, ch. 14). Biddulph writes: "The Men's Movement claims that men are massively wounded in normal life, from birth onwards." It is *"the Women's Movement's missing half"* (Biddulph, 2002: 25, 183; his emphasis). Its chief apologist is Robert Bly whose *Iron John* (1991) is quoted at length by Biddulph. See Biddulph (2002: 186) for a justification of initiation derived from Bly.
25 For example, there are constant references to American, Brazilian, and Australian indigenous cultures as well as stories of contemporary attempts to recreate a sense of ritual arrival at manhood. See Biddulph (1997: 170–71; 2002: 186–91).
26 For examples of celebrations of "the transition from boyhood to manhood" see N. Pizzini (1999) in the *Boys in Schools Bulletin*, 2(3); also *Boys in Schools Bulletin* (2000) 3(2). For getting out in Year 9 see *Boys in Schools Bulletin* (2000) 3(3) and (2001) 4(1). Perhaps the longest running example of its type in Australia is Geelong Grammar's "Timbertop" campus in alpine Victoria. See also Fletcher (2005) on why it is essential to be a male to be a role model for boys.

244 Notes

27 Attention Deficit Disorder; Attention Deficit Hyperactivity Disorder. Regarded as neuro-developmental disorders indicated by hyperactivity, impulsiveness, and inattentiveness, symptoms mostly exhibited by boys. Treatment is by psychostimulant drugs, behavioral therapy and educational intervention. Rowe and Rowe suggest the symptoms "may simply be a response to the way (boys) are being taught" (in Arndt, 2000b).
28 See also *The Age*, 8 February 2000; 11 September 2000 and especially Fletcher (2005: 34 – 35).
29 Dr Ken Rowe, at the time Principal Research Fellow at the Australian Council of Educational Research; also coauthored with his wife, Dr Kathy Rowe, who was the senior consultant paediatrician, Royal Children's Hospital, Melbourne.
30 See also *The Age*, 17 June 2000; 26 October 2000; 3 November 2000; 4 November 2000; 16–17 June 2001.
31 See also *The Age*, 8 February 2000.
32 For example, Fletcher to House of Representatives Inquiry:

> it is important that we convey to boys that men value learning ... The best way to do this is to have men demonstrate that ... (It) is not quite as convincing for a female teacher to tell the boy that men value learning as it is for him to see men doing it.
> (Commonwealth of Australia, 2002: 160).

33 For feminist rebuttals of these and similar claims together with suggestions on how boys and men might better understand their emotional response to gender reform, see Kenway (1995b; 1996), and Kenway *et al.* (1997).
34 See *The Age*, 8 May 2004; *The Age*, 6 June 2001. This issue was explicitly addressed in Recommendation 17 of the House of Representatives Inquiry (2002), especially pp. 160–64.
35 Also: "middle-aged, middle-class female teachers don't have a lot in common with adolescent boys with rampaging hormones, erratic attention spans and bizarre interests" (*The Age*, 3 May 2004).
36 "the truth is that for some of my male patients, schools remain a psychological wasteland where they don't feel safe, valued or listened to" (*The Age*, 19 July 2004).
37 The case for male mentors received a fillip in 2004 when Mark Latham, then leader of the Australian Labor Party, delivered a speech addressing the "crisis of masculinity" in which he proposed funding for "a national network of 'transition support workers' ... (who would) provide intensive personal support for at-risk early leavers, encouraging participation in education, training and work options" (*The Age*, 27 May 2004). See also West (2004) for his support for Latham and for bolstering "that web of authority" represented by fathers, churches, schools, and police.
38 Dr Tim Hawkes, Principal of The King's School; author of *Boy oh Boy. How to raise and educate boys* (2001b)
39 Quoted approvingly in *The Age* editorial, 27 October 2000. He was at the time the immediate past president of the Association of Heads of Independent Schools of Australia.
40 *The Age*, 7 March 2005; Paul Sheahan, then Principal of Melbourne Grammar School, who in referring to the "workaholic" father, wrote: "If you want the definitive account of this phenomenon, read the American poet and academic Robert Bly's wonderful book, *Iron John* ..." (*Australian Quarterly*, January–February (1999: 43).
41 See *The Sunday Age*, 27 October 2002. This view was put to the House of

Representatives Inquiry by a large delegation from Tintern and Southwood Schools, 26 October 2000. The crisis facing this discourse is seen when a single-sex school decides to become coeducational. See *The Age*, 30 July 2005 and *The Weekend Australian*, 27–28 February 2005 for responses to the decision by Mentone Grammar School in Melbourne to become coeducational. See also (Mills, 2000: 242) for further examples.

42 This view positions State schools as potential sites of failure relative to independent/private schools. In Victoria there is only one (selective) boys-only High School and three girls' High Schools. On the other hand, at the same time some previously single-sex independent schools have become coeducational. For the views of a Principal of the single boys-only state High School, see Willis (2005).

43 Note the observation by Francis and Skelton (2005) that

> Feminists have been extremely sceptical of, and often hostile to, concerns about boys' educational attainment . . . (In) Britain the feminist response to the media and policy furore on "boys' underachievement" can be characterized as initial hostility followed by scornful silence . . . Talk of boys' achievement is now often met with disdainful sarcasm in these circles.
>
> (p. 2)

44 Epstein *et al.* (1998) draw attention to this passage (p. 6). See also Gilbert and Gilbert (1998: 185).

3 WRITING THE SCHOOLBOY

1 On structural–functionalism see Sills (1968: 22) and Bruce and Yearley (2006: 292); on symbolic interactionism see Bruce and Yearley (2006: 296). Here I follow Atkinson's (1996) discussion (pp. 8–9 and 21). See also Hammersley and Atkinson (1995), Grant (1988), and Rock (2001). On neomarxism, see Aronowitz's Preface (1981) to the Morningside edition of Willis (1977).

2 This interpretation differs somewhat from that offered by Marcus (1992). For him, modernist ethnography is built around "the complex moral relationship of the observer to the observed" from which "a kind of ethical awareness" arises which ultimately has the power to remake the observer and the observed (p. 328). This has been influential in the work of Skeggs (1998, 2004) and at least indirectly in the work of Coffey (1999) and Atkinson (1996).

3 My selection of texts acknowledges their iconic status and could arguably have included Burgess (1983).

4 Lacey notes:

> Participant observation is a much maligned word, but in Manchester at the time it involved the fullest possible transfer; that is, the transfer of the whole person into an imaginative and emotional experience in which the fieldworker learned to live in and understand the new world he [sic] had chosen. I have not used the term "role-playing". I think in retrospect I would use the term "role-taking" (or role-making . . .) because this implies involvement of the self in an exposed and vulnerable position. There could be no clinical distancing, the fieldworker was expected to enter in and take punishment until he or she had learned to survive.
>
> (Lacey, 1976: 65–66)

This early reference to the ethnographic self nevertheless remained at the level of method and hardly intruded at all in his ethnographic opus.

5 Lacey (1976) wrote of his 1970 book:

> The review that follows is a personal statement. In it I explain some of the factors that led up to and shaped the study, and which are seldom discussed in sociological monographs. I hope to make clear the central ideas underlying my methodology.
>
> (p. 63)

6 Lacey and Hargreaves studied boys' schools while Lambart studied a girls' school. No theoretical justification for this division of labor (perhaps taken for granted) seems to have been published.

7 Frankenberg (1982), who had been influential in setting the terms of the Manchester studies, notes of Hargreaves:

> The earliest major work to emerge from this educational study . . . did not recognise its intellectual antecedents save for a brief reference to (one of the Manchester supervisors) and I here respect if I cannot share its author's implicit view that his periodic sharing of seminars and experience had had a negligible effect on his analysis.
>
> (p. 28)

This is a reference to Hargreaves' Introduction (1967) and may reflect the fact that Hargreaves entered the Manchester team a year later than the others when the direction of the research had already been determined, as much as any ideological differences or debate over method that there may have been with Frankenberg and Lacey.

8 See, for example, Lacey (1970: 181). The teaching profession appears masculinized almost without exception in the texts by Lacey and Hargreaves under discussion.

9 This revision appears in Lacey (1982: 168). In the original work boys appear as "pupils," "students," members of a subculture or peer group and more generally as persons to be socialized.

10 See Lacey (1970: 125).

11 It will emerge again in Wolpe's (1988a) work; see pp. 33–35.

12 Examples abound. See, for example, Lacey (1970: 86–87; 91).

13 Described as a "ritual of rebellion," this is the only example of a direct reference to Gluckman and the conceptual apparatus specific to social anthropology in the body of his text. (Lacey, 1970: fn. 32, 184).

14 See especially Lacey's (1976) comments on boys refusing to attend school, pp. 132–42, where his text departs in tone from that used in the more formal explication of his thesis.

15 "At first I suspected some of the boys were being rather rude to me, until I discovered that this was their natural mode of communication to the staff" (Hargreaves, 1967: 85). Hargreaves had previously taught briefly in a more genteel London Grammar school.

16 See especially pp. 202–05.

17 Ball's doctoral supervisor was Colin Lacey (Jackson, 1981: 287).

18 The commitment to symbolic interactionist theory is made clear in Ball (1984: 70; 86).

19 By 1990 Ball was self-consciously explicit about the researcher's self and its relation to both the construction of the ethnographic fieldwork experience and, in a limited way, the ethnographic text. See Ball (1990b).

20 Ball answers this criticism by pointing out that chapters covering methodology and theory were excised from the text at the publisher's insistence (Ball, 1984: 91–92). Autobiographical reflections on this and other ethnographic research show him to be keenly reflective. See Ball (1983) also.
21 By focusing almost exclusively on academic aspects of schooling, Ball admits that vast areas of student experience remain unexamined. Hence, "My account of the school is as a result profoundly distorted" (Ball, 1984: 76–77).
22 See, for example, Hall and Jefferson (1977) and Corrigan (1979).
23 A view also shared by Connell *et al.* (1985/1982) in terms such as "the working class experience" and the "collective experience" of schooling (pp. 45–46; 51; 172).
24 In the afterword to the American edition of *Learning to Labor* Willis wrote:

> The role of ethnography is to show the cultural viewpoint of the oppressed, their "hidden" knowledges and resistances as well as the basis on which entrapping "decisions" are taken with some sense of liberty, but which nevertheless help to produce "structure." This is, in part, the project of showing the capacities of the working class to generate . . . collective and cultural forms of knowledge not reducible to the bourgeois forms.
> (Willis, 1981: 203)

25 According to Skeggs (1992), Willis' text was the product of changing paradigms in sociology and the sociology of education and the critical analysis of education developed at the Centre for Contemporary Cultural Studies at Birmingham University in the 1970s. His work can be located firmly within the anthropological ethnographic tradition of youth cultural studies in Britain but with the added conceptual apparatus of Marxist theory. Thus he was concerned to explain and challenge the role of the educational system in reproducing inequality in a capitalist State.
26 He also interviewed their parents and teachers, and some boys in other nearby schools. See Willis (1977: 4–6). Nothing is said about how and why he came to choose the participants in his study (Whelen, 2008).
27 Marcus (1992) subsequently praised Willis for generating a sort of parallel text, or "negative image" of the text, in its margins (footnotes, asides, the afterword), which he saw as presaging a more experimental approach to writing ethnography (p. 324).
28 Meighan (1978) is particularly critical of Willis for his dogmatic style and too partial analysis of too small a sample of working-class youth in too limited an area.
29 Willis did extend his fieldwork to some homes and workplaces, but Walker's larger cohort and extended fieldwork, especially in social settings, far exceeded Willis'. Cusick (1973) similarly mixed with his students in many locations in and out of school, though over a much shorter period.
30 Walker chides Willis for overrapport with his subjects, inadequate triangulation, vagueness, and ambiguity in the use of the term "resistance," failure to question the boys' accounts, theoretical rigidity and for romanticizing the lads' actions and opinions (Walker, 1985, 1986).
31 As did Connell *et al.* (1985/1982) in another study of the relationship between schools, families, and social division.
32 No generic feminism is implied here. There were at the time, and still are, multiple feminist positions offering critiques of the everyday (Skelton and Francis, 2009).
33 See, for example, Hey (1997: 16–17) where a sense of outrage at the silencing and exclusion of girls and women from cultural studies is made clear.

34 Lesko (1988a) was similarly motivated. Her study "(gave) highest priority to students' experiences in school, while analyzing those events from a perspective of social integration, identity and system of thought" (p. 31). Lesko took what she called "structuralist approaches" (p. 23) in her analysis of girls' experiences in a Catholic High School in Midwestern America and was critical of studies that failed to examine the culture of schools from the views of participants. Her view of experience appears to be constructionist but in the sense that I have called prediscursive.

35 Similarly, in his study of "Why . . . teachers hate black kids" he had earlier criticized "white policy-makers and welfare practitioners, such as teachers (for not understanding) the 'different reality' that the black community experience" (Mac an Ghaill, 1988: 155).

36 Again, in his study of student–teacher relations in the schooling of black youth, Mac an Ghaill (1988) "developed the participant-observer role" (p. 8) well beyond the boundaries of the school to a variety of community spaces and occasions, including student access to his home (ibid. 8, 13).

37 There is more than a hint in his oblique reference to Foucault that the target of this criticism is poststructuralism generally, suggesting a pragmatic commitment to a modernist epistemology (Mac an Ghaill, 1994: 2–3).

38 This strategy was based on Aggleton's (1987) use of "purposive sampling" (p. 14). Mac an Ghaill is well aware of possible contradictions within such types and of the problems of reification and stereotyping (Mac an Ghaill, 1994: 161–62).

39 This is not a judgment Mac an Ghaill would necessarily agree with, as his final lines indicate (1994: 181). On plausibility and authenticity in qualitative research, see Skeggs (1998): "Research that listens to others rather than making assumptions about their existence is, I would argue, more plausible" (p. 33) than research judged by external criteria of validity.

40 Although not an ethnographic study, McLeod and Yates (2006) also take up a number of poststructuralist concerns in their study of student subjectivity.

41 Fordham's research, of course, can be located more broadly in the long tradition of critical ethnographic studies of African-American and other ethnic minority struggles in educational settings in America of which Fine's study referred to earlier is a clear example: see Anderson (1989); and for example, Weis (1985, 1988); Weis and Fine (1993; 2000). The socially critical and activist strain in ethnographies of education can be traced even further back to, for example, Rist (1973) who noted: "the system of public education in the United States is specifically designed to aid in the perpetuation of the social and economic inequalities found within the society" (p. 2).

42 In so far as Fordham here offers a critique of ethnography, her position seems to be anticipated to some extent in the following observation by James Clifford (1986): "The predominant metaphors in anthropological research have been participant-observation, data collection, and cultural description, *all of which presuppose a standpoint outside – looking at, objectifying, or, somewhat closer, 'reading' a given reality*" (p. 11; emphasis added). Similarly, Britzman (1995) writes that "For the poststructuralist, 'being there' does not guarantee access to truth. Thus, the tradition of ethnographic authority derived from participant observation becomes a site of doubt, rather than a confirmation of what exists prior to representation" (p. 232).

43 Paraphrasing Wexler (1992) earlier, they note: "we analyse how school students become some*bodies* some*where*" (p. 2; original emphasis).

44 This would seem to be a fundamental assumption of critical ethnography as the work of Fine, Fordham, and Skeggs referred to earlier shows, and indeed

4 OBSERVING PARTICIPATION

1. This and all other names in this study are pseudonyms.
2. Similarly, Gonick (2003) notes: "Our discussions were in effect often narratives of experience" (p. 51).
3. In addition to, for example, Willis (1977), see Abraham (1995: 30–33). By comparison, see Aggleton (1987) who suspended his teaching activities in order to gain access to a wide variety of sites and in the process develop a research persona quite distinct from the way he understood himself as a teacher.
4. See also Gonick (2003) who not only sat in on classes but met her subjects after school to see films, go skating, attend birthday parties and restaurants and who also met them at her home and university (pp. 33, 37).
5. Concern for what fieldnotes contain and the way they way are written arises from the understanding that, like the final texts, they too are constructed artefacts. See Delamont (1992); Britzman (1995: 230); Coffey (1999); Emerson, Fretz, and Shaw (2001).
6. This is very much the concern of Dwyer (1982) whose extended commentary on this "fieldwork confrontation" of Self to Other is exemplary (pp. xvii; 277: fn. 6).
7. The terms "lad" and "laddishness" have attracted a vast archive of research. As the term is most pertinent to British studies I will only use it in passing, but a useful review may be found in Francis (2000: 94 ff.)

PART II THAT UNSTABLE CONSTRUCT

5 MONDAY MORNING

1. According to Atkinson (1996: 27), arrival stories are a typical component of anthropologically informed ethnography in which the ethnographer constructs a sense of place, demarcates a "field" and constructs him or herself as "an archetypal 'stranger.'" My extension of the trope here to one of the students recognizes the cyclical, repetitive structure of the experience of coming to school. It foregrounds the "dailiness" of autobiographical and discursively grounded experience: see Okely (1992: 6; 14). MacLure (2003) sees arrival stories as first attempts to deconstruct such "stable opposites" as self/other, outsider/insider, "(constituting) a key ethnographic moment: the point at which the putative opposites first confront one another, marvel at the strangeness of their stark differences, and establish some sort of first contact" (p. 156). See Whelen (2008).
2. The question of identifying and delimiting discourses is regarded by Phillips and Jorgensen (2002) as more strategic than theoretical. They argue that the delimitation of discourses "entails understanding discourses as objects that the researcher constructs rather than as objects that exist in a delimited form in reality, ready to be identified and mapped" (p. 144). Thus, while I claim these discourses pervade and to a large degree constitute the site of research, other researchers might identify and privilege other discursive formations. For example, Francis and Skelton (2005: 47–49) identify the emergence of new discourses that to some extent displace those identified by Epstein *et al.* (1998)

See also Francis (1999b) for examples of how imprecise such distinctions may inevitably be and how contradictory discourses as rhetorical resources may be. See also Parker (1992). Youdell (2006b: 56), in seeking to unpack the effects of discourses in schools, acknowledges the contingent nature of such decisions.

3 Equivalent National Tertiary Entrance Rank; a numerical value with a maximum of 99.95 derived from students' study (subject) scores.
4 A document required of every State school by the Victorian Minister of Education setting out each school's goals (curriculum, environmental, management, accountability, and resources), priorities, curriculum profile, rights and responsibilities, reporting, and budget details. A heavy emphasis is placed on measurable outcomes and the demonstration of achievements.
5 As shown in the approaches of Mac an Ghaill (1994), Hey (1997), Gonick (2003), and Aggleton (1987). See Chapter 4.
6 Although we briefly continued conversations I did not include him in this study as my focus was on the possibility of following Year 8 boys through to Year 10.
7 My concern for appearance, voice, and embodiment – for presence – all in an attempt to construct rapport recalls Epstein's (1998a) approach to achieving a "least adult" role in her research with young children. For a similar concern with boys aged 11 to 14 years, see Phoenix and Frosh (2001: 29), and for slightly older students, see Aggleton (1987).
8 This section draws extensively on Whelen (2008).
9 Nor is the same as attending school for the first time, such as the move from primary to secondary school, the study of which has a long history in educational sociology. See, for example, Lacey (1970) in Chapter 4 earlier, Ball (1980), Delamont and Galton (1986), and Salo (2003).
10 For an example of how clothing and a sense of class contribute to this, see Phoenix and Frosh (2001: 32).
11 This is briefly acknowledged also in an incident observed by Francis (2000: 39).
12 See Appendix I for procedures adopted in transcribing interviews.
13 A novel: Marchetta, M. (2000) *Looking for Alibrandi*, Ringwood, Vic., Penguin. First published 1992; made into a film, 1999.
14 There is throughout this passage a sort of silence that intrudes between the words – what MacLure *et al.* (2010) refer to as "moments of *disconcertion* . . . points of unease or seeming failure in research encounters, where tacit expectations of 'proper' interview conduct or 'good' data are momentarily thrown into disarray . . ." (p. 495; original emphasis).

6 GEORGE

1 Technical and Further Education College, providing a variety of trade and service-oriented qualifications.
2 The primacy accorded friendship in students' accounts of liking school has been widely attested. See Lahelma (2002) and Riley and Docking (2004), but for an alternative view in relation to boys, see Francis (2000).
3 I shall return to this passage in Chapter 9.
4 I shall return to this passage also in Chapter 9.
5 Stuart Hall (1997) emphasizes that the apparent unity and internal homogeneity implied by the term "identity" are not foundational, or natural, "but a constructed form of closure." He goes on:

I use "identity" to refer to the meeting point, the point of *suture*, between on the one hand the discourses and practices which attempt to "interpellate", speak to us or hail us into place as the social subjects of particular discourses, and on the other hand, the processes which produce subjectivities, which construct us as subjects which can be "spoken". Identities are thus points of temporary attachment to the subject positions which discursive practices construct for us.

(pp. 5–6; original emphasis)

Clearly such a view of identity is non-essentialist and in no way implies a stable, or core self.
6 As Lather (1991) remarks, "Whatever 'the real' is, it is discursive" (p. 25).
7 "To deck" means to knock someone to the ground.

7 YEAR 9

1 This is generally reckoned to include his "genealogical" texts, such as *The History of Sexuality* (1990), especially the second and third volumes, but in this context particular attention is drawn to Foucault (1983a, 1983b, 1988).
2 Commenting on a paper by Abrahams, Bruner (1986) notes

we participate in the action but also report about it; we are part of the experience but also detached witnesses to that experience. This double consciousness is an essential condition of the ethnographer who participates as he or she observes. In ethnography, there are always at least two double experiences to be dealt with: on the one hand, our experiences of ourselves in the field, as well as our understanding of our objects; and on the other hand, our objects' experiences of themselves and their experience of us.

(p. 14)

3 Meyerhof and Ruby (1982) note that Clifford Geertz's classic study of a Balinese cockfight is just such a "moment of self-commentary."
4 This is a composite account of subschool assemblies over the period of a year.
5 A reference to the Year 7 Level assembly, lengthened to allow young students, new to the school, to become familiar with procedures and build a common identity at leisure.
6 "mad": really good, excellent.
7 Spitball: chewed up paper rolled into a ball with saliva and flicked around with the aid of a ruler; smaller ones blown through the shell of a ballpoint pen.
8 Knitted woollen cap.
9 Container for water made from specially folded paper.
10 Francis (2000) has observed much the same phenomenon, emphasizing how being a "class clown," or mucking about, is constitutive of gender (pp. 55ff).
11 This passage is quoted (in part) also by A. Hargreaves (ibid. 215) and by Farrell (1998) in her comments on "the power (exerted by) centralized examination . . . over curriculum and assessment" (p. 3) and its promotion of a society "in which everyone is encouraged to become 'people like us'" (ibid. 16). For a specific example of such individuating practices, see Meadmore (2000).

8 THE STUDENT BODY

1 Willis (2000) continues to locate his cultural critique in this domain, highlighting ways in which the "creative self activity" of individuals in their "everyday culture" takes place "within the new conditions of commodization of culture and its universal, saturating, electronic mediation" (pp. xvi–xvii). While not adopting a poststructuralist position, he nevertheless reflects a widespread concern with embodiment as a form of "creative self-activity."
2 See, for example, Epstein et al. (2001) on making masculinities and femininities in primary school playgrounds.
3 Once again, these observations seem to reinforce Connell's notion of body-reflexive practices. Examples abound: for example Connell (1996: 214 ff.) and Epstein et al. (2001: 164). Connell's notion of "masculinity vortices" (1996: 216), such as subject choice, school discipline and sport, around which dominant masculinity formation is evident, privileges the "social" in much the same way as Biddulph (see Chapter 2) privileges the biological. See also Connell (2000).
4 Resistance to the proper wearing of school uniforms has been the subject of comment by Meadmore and Symes (1996: 217) and Lesko (1988b), who focused on this issue especially in relation to girls.
5 Slang term: great, excellent.
6 Slang term: signifies southern European, usually Greek or Italian ethnic origin.
7 Slang term: signifies Anglo-Australian; derived from a 1970s television serial for children featuring a kangaroo named "Skippy."
8 It had a symbol of a marijuana leaf on the front.

9 THE ASPIRATIONAL SELF

1 Mac an Ghaill (1994) draws attention to the role of "social class judgements" made by teachers in deciding who might be an "ideal student" (p. 47).
2 McLeod and Yates (2006) draw attention to the broad social context within which such distinctions are made such that the "'good student' is constructed discursively and socially and takes differing forms in different schools" (p. 50). Furthermore, as Laws and Davies (2000) point out, "available repertoires for being a 'good school student' differ between classrooms and ... within classrooms" (p. 210).
3 Note also Mac an Ghaill's (1994) aside on the problems of representation and self-representation (p. 3) and Foucault's (1994) discussion of the question of representation and its relation to truth, again in the context of painting.
4 This section draws on role descriptions, school handbook, and student applications.

10 CONCLUSION

1 And as Francis (2000) asks, to what extent is it a debate about boys to the exclusion of girls? (pp. 9–10).
2 Useful commentary on such change can be found in Lingard (2003), Davies et al. (2006) and McLeod and Yates (2006: 78–79; 186–87).

Bibliography

NEWSPAPERS AND MAGAZINES

The Weekend Australian, 2001; 2005
The Weekend Australian Magazine, 2006
The Age, 1996–2005
The Sunday Age, 1995; 2002
Herald-Sun, 1996
The Bulletin, 2001

HILLSIDE HIGH SCHOOL – OFFICIAL DOCUMENTS

Annual Reports, 2003–05
Department of School Education (Victoria), Discipline Procedures, 1994
Prospectus, 2003
School Charters, 2003–05
Staff Procedures Handbook, 1997
Student Diary, 2003–06
Teacher Handbook, 2004
Year 9 Daybook, 2004
Year 10 Daybook, 2005

BOOKS AND JOURNAL ARTICLES

Abrahams, R. D. (1986) Ordinary and extraordinary experience, in: V. W. Turner and E. M. Bruner, (eds) *The Anthropology of Experience*, Urbana: University of Illinois Press.

Abraham, J. (1995) *Divide and School: Gender and Class Dynamics in Comprehensive Education*, London, The Falmer Press.

Aggleton, P. (1987) *Rebels without a Cause? Middle Class Youth and the Transition from School to Work*, London: Falmer.

Ailwood, J. (2003) A national approach to gender equity policy in Australia: Another ending, another opening? *International Journal of Inclusive Education*, 7: 1, 19–32.

Anderson, G. (1989) Critical ethnography in education: Origins, current status, and new directions, *Review of Educational Research*, 59: 3, 249–70.
Angrosino, M. V. and Mays de Perez, K. A. (2000) Rethinking observation: From method to context, in: N. K. Denzin and Y. S. Lincoln, (eds) *Handbook of Qualitative Research. Second Edition*, Thousand Oaks: Sage.
Arndt, B. (2000a) The trouble with boys, in *The Age*, 17 June, 2000.
Arndt, B. (2000b) Lessons for the boys, in *The Age*, 3 November, 2000.
Arndt, B. (2004) A boys' own champion, in *The Age*, 26 January, 2004.
Arnot, M. and Weiner, G. (eds) (1981) *Gender and the Politics of Schooling*, London: Unwin Hyman.
Aronowitz, S. (1981) Preface to morningside edition of P. Willis, *Learning to Labor*, New York: Columbia University Press.
Atkinson, P. (1991) *The Ethnographic Imagination: Textual Constructions of Reality*, London: Routledge.
Atkinson, P. (1996) *Sociological Readings and Re-Readings*, Aldershot: Avebury.
Atkinson, P., Coffey, A., and Delamont, S. (1999) Ethnography: Post, past, and present, *Journal of Contemporary Ethnography*, 28:5, 460–71.
Atkinson, P, Coffey, A., Delamont, S., Lofland, J., and Lofland, L. (eds) (2001) *Handbook of Ethnography*, London: Sage.
Atkinson, P., Delamont, S., and Hammersley, M. (1988) Qualitative research traditions: A British response to Jacob, *Review of Educational Research*, 58: 2, 231–50.
Atkinson, P. and Hammersley, M. (1994) Ethnography and participant observation, in: N. K. Denzin and Y. S. Lincoln (eds) *Handbook of Qualitative Research*, Thousand Oaks: Sage.
Ball, S. J. (1980) Initial encounters in the classroom, in: P. Woods (ed) *Pupil Strategies: Explorations in the Sociology of the School*, London, Croom Helm.
Ball, S. J. (1981) *Beachside Comprehensive: A Case-Study of Secondary Schooling*, Cambridge: Cambridge University Press.
Ball, S. J. (1983) Case study research in education: Some notes and problems, in: M. Hammersley, (ed) *The Ethnography of Schooling: Methodological Issues*, Driffield: Nafferton Books.
Ball, S. J. (1984) Beachside reconsidered: Reflections on a methodological apprenticeship, in: R. G. Burgess, (ed.) *The Research Process in Educational Settings: Ten Case Studies*, London: Falmer.
Ball, S. J. (1985) Participant observation with pupils, in: R. G. Burgess, (ed.) *Strategies of Educational Research: Qualitative Methods*, London; Falmer.
Ball, S. J. (1990a) *Foucault and Education: Disciplines and Knowledge*, London: Routledge.
Ball, S. J. (1990b) Self-doubt and soft data: social and technical trajectories in ethnographic fieldwork, *International Journal of Qualitative Studies in Education*, 3: 2, 157–71.
Barker, M. and Beezer, A. (eds) (1992) *Reading into Cultural Studies*, London: Routledge.
Barton, L. and Meighan, R. (eds) (1978) *Sociological Interpretations of Schooling and Classrooms: A Re-Appraisal*, Driffield: Nafferton Books.
Barton, L. and Walker, S. (eds) (1983) *Race, Class and Education*, London: Croom Helm.

Behar, R. and Gordon, D. A. (eds) (1995) *Women Writing Culture*, Berkeley: University of California Press.
Biddulph, S. (1994/2002) *Manhood: An Action Plan for Changing Men's Lives*, Sydney: Finch publishing.
Biddulph, S. (1995) Foreword, in: R. Browne and R. Fletcher, (eds) *Boys in Schools: Addressing the Real Issues – Behaviour, Values and Relationships*, Lane Cove: Finch publishing.
Biddulph, S. (1997) *Raising Boys*, Sydney: Finch publishing.
Bly, R. (1991) *Iron John: A Book About Men*, London: Element.
Britzman, D. P. (1995) The question of belief: Writing poststructural ethnography, *Qualitative Studies in Education*, 8: 3, 229–38.
Broadfoot, P. (ed.) (1986) *Profiles and Records of Achievement: A Review of Issues and Practice*, London: Holt, Rinehart & Winston.
Brod, H. (ed.) (1987) *The Making of Masculinities: The New Men's Studies*, Boston: Allen & Unwin.
Brod, H. and Kaufman, M. (eds) (1994) *Theorizing Masculinities*, Thousand Oaks: Sage.
Browne, R. (1995) Schools and the construction of masculinity, in: R. Browne and R. Fletcher, (eds) *Boys in Schools: Addressing the Real Issues – Behaviour, Values and Relationships*, Lane Cove: Finch Publishing.
Browne, R. (1997) Boys and the middle school, *Boys in Schools Bulletin*, 1: 1, 3–4.
Browne, R. and Fletcher, R. (eds) (1995) *Boys in Schools: Addressing the Real Issues – Behaviour, Values and Relationships*, Lane Cove: Finch Publishing.
Bruce, S. and Yearley, S. (eds) (2006) *The Sage Dictionary of Sociology*, London: Sage.
Bruner, E. M. (1986) Experience and its expressions, in: V. W. Turner and E. M. Bruner (eds) *The Anthropology of Experience*, Urbana: University of Illinois Press.
Buckingham, J. (1999) The puzzle of boys' educational decline: A review of the evidence, *Issue Analysis*, 9, 18 November, 1999, St. Leonards: The Centre for Independent Studies.
Buckingham, J. (2004) *Boys' Education: Research and Rhetoric*, St. Leonards: Centre for Independent Studies Occasional paper 89.
Burchell, G., Gordon, C., and Miller, P. (eds) *The Foucault Effect: Studies in Governmentality*, Chicago: The University of Chicago Press.
Burgess, R. G. (1983) *Experiencing Comprehensive Education: A Study of Bishop McGregor School*, London: Methuen.
Burgess, R. G. (ed.) (1984) *The Research Process in Educational Settings: Ten Case Studies*, London: Falmer.
Burgess, R. G. (ed.) (1985a) *Strategies of Educational Research: Qualitative Methods*, London: Falmer.
Burgess, R. G. (ed.) (1985b) *Field Methods in the Study of Education*, London: Falmer.
Burgess, R. G. (1988) Conversations with a purpose: The ethnographic interview in educational research, *Studies in Qualitative Methodology*, Vol. 1: 137–55.
Burr, V. (1998) *An Introduction to Social Constructionism*, London: Routledge.
Burroughs, C. B. and Ehrenreich, J. D. (eds) (1993) *Reading the Social Body*, Iowa City: University of Iowa Press.

Butler, J. (1990) *Gender Trouble: Feminism and the Subversion of Identity*, New York: Routledge.
Butler, J. (1993) *Bodies That Matter: On the Discursive Limits of Sex*, New York: Routledge.
Butler, J. (1997a) *Excitable Speech: A Politics of the Performative*, New York: Routledge.
Butler, J. (1997b) *The Psychic Life of Power*, Stanford: Stanford University Press.
Butler, J. and Scott, J. W. (eds) (1992) *Feminists Theorise the Political*, New York: Routledge.
Carr-Gregg, M. and Shale, E. (2002) *Adolescence: A Guide for Parents*, Lane Cove: Finch publishing.
Carrigan, T., Connell, B., and Lee, J. (1985) Toward a new sociology of masculinity, *Theory and Society*, 14: 5, 551–604.
Clark, H. H. (1996) *Using Language*, Cambridge: Cambridge University Press.
Clatterbaugh, K. (1990) *Contemporary Perspectives on Masculinity: Men, Women, and Politics in Modern Society*, Boulder: Westview Press.
Clatterbaugh, K. (1998) What's problematic about masculinities? *Men and Masculinities*, 1: 1, 24–45.
Clifford, J. (1983) On ethnographic authority, *Representations*, 1: 2, 118–46.
Clifford, J. (1986) On ethnographic allegory, in: Clifford, J. and Marcus, G. (eds) (1986) *Writing Culture: The Poetics and Politics of Ethnography*, Berkeley: University of California Press.
Clifford, J. and Marcus, G. E. (eds) (1986) *Writing Culture: The Poetics and Politics of Ethnography*, Berkeley: University of California Press.
Coffey, A. (1999) *The Ethnographic Self: Fieldwork and the Representation of Identity*, London: Sage.
Cole, M. (ed.) (1988) *Bowles and Gintis Revisited: Correspondence and Contradiction in Educational Theory*, London: Falmer.
Collins, C., Batten, M., Ainley, J., and Getty, C. (1996) *Gender and School Education*. A project funded by the Commonwealth Department of Employment, Education, Training and Youth Affairs, Canberra: AGPS.
Collins, C., Kenway, J., and McLeod, J. (2000) *Factors Influencing the Educational Performance of Males and Females in School and their Initial Destinations after Leaving School*, A project funded by the Commonwealth Department of Education, Training and Youth Affairs, Commonwealth of Australia.
Commonwealth of Australia, (2002) *Boys: Getting it Right: Report on the Inquiry Into the Education of Boys*, House of Representatives Standing Committee on Education and Training, October 2002: Canberra.
Commonwealth Schools Commission (1987) *National Policy on the Education of Girls in Australian Schools*, Canberra.
Connell, R. W. (1985) Theorising gender, *Sociology*, 19: 2, 260–72.
Connell, R. W. (1987) *Gender and Power: Society, the Person and Sexual Politics*, Sydney: Allen & Unwin.
Connell, R. W. (1989) Cool guys, swots and wimps: The interplay of masculinity and education, *Oxford Review of Education*, 15: 3, 291–303.
Connell, R. W. (1995) *Masculinities*, St. Leonards: Allen & Unwin.
Connell, R. W. (1996) Teaching the boys: New research on masculinity, and gender strategies for schools, *Teachers College Record*, 98: 2, 206–35.

Connell, R. W. (2000) *The Men and The Boys*, St. Leonards: Allen & Unwin.
Connell, R. W. (2001) Studying men and masculinity, *Resources for Feminist Research*, 29: 1–2, 43–55.
Connell, R. W., Ashenden, D. J., Kessler, S., and Dowsett, G. W. (1985/1982) *Making The Difference: Schools, Families and Social Division*, Sydney, George Allen & Unwin.
Corrigan, P. (1979) *Schooling the Smash Street Kids*, London: MacMillan.
Corrigan, P. (1988) The making of the boy: Meditations on what grammar school did with, to, and for my body, *Journal of Education*, 70: 3, 142–61.
Cox, E. (1995) Boys and girls and the costs of gendered behaviour, in: MCEETYA, *Proceedings of the Promoting Gender Equity Conference*, 22–24 February: Canberra.
Croxford, L., Tinklin, T., Frame, B., and Ducklin, A. (2003) Gender and pupil performance: Where do the problems lie? *Scottish Educational Review*, 35: 2, 135–47.
Cusick, P. A. (1973) *Inside High School: The Students' World*, New York: Holt, Rinehart & Winston.
Cuttance, P., Imms, W., Godhino, S., Hartnell-Young, E., Thompson, J., McGuiness, K., and Neal, G. (2006) *Boys' Education Lighthouse Schools: Stage Two Final Report*, Australian government: Canberra.
Davies, B. (1989) *Frogs and Snails and Feminist Tales: Preschool Children and Gender*, Sydney: Allen & Unwin.
Davies, B. (1992) Women's subjectivity and feminist stories, in: C. Ellis and M. G. Flaherty (eds) *Investigating Subjectivity: Research on Lived Experience*, Newbury Park: Sage.
Davies, B. (1993) *Shards of Glass: Children Reading and Writing Beyond Gendered Identities*, St. Leonards: Allen & Unwin.
Davies, B. (1997) The subject of post-structuralism: A reply to Alison Jones, *Gender and Education*, 9: 3, 271–83.
Davies, B. (2006) Subjectification: The relevance of Butler's analysis for education, *British Journal of Sociology of Education*, 27: 4, 425–38.
Davies, B. and Harré, R. (1990) Positioning: The discursive production of selves, *Journal for the Theory of Social Behaviour*, 20: 1, 43–63.
Davies, B., Dormer, S., Gannon, S., Laws, C., Rocco, S., Taguchi, H. L., and McCann, H. (2001) Becoming schoolgirls: The ambivalent project of subjectification, *Gender and Education*, 13: 2, 167–82.
Davies, B., Browne, J., Gannon, S., Hopkins, L., McCann, H., and Wihlborg, M. (2006) Constituting the feminist subject in poststructuralist discourse, *Feminism and Psychology*, 16: 1, 87–103.
Davies, L. (1984) *Pupil Power: Deviance and Gender in School*, London: Falmer.
Delamont, S. (1992) *Fieldwork in Educational Settings: Methods, Pitfalls and Perspectives*, London: The Falmer Press.
Delamont, S. (1999) Gender and the discourse of derision, *Research Papers in Education*, 14: 1, 3–21.
Delamont, S. (2002) *Fieldwork in Educational Settings: Methods, Pitfalls and Perspectives*, London: Routledge.
Delamont, S. (2004) Confessions of a ragpicker, in: H. Piper and I. Stronach (eds) *Educational Research: Difference and Diversity*, Burlington: Ashgate.

Delamont, S. and Atkinson, P. (1980) The two traditions in educational ethnography: Sociology and anthropology compared, *British Journal of Sociology of Education*, 1: 2, 139–52.

Delamont, S. and Atkinson, P. (1995) *Fighting Familiarity: Essays on Education and Ethnography*, Cresskill: Hampton Press.

Delamont, S. and Galton, M. (1986) *Inside the Secondary Classroom*, London: Routledge.

Delfos, M, (2005) About boys. The core of the matter, *The Boys in Schools Bulletin*, 8: 1, 36–39.

Denzin, N. (1997) *Interpretive Ethnography: Ethnographic Practices for the 21st Century*, Thousand Oaks: Sage.

Denzin, N. K. and Lincoln, Y. S. (1994) *Handbook of Qualitative Research*, Thousand Oaks: Sage.

Denzin, N. K. and Lincoln, Y. S. (2000) *Handbook of Qualitative Research: Second Edition*, Thousand Oaks: Sage.

Department of Education, Employment and Training (2001) *The Education of Boys: Improving Outcomes for All*, (Draft): State of Victoria.

Dewey, J. (1997/1938) *Experience and Education*, New York, Touchstone.

Dillabough, J-A., McLeod, J., and Mills, M. (2008) In search of allies and others: "Troubling" gender and education, *Discourse: Studies in the Cultural Politics of Education*, 29: 3, 301–10.

Donaldson, M. (1993) What is hegemonic masculinity? *Theory and Society*, 22: 643–57.

Dormer, S. and Davies, B. (2001) Desiring women and the (im)possibility of being, *Australian Psychologist*, 36: 1, 4–9.

Dreyfus, H. L. and Rabinow, P. (eds) (1983) *Michel Foucault: Beyond Structuralism and Hermeneutics*, Chicago: The University of Chicago Press.

Dwyer, K. (1982) *Moroccan Dialogues: Anthropology in Question*, Baltimore: The Johns Hopkins University Press.

Eder, D. with Evans, C. C. and Parker, S. (1995) *School Talk: Gender and Adolescent Culture*, New Jersey: Rutgers University Press.

Elium, D. and Elium, J. (1992) *Raising a Son: Parents and the Making of a Healthy Man*, Gloucestershire: Hawthorn Press.

Edmondson, R. (1984) *Rhetoric in Sociology*, London: MacMillan.

Edwards, J. (ed.) (1994) *Thinking: International Interdisciplinary Perspectives*, Highett: Hawker Brownlow Education.

Emerson, R. M., Fretz, R. I., and Shaw, L. L. (2001) Participant observation and fieldnotes, in: P. Atkinson, A. Coffey, S. Delamont, J. Lofland, and L. Lofland (eds) *Handbook of Ethnography*, London: Sage.

Epstein, D. (1997) Boyz' own stories: Masculinities and sexualities in schools, *Gender and Education*, 9: 1, 105–15.

Epstein, D. (1998a) Are you a girl or are you a teacher? The "least adult" role in research about gender and sexuality in a primary school, in: G. Walford (ed.) *Doing Research About Education*, London: Falmer Press.

Epstein, D. (1998b) Real boys don't work: "Underachievement", masculinity, and the harassment of "sissies", in: D. Epstein, J. Elwood, V. Hey and J. Maw (eds) *Failing Boys?* Buckingham: Open University Press.

Epstein, D., Elwood, J., Hey, V., and Maw, J. (eds) (1998) *Failing Boys? Issues in Gender and Achievement*, Buckingham: Open University Press.

Epstein, D., Kehily, M., Mac an Ghaill, M., and Redman, P. (2001) Boys and girls come out to play. Making masculinities and femininities in school playgrounds, *Men and Masculinities*, 4: 2, 158–72.

Fairclough, N. (2003) *Analysing Discourse: Textual Analysis for Social Research*, London: Routledge.

Farrell, L. (1998) Back to the future: School examinations, fairness and the question of identity, *Australian Educational Researcher*, 25: 2, 1–17.

Felski, R. (1995) *The Gender of Modernity*, Cambridge, Mass: Harvard University Press.

Fine, M. (1991) *Framing Dropouts: Notes on the Politics of an Urban Public High School*, New York: State University of New York Press.

Fletcher, R. (2005) Male role models. Emotional regulation, identity scaffolding and fathers' involvement in schools, *The Boys in Schools Bulletin*, 8: 2, 34–41.

Fontana, A. and Frey, J. H. (2000) The interview: From structured questions to negotiated text, in: N. K. Denzin and Y. S. Lincoln, (eds) *Handbook of Qualitative Research: Second Edition*, Thousand Oaks: Sage.

Fordham, S. (1996) *Blacked Out: Dilemmas of Race, Identity, and Success at Capital High*, Chicago: The University of Chicago Press.

Formaini, H. (1990) *Men: The Darker Continent*, London: Heinemann.

Foster, V., Kimmel, M., and Skelton, C. (2001) "What about the boys?" An overview of the debates, in: W. Martino and B. Meyenn (eds) *What About the Boys?* Buckingham, Open University Press.

Foucault, M. (1970) The order of discourse, in: R. Young (ed.) (1987) *Untying the Text: A Post-Structuralist Reader*, London: Routledge.

Foucault, M. (1972/1969) *The Archaeology of Knowledge*, Tavistock Publications.

Foucault, M. (1976) Two lectures, in: C. Gordon (ed.) (1980) *Power/Knowledge: Selected Interviews and Other Writings 1972–1977*, New York: Pantheon Books.

Foucault, M. (1978) Governmentality, in: G. Burchell, C. Gordon and P. Miller (eds) *The Foucault Effect: Studies in Governmentality*, Chicago: The University of Chicago Press.

Foucault, M. (1983a) The subject and power, in: H. L. Dreyfus and P. Rabinow (eds) *Michel Foucault: Beyond Structuralism and Hermeneutics*, Chicago: The University of Chicago Press.

Foucault, M. (1983b) On the genealogy of ethics: An overview of work in progress, in: H. L. Dreyfus and P. Rabinow, (eds) *Michel Foucault: Beyond Structuralism and Hermeneutics*, Chicago: The University of Chicago Press.

Foucault, M. (1987) The ethic of care for the self as a practice of freedom, *Philosophy and Social Criticism*, 12: 112–31.

Foucault, M. (1988) Technologies of the self, in: L. Martin, H. Gutman and P. Hutton (eds) *Technologies of the Self: A Seminar with Michel Foucault*, Amherst: The University of Massachusetts Press.

Foucault, M. (1990/1976) *The History of Sexuality, Volume 1: An Introduction*, New York: Vintage Books.

Foucault, M. (1991/1975) *Discipline and Punish: The Birth of the Prison*, London: Penguin Books.

Foucault, M. (1994/1966) *The Order of Things*, New York: Vintage Books.

Francis, B. (1999a) Modernist reductionism or post-structuralist relativism: Can

we move on? An evaluation of arguments in relation to feminist educational research, *Gender and Education*, 11: 4, 381–93.
Francis, B. (1999b) An investigation of the discourses children draw on in their construction of gender, *Journal of Applied Social Psychology*, 29: 2, 300–16.
Francis, B. (2000) *Boys, Girls and Achievement: Addressing the Classroom Issues*, London: Routledge/Falmer.
Francis, B. (2006) Heroes or zeroes? The discursive positioning of "underachieving boys" in English neo-liberal education policy, *Journal of Education Policy*, 21: 2, 187–2000.
Francis, B. (2008) Teaching manfully? Exploring gendered subjectivities and power via analysis of men teachers' gender performance, *Gender and Education*, 20: 2, 109–22.
Francis, B. and Skelton, C. (eds) (2001) *Investigating Gender: Contemporary Perspectives in Education*, Buckingham: Open University Press.
Francis, B. and Skelton, C. (2005) *Reassessing Gender and Achievement: Questioning Contemporary Key Debates*, London: Routledge.
Frank, B. (1987) Hegemonic heterosexual masculinity, *Studies in Political Economy*, 24: Autumn, 159–70.
Frankenbeg, R. (ed.) (1982) *Custom and Conflict in British Society*, Manchester: Manchester University Press.
Fraser, N. (1983) Foucault's body-language: A post-humanist political rhetoric? *Salmagundi*, 61: 55–70.
Frosh, S., Phoenix, A., and Pattman, R. (2002) *Young Masculinities: Understanding Boys in Contemporary Society*, Basingstoke: Palgrave.
Furlong, V. J. (1976) Interaction sets in the classroom: Towards a study of pupil knowledge, in: M. Stubbs and S. Delamont (eds) *Explorations in Classroom Observation*, Wiley & Sons.
Gender Equity Taskforce (1997) *Gender Equity: A Framework for Australian Schools*, Canberra.
Gergen, K. and Davis, K. E. (eds) (1985) *The Social Construction of the Person*, New York: Springer-Verlag.
Gergen, M. and Gergen, K. J. (eds) (2003) *Social Constructionism: A Reader*, London: Sage.
Gilbert, P. (1998) Gender and schooling in new times: The challenge of boys and literacy, *Australian Educational Researcher*, 25: 1, 15–36.
Gilbert, R. and Gilbert, P. (1998) *Masculinity Goes to School*, St. Leonards: Allen & Unwin.
Goertz, J. P. and Allen, J. (eds) (1988) *Qualitative Research in Education: Substance, Methods and Experience*, Athens: The University of Georgia.
Gonick, M. (2003) *Between Femininities: Ambivalence, Identity, and the Education of Girls*, Albany: The Sate University of New York Press.
Gordon, C. (ed.) (1980) *Power/Knowledge: Selected Interviews and Other Writings 1972–1977*, New York: Pantheon Books.
Gordon, T., Holland, J., and Lahelma, E. (2000) *Making Spaces: Citizenship and Difference in Schools*, London: Macmillan.
Gordon, T., Holland, J., and Lahelma, E. (2001) Ethnographic research in educational settings, in: P. Atkinson, A. Coffey, S. Delamont, J. Lofland and L. Lofland (eds) *Handbook of Ethnography*, London: Sage.

Gordon, T. and Lahelma, E. (1996) School is like an ant's nest: Spatiality and embodiment in schools, *Gender and Education*, 8: 3, 301–10.

Gough, A. (2004) Blurring boundaries: Embodying cyborg subjectivity and methodology, in: H. Piper and I. Stronach (eds) *Educational Research: Difference and Diversity*, Burlington: Ashgate.

Grant, B. (1997) Disciplining students: The construction of student subjectivities, in: C. O'Farrell (ed.) *Foucault: The Legacy*, Kelvin Grove: Queensland University of Technology.

Grant, L. (1988) Symbolic interactionist approaches to the study of education: An overview and assessment of trends in sociology, in: J. P. Goetz and J. Allen (eds) *Qualitative Research in Education: Substance, Methods and Experience*, Athens: The University of Georgia.

Guillaumin, C. (1993) The constructed body, in: C. B. Burroughs and J. D. Ehrenreich (eds) *Reading the Social Body*, Iowa City: University of Iowa Press.

Hall, S. (ed.) (1980) *Culture, Media, Language*, London: Hutchinson.

Hall, S. (1997) Introduction: Who needs "identity"? In: S. Hall and P. Du Gay (eds) *Questions of Cultural Identity*, London: Sage.

Hall, S. and Du Gay, P. (eds) (1997) *Questions of Cultural Identity*, London: Sage.

Hall, S. and Jefferson, T. (eds) (1977) *Resistance Through Rituals: Youth Subcultures in Post-War Britain*, London: Hutchinson in association with the Centre for Contemporary Cultural Studies, University of Birmingham.

Halpin, D. and Troyna, B, (eds) (1994) *Researching Education Policy: Ethical and Methodological Issues*, London: Falmer.

Hammersley, M. (ed.) (1983) *The Ethnography of Schooling: Methodological Issues*, Driffield: Nafferton Books.

Hammersley, M. (2006a) Review essay, recent radical criticism of interview studies: Any implications for the sociology of education? *British Journal of Sociology of Education*, 24: 1, 119–26.

Hammersley, M. (2006b) *Ethnography: Problems and Prospects*, Ethnography and Education, 1: 1, 3–14.

Hammersley, M. and Atkinson, P. (1995) *Ethnography: Principles in Practice*, London: Routledge.

Hammersley, M. and Turner, G. (1980) Conformist pupils? In: P. Woods (ed.) *Pupil Strategies: Explorations in the Sociology of the School*, London: Croom Helm.

Hammersley, M. and Woods, P. (eds) (1976) *The Process of Schooling*, London: Routledge & Kegan Paul.

Hammersley, M. and Woods, P. (eds) (1984) *Life in School: The Sociology of Pupil Culture*, Milton Keynes: Open University Press.

Harari, J. V. (ed.) (1980) *Textual Strategies: Perspectives in Post-Structuralist Criticism*, London: Methuen.

Haraway, D. (1985) A manifesto for cyborgs: Science, technology and socialist feminism in the 1980s, *Socialist Review*, No. 80: 65–107.

Hargreaves, A. (1986) Ideological: Record breakers? In: P. Broadfoot (ed.) *Profiles and Records of Achievement: A Review of Issues and Practice*, London: Holt, Rinehart & Winston.

Hargreaves, D. (1967) *Social Relations in a Secondary School*, London: Routledge & Kegan Paul.

Hargreaves, D. (1978) Whatever happened to symbolic interactionism? In: L. Barton and R. Meighan (eds) *Sociological Interpretations of Schooling and Classrooms: A Re-Appraisal*, Driffield: Nafferton Books.

Hargreaves, D. (1981) Unemployment, leisure and education, *Oxford Review of Education*, 7: 3, 197–210.

Harvey, D. (1997) *The Condition of Postmodernity: An Enquiry into the Origins of Cultural Change*, Oxford: Blackwell.

Hawkes, T. (2001a) Introduction, in: P. West, *Report on Best Practice in Boys' Education*, University of Western Sydney.

Hawkes, T. (2001b) *Boy oh Boy: How to Raise and Educate Boys*, Frenchs Forest: Pearson Education Australia.

Hayes, D. and Lingard, B. (eds) (2003) Introduction: Rearticulating gender agendas in schooling: An Australian perspective, *International Journal of Inclusive Education*, 7:1, 1–6.

Haywood, C. and Mac an Ghaill, M. (1996) Schooling masculinities, in: M. Mac an Ghaill (ed.) *Understanding Masculinities: Social Relations and Cultural Arenas*, Buckingham: Open University Press.

Haywood, C. and Mac an Ghaill, M. (1997) Materialism and Deconstructivism: Education and the epistemology of identity, *Cambridge Journal of Education*, 27: 2, 261–72.

Haywood, C. and Mac an Ghaill, M. (1998) The making of men: Theorizing methodology in "uncertain" times, in: G. Walford (ed.) *Doing Research About Education*, London: Falmer.

Hebdidge, D. (1979) *Subculture: The Meaning of Style*, London: Methuen.

Henriques, J., Hollwa, W., Urwin, C., Venn, C., and Walkerdine, V. (1984) *Changing the Subject: Psychology, Social Regulation and Subjectivity*, London: Methuen.

Hey, V. (1997) *The Company She Keeps: An Ethnography of Girls' Friendships*, Buckingham: Open University Press.

Hey, V. (2006a) Getting over it? Reflections on the melancholia of reclassified identities, *Gender and Education*, 18: 3, 295–308.

Hey, V. (2006b) The politics of performative resignification: Translating Judith Butler's theoretical discourse and its potential for a sociology of education, *British Journal of Sociology of Education*, 27: 4, 439–57.

Heyl, B. S. (2001) Ethnographic interviewing, in: P. Atkinson, A. Coffey, S. Delamont, J. Lofland, and L. Lofland (eds) *Handbook of Ethnography*, London: Sage.

Hodgetts, K. (2008) Underperformance or "getting it right"? Constructions of gender and achievement in the Australian inquiry into boys' education, *British Journal of Sociology of Education*, 29; 5, 465–77.

Holstein, J. A. and Gubrium, J. F. (1995) *The Active Interview*, Thousand Oaks: Sage.

Hoskin, K. (1979) The examination, disciplinary power and rational schooling, *History of Education*, 8: 2, 135–46.

Ireland, P. (1995) Nurturing boys, developing skills, in: R. Browne and R. Fletcher, *Boys in Schools: Addressing the Real Issues – Behaviour, Values and Relationships*, Lane Cove: Finch Publishing.

Jackson, A. Y. and Mazzei, L. A. (eds) (2009) *Voice in Qualitative Inquiry: Chal-*

lenging Conventional, Interpretive, and Critical Conceptions in Qualitative Research, Abingdon: Routledge.
Jackson, P. (1981) Review: Beachside comprehensive, British Journal of Sociology of Education, 2: 3, 285–90.
Jones, S. and Myhill, D. (2004) "Troublesome boys" and "compliant girls": Gender identity and perceptions of achievement and underachievement, British Journal of Sociology of Education, 25: 5, 547–61.
Kapferer, B. (1996) Performance and the structuring of meaning and experience, in: V. W. Turner and E. M. Bruner (eds) The Anthropology of Experience, Urbana: University of Illinois Press.
Keddie, A. (2005) A framework for gender justice: Evaluating the transformative capacities of three key Australian schooling initiatives, The Australian Educational Researcher, 32: 3, 83–101.
Keddie, A. (2010) Feminist struggles to mobilize progressive spaces within the "boy-turn" in gender equity and schooling reform, Gender and Education, 22; 4, 353–68.
Kenway, J. (1995a) Having a postmodernist turn or postmodernist angst: A disorder experienced by an author who is not yet dead or even close to it, in: R. Smith and P. Wexler (eds) After Postmodernism: Education, Politics and Identity, London: Falmer.
Kenway, J. (1995b) Masculinities in schools: Under siege, on the defensive and under reconstruction? Discourse: Studies in the Cultural Politics of Education, 16: 1, 59–79.
Kenway, J. (1995c) Taking stock of gender reform in Australian schools: Past, present and future, in: MCEETYA, Proceedings of the Promoting Gender Equity Conference, 22–24 February: Canberra.
Kenway, J. (1996) Reasserting masculinity in Australian schools, Women's Studies International Forum, 19: 4, 447–66.
Kenway, J. (ed) (1997) Will Boys Be Boys? Boys' Education in the Context of Gender Reform, Deakin West: Australian Curriculum Studies Association.
Kenway, J. (2000) Puzzling about gender, school and school life: Five Paradoxes for Policy, Australian Quarterly, October–December, 2000: 27–34.
Kenway, J. and McLeod, J. (2004) Bourdieu's reflexive sociology and "spaces of points of view": Whose reflexivity, which perspective? British Journal of Sociology of Education, 25: 4, 525–44.
Kenway, J. and Willis, S. (1997) Answering Back: Girls, Boys and Feminism in Schools, St. Leonards: Allen & Unwin.
Kenway, J. and Willis, S. with Blackmore, J. and Rennie, L. (1997) Are boys victims of feminism in schools? Some answers from Australia, International Journal of Inclusive Education, 1: 1, 19–35.
Kessler, S., Ashenden, D. J., Connell, R. W., and Dowsett, G. W. (1985) Gender relations in secondary schooling, Sociology of Education, 58, January: 34–48.
Kimmel, M. S. (1995) The Politics of Manhood: Profeminist Men Respond To The Mythopoetic Men's Movement (And The Mythopoetic Leaders Answer), Philadelphia: Temple University Press.
Kimmel, M. S. and Kaufman (1995) Weekend warriors: The new men's movement, in: M. Kimmel, The Politics of Manhood, Philadelphia, The Temple University Press.

Kondo, D. K. (1990) *Crafting Selves: Power, Gender, and Discourses of Identity in a Japanese Workplace*, Chicago: The University of Chicago Press.

Kvale, S. (1996) *Interviews: An Introduction to Qualitative Research Interviewing*, Thousand Oaks: Sage.

Lacey, C. (1966) Some sociological concomitants of academic streaming in a grammar school, *British Journal of Sociology*, September: 245–62.

Lacey, C. (1970) *Hightown Grammar: The School as a Social System*, Manchester: Manchester University Press.

Lacey, C. (1976) Problems of sociological fieldwork: A review of the methodology of Hightown Grammar, in: M. Shipman (ed.) *The Organisation and Impact of Social Research: Six Original Case Studies in Education and Behavioural Science*, London: Routledge & Kegan Paul.

Lacey, C. (1981) Foreword, in: S. J. Ball, *Beachside Comprehensive: A Case-Study of Secondary Schooling*, Cambridge: Cambridge University Press.

Lacey, C. (1982) Freedom and constraints in British education, in: R. Frankenberg (ed.) *Custom and Conflict in British Society*, Manchester: Manchester University Press.

Lahelma, E. (2002) School is for meeting friends: Secondary school as lived and remembered, *British Journal of Sociology of Education*, 23: 3, 367–81.

Lahelma, E. (2005) School grades and other resources: The "failing boys" discourse revisited, *Nordic Journal of Women's Studies*, 13: 2, 78–89.

Lambart, A. (1976) The sisterhood, in: M. Hammersley and P. Woods (eds) *The Process of Schooling*, London: Routledge & Kegan Paul.

Lambart, A. (1982) Expulsion in context: A school as a system in action, in: R. Frankenberg (ed.) *Custom and Conflict in British Society*, Manchester: Manchester University Press.

Lash, S. and Friedman, J. (eds) (1992) *Modernity and Identity*, Oxford: Blackwell.

Lather, P. (1991) *Getting Smart: Feminist Research and Pedagogy With/in the Postmodern*, New York: Routledge.

Laws, C. and Davies, B. (2000) Poststructuralist theory in practice: Working with "behaviourally disturbed" children, *International Journal of Qualitative Studies in Education*, 13: 3, 205–21.

Lesko, N. (1988a) *Symbolizing Society: Stories, Rites and Structure in a Catholic High School*, New York: Falmer.

Lesko, N. (1988b) The curriculum of the body: Lessons from a Catholic High School, in: L. G. Roman, L. K. Christian-Smith with E. Ellsworth (eds) *Becoming Feminine: The Politics of Popular Culture*, London: Falmer.

Lingard, B. (1998) Contextualising and utilising the "what about the boys?" backlash for gender equity goals, *Change: Transformations in Education*, 1: 2, 16–30.

Lingard, B. (2003) Where to in gender policy in education after recuperative masculinity politics? *International Journal of Inclusive Education*, 7: 1, 33–56.

Lingard, B. and Douglas, P. (1999) *Men Engaging Feminisms: Pro-Feminism, Backlashes and Schooling*, Buckingham: Open University Press.

Lingard, B., Martino, W., and Mills, M. (2009) *Boys and Schooling: Beyond Structural Reform*, Basingstoke: Palgrave MacMillan.

Ludowyke, J. and Scanlon, J. (1997) *Improving the School Performance of Boys*, Victorian Association of State School Principals.

Lyotard, J-F. (1999/1979) *The Postmodern Condition: A Report on Knowledge*, Minneapolis, University of Minnesota Press.

Mac an Ghaill, M. (1988) *Young, Gifted and Black: Student-Teacher Relations in the Schooling of Black Youth*, Milton Keynes: Open University Press.

Mac an Ghaill, M. (1989a) Beyond the white norm. The use of qualitative methods in the study of black youths' schooling in England, *Qualitative Studies in Education*, 2: 3, 175–89.

Mac an Ghaill, M. (1989b) Coming-of-age in 1980s England: Reconceptualizing black students' schooling experience, *British Journal of Sociology of Education*, 10: 3, 273–86.

Mac an Ghaill, M. (1991a) Young, gifted and black: Methodological reflections of a teacher/reseacher, in: G. Walford (ed.) *Doing Educational Research*, London: Routledge.

Mac an Ghaill, M. (1991b) Schooling, sexuality and male power: Towards an emancipatory curriculum, *Gender and Education*, 3: 3, 291–309.

Mac an Ghaill, M. (1994) *The Making of Men: Masculinities, Sexualities and Schooling*, Buckingham: Open University Press.

Mac an Ghaill, M. (ed.) (1996a) *Understanding Masculinities: Social Relations and Cultural Arenas*, Buckingham: Open University Press.

Mac an Ghaill, M. (1996b) What about the boys? Schooling, class and crisis masculinity, *The Sociological Review*, 44: 381–97.

MacLure, M. (2003) *Discourse in Educational and Social Research*, Buckingham: Open University Press.

MacLure, M., Holmes, R., Jones, L., and MacRae, C. (2010) Silence as resistance to analysis: Or, on not opening one's mouth properly, *Qualitative Inquiry*, 16: 6, 492–5000.

McCarthy, C. (1998) *The Uses of Culture: Education and the Limits of Ethnic Affiliation*, New York: Routledge.

McLeod, J. (2000a) Metaphors of the self: Searching for young people's identity through interviews, in: J. McLeod and K. Malone, (eds) *Researching Youth*, Hobart: Australian Clearing house for Youth Studies.

McLeod, J. (2000b) Subjectivity and schooling in a longitudinal study of secondary schools, *British Journal of Sociology of Education*, 21: 4, 501–21.

McLeod, J. and Yates, L. (2006) *Making Modern Lives: Subjectivity, Schooling and Social Change*, Albany: State University of New York Press.

McNay, L. (1992) *Foucault and Feminism: Power, Gender and the Self*, Cambridge: Polity Press.

McNay, L. (2000) *Gender and Agency: Reconfiguring the Subject in Feminist and Social Theory*, Cambridge, Polity Press.

McRobbie, A. (1980) Settling accounts with subcultures: A feminist critique, *Screen Education*, 34: 37–39.

McRobbie, A. and Garber, J. (1977) Girls and subcultures: An exploration, in: S. Hall and T. Jefferson (eds) *Resistance Through Rituals: Youth Subcultures in Post-War Britain*, London: Hutchinson in association with the Centre for Contemporary Cultural Studies, University of Birmingham.

Marchetta, M. (2000) *Looking for Alibrandi*, Ringwood: Penguin Books.

Marcus, G. (1986) Contemporary problems of ethnography in the modern world system, in: J. Clifford and G. E. Marcus, (eds) *Writing Culture: The Poetics and Politics of Ethnography*, Berkeley: University of California Press.

Marcus, G. (1992) Past, present and emergent identities: Requirements for ethnographies of late twentieth-century modernity worldwide, in: S. Lash and J. Friedman (eds) *Modernity and Identity*, Oxford: Blackwell.

Marcus, G. (1994) What comes (just) after "post"? The case of ethnography, in: N. K. Denzin and Y. S. Lincoln (eds) *Handbook of Qualitative Research*, Thousand Oaks: Sage.

Marcus, G. (1998) *Ethnography Through Thick and Thin*, Princeton: Princeton University Press.

Marcus, G. and Fisher, M. J. (1999) *Anthropology as Cultural Critique: An Experimental Moment in the Human Sciences*, Chicago: The University of Chicago Press.

Martin, L. H., Gutman, H., and Hutton, P. H. (eds) (1988) *Technologies of the Self: A seminar with Michel Foucault*, Amherst: The University of Massachusetts Press.

Martino, W. (1999) "Cool boys", "party animals", "squids" and "poofters": interrogating the dynamics and politics of adolescent masculinities in school, *British Journal of Sociology of Education*, 20: 2, 239–63.

Martino, W. (2001) "Powerful people aren't usually real kind, friendly, open people!" Boys interrogating masculinities at school, in: W. Martino and B. Meyenn (eds) *What About the Boys? Issues of Masculinity in Schools*, Buckingham: Open University Press.

Martino, W. and Meyenn, B. (eds) (2001) *What About the Boys? Issues of Masculinity in Schools*, Buckingham: Open University Press.

Martino, W. and Pallotta-Chiarolli, M. (2003) *So What's a Boy? Addressing Issues of Masculinity and Schooling*, Maidenhead: Open University Press.

Martino, W., Lingard, B., and Mills, M. (2004) Issues in boys' education: A question of teacher threshold knowledges? *Gender and Education*, 16: 4, 435–54.

Martino, W., Kehler, M., and Weaver-Hightower, M. B. (eds) (2009) *The Problem with Boys' Education: Beyond the Backlash*, New York: Routledge.

May, T. (ed.) (2002) *Qualitative Research in Action*, London: Sage.

Mazzei, L. A. and Jackson, A.Y. (2009) Introduction. The limit of voice, in: Jackson, A.Y. and Mazzei, L. A. (eds) *Voice in Qualitative Inquiry*, Abingdon: Routledge.

Meadmore, D. (1997) "This slender technique": Examining assessment policy, in: C. O'Farrell (ed.) *Foucault: The Legacy*, Kelvin Grove: Queensland University of Technology.

Meadmore, D. (2000) Testing bodies of knowledge, in: C. O'Farrell, D. Meadmore, E. McWilliam, and C. Symes (eds) *Taught Bodies*, New York: Peter Lang.

Meadmore, D. and Symes, C. (1996) Of uniform appearance: A symbol of school discipline and governmentality, *Discourse: Studies in the Cultural Politics of Education*, 17: 2, 209–25.

Meighan, R. (1978) Review of learning to labour, *Educational Review*, 30: 2, 183–85.

Messner, M. A. and Sabo, D. F. (eds) (1990) *Sport, Men, and the Gender Order: Critical Feminist Perspectives*, Champaign, Illinois: Human Kinetics Books.

Meyerhoff, B. and Ruby, J. (1982) Introduction, in: J. Ruby (ed.) *A Crack in the Mirror*, Philadelphia: University of Pennsylvania Press.

Middleton, S. (1998) *Disciplining Sexuality: Foucault, Life Histories, and Education*, New York: Teachers College Press.

Miller, P. and Rose, N. (2008) *Governing the Present: Administering Economic, Social and Personal life*, Cambridge: Polity Press.

Mills, M. (2000) Troubling the "failing boys" discourse, *Discourse: Studies in the Cultural Politics of Education*, 21: 2, 237–46.

Mills, M. (2003) Shaping the boys' agenda: The backlash blockbusters, *International Journal of Inclusive Education*, 7: 1, 57–73.

Mills, M. and Lingard, B. (1997) Masculinity politics, myths and boys' schooling: A review essay, *British Journal of Educational Studies*, 45: 3, 276–92.

Mills, M., Martino, W., and Lingard. (2007) Getting boys' education "right": The Australian Government's Parliamentary Inquiry Report as an exemplary instance of recuperative masculinity politics, *British Journal of Sociology of Education*, 28: 1, 5–21.

Ministerial Council on Education, Employment, Training and Youth Affairs (MCEETYA) (1995) *Proceedings of the Promoting Gender Equity Conference*, 22–24 February: Canberra.

Mishler, E. G. (1986) *Research Interviewing: Context and Narrative*, Cambridge: Harvard University Press.

Nagel, M. (2005) Frogs and snails and puppy dogs' tails, *The Boys in Schools Bulletin*, 8: 1, 36–39.

Nayak, A. and Kehily, M. J. (2008) *Gender, Youth and Culture: Young Masculinities and Femininities*, Basingstoke: Palgrave MacMillan.

Nicholson, L. J. (1990) *Feminism/Postmodernism*, New York: Routledge.

O'Doherty, S. (1994) *A Report To The Minister For Education, Training, and Youth Affairs on the Inquiry Into Boys' Education: Challenges & Opportunities: A Discussion Paper*, NSW Government Advisory Committee on Education Training and Tourism.

O'Donovan, D. (2006) Moving away from "failing boys" and "passive girls": Gender meta-narratives in gender equity policies for Australian schools and why micro-narratives provide a better policy model, *Discourse: Studies in the Cultural Politics of Education*, 27: 4, 475–94.

O'Farrell, C. (ed.) (1997) *Foucault: The Legacy*, Kelvin Grove: Queensland University of Technology.

O'Farrell, C. (2005) *Michel Foucault*, London: Sage.

O'Farrell, C., Meadmore, D., McWilliam, E., and Symes, C. (eds) (2000) *Taught Bodies*, New York: Peter Lang.

Okely, J. (1992) Anthropology and autobiography: Participatory experience and embodied knowledge, in: J. Okely and H. Callaway (eds) *Anthropology and Autobiography*, London: Routledge.

Okely, J. and Callaway, H. (eds) (1992) *Anthropology and Autobiography*, London: Routledge.

Parker, I. (1990) Discourse: Definitions and contradictions, *Philosophical Psychology*, 3: 2, 189–204.

Parker, I. (1992) *Discourse Dynamics: Critical Analysis for Social and Individual Psychology*, London: Routledge.

Parker, I. (1998) Realism, relativism and critique in psychology, in: I. Parker (ed.) *Social Constructionism, Discourse and Realism*, London: Sage.

Parker, I. (ed.) (1998) *Social Constructionism, Discourse and Realism*, London: Sage.

Pattman, R., Frosh, S., and Phoenix, A. (1998) Lads, machos and others: Developing "boy-centred" research, *Journal of Youth Studies*, 1: 2, 125–42.

Phoenix, A. and Frosh, S. (2001) Positioned by "'hegemonic' masculinities: A study of London boys" narratives of identity, *Australian Psychologist*, 36: 1, 27–35.

Phillips, L. and Jorgensen, M. W. (2002) *Discourse Analysis as Theory and Method*, London: Sage.

Piper, H. and Stronach, I. (eds) (2004) *Educational Research: Difference and Diversity*, Burlington: Ashgate.

Pizzini, N. (1999) Making the transition from boyhood to manhood, *Boys in Schools Bulletin*, 2: 3, 16–18.

Pollack, W. (1999) *Real Boys: Rescuing Our Sons from the Myths of Boyhood*, Melbourne: Scribe.

Porter, S. (2002) Critical realist ethnography, in: T. May (ed.) *Qualitative Research in Action*, London: Sage.

Potter, J. (1998) Fragments in the realisation of relativism, in: I. Parker (ed.) *Social Constructionism, Discourse and Realism*, London: Sage.

Potter, J., Wetherell, M., Gill, R., and Edwards, D. (eds) (1990) Discourse: Noun, verb or social practice? *Philosophical Psychology*, 3: 2, 205–17.

Prideaux, J. (ed.) (2005) *More Than Just Marks: Boys' Education*, Essendon: Pennon Publishing.

Rabinow, P. (ed.) (1991) *The Foucault Reader: An Introduction to Foucault's Thought*, London: Penguin.

Ramazanoglu, C. (ed.) (1993) *Up Against Foucault: Explorations of Some Tensions between Foucault and Feminism*, London: Routledge.

Ramazanoglu, C. and Holland, J. (1999) Tripping over experience: Some problems in feminist epistemology, *Discourse: Studies in the Cultural Politics of Education*, 20: 3, 381–92.

Ransom, J. (1993) Feminism, difference and discourse: The limits of discursive analysis for feminism, in: C. Ramazanoglu (ed.) *Up Against Foucault: Explorations of Some Tensions between Foucault and Feminism*, London: Routledge.

Raulet, G. (1983) "Structuralism and post-structuralism: An interview with Michel Foucault," *Telos*, 55: 195–211.

Reay, D. (2002) Shaun's story: Troubling discourses of white working-class masculinities, *Gender and Education*, 14: 3, 221–34.

Redman, P. and Mac an Ghaill, M. (1996) Schooling sexualities: Heterosexual masculinities, schooling, and the unconscious, *Discourse: Studies in the Cultural Politics of Education*, 17: 2, 243–56.

Reichert, M. C. (2001) Rethinking masculinities: New ideas for schooling boys, in: W. Martino and B. Meyenn (eds) *What About the Boys? Issues of Masculinity in Schools*, Buckingham: Open University Press.

Renold, E. (2004) "Other" boys: Negotiating non-hegemonic masculinities in the primary school, *Gender and Education*, 16: 2, 247–66.

Riley, K. and Docking, J. (2004) Voices of disaffected pupils: Implications for policy and practice, *British Journal of Educational Studies*, 52: 2, 166–79.

Rist, R. (1973) *The Urban School: A Factory for Failure*, Cambridge, Massachusetts: MIT Press.

Rock, P. (2001) Symbolic interactionism and ethnography, in: P. Atkinson, A. Coffey, S. Delamont, J. Lofland, and L. Lofland (eds) *Handbook of Ethnography*, London: Sage.

Roman, L. G. (1993) Double exposure: The politics of feminist materialist ethnography, *Educational Theory*, 43: 3, 279–308.

Roman, L. G., Christian-Smith, L. K. with Ellsworth, E. (eds) (1988) *Becoming Feminine: The Politics of Popular Culture*, London: Falmer.

Rose, N. (1989) Individualising psychology, in: J. Shotter and K. J. Gergen (eds) *Texts of Identity*, London: Sage.

Rose, N. (1996) *Inventing Our Selves: Psychology, Power and Personhood*, Cambridge: Cambridge University Press.

Rose, N. (1999) *Governing the Soul: The Shaping of the Private Self*, London: Free Association Books.

Ruby, J. (ed.) (1982) *A Crack in the Mirror*, Philadelphia: University of Pennsylvania Press.

St Pierre, E. A. (2000) Poststructural feminism in education: An overview, *International Journal of Qualitative Studies in Education*, 13: 5, 477–515.

Salih, S. (ed.) with Judith Butler (2004) *The Judith Butler Reader*, Oxford: Blackwell.

Salo, U-M. (2003) Becoming a pupil, in: D. Beach, T. Gordon and E. Lahelma (eds) *Democratic Education: Ethnographic Challenges*, London: Tuffnell Press.

Sarup, M. (1993) *An Introductory Guide to Post-Structuralism and Postmodernism*, Athens: University of Georgia Press.

Saukko, P. (2003) *Doing Research in Cultural Studies: An Introduction to Classical and New Methodological Approaches*, London: Sage.

Scheurich, J. J. (1995) A postmodern critique of research interviewing, *Qualitative Studies in Education*, 8: 3, 239–52.

Schostak, J. and Logan, T. (eds) (2001) *Pupil Experience*, Sydney, Croom Helm.

Scott, J. (1992) Experience, in: J. Butler and J. W. Scott (eds) *Feminists Theorise the Political*, New York: Routledge.

Sharp, R. (1981) Review: Beachside comprehensive, *British Journal of Sociology of Education*, 2: 3, 278–85.

Shipman, M. (ed.) (1976) *The Organisation and Impact of Social Research. Six Original Case Studies in Education and Behavioural Science*, London: Routledge & Kegan Paul.

Shotter, J. and Gergen, K. J. (eds) (1989) *Texts of Identity*, London: Sage.

Sills, D. L. (ed.) (1968) *International Encyclopedia of the Social Sciences*, The Macmillan Company & The Free Press.

Silverman, D. (ed.) (1998) *Qualitative Research: Theory, Method and Practice*, London: Sage.

Silverman, D. (2000) Analyzing talk and text, in: N. K. Denzin and Y. S. Lincoln (eds) *Handbook of Qualitative Research: Second Edition*, Thousand Oaks: Sage.

Skeggs, B. (1989) Review of louts and legends, *British Journal of Sociology of Education*, 10: 4, 484–90.

Skeggs, B. (1991) Postmodernism: What is all the fuss about? *British Journal of Sociology of Education*, 12: 2, 255–67.

Skeggs, B. (1992) Paul Willis, learning to labour, in: M. Barker and A. Beezer, (eds) *Reading into Cultural Studies*, London: Routledge.

Skeggs, B. (1994) The constraints of neutrality: The 1988 Education Reform Act and feminist research, in: D. Halpin and B. Troyna (eds) (1994) *Researching Education Policy: Ethical and Methodological Issues*, London: Falmer.
Skeggs, B. (ed.) (1995a) *Feminist Cultural Theory: Process and Production*, Manchester: Manchester University Press.
Skeggs, B. (1995b) Theorising, ethics and representation in feminist ethnography, in: B. Skeggs (ed.) *Feminist Cultural Theory: Process and Production*, Manchester: Manchester University Press.
Skeggs, B. (1998) *Formations of Class and Gender: Becoming Respectable*, London: Sage.
Skeggs, B. (2001) Feminist ethnography, in: P. Atkinson, A. Coffey, S. Delamont, J. Lofland, and L. Lofland (eds) *Handbook of Ethnography*, London: Sage.
Skeggs, B. (2002) Techniques for telling the reflexive self, in: T. May, *Quantitative Research in Action*, London: Sage.
Skeggs, B. (2004) *Class, Self, Culture*, London: Routledge.
Skelton, C. and Francis, B. (2009) *Feminism and "The Schooling Scandal,"* Abingdon: Routledge.
Slade, M. (2001) Listening to the boys, *The Boys in Schools Bulletin*, 4: 1, 10–18.
Slade, M. (2002) *Listening to the Boys: Issues and Problems Influencing School Achievement and Retention*, Flinders University: Institute of International Education.
Slade, M. and Trent, F. (2000) What the boys are saying. An examination of the views of boys about declining rates of achievement and retention, *International Education Journal*, 1: 3, 201–29.
Smith, D.(1988) Femininity as discourse, in: L. G. Roman, L. K. Christian-Smith with E. Ellsworth (eds) *Becoming Feminine: The Politics of Popular Culture*, London: Falmer.
Smith, D. (2002) Institutional ethnography, in: T. May (ed.) *Qualitative Research in Action*, London: Sage.
Smith, R. (1992) *Inhibition: History and Meaning in the Sciences of Mind and Brain*, Berkeley: University of California Press.
Smith, R. and P. Wexler (eds) (1995) *After Postmodernism: Education, Politics and Identity*, London: Falmer.
Spindler, G. (ed.) (1982) *Doing the Ethnography of Schooling: Educational Anthropology in Action*, New York: Holt, Rinehart and Winston.
Stronach, I. and MacLure, M. (1997) *Educational Research Undone: The Postmodern Embrace*, Buckingham: Open University Press.
Sunderland, J. and Litosseliti, L. (2002) Gender identity and discourse analysis: Theoretical and empirical considerations, in: L. Litosseliti and J. Sunderland (eds) *Gender Identity and Discourse Analysis*, Amsterdam: John Benjamins.
Swann, J. (2002) Yes, but is it gender? In: L. Litosseliti and J. Sunderland (eds) *Gender Identity and Discourse Analysis*, Amsterdam: John Benjamins.
Tedlock, B. (1991) From participant observation to the observation of participation: The emergence of narrative ethnography, *Journal of Anthropological Research*, 47:1, 69–94.
Tedlock, B. (2000) Ethnography and ethnographic representation, in: N. K. Denzin and Y. S. Lincoln, (eds) *Handbook of Qualitative Research: Second Edition*, Thousand Oaks: Sage.

Teese, R., Davies, M., Charlton, M., and Polesel, J. (1995) *Who Wins at School? Boys and Girls in Australian Secondary Education*, Melbourne: Department of Education Policy and Management, Melbourne University.

Teese, R., Davies, M., Charlton, M., and Polesel, J. (1997) Who wins at school: Which boys, which girls? In: J. Kenway (ed.) *Will Boys be Boys? Boys' Education in the Context of Gender Reform*, Deakin West: Australian Curriculum Studies Association.

Teese, R., McLean, G., and Polesel, J. (1993) *Equity Outcomes: A Report to the Schools Council's Task Force on a Broadband Equity Program for Schools*, Canberra: National Board of Employment, Education and Training.

Tsolidis, G. (2006) *Youthful Imagination: Schooling, Subcultures, and Social Justice*, New York: Peter Lang.

Turner, G. (1983) *The Social World of the Comprehensive School: How Pupils Adapt*, London: Croom Helm.

Turner, T. S. (1993) The social skin, in: C. B. Burroughs and J. D. Ehrenreich (eds) *Reading the Social Body*, Iowa City: University of Iowa Press.

Turner, V. W. and Bruner, E. M. (eds) (1986) *The Anthropology of Experience*, Urbana: University of Illinois Press.

Tyler, S. (1986) Post-modern ethnography: From document of the occult to occult document, in: J. Clifford and G. Marcus (eds) *Writing Culture: The Poetics and Politics of Ethnography*, Berkeley: University of California Press.

Van Maanen, J. (1988) *Tales of the Field: On Writing Ethnography*, Chicago: University of Chicago Press.

Van Manen, M. (1990) *Researching Lived Experience: Human Science for an Action Sensitive Pedagogy*, New York, State University of New York Press.

Van Manen, M. (1999) The language of pedagogy and the primacy of student experience, in: J. Loughnan (ed) *Researching Teaching: Methodologies and Practices for Understanding Pedagogy*, London, Falmer.

Velody, I. and Williams, R. (eds) (1998) *The Politics of Constructionism*, London: Sage.

Walford, G. (ed) (2002) *Doing a Doctorate in Educational Ethnography*, Amsterdam, Elsevier Science Ltd.

Walker, J. C. (1985) Rebels with our applause? A critique of resistance theory in Paul Willis's ethnography of schooling, *Journal of Education*, 167: 2, 63–83.

Walker, J. C. (1986) Romanticising resistance, romanticising culture: Problems in Willis's theory of cultural production, *British Journal of Sociology of Education*, 7: 1, 59–80.

Walker, J. C. (1988) *Louts and Legends: Male Youth Culture in an Inner-City School*, Sydney: Allen & Unwin.

Walkerdine, V. (1981) Sex, power and pedagogy, in: M. Arnot and G. Weiner (eds) *Gender and the Politics of Schooling*, London: Unwin Hyman.

Walkerdine, V. (1986) Poststructuralist theory and everyday social processes: The family and the school, in: S. Wilkinson (ed.) *Feminist Social Psychology: Developing Theory and Practice*, Milton Keynes: Open University Press.

Walkerdine, V. (1989) Femininity as performance, *Oxford Review of Education*, 15: 3, 267–79.

Walkerdine, V. (1990) *Schoolgirl Fictions*, London: Verso.

Walkerdine, V. (1993) Beyond developmentalism? *Theory and Psychology*, 3: 4, 451–69.

Walkerdine, V. (1994) Reasoning in a post-modern age, in: J. Edwards (ed.) *Thinking: International Interdisciplinary Perspectives*, Highett: Hawker Brownlow Education.

Walkerdine, V. (ed.) (2002) *Challenging Subjects: Critical Psychology for a New Millenium*, Basingstoke: Palgrave.

Walkerdine, V., Lucey, H., and Melody, J. (2001) *Growing Up Girl: Psychosocial Explorations of Gender and Class*, New York: New York University Press.

Walkerdine, V., Lucey, H., and Melody, J. (2002) Subjectivity and qualitative method, in: T. May (ed.) *Qualitative Research in Action*, London: Sage.

Walpole, S. (1995) Gender equity in education: A view from outside the classroom, in: MCEETYA, *Proceedings of the Promoting Gender Equity Conference*, February 22–24, 1995: Canberra.

Watson, N. and Cunningham-Burley, S. (eds) (2001) *Reframing the Body*, London: Palgrave.

Weaver-Hightower, M. B. (2003) Crossing the divide: Bridging the disjunctures between theoretically oriented and practice-oriented literature about masculinity and boys at school, *Gender and Education*, 15: 4, 407–23.

Weaver-Hightower, M. B. (2009) Issues of boys' education in the United Sattes: Diffuse contexts and futures, in: Martino, W., Kehler, M., and Weaver-Hightower, M. B. (eds) *The Problem with Boys' Education. Beyond the Backlash*, New York: Routledge.

Weis, L. (1985) *Between Two Worlds: Black Students in an Urban Community College*, Boston: Routledge & Kegan Paul.

Weis, L. (ed.) (1988) *Class, Race, and Gender in American Education*, New York: State University of New York Press.

Weis, L. and Fine, M. (eds) (1993) *Beyond Silenced Voices*, New York: State University of New York Press.

Weis, L. and Fine, M. (eds) (2000) *Construction Sites: Excavating Race, Class, and Gender Among Urban Youth*, New York: Teachers College Press.

Weedon, (1997) *Feminist Practice and Poststructuralist Theory*, second edition, Oxford: Blackwell.

West, P. (2000) Raising boys: Who will we listen to? *Australian Quarterly*, October–December, 2000: 35–38.

West, P. (2001) *Report on Best Practice in Boys' Education*, Sydney: University of Western Sydney.

West, P. (2002a) *What is the Matter with Boys? Showing Boys the Way Towards Manhood*, Marrickville: Choice Books.

West, P. (2002b) Motivating boys in the secondary school: What's the problem? *Principal Matters*, May 2002; 25–26.

West, P. (2004) Kids need parents, and parents may need help, *The Age*, 29 January, 2004.

Wexler, P. (1992) *Becoming Somebody: Towards a Social Psychology of School*, London: Falmer.

Whelen, J. (2006) *The Social and Discursive Construction of Boys' Experience of their Schooling*. Unpublished PhD thesis, Monash University.

Whelen, J. (2008) On the margins of education, or two stories of arriving at school, *Ethnography and Education*, 3:3, 297–312.

Whitson, D. (1990) Sport in the social construction of masculinity, in: M. A.

Messner and D. F. Sabo (eds) *Sport, Men, and the Gender Order: Critical Feminist Perspectives*, Champaign, Illinois: Human Kinetics Books.

Wilkinson, S. (ed.) (1986) *Feminist Social Psychology: Developing Theory and Practice*, Milton Keynes: Open University Press.

Willis, P. (1977) *Learning to Labour: How Working Class Kids Get Working Class Jobs*, Aldershot: Gower.

Willis, P. (1978) *Profane Culture*, London: Routledge & Kegan Paul.

Willis, P. (1980) Notes on method, in: S. Hall (ed.) *Culture, Media, Language*, London: Hutchinson.

Willis, P. (1981) *Learning to Labor: How Working Class Kids Get Working Class Jobs*, New York: Columbia University Press.

Willis, P. (1983) Cultural production and theories of reproduction, in: L. Barton and S. Walker (eds) *Race, Class and Education*, London: Croom Helm.

Willis, P. (2000) *The Ethnographic Imagination*, Cambridge: Polity.

Willis, R. (2005) Learning to "think with your heart", in: J. Prideaux (ed.) *More Than Just Marks: Boys' Education*, Essendon: Pennon Publishing.

Wolpe, A. M. (1988a) *Within School Walls: The Role of Discipline, Sexuality and The Curriculum*, London: Routledge.

Wolpe, A. M. (1988b) "Experience" as analytical framework: Does it account for girls' education? In: M. Cole (ed.) *Bowles and Gintis Revisited: Correspondence and Contradiction in Educational Theory*, London: Falmer.

Woods, P. (1985) Ethnography and theory construction in educational research, in: R. G. Burgess, (1985) *Field Methods in the Study of Education*, London: Falmer.

Woods, P. (1986) *Inside Schools: Ethnography in Educational Research*, London: Routledge & Kegan Paul.

Yon, D. A. (2000) *Elusive Culture: Schooling, Race, and Identity in Global Times*, Albany: State University of New York.

Youdell, D. (2003) Identity traps or how black students fail: The interaction between biographical, sub-cultural, and learner identities, *British Journal of Sociology of Education*, 24: 1, 3–20.

Youdell, D. (2004) Engineering school markets, constituting schools and subjectivating students: The bureaucratic, institutional and classroom dimensions of educational triage, *Journal of Education Policy*, 19: 4, 407–31.

Youdell, D. (2005) Sex-gender-sexuality: How sex, gender and sexuality constellations are constituted in secondary schools, *Gender and Education*, 17: 3, 249–70.

Youdell, D. (2006a) Diversity, inequality and a post-structural politics for education, *Discourse: Studies in the Cultural Politics of Education*, 27: 1, 33–42.

Youdell, D. (2006b) *Impossible Bodies, Impossible Selves: Exclusions and Student Subjectivities*, Dordrecht: Springer.

Youdell, D. (2006c) Subjectivation and performative politics – Butler thinking Althusser and Foucault: Intelligibility, agency and the raced-nationed-religioned subjects of education, *British Journal of Sociology of Education*, 27: 4, 511–28

Youdell, D. (2010) Queer outings: Uncomfortable stories about the subjects of post-structural school ethnography, *International Journal of Qualitative Studies in Education*, 23: 1, 87–100

Young, R. (ed.) (1987) *Untying the Text: A Post-Structuralist Reader*, London: Routledge.

Index

Abraham, J. 96
agency 13, 16, 18, 78, 85–6, 122, 147, 167, 226, 229
Aggleton, P. 98, 248, 249, 250
Ailwood, J. 230
Angrossino, M.V. 22–3
Arndt, 41, 242, 244
Aronowitz, S. 73, 245
arrival (stories) 30, 88, 101–103, 249
assemblies 102, 104–5, 108, 110, 124, 148–155, 162–63, 174, 183, 215, 251
Atkinson, P. 7, 13, 20, 22, 60–1, 70, 76–7, 96–7, 111, 245, 249

Ball, S. 16, 61, 72, 75, 78, 83, 95, 98, 174, 202, 246, 247, 250
Behar, R. 21, 83
Biddulph, S. 4, 32–3, 35, 45–9, 52, 54, 227, 242–43, 252
Bly, R. 33, 35, 243, 244
body (bodies) 180, 182–91; care of 196–99, 204
boys (see also schoolboys); achievement of 3, 11, 29, 32–3, 37–42, 54–5, 59, 90, 202–03, 226; anti-school ethic 8–9, 41–5, 50, 54, 74; behaviour of 8, 10–12, 26, 37, 40–2, 54–5, 91, 94, 125, 159, 165, 182, 202–04, 212, 130, 233; "cool to be a fool" 4, 233; "crisis", plight of 3–6, 34–5, 41–2, 44–5, 50; as modernist subject 36; male role models for 243; as victim 55; "what about the boys?" 9, 13, 24, 29, 30, 32, 34; see experience; "which boys?"
Britzman, D. 26–7, 61, 86–7, 89, 248, 249

Broadfoot, P. 174
Brod, H. 44
Browne, R. 45–8, 50, 52–3, 242, 243
Bruce, S. 245
Bruner, E.M. 28, 241, 251
Buckingham, J. 52, 243
Burgess, R.G. 20, 22, 245
Burr, V. 158
Burroughs, C.B. 180–81
Butler, J. 4, 17, 18–20, 28–9, 122, 138, 180–81, 203, 228, 233, 239, 240

Carr-Gregg, M. 53, 242
Carrigan, T. 11, 240
Clark, H.H. 119
Clatterbaugh, K. 44, 238
Clifford, J. 21, 83, 248
Coffey, A. 21, 60, 88, 90, 97, 111–12, 245, 249
Collins, C. 38, 40–1, 57
Connell, R.W. 10–12, 17, 29, 35, 52, 84, 98, 113, 180–81, 238, 240, 242, 243, 247, 252
Corrigan, P. 241, 247
Cox, E. 45
Croxford, L. 29
Cunningham-Burley, S. 180
Cusick, P.A. 247
Cuttance, P. 230

Davies, B. 9, 15–17, 19, 28, 86–7, 122, 139, 231, 240, 252
Davies, L. 80–3, 90, 202
Delamont, S. 7, 20, 23, 60–1, 70, 98, 111, 241, 249, 250
Delfos, M. 243
Denzin, N. 13, 21–2, 60–1, 83, 87, 96

desire 215–224
Dewey, J. 231
Dillabough, J-A. 231
Discourse 103–04; of adolescence 187, of appearance 182–83; of care 106–08, 154, 215; of community 105–06, 199; of contempt 167, 173, 179; of doing well and being good 214; of excellence 104–05, 217; of failure and disadvantage 44; of friendship 135, 154, 165, 173, 189, 191; of gender equity 3; of normative school 103
Docking, J. 250
Donaldson, M. 238
Dormer, S. 139
Douglas, P. 10, 33–6, 44, 57, 230, 231
Dwyer, K. 249

Eder, D. 241
Edmondson, R. 76–7, 85
Ehrenreich, J.D. 180–81
embodiment 31
Emerson, R.M. 249
Enlightenment subject 4, 12–14, 148, 231, 233; see also subject
Epstein, D. 29, 44, 124, 226, 245, 249, 250, 252
essentialism 3, 4, 33, 35–6, 41, 44–52, 57–9, 226, 229, 231
ethics 21, 23–6, 71, 94, 96; of representation 87; of research 102, 111
ethnicity 31, 191–94, 226, 229, 234, 241
ethnography 4, 8, 13, 20–3, 27, 59, 87 90; entry to site 24, 88; feminist critique of 79–80; fieldwork 111–113, 246; fieldwork body 112; fieldwork persona 112, 249; male ethnographers 21, 79, 83, 89, 96; modernist 60ff, 202, 228, 245; recruiting participants 11–12, 92, 103, 111–17; as text 60, 67, 68, 70, 74–5, 77, 82, 85; writing 86, 97, 107; see ethics
examinations 174–79, 241
experience 4, 7, 9, 13, 17, 26–8, 73, 77, 93, 113, 148, 154, 199, 225, 227, 234, 241; and boys 3, 58, 72, 128, 227, 231; and difference 85; and girls 81, 248;
and ethnography 28, 88, 139; and researcher 95–6

Fairclough, N. 239
Farrell, L. 251
Felski, R. 86
fights 194–96
Fine, M. 21, 85, 248
Fletcher, R. 45–8, 50–4, 242–44
Fontana, A. 22
Fordham, S. 23, 86–8, 248
Formaini, H. 243
Foster, V. 29
Foucault. M. 4, 14–18, 82, 103–04, 107–08, 122–23, 174, 180, 183, 203, 225, 227, 239, 251, 252
Francis, B. 29, 38, 53, 90, 98, 203, 231, 238–42, 245, 247, 249–52
Frank, B. 238
Frankenberg, R. 62, 246
Fraser, N. 239
Fretz, R.I. 249
Frey, J.H. 22
friendship, friends (mates) 130–138, 140–42, 154, 164–65, 173, 177–79, 198, 225, 232, 234; see discourse
Frosh, S. 11, 238, 250
Furlong, V.J. 202

Galton, M. 250
Garber, J. 79
gender 10–11, 33, 43, 48, 51–3, 58, 83–4; equity, 29; equity policy 30–1, 33, 36–44, 49, 59, 231; "gender wars" 41; reform 34; regime 187; see social construction
Gilbert, R. and Gilbert, P. 34–5, 58, 83, 245
girls 3, 4, 8, 10, 33–4, 36–43, 46–8, 52–6, 79–82, 86, 90, 93, 98, 109, 132–34, 149–50, 187–91, 210–11, 213, 226–27, 247–48, 252; "girl friendly" assessment 50; see experience
Gluckman, M. 61–2, 246
Gonick, M. 24, 86–8, 249–50
Gordon, D.A. 21, 83
Gordon, T. 20, 29, 88, 115, 181
Gough, A. 181
Grant, B. 225
Grant, L. 245
grief 31, 157–62, 179, 234
Gubrium, J.F. 241
Guillaumin, C. 181

276 Index

Hall, S. 147, 203, 247, 250
Hammersley, M. 20, 22, 77, 96–7, 202, 245
Harari, J.V. 71
Haraway, D. 180
Hargreaves, A. 174, 251
Hargreaves, D. 60–7, 70–1, 75, 78, 80–3, 90, 95–6, 98, 246
Harré, R. 17, 240
Hawkes, T. 54, 244
Hayes, 33
Haywood, C. 83
Hebdidge, D. 180
Henriques, J. 13
Hey, V. 86–7, 202, 205, 228, 235, 247, 250
Heyl, B.S. 7, 22
Hodgetts, K. 230
Holland, J. 241
Holstein, J.A. 241
Hoskin, K. 174
House or Representatives, inquiry 41–3, 50–1, 54, 57

ideal types, see sampling
identity 11, 27, 83–5, 138–146, 147–48, 170–71, 173, 179–80, 197, 204–05, 224–27, 229, 250–51; see schoolboys
interpellation 18–19, 86, 104, 117, 130, 138, 147, 229, 234, 251
interviews 22, 86, 93, 240–41
Ireland, P. 47

Jackson, A.Y. 87, 96
Jackson, P. 246
Jefferson, T. 247
Jones, S. 29
Jorgensen, M.W. 249

Kapferer, B. 241
Kaufman, M. 44, 243
Keddie, A. 58, 230
Kehily, M.J. 86
Kenway, J. 9, 33–5, 38, 45, 53, 58–9, 86, 231, 239–40, 242, 244
Kessler, S. 84, 240
Kimmel, M.S. 44, 49, 243
Kondo, D.K. 21, 148
Kvale, S. 22

Lacey, C. 61–4, 67–72, 75–6, 78, 83, 85, 90, 95–6, 98, 202, 245–46, 250
Lahelma, E. 29, 115, 181, 241, 250

Lambart, A. 61–2, 246
Lather, P. 86, 104, 139, 251
Laws, C. 9, 19, 86, 231, 252
Lesko, N. 248, 252
Lincoln, Y.S. 21–2, 60, 83, 87, 96
Lingard, B. 10, 33–6, 42, 44, 57, 230–31, 252
Litoseliti, L. 238–39
Logan, T. 241
loss 31, 162–64, 179, 225
Ludowyke, J. 42–3, 51, 242

Mac an Ghaill, M. 10, 12, 24, 29, 70, 83–5, 98, 113, 181, 248, 250, 252
MacLure, M 23, 61, 109, 139, 239, 240–41, 249, 250McCarthy, C. 35
McLeod, J. 24, 29, 183, 203, 240, 248, 252
McNay, L. 17
McRobbie, A. 79, 80–1
Marchetta, M. 250
Marcus, G. 13, 75–6, 83, 96, 138, 245, 247
Martino, W. 11, 44, 98, 113, 158, 230–31
masculinity, hegemonic 10, 32–4, 58; recuperative 34–5, 44, 57, 59
Mays de Perez, K.A. 22–3
Mazzei, L.A. 86, 96
Meadmore, D. 174, 183, 251–52
Meighan, R. 247
mentors, for boys 244; see parenting, teachers
Meyenn, B. 44
Meyerhof, B. 151, 251
Middleton, S. 16
Miller, P. 4, 228
Mills, M. 33, 230, 245
Mischler, E.G. 22, 25
Myhill, D. 29

Nagel, M. 243
Nayak, A. 86

observation 22–3, 86, 93; participant 20, 28, 61–2, 68, 71, 73, 82, 87, 89, 94, 96, 103, 111, 202, 248; ethics of 205
O'Doherty, S. 37–8, 40, 42–3, 58, 242
O'Donovan, D. 33, 230
O'Farrell, C. 14, 16
Okley, J. 249

Palotta-Chiarolli, M. 11
parenting 45; families 51;
    fathers, 48–9, 53; initiation 49;
    mothers and sole parenting 52
Parker, I. 239, 250
Pattman, R. 241
performativity, discursive 18–20; and
    ethnography 19–20
Phillips, L. 249
Phoenix, A. 11, 238, 250
Pizzini, N. 243
policy, see gender
Pollack, W. 54, 243
Potter, J. 10, 239
profeminism 30, 32–5, 38, 45, 58–9,
    226, 230
professional development 6, 10, 37,
    45

qualitative research 7, 13, 73

Rabinow, P. 16
Ramazanoglou, C. 239, 241
Ransom, J. 239
rapport 21–2, 26, 61, 70–1, 83, 89,
    94, 96, 98, 103, 122, 128, 154,
    165
Reay, D. 29
Redman, P. 83
reflexivity 4, 20–1, 70, 73, 83, 86–7,
    96, 151, 240
Reichert, M.C. 158
research design 25, 84; research
    paradigm 60–1, 65
Riley, K. 250
Rist, R. 248
Rock, P. 245
Roman, L.G. 25
Rose, N. 4, 18, 35, 228, 231
Rowe, K. 51, 55–6, 244
Ruby, J. 96, 151, 251

St.Pierre, E.A. 86
Salih, S. 180
Salo, U-M. 250
sampling 68–9, 76, 82, 85, 248
Saukko, P. 22
Scanlon, J. 42–3, 51, 242
Scheurich, J.J. 86
school(s) 18,44, 75; "boy
    friendly" 53; feminization of 3, 6,
    49–52, 54, 227; gender regime 10–
    12, 48; gendered curriculum 10;
    masculinising institutions 12,
    53, 83–4; microcultures 84;
    normative 18, 30–1, 124, 134,
    138–39, 141, 148, 151, 157, 162,
    178, 182, 196–97, 202, 215,
    217, 233–34; pathological 18,
    30, 124; patriarchal values 81;
    single sex 55; social system 63–4;
    uniform 106, 110, 122, 117–123,
    125, 182–85, 193, 232, 252
schoolboys 12, 68, 203, 224, 229;
    and change 230, 232; gay 83–4;
    textual identities 71; unitary
    subjects 228
schooling 3, 11, 26, 28, 83, 228
Schostak, J. 241
Scott, J. 27–8
self, selves 15–17, 23, 28–9, 31, 122,
    147–48, 173, 179, 203–04, 227;
    ethnographic/fieldworker self 103,
    111, 114–15, 246; researcher
    70–1, 96–7, 139, 154, 184, 200;
    students 71, 142, 165, 167, 171,
    225, 229
self-improvement 217
Shale, E. 242
Shaw, L.L. 249
Sills, D.L. 245
Silverman, D. 22, 25
Skeggs, B. 21, 76–80, 83, 85–6, 89–
    90, 235, 240, 245, 247–48
Skelton, C. 29, 38, 90, 231, 240–41,
    245, 247, 249
Slade, M. 40–1, 43, 58, 242
Smith, D. 203, 231, 241
social anthropology 61–2
social construction(ism) 9–10, 33, 52,
    71; and gender 47, 58, 180, 226,
    243
Spivak, G.C. 28
students 109–111; good student 94,
    ch. 9 passim, 252
subject of modernism 15, 17–18, 83;
    humanist 4, 12, 16, 147, 231; of
    schooling 86, 228; unitary 226; see
    boys; Enlightenment subject
subjectification 3–4, 9, 12–13, 16, 18,
    20, 27–9, 31, 86, 89, 103–04, 122,
    124, 141, 154, 181, 203, 225,
    227–29, 232–33; see Butler,
    Foucault
Swann, J. 13, 199
Sunderland, J. 238–39
symbolic interactionism 61–2
Symes, C. 183, 252

teacher-researcher 4–5, 7–9, 11, 13, 20, 24, 94, 96, 102–03, 111, 115, 130, 227; "teacher persona" 70, 95–6
teachers 108–09; interpellation as 104; lack of men 50; mentors, role models 42, 45, 48, 53, 106; women 49, 52, 54–5
Tedlock, B. 7, 97, 241
Teese, R. 36–41; 43, 51–2
textual turn 4, 14, 75, 83, 89–90; textuality 96
Trent, F. 40–1, 43, 58
trouble, getting into 131, 138–39, 153, 164–173
Tsolidis, G. 86
Turner, G. 202
Turner, T.S. 181, 202
Turner, V. 28
Tyler, S. 97

Van Manen, M. 241

Walford, G. 25
Walker, J.C. 70, 77–9, 83, 85, 89, 98, 247

Walkerdine, V. 7, 12, 16–17, 21–2, 203, 225, 235, 238, 240
Walpole, S. 9
Watson, N. 180
Weaver-Hightower, M.B. 10, 29, 241
Weis, L. 248
West, P. 52–7, 242, 244
Wexler, P. 248
Whelen, J. 247, 249, 250
"which boys?" 24, 29–30, 32–3, 38, 41–2, 50–1, 57, 59, 113, 226
Whitson, D. 181
Willis, P. 29, 70, 73–83, 85, 88–9, 98, 101, 113, 233, 245, 247, 249, 252
Willis, S. 9, 34–5, 45, 53, 58–9, 231
Wolpe, A.M. 79, 82, 85, 90, 246
Woods, P. 22, 25, 202

Yates, S. 183, 248, 252
Yearly, S. 245
Yon, D. 24
Youdell, D. 19, 27–8, 86, 104, 108, 180–81, 183, 230–32, 250
Young, R. 14–15

An environmentally friendly book printed and bound in England by www.printondemand-worldwide.com

PEFC Certified

This product is
from sustainably
managed forests
and controlled
sources

www.pefc.org

PEFC/16-33-415

MIX
Paper from
responsible sources
FSC® C004959

www.fsc.org

This book is made entirely of chain-of-custody materials. The cover is made using FSC materials whilst the text pages are PEFC mat

#0020 - 050712 - C0 - 229/152/16 - CB